The Social Welfare of Women and Children with HIV and AIDS

Legal Protections, Policy, and Programs

Theodore J. Stein

New York   Oxford
OXFORD UNIVERSITY PRESS
1998

Oxford University Press

Oxford   New York

Athens   Auckland   Bangkok   Bogota   Bombay   Buenos Aires
Calcutta   Cape Town   Dar es Salaam   Delhi   Florence   Hong Kong
Istanbul   Karachi   Kuala Lumpur   Madras   Madrid   Melbourne
Mexico City   Nairobi   Paris   Singapore   Taipei   Tokyo   Toronto   Warsaw

and associated companies in
Berlin   Ibadan

Copyright © 1998 by Oxford University Press, Inc.

Published by Oxford University Press, Inc.,
198 Madison Avenue, New York, New York 10016

Oxford is a registered trademark of Oxford University Press

Library of Congress Cataloging-in-Publication data
Stein, Theodore J.
The social welfare of women and children with HIV and AIDS : legal
protections, policy, and programs / Theodore J. Stein.
p.   cm.
Includes bibliographical references and index.
ISBN 0-19-510941-4 (cloth). — ISBN 0-19- 510942-2
(paper)
1. AIDS (Disease)—Patients—Legal status, laws, etc.— United
States. 2. HIV infections—Patients—Legal status, laws, etc.-
-United States. 3. Women patients—Legal status, laws, etc.- -United
States. 4. Children of AIDS patients—Legal status, laws, etc.-
-United States. 5. AIDS (Disease)—Patients—Services for— United
States. 6. Women patients-Services for—United States. I. Title.
KF3803.A54S74   1998
344.73'0321969792—DC21   96-50095
                                                              CIP

1 3 5 7 9 8 6 4 2

Printed in the United States of America
on acid-free paper

The Social Welfare of Women and Children with HIV and AIDS

Child Welfare
A series in child welfare practice, policy, and research
Duncan Lindsey, *General Editor*

The Welfare of Children
Duncan Lindsey

The Politics of Child Abuse in America
Lela B. Costin, Howard Jacob Karger, and David Stoesz

Combatting Child Abuse: International Perspectives and Trends
Neil Gilbert, Editor

**The Social Welfare of Women and Children with HIV and AIDS:
Legal Protections, Policy, and Programs**
Theodore J. Stein

CONTENTS

List of Tables		**vii**
Preface		**viii**
Acknowledgments		**xiii**
Chapter 1	**Introduction**	1
	Part I. The Emergence of AIDS in the United States and the Response of the Federal Government	1
	Part II. The Emergence of HIV	7
	Part III. Summary	12
Chapter 2	**The Policy Framework: Status-Conferring Policies**	**14**
	Introduction	14
	Part I. Overview of Statutory Provisions	15
	Part II. Statutory Terms and Their Application by the Courts	20
	Part III. Summary	34
Chapter 3	**The Policy Framework: Benefit-Conferring Policies**	**38**
	Introduction	38
	Part I. Financial Assistance	39
	Part II. Medical Care	43
	Part III. Social Services and Housing	53
	Part IV. Summary	61
Chapter 4	**The Care of Children and the Child Welfare System**	**64**
	Introduction	64
	Part I. Child Care and Long-Range Planning	65
	Part II. Child Welfare System	71
	Part III. Summary	87

Chapter 5   **Confidentiality, Testing, and Reproductive**
                   Choice   **89**
                   Introduction   89
                   Part I. Testing and Confidentiality   90
                   Part II. Testing and Confidentiality: The Legal
                          Framework   92
                   Part III. Reproductive Choice   105
                   Part IV. Summary   113

Chapter 6   **Adolescents and HIV and AIDS: Population**
                   Demographics and Prevention Strategies   **116**
                   Introduction   116
                   Part I. The Incidence and Prevalence of HIV and
                          AIDS Among Adolescents   117
                   Part II. AIDS Education Programs   124
                   Part IV. Summary and Conclusion   137

Chapter 7   **Welfare Reform and Its Effects on Women and**
                   Children with HIV and AIDS   **140**
                   Introduction   140
                   Part I. Welfare Reform and the Temporary Assistance
                          to Needy Families Block Grant   141

Notes   **154**
Table of Cases   **218**
Bibliography   **227**
Index   **247**

LIST OF TABLES

6.1   Number and Percentage of Asymptomatic Young Women and
        Men by Method of Exposure to HIV by Age   119

6.2   Number of Females and Males with AIDS by Race and Age
        Categories of 13 to 19 and 20 to 29 and Percentage of These
        Groups by Racial Categories Compared to All Cases of AIDS—
        As of December 1995   120

6.3   Number and Percentage of Cases of AIDS by Exposure
        Category by Age Through December 1995   121

PREFACE

This book is about women and children and the Acquired Immune Deficiency Syndrome (AIDS) epidemic. The framework I use for reporting and analysis is derived from federal statutes that protect the civil rights of women and children with the Human Immunodeficiency Virus (HIV) and AIDS and that identify the financial, medical, and social services that are available to them. Selected state statutes illustrate matters such as child custody, testing for HIV, and confidentiality of medical records.

AIDS has been perceived mainly as a disease of gay men and intravenous drug users (IVDUs), and the image of a woman with HIV or AIDS is intertwined with that of a woman who is an IVDU. This image is correct but it is limited. Its origins lie, in part, in the way in which the Centers for Disease Control classifies cases by means of exposure to the HIV and in part in the lack of media attention to the role of heterosexual intercourse in transmitting the virus. Through December of 1995, heterosexual contact accounted for 38 percent of all cases of AIDS in women ever reported to the CDC and for more than 50 percent of new cases reported in 1994 and 1995 (chapter 1).

While men with HIV and AIDS outnumber women, since the late 1980s the incidence of AIDS has grown faster among women than it has among men. Among adolescents the percentage of cases accounted for by females is striking. Young women between the ages of 13 and 19 account for 35 percent of cases of AIDS compared to 14 percent of cases represented by women regardless of age (chapter 1).

Roughly three-quarters of women with AIDS have children, and it is estimated that between 125,000 and 150,000 children will be orphaned by the AIDS epidemic by the turn of the century (chapter 4). Each year there are approximately 2,000 new cases of AIDS among infants, although data released in 1996 suggest that the number of new cases of perinatal AIDS may be declining.

Women with the Human Immunodeficiency Virus (HIV) and AIDS have confronted a series of gender-specific problems including: (1) their exclusion from programs testing new AIDS treatments because it was assumed that women of childbearing age needed protection from exposure to exper- imental drugs; (2) inattention by the scientific community to whether or not HIV progressed differently in women than in men, resulting in the fail- ure to correctly diagnose HIV-disease in women; (3) denial of federal fi- nancial aid because criteria for eligibility for aid were based on the signs and symptoms of HIV in men; and (4) the myriad problems that poor women raising children on their own confront that are compounded by family ill- ness.

The first chapter covers the emergence of the AIDS epidemic in the United States and describes the responses of the general public and the federal government to people with HIV and AIDS in the first decade of the epidemic. The methods used by the CDC to compile data on the number of AIDS cases and to estimate the rate of HIV-infection is described and the incidence and prevalence of HIV and AIDS in women is discussed, includ- ing methods of exposure and the geographic distribution of AIDS cases in the United States.

The stigma associated with HIV and AIDS and the discrimination ex- perienced by people with either condition is well documented. Protection from illegal discrimination is found in a series of civil rights statutes, in- cluding the Americans with Disabilities Act, the Fair Housing Act, and laws that protect children from discrimination in education. These are the sub- ject of chapter 2.

Approximately 75 percent of women with HIV have children, 50 per- cent have more than one child, and most are single parents. Approximately 70 percent of single women who are raising children are poor. As a woman's health or the health of her child deteriorates, government policies that pro- vide financial assistance, medical assistance, and social services play an important role in her life and her ability to maintain her family intact. The federal and state policies through which such assistance is available are covered in chapter 3.

Chapter 4 covers a number of issues related to child care. First, the question "Who is caring for children when a parent has HIV?" is addressed, followed by a review of planning options that are available to an HIV- positive woman who wishes to plan for her child's future. A number of women with HIV-disease in their families will become involved with the child wel- fare system, which is also discussed in chapter 4. For some women such in- volvement will be involuntary, initiated by a medical provider because a child was born with a positive toxicology for drugs or displaying signs or symptoms associated with fetal alcohol syndrome. Other women will turn to the child welfare system to seek help as their health deteriorates.

Chapter 5 deals with the subjects of testing for HIV, including argu- ments that are made to justify why a woman should be tested, and the sub- ject of confidentiality of information regarding a woman's HIV-status. There is evidence that some women who test positive for HIV have been "en- couraged" to terminate their pregnancies, and some medical providers ex- press the opinion that the state should use its coercive powers on behalf of a fetus, including active surveillance of the behavior of pregnant women outside the hospital during the last trimester of pregnancy and forced intervention to protect a woman's fetus. The subject of reproductive choice and the issues that arise for a woman who is HIV-positive or diagnosed with AIDS are also covered in chapter 5.

In 1995, one-half of all cases of AIDS that were reported to the CDC occurred in young people under the age of 25. Since the latency between exposure to the HIV and development of symptoms suggestive of AIDS is approximately ten years, it is assumed that these young people were exposed to HIV in their adolescence. Chapter 6 covers the subject of HIV and AIDS in adolescents, including the subject of AIDS prevention through education.

In the spring and summer of 1996, federal legislation that controls the operations of programs through which financial assistance is provided to able-bodied and disabled women was changed, and changes were made in the regulations that govern the provision of financial aid to disabled children. The changes are described in chapter 7 where I speculate on how women and children with HIV and AIDS may be affected by the revisions to the law.

SUBJECTS NOT ADDRESSED

Throughout this text I report court decisions to illustrate the application of statutes such as the Americans with Disabilities Act, the Fair Housing Act, and statutes that mandate reporting as abused a child born with a positive toxicology for drugs. However, I have been selective in choosing what issues to cover and what cases to report, in large part because HIV and AIDS have generated more legal cases than any other disease in American history (Gostin, 1990) and a comprehensive review of case law on this subject is beyond the scope of this text. Topics such as litigation against blood banks brought by people who allege that they contracted HIV because a blood bank was negligent in monitoring the blood supply and litigation against employers brought by hospital personnel who claim that they contracted HIV on the job because of employer negligence are not covered. Likewise, it is beyond the scope of this text to review each state's antidiscrimination laws that have relevance to people with HIV and AIDS.

I used two criteria in choosing cases to report. First, rulings of the United States Supreme Court and federal circuit courts of appeals that have direct bearing on HIV and AIDS are reported except for those dealing with excluded matters such as negligence. Second, regardless of whether the court is a federal or a state court and regardless of its ranking in the hierarchy of courts, I report decisions that are "unique" even though they may not bear directly on the subject of HIV or AIDS. For example, in 1996 the Supreme Court of South Carolina ruled that the mother of a child born with a positive toxicology for cocaine could be charged under the state's criminal laws and be imprisoned for "delivering" cocaine to another person. In light of the relationship between drug use and HIV and AIDS, the relevance of this court ruling for pregnant women is inescapable.

Some final points on the use of case law. First, many cases are never officially reported, for example, cases from a state's juvenile or family court. As a consequence, information about how a state resolves child custody disputes that implicate a woman with HIV or AIDS may be limited. Next, many cases that involve disputes about eligibility for financial or medical assistance and cases alleging employment or housing discrimination receive a first hearing before an administrative body and these cases are not routinely reported, providing a further information gap. A final point is that many cases are settled with no official report of the settlement, although the facts of the case may appear in official publications. This may result in frustration for the reader who wants to know how a case turned out but where this information is not available.

A NOTE ON TERMINOLOGY

In writing this text I have avoided using the conventional "HIV/AIDS" as a formulaic way of referring to these phenomena. There is a great deal of difference between testing positive for HIV and being diagnosed with an opportunistic infection, which defines the condition referred to by the acronym AIDS. The latency between exposure to HIV and the development of symptoms that are AIDS defining can be ten years or longer and a person may live all those years ignorant of her condition. Moreover, in the law, if not in everyday life, the distinction between HIV and AIDS is significant. For example, a woman with HIV is protected from discrimination under civil rights statutes such as the Americans with Disabilities Act or the Fair Housing Act, but she is not, based on a diagnosis of HIV alone, eligible for assistance under disability-based income maintenance programs.

Throughout the text when I refer to the Supreme Court I am referring to the United States Supreme Court. In instances where a state supreme court is referred to I include the name of the state, as in the Supreme Court of New York. Since most women with AIDS who have children are single parents, I use the singular parent and for convenience sake, I use the singular child although many women with HIV have more than one child. Terms used in this text that refer to race or ethnicity are those used by the source that is cited, although I do not routinely use quotation marks around the descriptions "African American," "Hispanic," and so forth.

I cite the "AIDS Daily Summary" in several places. The summary is produced by the Centers for Disease Control and distributed, free of charge, via electronic mail. The interested reader should contact the CDC at aidsnews@cdcnac.aspensys.com.

For convenience sake I have included at the end of this preface a glossary which includes acronyms used for federal statutes and federal agencies as well as terms born of the epidemic.

GLOSSARY

AACWA	Adoption Assistance and Child Welfare Act
ACTG	AIDS Clinical Trials Group
ADA	Americans with Disabilities Act
ADAMHA	Alcohol, Drug Abuse and Mental Health Administration Reorganization Act
AFDC	Aid to Families with Dependent Children
AIA	Abandoned Babies and Abandoned Infants Act
AIDS	Acquired Immune Deficiency Syndrome
AZT	Azidothymidine also called Zidovudine (ZDV). AZT inhibits replication of HIV. Retrovir is the drug's trade name.
CAPTA	Child Abuse Prevention and Treatment Act
CARE Act	Ryan White Comprehensive AIDS Resources Emergency Act
Case Law	Any court decision or body of court decisions. For example, all decisions involving employment discrimination brought by people with HIV and AIDS are the body of case law on that subject.
CDC	Centers for Disease Control
EAHCA	Education for All Handicapped Children Act
EPSDT	Early and Periodic Screening, Diagnosis, and Treatment
FAS	Fetal Alcohol Syndrome
FHA	Fair Housing Act
GAO	General Accounting Office
HHS	U. S. Department of Health and Human Services
HIV	Human Immunodeficiency Virus
HOPWA	Housing Opportunities for People with AIDS
IDEA	Individuals with Disabilities Education Act
IVDU	Intravenous Drug User
PCP	*Pneumocystis carinii* pneumonia
PRA	Personal Responsibility and Work Opportunity Act
SSA	Social Security Administration
SSBG	Social Services Block Grant
SSDI	Supplemental Security Disability Income
SSI	Supplemental Security Income
STD	Sexually transmitted diseases
TANF	Transitional Assistance for Needy Families
VRA	Vocational Rehabilitation Act
ZDV	See AZT

ACKNOWLEDGMENTS

I want to thank a number of people at the Centers for Disease Control, the United States Department of Housing and Urban Development, the United States Department of Health and Human Services, the Office of AIDS Research, and the White House Office on AIDS for responding by FAX and by overnight mail and for returning my telephone calls, in my quest for information and my need to have immediate answers to all of my questions.

Special thanks go to Mary Lee Allen of the Children's Defense Fund for sending information and for providing good "leads" to other sources for information to Jodie Epstein at the Center for Law and Social Policy for taking the time to speak with me on the telephone and for the publications she sent to me, and to Professor Nancy Mudrick of the Maxwell School, Syracuse University, for helping in my search for cases where women with HIV and AIDS experienced employment discrimination. I am indebted to Gioia Stevens, my editor at Oxford University Press, for all the help she provided and in general for paving the way from prospectus to publication.

And my never-ending gratitude goes to my partner, friend, reviewer, critic, and constant source of support, Gary David Comstock.

CHAPTER 1

Introduction

Since brought to public attention in 1981, AIDS has been a political as well as a medical issue. The response of the federal government in the first decade of the epidemic was affected as much by negative attitudes toward gay men and intravenous drug users (IVDUs) as it was by public health concerns.

In Part I of this chapter the federal response to the AIDS epidemic in its first decade is discussed and similarities are drawn between the AIDS epidemic and venereal disease epidemics in the early part of the twentieth century. In Part II the methodologies that are used by the Centers for Disease Control (CDC) to compile data describing the incidence (the number of new cases within a specified time period) and prevalence (the proportion of a population that is infected) of HIV and AIDS are described; then, using available data, the impact of HIV on women and children is reported. The modes of transmission of HIV and the geographic distribution of AIDS cases are the last topics reviewed.

PART I. THE EMERGENCE OF AIDS IN THE UNITED STATES AND THE RESPONSE OF THE FEDERAL GOVERNMENT

AIDS came to public attention on June 5, 1981, when the Centers for Disease Control (CDC) reported that five cases of a rare form of pneumonia (*Pneumocystis carinii* pneumonia [PCP]) had been diagnosed in homosexual men. The first cases of HIV in women were reported in 1982, and pediatric AIDS, defined as AIDS in children younger than 13 years of age, was first described in 1983.

Throughout the first decade of the epidemic, criticism was levied at the federal government. Appropriated funds were viewed as insufficient by some,[1] and the manner in which funds were allocated for research purposes had been a source of concern.[2] However, the most serious critique of the federal role was reserved for its failure of leadership. At Congressional hearings in 1987, 1990, and 1992, members of Congress, health care providers and health care organizations, the Presidential Commission on the HIV Epidemic, and people with AIDS, among others,[3] called for the federal government to assume a leadership role. For example, in 1990, at hearings held by the House Subcommittee on Human Resources and Intergovernmental Relations (hereafter, House Subcommittee Report), committee members, after acknowledging the federal role in providing funds for AIDS research, said:

> Leadership has not been forthcoming. Through two Administrations, neither the President nor any other Federal official, at the highest levels to which the American public looks for direction in times of crisis, has taken responsibility for the strategic planning necessary to control the epidemic and provide treatment and care to its casualties. We urge the President to provide the overarching leadership that is fundamental to winning the fight against AIDS.[4]

In 1992, the same subcommittee, in a report titled *The Politics of AIDS Prevention: Science Takes a Time Out,* criticized the federal government, including the executive branch. The role played by the federal government in the 1980s was referred to as a "huge scar on American history . . . and an international disgrace," because two United States presidents at best ignored and at worst interfered with policy to combat the epidemic.[5]

Specific problems that were attributed to the lack of leadership included a near breakdown in some urban hospitals, which were described by Senator Lautenberg of New Jersey as overburdened, understaffed, and forced to provide care in a "Calcutta-like" environment where patients spent weeks lying in the corridors waiting for hospital beds.[6] In 1990, Dr. C. Everett Koop, the former Surgeon General of the United States, echoing a theme raised in 1986 by the National Academy of Sciences, told Congress that "we do not have a Federal policy on AIDS [and it is] incredible that the Federal government has not had a dialogue with the states, and with certain municipalities about how the costs of the epidemic will be paid."[7]

The suggestion that the federal government defaulted in its role was not universally held. In 1990, six senators dissenting to the 1992 House Subcommittee Report argued that transmission of HIV is preventable in the great majority of cases and said that federal aid should be made contingent on local units of government "clearly demonstrating that they are taking concrete public health measures to prevent the continued growth of AIDS."[8] Senator Helms of North Carolina faulted the government for spending more on AIDS-related research than on other conditions and diseases such as heart disease, cancer, and Alzheimer's disease,[9] although the senator's views were not shared by members of the scientific community who were surveyed by the Federal Office of Technology Assessment.[10]

The reluctance of top officials to become involved in AIDS policy making was not confined to the national level. Backstrom and Robins (1996) surveyed legislators who chaired state health committees. Only 19 percent of legislative chairs reported that the governors of their states were influential in formulating AIDS policy and 27 percent said that the governor had little if any influence. From interviews they conducted in six states, they learned that AIDS was a subject that governors wanted to keep out of, forfeiting their chance to influence public policy.[11]

The Government's Response in Historical Context

The federal response is best understood if viewed in a historical context and then with reference to the groups identified as being at greatest risk for the HIV. Brandt (1988) finds parallels between the epidemic of venereal disease that confronted the United States in the early part of the twentieth century and the AIDS epidemic.[12] In both periods of history, there was a general fear of contagion; a publically held belief, despite evidence to the contrary, that casual contact provided a route of infection; and a conviction that there was a responsible "other," an outsider, who was the source of contamination. In 1907, a gynecologist at Johns Hopkins described the problem of venereal disease in the following terms:

> The tide of [venereal disease] has been raising [*sic*] owing to the inpouring of a large foreign population with lower ideals . . . these countless currents flowing daily from the houses of the poorest into those of the richest and forming a sort of civic circulatory system expressive of the body politic, a circulation which continually tends to equalize the distribution of morality and disease.[13]

In the early part of the twentieth century, medical opinion held that sexually transmitted diseases were communicated "by pens, pencils, toothbrushes, towels and bedding." The navy removed doorknobs from its battleships during World War I because they were claimed to be a source of infection.[14]

Anyone who views this kind of thinking as a relic of history should consider the following events that occurred in the late 1980s and mid-1990s:

> In 1987, testifying before Congress, Louise Ray described the experiences of her family after her sons tested positive for the HIV. The . . . barber refused to cut their hair, the family pastor advised them to stop coming to church, and school officials told the boys to stay home. . . . There were two bomb threats . . . threatening phone calls. . . . [our] house burned down and [we] lost everything. The fire was determined to be arson. The nightmare continued when [we] moved to a motel after the fire, [and] were asked to leave because of the boys.[15]

> In 1995, forty gay and lesbian leaders who were invited to the White House to confer with President Clinton were greeted by members of the Secret Service wearing rubber gloves. . . . The guards presumably thought they were protecting themselves against the AIDS virus should any of the visitors be infected.[16]

Arrangements were made to send 50 HIV-infected children from New York City to camp in the summer of 1995. In an example of the enduring, tenacious stigma attached to HIV and AIDS, the private campground that agreed to give the kids a free week of fun decided . . . to turn them away. The reason given . . . was [that] the brief visit would scare others away from using the camp in the future.[17]

The view that the carrier of disease is an outsider is a tenacious one, neither informed by nor subject to change on the basis of facts. For example, the view of immigrants as responsible for bringing venereal disease into the United States was held despite medical information compiled at ports of entry that did not support this suggestion, and prostitutes were quarantined in both world wars although this practice had no effect on venereal disease rates.[18] In 1990, community residents in Puerto Rico objected to the placement of an AIDS hospice in their neighborhood, because they thought that AIDS could be transmitted by mosquitoes and that the hospice posed a danger to students attending a nearby school. Community residents refused to meet with a local physician who asked for a meeting to educate them about HIV transmission.[19]

Intravenous drug users, their sex partners, and gay and bisexual men have replaced immigrants as the outsiders or carriers of disease and prostitutes have again been targeted for blame. Some states have statutes that mandate testing for HIV for any person convicted of prostitution, and a number of states have adopted statutes that criminalize behavior that could result in transmission of HIV.[20] The focus on prostitutes occurs even though there is no evidence to suggest that their clients are at special risk of infection. The CDC reports that prostitution, despite its long association with the transmission of syphilis, has played a minor role in the epidemiology of that disease.[21] Moreover, arguments that prostitutes are sources of HIV-transmission ignore the fact that male-to-female transmission is twice as likely as female-to-male transmission. The risk for prostitutes is greater than for their male clients.*

The focus on the epidemic as confined to outsiders and caused by contact with outsiders is dangerous to the extent that it suggests that one is free of risk by avoiding contact with members of groups closely associated with the epidemic. There are data on the percentage of women with HIV or AIDS who report no identification or contact with an "outsider" group. As of December 31, 1995, 22 percent of HIV-infected women, compared to 15 percent in 1994, reported no such contact or identification.[22]

Condemnation of the outsider pervades public opinion. In 1992, Blendon and his colleagues, reporting the results of twenty national opinion polls, informed us that the great majority of those surveyed agreed with the statement that people with AIDS should be treated with compassion; and only

---

*The Centers for Disease Control defines prostitutes as females, counting male prostitutes as homosexual or bisexual men. Field, Martha, A., "Testing for AIDS: Uses and Abuses," *American Journal of Law & Medicine* 16 (1990): 91.

6 percent disagreed with this proposition.[23] But the percentage of disagreement increased to 24 percent if the person with HIV contracted it
through sexual relations with a drug user, to 27 percent if the disease was
contracted through homosexual activity, and to 30 percent if drug use was
causal to contracting the virus. Public sympathy was greatest toward those
who contracted HIV through blood transfusions, with only 3 percent of survey respondents failing to view this group with sympathy.

Comparing data they compiled in the late 1980s with their 1992 data,
Blendon and his colleagues report that hostility toward people with AIDS
declined or remained the same between these time periods. For example,
in 1987, 25 percent of Americans, compared to 21 percent in 1991, agreed
with the proposition that employers should have the right to fire a worker
with AIDS. There was a significant decrease in the percentage of people
who said that they would not work alongside a person with AIDS (25 percent to 16 percent, 1988 to 1992, respectively), and the percentage of people who believed that a child with AIDS should not be allowed to attend
school dropped from a 1985 high of 39 percent to a low of 9 percent in
1992.[24]

Public sympathy toward those who contract HIV through blood transfusions reflects the tendency to classify people with HIV as victims versus
those responsible for their condition. However, those classified as victims
are not always viewed with sympathy. Children, for example, have experienced considerable discrimination despite their victim status and the overwhelming evidence that HIV is not easily transmissible in school settings.
(See chapter 2.) Clemo (1992) interviewed forty lobbyists in Washington,
D. C., who represent groups advocating for children's issues. In response to
questions regarding the effectiveness of their lobbying efforts in general
compared to their effectiveness on AIDS issues, only 3 percent of lobbyists
reported that they were effective on AIDS-related matters compared to 71
percent reporting that their lobbying efforts were successful on other children's issues.[25] Clemo concluded that politicians generalize their moral condemnation of adults with HIV and AIDS to children.

Public Policy and Acts of Discrimination

At both the federal and state levels public policy concerning HIV and AIDS
was designed in the late 1980s. Policy was shaped in part by the compassion of a number of legislators and in part as an accommodation to the practical needs of government and to the fears and needs of people with HIV.
Agencies of government with responsibility for tracking the spread of the
epidemic and for testing experimental treatments needed the cooperation
of people who were HIV-positive. However, based on a history of less than
exemplary treatment by agencies of government, coupled with documented
instances of AIDS-related discrimination and calls for quarantine and other
forms of coercive intervention, it was assumed that cooperation would not
be forthcoming absent guarantees of confidentiality and statutory protections against discrimination. (See chapters 2 and 5.) According to the Pres-

ident's Commission on AIDS, discrimination against people with HIV and AIDS was the greatest obstacle to progress in halting the epidemic, because people were not likely to cooperate with public health officials if they feared loss of their homes and jobs.[26]

Fear of people with HIV has spurred calls for legislation that would make it a felony for any person in a high-risk group to donate blood, for prohibitions on anyone with AIDS from working in the health care industry, for denying federal funds to cities that did not bar children with AIDS from public schools,[27] and for permitting funds allocated for research on AIDS to be diverted to closure or quarantine of massage parlors and bathhouses.[28] It has been suggested that laws criminalizing behavior which could result in transmitting HIV were "hastily conceived for political expedience . . . to calm the fears of the populace."[29] The result of the latter may be poorly drafted and ill-conceived statutes. There have been calls for quarantine of people with HIV, and public opinion polls conducted in the mid-1980s showed that a majority of Americans favored quarantine of AIDS patients, with many supporting the use of tattoos to mark those with AIDS.[30] At least twelve states enacted new legislation or amended existing legislation to bring HIV within quarantine statutes,[31] and instances of quarantine were documented, including, in the early 1980s the federal quarantine of approximately 200 HIV-positive Haitian immigrants until a federal judge ruled that the detention violated the federal Constitution.[32]

Discriminatory treatment of people with HIV and AIDS includes: (1) denying medical treatment; (2) counseling HIV-positive women to have abortions; and (3) terminating the employment of people: (a) perceived as HIV-positive; (b) known to be HIV-positive; (c) associated with people who were HIV-positive; or (d) advocating for providing medical services to people with HIV or AIDS.

Other HIV- and AIDS-based discrimination claims include: (1) limiting health care benefits; (2) voiding marriages; (3) limiting access to public schools of children with AIDS; (4) discriminating against children with AIDS in foster-care placement and access to adoption services; (5) failing to provide biological and foster families of children with AIDS the services and training they need to care for the children as well as failing to recruit foster parents for children with HIV and AIDS; (6) failing to provide qualified interpreters so that hearing-impaired prisoners can understand what medical and mental health treatments were to be provided to them, and testing them for the HIV without their knowledge and consent; and (7) marking the personal belongings of prisoners so as to identify them as HIV-infected.[33]

Public policy to protect people with HIV and AIDS from discrimination in employment is rooted in a 1987 decision of the Supreme Court that set the stage for classifying HIV-infection as a disability. (See chapter 2.) In 1990, Congress codified the high court's decision into civil rights statutes which protect people with HIV from discrimination in matters such as employment, access to housing and places of public accommodation, and receipt of medical care. HIV-disease was included in definitions of disability that are used to determine eligibility for benefit-conferring programs that provide cash and medical assistance. (See chapter 3.) In August of 1990, Congress passed the first comprehensive legislation affecting people with HIV and AIDS when it enacted the Ryan White Comprehensive AIDS Resources Emergency Act through which funds are made available to the states for a variety of social services. (See chapter 3.)

PART II. THE EMERGENCE OF HIV

Surveillance data which describe the incidence and prevalence of AIDS and HIV are compiled by the CDC in collaboration with the states and certain federal entities such as the Departments of Defense and Labor.

Data on AIDS

Confirmed cases of AIDS are reported to the CDC by all of the states. The CDC estimates that "about 50 percent of all AIDS cases [are] reported . . . within 3 months of diagnosis, with about 20 percent being reported more than one year after diagnosis."[34]

The CDC employs a hierarchical scheme for categorizing people by method of exposure to HIV. Cases are counted only once. If a person identifies more than one means of exposure, she or he is placed in that category listed first in the hierarchy. In descending order the categories are: men who have sex with men (which includes homosexual and bisexual men); injecting drug users; men who have sex with men and inject drugs; hemophiliacs; women and men who have heterosexual contact with a person with or at increased risk for HIV infection; blood product recipients; and undetermined.[35] In addition, there are four categories which identify means of exposure for cases of pediatric AIDS, including: hemophilia; mother who has or is at risk for HIV-infection; blood product recipients; and undetermined. There is no category for women who have sex with women. Ninety percent of lesbians with AIDS are said to have contracted HIV through IVDU and they would be classified as injection drug users in the CDC's scheme.[36] No information regarding a woman's sexual orientation would be recorded.[37] The exposure category for a lesbian who contracted AIDS through sexual contact with a woman who was an IVDU or bisexual would be classified as "risk unknown," since sexual contacts involving women are restricted to heterosexual contacts. The CDC classification scheme is weighted against recording heterosexual contact as a method of exposure in two ways. First, by classifying bisexual males in the category "men who have sex with men," and second, by classifying as an IVDU a woman who reports that in addition to IVDU she has had sexual contact with a man with or at increased risk for HIV-infection.

Data on HIV

Data on HIV are compiled in two ways. The first method estimates the infection rate using AIDS incidence data as a baseline. Rates of HIV-infection are "back-calculated" from these data using assumptions about the incubation period, and projections are made of the prevalence of HIV- infection.[38]

In the second approach, the CDC, acting through the states, gathers information through anonymous surveys of specific segments of the population in its "Family of Surveys."[39] Blood samples are collected and analyzed for the presence of antibodies to HIV after information identifying the person is removed. Demographic and behavioral information are preserved. Blood samples are collected at a variety of sites such as sexually transmitted disease (STD) clinics, family planning clinics, Indian Health Service clinics, drug treatment centers, hospitals, blood collection centers, laboratories, and screening programs that are operated by the Departments of Defense and Labor. Because identifying information is not maintained, informed consent is not seen as necessary and the sampling bias that would result from refusals to cooperate is eliminated.

The data that are collected through the Family of Surveys provide information describing rates of infection in readily accessible populations. For example, the Family of Surveys includes the Survey of Childbearing Women, which compiles data on all newborns by using blood that is drawn from newborns for general screening purposes. Active-duty military personnel are screened for HIV, and screening is routine for those applying for military services and the Job Corps and those seeking to donate blood. Information provided by STD clinics, health care clinics, and hospitals yields information on select but diverse populations including IVDUs; the homeless; women who seek prenatal care, family planning services, and abortion services; primary care patients; and blood donors. In addition, with the informed consent of the tested party, nonblinded surveys are conducted in areas where the prevalence of HIV is high. They allow for the collection of more detailed social and behavioral information than is possible through blinded surveys.

Newborns and their mothers, except for women who deliver outside of formal medical networks, are the only groups where an entire universe is tested. While testing of all military recruits and applicants to the Job Corps takes place, neither group can be assumed to represent the universe from which applicants are drawn. All other collected data are limited because each survey method depends on a process of self-selection that includes only a segment of the population that seeks a medical or social service where blood samples are drawn. Moreover, many of the sites chosen for collection are those frequented by populations already known to be at risk, and the sites chosen are not randomly selected but are designated by state health officials.[40] Data that describe incidence and prevalence by risk category are circular to the degree that the reported numbers will reflect increases in those populations originally identified as at risk, not necessarily because their numbers are increasing relative to other groups, but because data are collected at sites that serve these populations. Others, not in a known risk category, are not necessarily accessible for testing.

There is evidence that the sampling methodology used yields an undercount. The CDC estimates that cases of AIDS are undercounted by as much as 18 percent.[41] Using cause of death as reported on death certificates as an indicator of the accuracy of reporting of cases of AIDS, the CDC claims that studies show that deaths for which HIV-infection was designated the underlying cause of death represent approximately two-thirds to three-quarters of deaths actually attributable to HIV.[42] In addition, evidence of a self-selection bias comes from a study conducted at an STD clinic in San Francisco where all of the clients were tested but where only 67 percent ($n = 568$) volunteered to be tested. The rate of seroprevalence was lower among the volunteers than among the group as a whole (9.5 percent compared to 14.5 percent).[43]

The CDC made an effort in 1987 to conduct a national "household" survey to determine the extent of HIV in the population. The household survey was to be voluntary and therefore biased but nonetheless might have revealed information on HIV prevalence in the entire population. The survey did not get much beyond the stage of pilot testing, because of concerns that were raised by minority communities. Hurley and Pinder (1992), discussing the failed effort, stress the relevance of social context in efforts to elicit involvement of those communities without whose cooperation data collection efforts are doomed to fail. These authors attribute lack of cooperation from minority groups to the "effects of discrimination and persecution . . . bolstered by the idea of quarantining HIV-positive people emanating from the highest halls of government [where] the purest of scientific motives may, and probably should, be questioned."[44]

The Numbers   Cases of HIV and AIDS are classified as either pediatric or adolescent/adult. The method of exposure to HIV distinguishes these categories. Pediatric cases consist of children younger than 13 who presumably contracted HIV in utero or through transfusion with contaminated blood products before testing of the blood supply became routine. Those 13 years of age and older contract HIV through the same modes of transmission, discussed below, that affect adults. Of the 2,354 cases of AIDS in 13- to 19-year-olds that were diagnosed through December of 1995, twenty-nine cases were determined to have been exposed to HIV in utero.[45]

Through December of 1995, 513,486 cases of AIDS were reported to the CDC.[46] One-half of these cases were reported in the period 1993 through 1995.[47] New diagnostic criteria implemented by the CDC in 1993 accounted for a significant portion of the increase in new cases.[48] Karon and colleagues (1996)estimate that in 1992 the number of HIV-positive people in the United States was between 650,000 and 900,000. The overall rate of infection at that time for people over 12 years of age was estimated to be 1 in 300 with a rate of 1 in 1,000 for women and 1 in 160 for men.[49]

Women with AIDS account for 71,818 cases, approximately 14 percent of the total of 513,486 cases reported through December of 1995. The incidence of AIDS is increasing more rapidly among women than men. Of the 73,380 cases of AIDS in adults and adolescents (13 years of age and older) that were first diagnosed in 1995, 13,764 (19 percent) were women, the highest proportion of cases among women ever reported in a single year.[50] This finding continues a trend, accentuated by the new diagnostic criteria implemented in 1993, where cases of AIDS in women have reflected an in-

creasing proportion of all reported AIDS cases. In 1994, the proportionate
increase among women was nearly three times greater than it had been in
1985.[51] The World Health Organization estimates that worldwide, women
of childbearing age account for approximately 50 percent of all adults with
HIV-infection.[52]

By the end of 1995, 319,849 people in the United States, representing
62 percent of reported cases of AIDS, had died.[53] AIDS is the eighth leading cause of death overall and the leading cause of death among people age
25 to 44.[54] For women age 25 to 44, AIDS is the third leading cause of death
overall, the fifth leading cause of death for white women, and the leading
cause of death for black women.[55] Mortality data for Hispanic, Asian, and
Native-American women were not separately reported.[56] AIDS is the leading cause of death among women in prison.[57] Among children, it is the leading cause of death for 1- to 4-year-olds[58] and the fifth leading cause of death
in youngsters less than 15 years of age.[59]

Of adult and adolescent AIDS cases reported through 1995, approximately 55 percent of women were black, not Hispanic; 24 percent were white,
not Hispanic; 20 percent were Hispanic; and less than 1 percent each were
Asian/Pacific Islander, American Indian/Alaskan Native, and unknown.[60]

The subject of AIDS in adolescents is dealt with extensively in chapter
6. It is worth noting here that of all cases reported to the CDC through December of 1995, in the 13- to 19-year-old age group, young women accounted
for 35 percent of cases, in the 20- to 29-year-old age group, women accounted
for 18 percent of cases, whereas for all age groups women accounted for 14
percent of cases.[61] The percentage of women in the 13- to 19-year-old age
group is almost twice that of women in the 20- to 29-year-old age group and
two and one-half times greater than that of women in all age groups.

Pediatric AIDS is defined as AIDS in children less than 13 years of age.
Data from the Survey of Childbearing Women measure the prevalence of
HIV-infection among women giving birth to live infants in the United
States. The survey is anonymous and unlinked. Blood specimens collected
from newborns for routine metabolic screening are tested for the HIV-
antibody after all personal identifiers are removed. Between 70 and 75 percent of children born to women who are HIV-positive will, within eighteen
months of birth, seroconvert, leaving between 25 and 30 percent of newborns, or about 2,000 children a year, HIV-positive. Through September
of 1996, 7,472 cases of pediatric AIDS were reported.[62] The race or ethnicity of these cases was 58 percent black, not Hispanic; 18 percent white, not
Hispanic; 23 percent Hispanic; and less than 1 percent each Asian/Pacific
Islander; American Indian/Alaskan Native, and unknown. Gender distribution was equal and the great majority of children (80 percent) were under
5 years of age.

Modes of Transmission and Symptoms

HIV may be transmitted through: (1) intimate sexual contact with an infected person; (2) needle sharing; (3) in utero mother-to-infant transmission; (3) blood product transfusions; (4) breast-feeding; and (5) artificial in-

semination. Because donated blood is now screened for HIV the likelihood that HIV-disease will be contracted through use of contaminated blood products is reduced significantly. Likewise, the risk of infection through artificial insemination seems low. Worldwide, of approximately 1 million donor inseminations, twelve cases of HIV contracted through artificial insemination have been reported.[63] While HIV can be transmitted through breast-feeding, such occurrences are said to be uncommon and the risk of infection through breast-feeding is said to be low.[64]

Risk of in utero transmission is increased for women who practice unprotected sex during their pregnancy, for women who contract sexually transmitted diseases during their pregnancy, and for women exposed to invasive surgical procedures such as amniocentesis.[65]

An individual's risk of becoming infected with HIV depends on a number of factors. Focusing on those at risk due to sexual contact, factors of concern are: (1) the number of sex partners; (2) the prevalence of infection in these partners; and (3) the likelihood that the virus will be transmitted during sexual contact. The latter is affected by considerations such as whether either person has an STD; the type of sex practiced; whether condoms are used; and the amount of the virus in the infected partner, which is itself related to the clinical stage of the disease. According to the CDC, these factors indicate that those at greatest risk are regular sex partners of a person with HIV; people who have sex with others with risk factors; people who have multiple sex partners from urban settings where the prevalence of IVDU and "crack" cocaine use is high; and individuals with other STDs.[66] As with other STDs, women who have sex with men are at greater risk than their male partners. Male-to-female transmission of HIV is "twice as effective as female-to-male transmission."[67]

Because they inherit their mothers' antibodies, virtually all newborns of HIV-positive women will test positive for HIV, but, as noted above, between 70 and 75 percent will seroconvert by 18 months of age.[68] Thus chances are good that a child born to a mother with HIV or AIDS will not be HIV-infected. However, screening of the blood supply makes infection through transfusion highly unlikely. Thus the mother of a child who tests positive at birth will in all likelihood be HIV-positive herself. An estimated 92 percent of all new cases of HIV-infection in newborns occur through vertical transmission.[69]

In 1995, 13,764 cases of AIDS among adult and adolescent women were reported to the CDC. Reported risk factors were IVDU ($n = 5,204$) and heterosexual contact ($n = 5,253$), with each method of exposure accounting for 38 percent of cases. No known risk factor ($n = 2,987$) accounted for 22 percent of cases, and exposure through contaminated blood products ($n = 320$) accounted for 2 percent of cases.[70]

A total of 61,028 people with AIDS have ever been classified as no known risk factor. Local health departments investigate these cases, and, if information becomes available, people are reclassified according to a known risk factor.[71] Over 33,000 cases (55 percent) have not been reclassified. Of these, 68 percent were under investigation at the end of 1995. Forty-five percent of cases have been reclassified. Women represent 6,218 of the reclassified cases (22 percent). These women were found to have been exposed to HIV through IVDU (28 percent); heterosexual contact (66 percent); blood products (6 percent); and other means (less then 1 percent).[72]

The Geography of AIDS

In the early years of the epidemic, AIDS was considered an urban problem, with more than one-half of all cases located in New York City and San Francisco. In 1987, the rate of AIDS per 100,000 population was relatively low, between 0 and 3.9 cases in more than one-half of the continental United States. By 1992, the number of states falling into this low-end category was reduced to nine,[73] and in 1994 only one state had a rate per 100,000 population of 0 to 3.9 cases.[74] In 1995, more than one-half of AIDS cases reported nationwide were outside of the original centers of the epidemic, with 17 percent of cases reported in small cities, towns, and rural areas throughout the country.[75] The greatest number of cases reported and the greatest proportionate increase of cases in the reporting periods 1988 to 1992 and 1993 to 1995 came from the South (31 percent), compared to proportionate increases in the Midwest, Northeast, and West of 22 percent, 20 percent and 15 percent, respectively.[76] Moreover, the highest proportion of cases of AIDS among adolescents and young adults, defined as those 13 to 29 years of age, was reported from small metropolitan areas with populations between 50,000 and 500,000, accounting for 27 percent of cases, and rural areas, accounting for 24 percent of cases compared with 9 percent reported in the Northeast and 11 percent in the West.[77]

Of cases reported in 1994, the greatest percentage of AIDS cases among women (44 percent) was reported from the Northeast, followed by the South (36 percent), the West (9 percent), the Midwest (7 percent), and Puerto Rico and the territories (4 percent).[78]

PART III. SUMMARY

The public response to HIV and AIDS has been similar to the public response to the venereal disease epidemic in the early part of the twentieth century. Then, as now, fear of contagion was not rationally related to the ways in which the disease was spread; an "outsider" was blamed for the epidemic as though the disease deliberately selected its victims; and measures to restrict the freedom of those presumed to be carriers of disease were proposed. Disapprobation has not been limited to members of disfavored groups but has been extended to children with AIDS.

HIV-disease is associated with disfavored groups and with behaviors not mentioned in polite society. This results in avoidance of the issue and helps to explain why ten years elapsed between the time the first cases of AIDS were diagnosed and the first federal policy directly affecting people with HIV and AIDS was passed. These factors explain also the absence of federal leadership in developing a plan to manage and coordinate the provision of health care services and social services and in establishing a plan to coordinate research into the causes of and treatments for HIV.

By the end of 1995, more than a half-million cases of AIDS were diagnosed in the United States and more than one-half of the people diagnosed with AIDS had died. The number of deaths caused by AIDS may be underestimated by as much as 18 percent according to the CDC.

An estimated 650,000 to 900,000 people in the United States are infected with HIV. Estimates of the rates of HIV-infection are drawn from diverse samples, but there are no data drawn from a probability sample that would lead one to conclude that estimates are accurate.

AIDS, once confined to major urban areas, has spread across the United States with more than one-half of the cases reported in 1995 coming from outside of the original centers of the epidemic. The South, followed by the Midwest have accounted for the greatest proportionate increase in cases since the late 1980s.

The notion that AIDS is a disease of men is being rapidly dispelled. AIDS is increasing more rapidly among women than any other group. In 1995, 19 percent of newly diagnosed cases occurred among women, the greatest proportionate increase in women with AIDS in any single year. As age decreases, the percentage of women with AIDS increases. Young women in their adolescence account for 35 percent of cases and women 20 to 29 years of age account for 18 percent of cases, compared to 14 percent of cases represented by women overall. While AIDS is the third leading cause of death for women age 25 to 44, it is the leading cause of death for black women and the fifth leading cause of death for white women in this age group.

Pediatric AIDS is AIDS in youngsters under the age of 13. By the end of 1995, almost 7,000 cases of pediatric AIDS were reported to the CDC. The younger the age of the adolescent or young adult with AIDS, the more likely she or he is to come from a small metropolitan area or rural part of the country.

Finally, the CDC's scheme for classifying cases by method of exposure has the unfortunate consequence of downplaying the role of heterosexual contact in transmission of HIV. Women are at greater risk of infection through sexual contact than are men, but women may develop a false sense of security because of the emphasis on intravenous drug users and transmission of the virus through intravenous drug use.

CHAPTER 2

The Policy Framework:
Status-Conferring Policies

INTRODUCTION

All social policy confers some type of benefit. The conferred benefit is often concrete and takes the form of cash, food, or payment for medical services. However, there are policies whose benefits are less tangible but of critical importance, such as those that seek to eliminate discrimination in employment, housing, and education by providing avenues of legal redress for people who are subject to discrimination. These policies or statutes confer "status" because their goal is to place all members of society on an equal footing by eliminating discrimination that is based on stereotypes where a person's physical condition or membership in a group (based on gender or race, for example) underpins decisions denying equal access.

The focus of this chapter is on federal statutes whose goal is the elimination of disability-based discrimination in housing, employment, education, and medical care; the provisions in these policies that determine when discrimination is illegal; and how women and others with HIV and AIDS are affected by these statutes.

The Vocational Rehabilitation Act of 1973 (VRA) was the first federal legislation to confer status on disabled people. The VRA offered protection from discrimination in employment, in education, and in access to public transportation, public accommodations, and health and social services by outlawing discrimination by entities such as employers, hospitals, and social service agencies (hereafter, entities) who receive federal funds.[1] The VRA will be discussed in tandem with the Americans with Disabilities Act (ADA) of 1990, which extended the protections in the VRA by outlawing discrimination by entities regardless of whether they received federal funds.[2] The Fair Housing Act of 1988 (FHA) expanded federal protections for the disabled to include protection against discrimination in the sale or rental of housing.[3] Women with HIV and AIDS are covered under all three statutes.[4] The Education for All Handicapped Children Act (EAHCA) of 1975[5] [renamed the Individuals with Disabilities Education Act (IDEA)] covers HIV-positive children who are symptomatic. The educational rights of HIV-positive but asymptomatic children are protected by either the VRA or ADA.

This chapter is divided into three parts. The material in Part I describes the basic provisions of the FHA, ADA, and education statutes and highlights the distinctions between the VRA and ADA. The reader will gain familiarity with the framework within which protection is offered to women and children with HIV and AIDS, including the limits of the protections that are offered. The VRA, ADA, and FHA share key terms, which are defined in Part II. Court decisions will be used to illustrate the application of these laws. A summary of the chapter appears in Part III.

PART I. OVERVIEW OF STATUTORY PROVISIONS

The Fair Housing Act

The Fair Housing Act (FHA) of 1968 proscribed housing practices that discriminated on the basis of race, color, national origin, or religion. The FHA was amended in 1974 by adding gender as a protected class and again in 1988 when protection was extended to disabled individuals and to families with children, including foster families. The FHA's protections extend beyond the disabled individual to protect also those who reside with or associate with the individual who has a disability.[6]

The FHA prohibits discrimination: (1) in the sale or rental of a building or part of any building which is used, designed, or intended to be a residence for one or more families, and any vacant land which is offered for sale or lease for the construction of a residential building;[7] and (2) in activities associated with the rental and sale of housing such as advertising, financing, and the provision of brokerage services.[8] Precluded also are actions that coerce, intimidate, threaten, or interfere with the rights of any person covered by the FHA, or of a person who assists another in exercising his or her rights.[9]

Exempt from coverage are: (1) noncommercial buildings that are owned or operated by religious organizations; (2) private clubs whose facilities are not open to the public; (3) housing for older persons; and (4) single-family housing sold or rented by an owner, if the owner does not own more than three single-family houses at the same time.[10]

The law sets standards for construction of new multifamily dwellings, which are buildings with four or more units with elevators, or ground floor units in nonelevator buildings, and requires that residential units be accessible and adaptable. For example, doors and hallways must be wide enough to accommodate wheelchairs and light switches must be in convenient locations. A disabled person should be able to make changes easily by installing grab bars in the bathroom, if needed, without major renovations or changes in the structure of the dwelling.[11]

A property owner's obligation to a prospective tenant does not extend to the person whose tenancy creates a direct threat and substantial risk of harm to the health and safety of others because of current conduct or a history of overt acts. However, generalizations about disabled people and assumptions, subjective fears, and speculation are not enough to establish that a person poses a direct threat. The property owner must obtain references to aid in evaluating an applicant as a candidate for tenancy. Inferences that a recent history of a physical or mental illness or disability, or treatment for such illnesses or disabilities, constitutes proof that an applicant will be unable to fulfill her tenancy obligations may not be drawn.[12]

Moreover, the proviso that a property owner need not rent to a person who poses a direct threat does not give the property owner a grant to query prospective tenants about matters that are unrelated to their ability to meet requirements for tenancy. Permissible questions include those regarding a person's rental history or inquiries that focus on whether a person has acted in a manner that would pose a direct threat to the health or safety of other tenants, but blanket questions about whether an individual has a disability are illegal. And a property owner may not make inquiries that would require the individual to disclose or waive her right to confidentiality concerning her medical condition or history. The only exception is that a prospective tenant may be asked about current illegal abuse of or addiction to controlled substances.

The Americans with Disabilities Act and the Vocational Rehabilitation Act

In 1990, Congress passed the Americans with Disabilities Act (ADA) to protect the civil rights of the approximately 43 million Americans with disabling conditions.[13] The ADA became effective in 1992.[14] The protections in the ADA are set forth in a series of Titles. Those of concern here preclude discrimination in employment (Title I), in access to public services and programs that are run by state and local government (Title II), and in access to places of public accommodation such as social service agencies, homeless shelters, and restaurants, hotels, theaters, museums, schools, stores, and professional offices of health care providers (Title III).[15] The ADA and the VRA coexist. A discussion of the provisions contained in the various Titles of the ADA follows a brief exploration of the relationship of the two statutes and the distinctions between them.

The ADA and the VRA Compared   The ADA and the VRA share a common definition of disability (shared also by the FHA), and provisions for determining the rights of the disabled are essentially similar under both statutes. Thus when the ADA was passed, it inherited a developed body of case law from the VRA, which, with few exceptions, serves to guide courts in interpreting the ADA. In fact, it was the express intent of Congress that the ADA be construed by the courts to apply at least the same standard of protection that had been applied under the VRA or its regulations.[16] When judicial decisions are discussed, unless otherwise noted, the reader should assume that the reasoning courts apply to cases brought under the VRA will be the same under the ADA.

The most far-reaching distinction between the VRA and the ADA lies in the employment provisions. Whereas the VRA's prohibition against discrimination is limited to entities receiving federal funds, coverage under the ADA extends to both private and public sector employers. A further distinction is found in the definition of *employer*, which in the ADA includes the Congress but not the executive branch of the federal government, a corporation wholly owned by the federal government, an Indian Tribe, or a bona fide private membership club (other than a labor organization).[17] Protection against discrimination by the executive branch of the federal government is found in the VRA. And where the VRA requires affirmative action for the disabled, this provision is absent in the ADA.[18]

Finally, the VRA requires that all of the programs of a recipient of federal financial assistance be available to persons with disabilities. This statute requires major structural changes in existing facilities if other means are ineffective in achieving program access. In contrast, the ADA adopts a lower standard of access to public accommodations for existing buildings. Access must be provided only if it can be provided in a manner that is "readily achievable,"[19] that is, if it can be easily accomplished without much difficulty or expense. Examples of readily achievable include:

> Coming to the door to receive or return dry cleaning; allowing a disabled patron to be served beverages at a table even though nondisabled persons having only drinks are required to drink at the inaccessible bar; providing assistance to retrieve items in an inaccessible location; and rotating movies between the first floor accessible theater and a comparable second floor inaccessible theater and notifying the public of the movie's location in any advertisements.[20]

The Titles of the ADA

Title I The employment provisions in the ADA provide that an employer, defined as one with fifteen or more employees,[21] may not discriminate against qualified individuals with disabilities in the "terms, conditions, and privileges of employment."[22] Two-thirds of the states have declared AIDS-related discrimination illegal[23] under their own laws. Some states—New York, for example—define as an employer one who employs four or more persons, thus sweeping a greater number of employers under the umbrella provided by the law.[24]

The ADA protects the "otherwise qualified person with a disability" against employment discrimination. An otherwise qualified person is one who has the requisite knowledge or skills, experience, education, and other job-related requirements and who, with or without reasonable accommodation, can undertake the essential functions of the job[25] or is able to meet all of a program's requirements in spite of her handicap.[26]

"Essential job functions" are fundamental job duties, not marginal ones. A function may be considered essential if: (1) the position exists to perform the function; (2) there are a limited number of employees available to perform the function; or (3) the function is highly specialized.[27]

"Reasonable accommodation" may include: (1) making existing facilities used by employees readily accessible to and usable by individuals with disabilities; (2) restructuring jobs, including part-time or modified work schedules; (3) reassigning individuals to a vacant position; (4) acquiring or modifying equipment or devices; (5) adjusting or modifying as appropriate examinations, training materials, or policies; (6) providing qualified readers or interpreters; and (7) making other similar accommodations for individuals with disabilities.[28]

Employment discrimination under Title I includes also: (1) excluding from consideration an applicant because of her association or relationship with a disabled person; (2) utilizing selection criteria that screen out disabled individuals unless the criteria are shown to be job related; (3) conducting medical examinations or making inquiries of an applicant or current employee as to whether she has a disability; and (4) administering tests in a manner that highlights disabilities to the detriment of the applicant's abilities.[29]

The statutory provisions that forbid efforts to limit the employment opportunities of a disabled person because of her or his disability include also an employer's participation in contractual arrangements or relationships. These include a relationship with an employment or referral agency, a labor union, an organization providing fringe benefits to an employee, or an organization providing training and apprenticeship programs.[30]

The employer's obligations to the disabled applicant or employee are balanced against rights retained by the employer or prospective employer, which are reviewed further on in this chapter.[31]

Title II   Title II provides that qualified individuals with disabilities should not be excluded because of their disability from "services, programs or activities of a public entity."[32] A qualified individual is one who meets the eligibility criteria for the service or program they are seeking.[33] For example, a child who is in foster care cannot be excluded from an adoption program due solely to her disability. Public entities, which include state or local government, those acting to achieve governmental ends, and the National Rail Road Passenger Corporation,[34] are obliged, when necessary, to make reasonable modifications to "rules, policies or practices, including the removal of architectural, communications or transportation barriers, or the provision of auxiliary aids and services."[35]

Titles II and III contain some similar provisions. For example, transportation provisions affecting public transportation systems exclusive of public school transportation systems[36] are found in Title II; and transportation provisions affecting private transportation systems (exclusive of airlines, which are covered by the Air Carrier Access Act)[37] are found in Title III. In a like manner, medical services provided by a publicly funded clinic or hospital are covered under Title II, while similar services offered by a practitioner in private practice are covered by Title III.

The ADA sets standards for both public and private transportation systems that govern accessibility for new, used, and remanufactured vehicles[38] operated on fixed route systems (i.e., any system that travels a standard route on a regular schedule), for (1) paratransit systems which public entities must, absent a financial hardship waiver, operate[39] as a complement to fixed route systems to provide transportation to people whose disability precludes use of a fixed route system, and (2) for demand-responsive systems, which are any systems that do not meet the definition of a fixed route system.[40]

Title III   Title III protects people with disabilities against discrimination in the "full and equal enjoyment of the goods, services, facilities, privileges, advantages or accommodations of any place of public accommodation."[41] Public accommodations include places where people seek: (1) lodging; (2) entertainment; (3) food, clothing, hardware, and other services (e.g., laundromat, dry-cleaner, gas station); (4) education; (5) social services; (6) medical services; and (7) access to public transportation.[42]

The removal of architectural barriers is required by Title III when removal is "readily achievable."[43] Readily achievable means "easily accomplishable and able to be carried out without much difficulty or expense."[44] The legislative history of the ADA shows that Congress was concerned that the barrier removal provisions in the law not result in businesses closing and the resultant loss of jobs and community services if compliance necessitated significant monetary investment. This problem was anticipated in depressed or rural areas where business might operate "at the margin or at a loss."[45] In each case, factors to be considered in determining whether barrier removal is readily achievable involve balancing the nature and cost of the action against the financial resources, number of employees, and business size of the affected entity.[46]

Education

In 1971, a federal district court ruled that once a state assumes responsibility for providing a free public education to its children, it cannot exclude disabled children and must provide education and training appropriate to the child's abilities.[47] A disabled child's right to receive a free public education was codified in 1975 in the Education for All Handicapped Children Act (EAHCA), renamed the Individuals with Disabilities in Education Act (IDEA). The IDEA requires, to the extent possible, that disabled children be educated with nondisabled children. This requirement imposes on a school district the obligation to educate disabled children in the least restrictive environment. Each disabled child is entitled to an individualized education plan which contains specific educational goals.[48]

A child with HIV or AIDS has a right not to be discriminated against in receipt of a public education. Whether this right is protected under the IDEA, the VRA (applicable to educational programs that receive federal funds),[49] or the ADA (either Title II, applicable to public school programs, or Title III, applicable to private school programs), depends on whether the child is HIV-positive but asymptomatic or is suffering an AIDS-related disability. Both the VRA and the ADA prohibit discrimination against the qualified disabled child and require, where necessary and not unduly burdensome, that reasonable accommodation be made to permit her or him to attend school.[50]

The IDEA guarantees a right to a free, appropriate public education for a handicapped child[51] but defines handicap to focus on children whose health is impaired to the extent that they require special education services. "Health impaired" means having "limited strength, vitality or alertness due to chronic or acute health problems . . . which adversely affect a child's educational performance."[52] This definition is too narrow to embrace children who are asymptomatic carriers of HIV, since they do not, by definition, experience the physical limitations identified in the IDEA.[53] A child with HIV-infection could meet this definition if she had another disability[54] or if her condition deteriorated because of her HIV-infection. Children with HIV who are asymptomatic are covered by the broader definition of handicap found in the VRA or the ADA. Either statute defines as disabled a person with a physical impairment which includes disorders that affect the blood or lymphatic systems. Since HIV and AIDS destroy lymphocytes, a child with either condition is physically impaired and cannot be excluded from the classroom solely because of her status as HIV-infected.[55]

PART II. STATUTORY TERMS AND THEIR APPLICATION BY THE COURTS

All decisions that are adverse to a woman or a child with a disability do not constitute illegal discrimination. Whether the person who alleges disability-based discrimination will find legal protection depends upon a number of factors, including whether the charged entity is covered by the law, whether the person is disabled as defined by the law, and whether the complained of actions fall within those proscribed by the law. In reviewing the terms of the IDEA, for example, I said that its definition of handicap is too narrow to offer legal protection to the asymptomatic HIV-infected child. As will become clear in the remainder of this chapter, court interpretations of key statutory terms, such as *otherwise qualified, reasonable accommodation,* and *direct threat*, determine whether or not the person with HIV or AIDS has a legal claim.

The VRA, FHA, and ADA share a number of common terms. The use of consistent language permits the body of case law that has developed since 1973 under the VRA to be applied to actions later brought under the FHA and the ADA. These terms are reviewed next and their application illustrated with judicial decisions. Before beginning, a caveat is in order.

Under either the VRA or Title I of the ADA, women have alleged employment-based discrimination because they had: (1) tuberculosis;[56] (2) epilepsy;[57] (3) "melt down" caused by inability to handle job pressures;[58] (4) blindness;[59] (5) narcolepsy;[60] (6) severe visual disability;[61] and (7) pregnancy.[62] To date, very few cases have been reported in which a woman with HIV or AIDS has alleged employment discrimination, although women report having lost their jobs when they tried to assist others with HIV or AIDS. For example, Joanne Finley, the Director of Medical Services for Rockland County, New York, sued the county by alleging that she was fired because she tried to provide health care services to people with AIDS.[63] In another case, a 64-year-old social worker was fired when she took a patient with AIDS who had been confined to his room for more than ten months out of his room so he could telephone his children. She was discharged because her supervisors feared that the nursing home would go out of business if others learned that services were being provided to individuals with AIDS.[64]

The limited number of cases of employment-based discrimination brought under federal law by women with HIV and AIDS may be due to several factors.* First, most women with HIV are poor and may not have access to legal counsel. They may not be aware of their legal rights or may not wish to exercise their rights. Second, because drug use accounts for approximately 40 percent of cases of AIDS among women, women whose drug use is excessive may not be in the paid labor force. In addition, women have represented a relatively small percentage of people with HIV and AIDS, although this is changing. (See chapter 1.) The number of cases brought by women alleging employment-based discrimination may increase because of: (1) the increased number of women with HIV and AIDS; (2) the fact that regardless of gender, the majority of people with HIV and AIDS are in their prime working years (73 percent are age 25 to 44);[65] and (3) the large number of U. S. employers who report having HIV-positive employees.[66] Finally, because the process of litigating employment-based discrimination cases is slow, there may be unreported cases in the pipeline.

That most of the employment cases that are reviewed involve men does not detract from their importance to the rights of women. The precedents set by these cases are gender neutral and relevant to the concerns that may be raised by women.

---

*To see if women were more likely to file claims under state law, I researched reported cases that were filed in state courts in the twelve states with the highest rates of AIDS among women, plus the case law in Puerto Rico and the District of Columbia. The states are California, Florida, New York, Georgia, New Jersey, Massachusetts, South Carolina, Texas, Rhode Island, Connecticut, Delaware, and Maryland. I found only one case involving a woman who was removed from an AFDC work-experience program because of rumors that she was HIV-positive [*Rice v. The School District of Fairfield*, 452 S.E. 2d 352 (S.C.App., 1994), *cert* denied (1995).]

The Definition of Disability

A woman seeking to avail herself of the protections found in antidiscrimination statutes must establish first that she is a member of the class the statute seeks to protect. The VRA, FHA, and ADA** cast a very broad net by affording protection against disabilities-based discrimination to over 40 million Americans.[67] These statutes define as disabled a person with a physical or mental impairment that limits significantly her or his ability to undertake a major life activity that the average person can perform with little or no difficulty, such as "caring for oneself, performing manual tasks, walking, seeing, hearing, speaking, breathing, learning and working."[68] The definition also includes those who have a "record" of an impairment. A record may be found where an individual has a history of an impairment or has been misclassified as having a mental or physical impairment that substantially limits one or more major life activities.[69] Covered also are people who are "regarded" as having an impairment.[70] The latter category covers those who have: (1) physical disabilities which do not substantially limit a major life activity but who are treated as though they are so limited; (2) physical or mental disabilities that substantially limit a major life activity only as a result of the attitudes of others toward the disability; or (3) no impairments but who are treated as having a substantially limiting impairment.

Neither the FHA nor the ADA cover anyone who is convicted of illegally manufacturing or distributing controlled substances[71] or who is illegally using or addicted to controlled substances,[72] except for recovering drug abusers who are in treatment programs and not currently using illegal drugs. The exemption does not affect anyone who is using drugs that are prescribed by a physician.[73] Because the VRA, when originally passed, did not exclude from coverage persons currently engaged in the illegal use of drugs, provisions in the ADA require that the language it contains and the language in the VRA be consistent on this subject.

Homosexuality, bisexuality, and transvestism are not, by themselves, disabilities, and conditions such as exhibitionism, voyeurism, compulsive gambling, and kleptomania are excluded from coverage under the ADA.[74]

Otherwise Qualified

The disabled individual seeking protection against discrimination in employment, education, housing, or medical care must be qualified for the opportunity she is seeking or she cannot proceed on a claim under the FHA, VRA, or ADA.[75] For example, a job applicant who has the knowledge or skills to do the work, a child who meets the basic requirements for admission to school, or an applicant for housing is "otherwise qualified" unless she poses a direct threat to the health or safety of others which cannot be remedied by reasonable accommodation.

**The IDEA's definition of disability is narrower. See notes 51–54 and accompanying text.

The basic rule for determining whether a disabled person is otherwise qualified was announced by the Supreme Court in 1987 and subsequently codified into disabilities statutes.[76] In *School Board of Nassau County v. Arline*,[77] a teacher who was susceptible to tuberculosis was fired from the teaching job she had held for 13 years, after she suffered a relapse of her illness. She sued the school district by alleging employment discrimination. The Supreme Court held that a contagious disease is a handicap under the VRA. To balance the rights of individuals with contagious diseases not to be discriminated against, against the rights of others to be safe from exposure to a contagious disease, the Court established a test for determining whether the disabled person is otherwise qualified. The test is to be applied on a case-by-case basis. The analysis of risk to others is framed by a set of questions, the answers to which should be informed by reasonable medical judgment given the state of medical knowledge about:

> (a) the nature of the risk (how the disease is transmitted), (b) the duration of the risk (how long is the carrier infectious), (c) the severity of the risk (what is the potential harm to third parties), and (d) the probabilities the disease will be transmitted and will cause varying degrees of harm.[78]

The pivotal case for determining the employment rights of a person diagnosed with AIDS is *Chalk v. United States*.[79] Following a diagnosis of AIDS, Vincent Chalk, a special education teacher, was placed on administrative leave and subsequently reassigned from classroom teaching to an administrative position. Insisting on his right to return to classroom teaching, Chalk sought to enjoin the school district's ban. He argued that his reassignment violated the VRA. Based on the Supreme Court decision in *Arline*, the district court concluded and the school board did not contest that AIDS was a handicap under the VRA.[80] The circumstances under which a person with a contagious disease may be otherwise qualified became the core issue considered by the trial court, which found Chalk unqualified for classroom teaching because some risk existed, even a small risk of infection through casual contact.[81]

In reviewing this case, the Ninth Circuit Court of Appeals held that the trial court had not followed the standard set out in *Arline* and had placed on Chalk the "impossible burden"[82] of proving no risk of transmission. The *Arline* standard provides for exclusion of an employee only when there is a significant risk of transmission which cannot be controlled through reasonable accommodation; and *Chalk*, through expert testimony, carried his burden of showing that there was no significant risk of transmission. The court granted Chalk's request to return to the classroom.

Under Title I, a prospective employer may not require a preemployment medical examination, question the applicant about a disability, nor inquire into the nature or severity of a disability to determine whether a person is otherwise qualified.[83] Once a job offer has been made and before work begins, a medical exam may be required under certain conditions,[84] and an employee may be required to undergo a medical examination if the examination is shown to be job-related and consistent with business necessity.[85]

An impermissible inquiry into an employee's medical condition is grounds for suit. A federal district court ruled that an attorney could pursue a claim of discriminatory discharge based on his allegation that his office was searched, that a letter from an AIDS services group was found and placed in his personal file, and that these actions constituted an impermissible medical inquiry.[86] Also based on an impermissible medical inquiry, another federal district decision held that Jane and John Doe, two applicants for positions as police officers in the city of Chicago, could sue the city, whom they alleged had tested them for HIV without their permission.[87]

When the medical inquiry is job-related and consistent with business necessity, an employer may require an employee to submit the results of an HIV-test.[88] On this basis, a court found persuasive a hospital's argument that guidelines for health care workers issued by the Centers for Disease Control (CDC), as well as the hospital's own policies, which seek to protect patients from exposure to communicable diseases and health care workers with compromised immune systems from exposure to infection from patients, were sufficient to require health care workers to submit the results of an HIV-test when the hospital learned that the employee was at risk of having HIV.

Whether a determination by the Social Security Administration (SSA) that a person is disabled and entitled to receive disability benefits is synonymous with a determination that she or he is not otherwise qualified to work has been addressed in two cases, with courts reaching different conclusions. In the first case, after a man was awarded disability benefits a federal court ruled that the award did not mean that he was unable to work.[89] Such a conclusion, the court said, would force a disabled individual to choose between the right to seek disability benefits and the right to pursue a claim of discriminatory discharge. Expressly disagreeing with this conclusion, another federal district court found another man not otherwise qualified to continue his employment because he was receiving disability benefits and had, in order to qualify as a recipient, declared himself "totally and permanently disabled."[90] A person cannot, the court ruled, be simultaneously unable to work and otherwise qualified.

A number of cases have considered whether a child with HIV or AIDS is otherwise qualified to attend public school. Parents are understandably concerned that their children not be exposed to infectious diseases. Since one of the modes of transmission of HIV is through blood, concern about transmission is acute with very young children, whose rough and tumble play may result in cuts and bruises, as it is with children who are not able to control their bodily functions. Concern is not limited to the risk confronting the HIV-negative child but extends to the HIV-positive child whose compromised immune system creates a danger that she or he may contract illnesses to which an HIV-negative child is not vulnerable. Addressing the latter concern, a federal court in Florida had the following to say:

> A child who is HIV-positive confronts certain risks in attending school as does a child whose immune system is suppressed from other conditions such as cancer. The risks to the child's health must be balanced

against the benefits which flow from school attendance. Keeping a child out of school does not guarantee her safety and long life; death if it seeks and takes Eliana may come from various sources which are available to her without restriction: the park, the mall, or her home. Upon conscientious consideration of the issue from all sides, the Court cannot find that the risk is significant enough to counterbalance the benefit and rights to this child inherent in attending school with other children.[91]

Other courts, considering whether children with HIV and AIDS are otherwise qualified to attend public school, have answered in the affirmative.[92] Courts rely on expert testimony[93] and guidelines issued by the CDC and the American Academy of Pediatrics, which provide the medical judgments called for by the Supreme Court in its *Arline* ruling. When the public interest in providing all children with an appropriate education in a nondiscriminatory manner is balanced against the public interest in protecting the health and safety of children who are not HIV-infected, the balance tips in favor of the HIV-infected child's right to receive an education in a nonsegregated environment.[94] Because HIV is not easily transmitted, there is no significant risk that a person will contract it in the classroom setting.[95] Therefore, children with HIV and AIDS are qualified to attend regular classes.

This determination holds even if the HIV-infected child is mentally retarded, as long as she can be toilet trained and learn a degree of personal hygiene. This conclusion was reached in a case concerning a 7-year-old who was mentally retarded and HIV-infected. At the original trial, the court found that there was a "remote theoretical possibility of transmission from tears, saliva and urine"[96] and ordered that the child be segregated from others and taught in a separate room within the classroom. The room was to have a large picture window that would give the child a clear view of the main classroom and a sound system. The Court of Appeals for the Eleventh Circuit overruled the trial court by finding that the theoretical possibility of transmission does not create the kind of significant risk that is necessary to justify exclusion from the classroom.

Reconsidering its decision based on the ruling of the appellate court, the trial court found that the child, who had demonstrated the ability to be trained in matters of personal hygiene, was otherwise qualified to attend a regular class for mentally retarded children and that any questions about the child's presence on any given day should be resolved by the school nurse.[97]

Just as the job or housing applicant or the child seeking to enroll in school must be otherwise qualified, so too the person who is seeking medical treatment must be qualified for the treatment sought. But the concept of otherwise qualified is more difficult to apply in medical settings than it is in situations involving employment, housing, and education. In the latter situations, answering the question "Is the applicant otherwise qualified?" turns on whether she has the requisite skills and or knowledge to perform the required work or to participate in the classroom, or on whether her occupancy of a residence poses a direct threat to others. The applicant argues that she is otherwise qualified and that the only reason that she is being denied the sought-after opportunity is because of her disability. Stated otherwise, the argument is that "but for" my disability I would have received the job offer, the housing, or the classroom admission.

When a woman seeking medical services requests assistance for reasons unrelated to her disability, her situation parallels that of the otherwise qualified job, housing, or school applicant. But the application of the otherwise qualified standard to cases involving medical care is complicated when the disability itself is the reason that treatment is sought. The suggestion that one must be qualified but for one's disability makes little sense where the disability creates the need for the required service.[98] Court decisions addressing the application of the otherwise qualified standard to cases involving HIV or AIDS generally have to contend with a 1984 decision by the Second Circuit Court of Appeals in *United States v. University Hospital*.[99] That case was concerned with the provision of medical treatment to a newborn who had serious birth defects. The court held that the otherwise qualified standard cannot be applied to medical treatments which are "fluid, without distorting the meaning of the concept [and that] where the handicapping condition is relevant to the condition to be treated it will rarely if ever be possible to say with certainty that a particular decision was discriminatory."[100] Providers of medical care cite this case for the proposition that a disabled person cannot claim discriminatory treatment under the VRA[101] and, by extension, under the ADA.

In deciding cases involving HIV and AIDS, some courts have rejected the holding in *University Hospital*. A federal court in Massachusetts, considering whether a patient with AIDS who was denied ear surgery could bring suit under the VRA, answered in the affirmative because it found persuasive the reasoning of a dissenting justice in *University Hospital*.[102] The Massachusetts court said that the majority view ignored the Congressional mandate to treat disabled people in the same manner as people without disabilities. While the VRA does not permit a court to override a medical decision, it does permit an inquiry into whether a medical decision is bona fide. A federal court in Virginia, citing the finding of the Massachusetts court, held that an infant in need of ventilation treatment was otherwise qualified to receive the treatment.[103]

Another federal court confronted the question of whether a person with HIV is otherwise qualified, when it reviewed a claim made by John Woolfolk, who alleged that because of his HIV-status he was treated like an "outcast" and that the physician to whom he had gone for treatment never made a good faith medical determination about his condition.[104] The physician argued that Woolfolk could not be otherwise qualified for medical treatment, since his HIV-status was central to the treatment that he sought. The court found that Woolfolk was otherwise qualified. Where medical services are at issue, the court said, "disability alone is not a permissible ground for withholding medical treatment."[105] The court expressed its concern with the implications of an alternative holding in the evolving system of medical care where a primary care physician in a managed care setting is the gatekeeper to almost all of the medical services that a patient might need if the patient were deemed not to be otherwise qualified.

Reasonableness Requirement

The law requires employers, educators, and property owners to make reasonable accommodation to the disabled individual, but the concept of reasonableness has different meanings in different contexts.[106] The following review addresses the concept of reasonableness in four situations: (1) primary and secondary education; (2) employment; (3) housing; and (4) higher education.

Primary and Secondary Education   In the early stages of litigation concerning children with HIV or AIDS, accommodations that were made in educational settings responded to fear of transmission. These accommodations resulted in segregating children and consigning them to receive instruction through homestudy,[107] via telephone,[108] in the school house but segregated in a modular classroom where there was neither visual nor auditory contact with other children,[109] or in a separate classroom[110] including a separate classroom constructed within the regular classroom with a window and sound system.[111] Reported court decisions stand for the proposition that these accommodations were not necessary and that the child with HIV-infection can be integrated into the regular classroom.[112]

Employment   When the allegation is employment discrimination against a person with HIV, the question "What is reasonable?" raises different issues depending upon the type of work performed or to be performed. Two federal courts have ruled that when performing invasive medical procedures is among the essential functions of a job, a hospital may, as a reasonable accommodation, reassign to a position that does not involve patient contact those surgical technicians who are HIV-infected and whose jobs include assisting during surgery in such a manner as to have direct contact with open surgical wounds.[113] Other courts have held that a hospital may require a surgeon to inform his patients of his HIV-status before performing surgery[114] and that a medical school may terminate a dental student from its program.[115] Also, the practice of neurosurgery was deemed to create a significant risk to the health or safety of others that could not be eliminated by reasonable accommodation and a hospital's termination of a surgical residency was not therefore illegal discrimination.[116]

A federal court in eastern Pennsylvania held that it is a reasonable accommodation to place an HIV-infected employee on a medical leave of absence until he could return to his job or until his absence posed an undue hardship for his employer.[117] In reaching this conclusion, the court noted that the situation confronting the employer with an employee who was hospitalized for an HIV-infection was not different from when an employee takes a pregnancy leave. In this case, others in the firm could have taken on the attorney's duties and enabled him to fulfill some of his job responsibilities by phone or by sending staff to visit him in the hospital or at home. The court said: "Such temporary modifications in scheduling and duties and the provision of additional assistance are plainly contemplated by the reasonable accommodation doctrine."[118]

Housing   The accommodation required by the Fair Housing Act (FHA) is different in that the property owner's obligation is to permit the tenant with a disability to make reasonable modifications to the premises, at her or his own expense, if the modification is necessary for the "full enjoyment of the premises."[119] For example, a person who has a hearing disability may install a flashing light to "see" that someone is ringing the doorbell, an elderly individual with severe arthritis may replace the doorknobs with lever handles, and a person in a wheelchair may install fold-back hinges in order to be able to go through a door or may build a ramp to enter a residence. The modifications must be reasonable and must be made at the expense of the individual with the disability. In the case of rental property, the property owner may, where it is reasonable to do so, grant permission to make the change contingent upon the renter agreeing to restore the premises to the condition that existed before the modification. It would constitute discrimination for a property owner to refuse to permit such reasonable accommodations, when they are necessary to afford a disabled person with the opportunity to use and enjoy a dwelling.

Higher Education   In 1979, the U.S. Supreme Court, in *Southeastern Community College v. Davis*,[120] held that educational programs are not required to make major adjustments to existing programs to accommodate disabled people. *Southeastern* involved an applicant to the college's nursing program who suffered from a severe hearing disability and who challenged the college's denial of her application as discriminatory under the VRA. She argued that federal regulations required the institution to modify its program to accommodate handicapped individuals. The Supreme Court found that the degree of accommodation required by Ms. Davis, if she were to participate in the school's clinical program (i.e., "close individualized attention by a nursing instructor"),[121] was not required by the law, but also that if she were allowed to take only academic courses absent the clinical training she would not receive the kind of training the program normally provided. The Court acknowledged that there might be a situation where an unwillingness to modify an existing program could constitute unreasonable discrimination; however, the law does not require an educational institution "to lower . . . or effect substantial modifications of standards to accommodate a handicapped person."[122] The Court held that denying admission to the school's nursing program to an applicant with a serious hearing disability was not discrimination, because the law does not require the educational institution to make "major adjustments in its program"[123] to accommodate the needs of the applicant.

The question "What constitutes reasonable accommodation in an education program when an applicant has HIV?" arose when John Doe, an HIV-positive dental student, was terminated from Washington University's dental program, because the invasive procedures performed by a dentist created an unacceptable degree of risk of transmission.[124] A committee at the dental school considered what reasonable accommodations might be made for Doe, i.e., whether he could complete the program without performing invasive procedures or whether he could participate in a clinic whose patients were all HIV-infected. They concluded that he could not avoid the former and that the patient pool was not large enough for Doe to treat only HIV patients. The school also offered him admission to "related medical career programs"[125] not involving invasive procedures. After acknowledging that risk of transmission was minimal, the court held nonetheless that "there is still some risk of transmission"[126] and that this risk was sufficient to sustain the school's determination that Doe could not successfully complete the dental program.

When Is Saying "No" Not Discriminaton?

An employer, property owner, school district, or other entity has available defenses to a charge of discriminatory conduct. As discussed earlier, the FHA says that a property owner need not rent to a person who poses a direct threat to others. And neither the VRA nor the ADA requires a prospective employer to hire a person who is not qualified for the position sought, if the established qualifications are necessary for job performance; nor is an employer required to maintain in a position a person who poses a direct threat to others. A religious institution may give hiring preference to a person of a particular religion to perform work connected with the carrying on of the institution's activities or it may require that employees conform to the organization's religious tenets.[127] But a religious organization may not discriminate against an individual who satisfies the permitted religious criteria because that individual is disabled.[128]

Nor is it required of a prospective employer that she undertake an undue hardship to employ a disabled person. Whether an accommodation creates an undue hardship is calculated by taking account of a number of factors, including the nature and cost of the accommodation balanced against available resources and the effect of the accommodation on the overall operation of the business or other entity.[129] The defense of "undue hardship" has not been raised in any reported federal cases implicating HIV or AIDS, although it was the subject of a lawsuit brought against the state of Pennsylvania by three blind income-maintenance workers. This suit is an example of how one court struck a balance between available resources and the cost of the required accommodation. In *Nelson v. Thornburgh*[130] the court held that it would not be an undue hardship for the state of Pennsylvania to pay the salaries for readers for income-maintenance workers who had been paying the readers themselves. The salaries, which ranged from a low of $1,000 per year to a high of $5,000 per year, were a fraction of the $300 million budget of the department and would not be an undue burden for the department.

Whether the matter at hand is employment, housing, or education, fear of transmission of HIV has been cited more than any other factor to explain why a decision that is adverse to an applicant should not be viewed as discriminatory. As previously noted, the employer, property owner, or educational institution is not required to accommodate a person who poses a direct threat to the health or safety of others,[131] if the threat cannot be reduced or eliminated.

Because risk of transmitting HIV is central to defending against claims of discrimination, a digression to consider studies on this subject and to consider risk-reduction guidelines that have been promulgated by professional organizations is in order. After such discussion, our attention turns to review cases that illustrate how the courts assess the direct threat defense. The question "Do children in elementary and secondary educational settings pose a direct threat of transmitting HIV?" was dealt with earlier and will not be revisited. As shown previously, children with HIV and AIDS who were segregated from others for fear of transmission were returned to appropriate classroom settings.

Studies of Transmission in Health Care Settings and Professional Guidelines to Reduce Transmission

The CDC has studied transmission of the HIV from health care workers (HCWs) to patients.[132] As of March 1993, 19,036 individuals who were treated by dentists, dental students, physicians, medical students, and surgeons had been tested. Ninety-five patients (less than 1 percent) were HIV-positive. As of July 1993, follow-up studies had been conducted on eighty-six of the ninety-five infected patients. Eight had become infected before receiving care; fifty-four had previously established risk factors; and nineteen may have been exposed to HIV through sexual contacts or drug use. Five of those who tested positive had no risks identified. The CDC estimates that the risk of surgeon-to-patient transmission is between two and twenty-four cases for every million operations. However, there are no documented cases of transmission by surgeons with HIV to their patients.[133]

Concerning transmission from patients to HCWs, as of June 1994, forty-two reports of occupationally acquired HIV-infection were reported to the CDC. Those infected were laboratory workers ($n = 17$); nurses ($n = 13$); non-surgical physicians ($n = 6$); surgical technicians ($n = 2$); and HCWs in other areas of medicine ($n = 4$).[134]

The CDC, the American Academy of Pediatrics, and the Child Welfare League of America have issued risk-reduction guidelines covering the provision of medical services and guidelines for use in schools, preschools, and foster care.[135] School districts in forty-one states have adopted policies governing this subject.[136] The United States Department of Health and Human Services, because it determined that there is no risk of transmission of HIV through food handling,[137] has not issued guidelines.

After determining that the risk of HCW-to-patient transmission of HIV was slight, the CDC recommended that HIV-positive HCWs not be barred from performing most surgical procedures. Instead, strict adherence to "universal precautions" including hand-washing, wearing of protective barriers such as gloves and masks, and care in the use of needles and other sharp instruments is recommended. Provided that the universal precautions are followed, the CDC concluded that "currently available data provide no basis for recommendations to restrict the practice of HCWs infected with HIV . . . who perform invasive procedures."[138]

However, the CDC distinguished between the large class of invasive procedures (ranging from insertion of an intravenous line to most types of surgery) and a more limited class of "exposure-prone" procedures (e.g., those posing a greater risk of percutaneous or skin-piercing injury). Although the CDC did not attempt to identify exposure-prone procedures, it did provide a general definition of the term to include the presence of the HCW's fingers and a "needle or other sharp instrument or object in a poorly visualized or highly confined anatomic site [and cautioned that] performance of exposure-prone procedures presents a recognized risk of percutaneous injury to the HCW, and—if such an injury occurs—the HCW's blood is likely to [make] contact with the patient [in a manner that creates the possibility of risk]."[139] The CDC recommended that health care organizations identify which procedures performed at their facilities are exposure-prone and that they determine whether, and under what circumstances, HIV-positive HCWs should perform such procedures.

The guidelines that focus on the risk of transmission in school settings and foster care are based on reports stating that there is no evidence of transmission of HIV by urine, feces, saliva, tears, or sweat even in communities with a high prevalence of HIV-infection.[140] There are no studies reported in the literature nor have reports been made to the CDC that suggest that transmission of HIV has occurred in

> school or day-care settings or during contact sports such as football, boxing, or wrestling; nor through close household contact, even when personal items such as razors, toothbrushes, towels, clothes, eating utensils, and drinking glasses or bedroom, bathroom, and kitchen facilities were shared, or when a family member helped the infected person bathe, dress, and eat and interact[ed] with hugs, kisses on the cheek, and kisses on the lips.[141]

Thus guidelines state as a general rule that HIV-infected children be allowed to attend school in unrestricted settings and that children with the HIV be allowed to attend day care if their "health, neurological development, behavior and immune status are appropriate."[142]

For infected preschool-age children and neurologically disabled children who lack control of their body secretions or who display biting behavior, and for those children who have uncoverable, oozing lesions, a more restricted environment is advisable until more is known about transmission in these settings. Decisions regarding a specific child are best made by a team including the child's physician, public health personnel, the child's parent or guardian, and personnel associated with the proposed care or educational setting. In each case, risks and benefits to both the infected child and to others in the setting should be weighed.

Because the risk of transmission from a single exposure to blood from a school-age child or adolescent with unknown serologic status is minute, the only mandatory precautionary action should be washing exposed skin with soap and water. Lacerations and other bleeding lesions should be managed in a manner that minimizes direct contact of the care giver with blood. Schools in high-prevalence areas should provide access to gloves so that individuals who wish further to reduce such minute risk may opt for their use. Under no circumstance should the urgent care of a bleeding child be delayed because gloves are not immediately available.

Risk of Transmission and Housing Discrimination

Housing discrimination against people with AIDS has been documented and includes actions by property owners against tenants and actions taken by city and town officials against groups trying to create congregate housing for homeless people with HIV and AIDS. Property owners have been accused of evicting people with AIDS from their homes because of their belief that the tenants pose a risk to the health of others and of refusing to make repairs for HIV-positive tenants.[143] Real estate agents have been accused of directing prospective home buyers away from homes in which people with HIV have previously resided,[144] and municipalities have been accused of changing zoning ordinances to prevent the opening of group homes.

Data on the number of homeless people with the HIV are imprecise and there are no data that provide an estimate of the number of homeless women with HIV or AIDS. Estimates of seroprevalence among the homeless range from a low of less then 1 percent to a high of 62 percent.[145] Likewise, there are no data on the number of women with HIV on whose behalf litigation has been brought under the FHA, although women were among the plaintiffs in class action litigation concerned with creating group living arrangements and hospices for people with HIV and AIDS.[146]

In 1989, a federal district court in Illinois prevented the city of Belleville from denying a permit for a hospice. The court dismissed as lacking merit a claim by the city that a hospice would constitute a direct threat to the health or safety of the community after experts testified that HIV-positive people do not pose a risk of transmission. The court held that the city was motivated to deny the permit, in part, by an irrational fear of AIDS and that the actions of the City Council were "intentionally and specifically designed to prevent persons with AIDS from residing in the hospice"[147]

In 1992, Support Ministries for Persons with AIDS sued the village of Waterford, New York, alleging discrimination when the village refused to allow them to open a residence for homeless persons with AIDS. The isolation experienced by people living in shelters or on the street as well as the erratic care they receive which can "hasten their demise"[148] were offered as evidence of the need for the residence. Support Ministries made efforts to explain the purpose of the residence at two public meetings, but they encountered a hostile crowd whose opposition included speculation that "HIV and AIDS was an illness that people brought on themselves. . . . [that] it was a punishment from God and [that the community] had no obligation to respond compassionately."[149]

Village officials and residents considered various ways to block the application for the hospice, including amendments to zoning laws to prevent use of the residence for a hospice. They settled on an amendment which altered the meaning of the term boarding house so as to deny the Ministries' request.[150] The court found that the amendment to the zoning ordinance served only one purpose: to prevent the opening of a residence for people with AIDS. Furthermore, the HIV-status of the future residents of the house was "at least one factor, and probably the primary factor, for the enactment of the new zoning law,"[151] whose passage was proof of an intent to discriminate in violation of the FHA. Finding for Support Ministries, the court permanently enjoined village officials from interfering with use of the property as a residence for homeless people with AIDS.

Risk of Transmission and Employment Discrimination

Employment cases that were reviewed earlier illustrated how courts interpret and apply the statutory provisions regarding "otherwise qualified" and "reasonable accommodation." They also illustrate the "direct threat" defense. In the reviewed cases whether the person with HIV or AIDS poses a risk of transmission to others is expressly or implicitly raised. For example, in holding that surgical technicians are not otherwise qualified to participate in surgical procedures, that a hospital may require a surgeon to inform his patients of his HIV-status before performing surgery, that a medical school may terminate a dental student from its program, and that a hospital may terminate a nurse for refusing to provide the results of an HIV-test, the courts are dealing with the issue of risk of transmission.

Courts judge risk on a case-by-case basis by applying the four-part test set forth by the Supreme Court in *Arline* to the facts of each case. The *Arline* standard requires that reasonable medical judgment and current medical knowledge inform the decision regarding risk. Medical judgment and medical knowledge regarding the transmissibility of HIV are made known to the court through expert testimony and through guidelines issued by professional organizations. Experts are nearly unanimous in claiming that the person with the HIV or AIDS does not pose a risk to others.[152] The case of John Doe, whose residency in neurosurgery was terminated by the University of Maryland, illustrates how courts apply the *Arline* test. Doe did not dispute that the first three *Arline* factors weighed against him. He did not, for example, dispute that HIV could be transmitted through surgery (factor one), that the absence of a "cure" for HIV means that the risk is of indefinite duration (factor two), nor that the potential harm is the presumed fatality associated with all AIDS cases (factor 3).[153] Doe's dispute centered on the fourth factor, which directs courts to consider the probability that the disease will be transmitted and the harm it will cause. Dr. Doe argued that the risk that he would transmit HIV was "so infinitesimal that it could not, regardless of the degree of harm involved, be considered a significant risk."[154] The court disagreed and supported its position by referring to guidelines issued by the CDC which say, on the one hand, that HIV-positive surgeons should be allowed to practice invasive procedures but which recommend, on the other hand, that hospitals identify exposure-prone procedures they view as creating an unacceptable degree of risk to a patient and that a hospital may bar HIV-positive surgeons from performing.[155]

Cases that involve risk of transmission in the context of surgery represent an extreme workplace situation. In other employment contexts, courts have shown little sympathy to employers who argue that people with HIV and AIDS pose a threat of transmitting HIV to others.

The California Court of Appeals held that fear that an employee with AIDS placed others at risk could not justify the employee's dismissal. In this case, Chadbourne, a quality assurance investigator for Raytheon, was discharged despite the fact that he had consistently received good performance reviews and the maximum pay increases available.[156] Although medical data compiled by Raytheon, indicated that he did not pose a risk to others, its medical director recommended that Chadbourne not be permitted to return to work. Raytheon defended its dismissal by arguing that other employees were at risk of infection. Finding for Chadbourne, the court said:

> All the . . . information . . . established that AIDS was not transmissible in the workplace and that Chadbourne could return to his job without risk to his fellow workers. Any other conclusion about the transmissibility of the HIV virus would have been pure speculation unsupported by any reasonable medical judgment or knowledge. Raytheon's failure to reinstate Chadbourne . . . was based upon an irrational and unsupported belief that he posed a risk to the health and safety of other workers.[157]

In other cases, two federal courts in the District of Columbia found the risk of transmission by firefighters performing rescue duties to be negligible. *Doe v. District of Columbia* illustrates this issue.[158] Doe was offered a position as a firefighter, only to have the offer withdrawn after he informed the department that he was HIV-positive. The assumption that his condition would interfere with his ability to perform as a firefighter was the basis for withdrawing the offer; and the court, finding for Doe, held that risk of HIV-transmission must be "measurable"[159] and refused to regard the "theoretical or remote possibility of transmission of HIV as a basis for excluding HIV-infected persons from employment or educational opportunities."[160]

PART III. SUMMARY

The Fair Housing Act (FHA), Vocational Rehabilitation Act (VRA), and the Americans with Disabilities Act (ADA) seek to confer status on disabled individuals, including those with HIV, by offering legal protection against actions that are discriminatory, i.e., based on a person's disability and not on an objective assessment of an applicant. Prohibitions against discrimination extend to: (1) the workplace; (2) places of accommodation, including hospitals, doctors' offices, social service agencies, hotels, and the like, whether publicly or privately operated; (3) housing; and (4) educational settings. The law extends its protection to those who are otherwise qualified and who do not pose a direct threat to the health and safety of others, but the law requires efforts to accommodate the individual with a disability as long as the accommodation does not pose an undue hardship on the covered entity. The protections that are offered in the Individuals with Disabilities Education Act (IDEA) apply to children with AIDS and other serious disabilities and guarantee them an education in the least restrictive environment.

The remainder of this chapter summarizes the findings reported above and highlights the conclusions that may be drawn from the reviewed material about the civil rights of women and children with HIV and AIDS. The summary is organized by the areas of education, employment, medical issues, and housing.

Education

A disabled child's right to a free public education is protected under the VRA, the ADA, or the IDEA. The cases reviewed in this chapter describe events that took place in the 1980s. With no new cases reported in the 1990s, it is reasonable to conclude that the right of a child with HIV or AIDS to attend public school is a settled matter. Moreover, special accommodations that segregated children with HIV or AIDS have been deemed unnecessary. Children with either condition can, with few exceptions, be integrated into appropriate classrooms.

The fear of AIDS transmission that compelled school districts to segregate children with HIV may have been allayed through a combination of events including: (1) court decisions finding segregation unnecessary; (2) educational campaigns through which people learned that HIV is not easily transmitted; (3) adoption by school districts of guidelines issued by professional organizations; and (4) adoption of school attendance policies by forty-one states.

Employment

There are very few reported cases of employment-based discrimination that have been brought by women with HIV and AIDS under either state or federal law. If the number of women with HIV continues to increase as it has in recent years (chapter 1), coupled with the fact that the great majority of cases involve women in their prime working years, the number of cases brought by women may increase. The framework used by the courts in analyzing claims of disability-based discrimination are gender neutral and the issues that have been addressed in this chapter are relevant to women.

Allegations of employment-based discrimination go hand-in-hand with concerns of workplace transmission of HIV. The likelihood of transmission depends on the work that is performed; and, as the reported cases show, expert testimony is crucial to helping the courts understand issues of transmission and risk.

If rules governing universal precautions are followed, the present state of medical knowledge does not support a hypothesis that there is a risk of HIV-transmission in work situations that do not involve invasive medical procedures.[161] Health care workers (HCWs) whose essential job functions involve "exposure-prone" procedures may be subject to job loss or job reassignment if they refuse to provide information regarding their health status.

Courts considering risk in classroom settings, office work, and firefighting work have been consistent in concluding that expert opinion does not support a suggestion of significant risk of transmission and have concluded that neither HIV-infection nor diagnosis of AIDS renders an applicant or employee unqualified.

Medical Care

The VRA and the ADA provide a framework for the woman who is denied medical care based on her HIV-status to sue the hospital or other medical provider for its refusal to treat her. Hospitals and physicians' offices are places of public accommodation that are covered by the antidiscriminatory provisions in either the VRA or the ADA.

A number of issues that are germane to receiving medical care, including insurance to cover the costs of care, physicians' attitudes toward treating people with HIV, and problems in receiving proper care that are unique to women with HIV, are covered in the next chapter. In this chapter, the addressed medical issues asked whether a woman with HIV or AIDS is otherwise qualified for the medical care she is seeking. This question must be answered in the affirmative before a woman with a disability will be able to avail herself of the protections that are offered in the VRA and the ADA.

As to whether a woman with HIV or AIDS is otherwise qualified to receive medical care, I reported that applying the concept of otherwise qualified to medical care decisions has been problematic. One federal circuit court ruled that such an effort was not appropriate and left open the possibility that people who are HIV-positive and in need of routine medical care may not have recourse to the courts if care is denied.[162] Other courts, considering it unlikely that Congress intended to exclude medical services from coverage under the VRA or ADA, have ruled otherwise. This issue could ultimately be resolved by Congress making clear its intention or by the Supreme Court in ruling on a case that raises this issue.

Housing

The FHA protects people with HIV from housing discrimination. A woman who is HIV-positive has a right to rent a dwelling and to modify the rented space at her own expense to accommodate her disability. The protections in the FHA prevent communities from barring group residences for people with HIV.

The issues that are raised by community members who are opposed to the opening of a hospice throw into bold relief the mix of fear and prejudice that has governed the response of some members of the general public to the AIDS epidemic, whether the issue at hand is housing, employment, or medical care. Opposition to creating residential facilities for people with HIV and AIDS has caused community members to pressure municipal officials to alter zoning ordinances so that permits to open a group residence could be denied. Community opposition to group residences is not confined to matters involving HIV;[163] and while the law is on the side of those who wish to create residential options, it is not clear that we have seen the last of these cases. Courts have admonished officials who are responsible for enforcing zoning laws that they are bound to base their decisions on the law and not to mold them to conform to community prejudice. They reiterate a point that was made by the Supreme Court in 1985 when it said that officials who deny permits to group home operators must have a rational basis for their decision. Intentional prejudice is not such a basis.[164]

CHAPTER 3

The Policy Framework: Benefit-Conferring Policies

INTRODUCTION

Social policies through which benefits are made available to eligible individuals with HIV and AIDS are the subject of this chapter. Benefits fall into three categories: cash; in-kind; and services. An example of the first is the Supplemental Security Income program, through which funds are provided to eligible individuals with disabilities to help them defray daily living expenses. "In-kind" benefits provide a specific and concrete type of aid, illustrated by payments that are made to providers of medical services through the Medicaid program or Food Stamps which the recipient can trade for food products at grocery stores.

The category of "services" is broad, covering various forms of assistance, such as help in finding and maintaining housing, assistance in the family home to enable a mother during periods of illness to maintain her children in her home, legal assistance to help her make out a will, drug abuse treatment, and counseling regarding the meaning of being diagnosed as HIV-positive.

The provisions in some of the policies reviewed in this chapter complement each other, as they do some of the policies reviewed in chapter 2. For example, the Ryan White Comprehensive AIDS Resources Emergency Act (CARE Act), reviewed below, allows federal funds to be used to provide certain outpatient health and support services to prevent unnecessary hospitalizations, thus supporting the health services that are available through the Medicaid program, which is reviewed below. Both the Americans with Disabilities Act (ADA) and the Vocational Rehabilitation Act (VRA) (chapter 2) have implications for medical care, since both ensure nondiscriminatory access to care. Certain services of importance to women raising children while coping with HIV and AIDS are dealt with in the next chapter, where issues related to planning for guardianship of children is discussed as are the policies that govern the provision of child welfare services.

Women with HIV tend to be poor. For this reason, they or their children are likely to participate in some federal or state social welfare program at the time a family member tests positive for HIV or is diagnosed with AIDS. Others, not initially recipients of social welfare benefits, are likely to turn to the public or voluntary social service sector for aid as the health of a family member deteriorates. Of the 541 HIV-positive women who were interviewed as part of the CDC's HIV/AIDS Surveillance Project most reported reliance on public resources for health care and financial support.[1]

This chapter is divided into four parts. Part I covers financial assistance that is available because of disability. In Part II medical issues are addressed, including policies through which medical benefits are available. The focus of Part III is on policies that provide for a variety of services, including housing, services to prevent unnecessary hospitalizations, and services for substance abusing women. The chapter is summarized in Part IV. Before beginning, a caveat is in order. In 1996, legislation was enacted that ended the Aid to Families with Dependent Children program (AFDC) and that modified the Supplemental Security Income program (SSI). AFDC has been a main source of income for many single women raising children and the major source of public assistance for HIV-positive but asymptomatic women who are not eligible for financial aid under disability-based income programs. In addition to ending the AFDC program, Congress made changes to the SSI program that may affect women and children with HIV. The description of the SSI program in this chapter includes the statutory changes made in 1996. The implications of these changes are discussed in chapter 7, where the federal program that replaces the AFDC program is also described and the implications of the changes that were made are considered.

PART I. FINANCIAL ASSISTANCE

Supplemental Security Income and Title II Disability Income

Financial assistance for a child or adult who has HIV or AIDS may be available under either the Title II Social Security Disability Insurance program (SSDI)[2] or the Title XVI Supplemental Security Income program (SSI).[3] Both programs are part of the Social Security Act, both are administered by the SSA, and both are entitlement programs. In an entitlement program all who apply receive assistance if they meet the categorical and financial need standards established. This means that the number of beneficiaries is limited only by eligibility rules, not by available funds. Stated otherwise, the only way to reduce the number of people benefiting from an entitlement program is to change the eligibility rules, for example, by decreasing the amount of earned income that is used to calculate eligibility. As the earned-income ceiling is lowered, fewer people qualify for program benefits.

SSDI is an insurance program that provides monthly cash benefits to an insured worker and under certain circumstances to the worker's family. Program contributions are made by employers and by employees from whose paychecks Federal Insurance Contribution taxes are withheld. SSI, in contrast, is linked to disability and financial need, not to an individual's work history. SSI provides a subsistence level of income to disabled, aged, or blind individuals whose income and resources fall below standards that are set by the SSA.

Not everyone with HIV is eligible for financial assistance under either program. If a woman has earned income or while unemployed is not suffering a severe impairment, she is not eligible for aid. Once she establishes that she is HIV-positive and unemployed or minimally employed, she is eligible for financial aid if she suffers from a severe impairment which matches a list of impairments used by the SSA to determine eligibility or if she suffers from a medical condition that is the medical equivalent of a listed condition.[4] The listed conditions include opportunistic infections such as *Pneumocystis carinii* pneumonia (PCP), cervical cancer, T-cell count of less then 200, pulmonary tuberculosis, and recurrent bacterial pneumonia.

The claimant for SSI or SSDI must: (1) be disabled; (2) be categorically eligible; (3) pass a "means-test" if applying for SSI; and (4) for either program, survive a multistep evaluation process.

Definition of Disability   Both statutes define a disabled adult as one who cannot continue to do her or his previous work or other work in the national economy because of a "Medically determinable physical or mental impairment which [is likely] to result in death or which has lasted or can be expected to last for [at least] 12 months."[5] A disabled child is an individual under the age of 18 who, like the adult, has a medically determinable physical or mental impairment. The child's impairment must "result in marked and severe functional limitations," and as with the adult, the disability must be expected to result in death or must have lasted or be expected to last for a continuous period of not less than twelve months.[6]

Categorical Eligibility   The applicant for SSI or SSDI must be a member of an eligible category, but the categories of eligibility differ for each program. Because SSDI eligibility rests on a person's employment history, the relevant categories address that history. Eligibility is contingent on the applicant being: (1) a disabled worker (in general, one who has worked for at least forty quarters);[7] (2) the unmarried child of a disabled worker who is under the age of 18;[8] (3) the child of a disabled worker who is 18 years or older and has a disability that began before the age of 22 years and whose physical or mental impairment is expected to result in death or to last for at least twelve months;[9] or (4) the widow or widower of an insured worker who has a disability and who is at least 50 years of age,[10] including the el-

igible not-married divorced widow or widower.[11] The disabled worker who
has worked the requisite period of time is entitled to receive benefits under the SSDI program.[12] Those categorically eligible for SSI are the disabled, aged, or blind who must be United States citizens (see chapter 7 on
the status of people legally in the United States under the 1996 program
reforms).

Means-Test for SSI Eligibility for a means-tested program focuses on
the applicant's income and assets and bears no relation to work history.
Earned and unearned income (and in some situations, contributions such
as food or clothing) are considered in determining eligibility for SSI. Any
woman with earned income runs the risk of being disqualified, not on the
basis of amount earned, but because her earnings may be considered evidence that she is able to engage in substantial gainful employment. In general, earnings in excess of $300 per month raise a rebuttable presumption
of ability to engage in substantial gainful employment and the application
will be denied unless the applicant successfully rebuts the presumption.[13]

The income and resource tests are complex. In general, a single disabled woman is eligible for benefits if her combined income from all sources
does not exceed the maximum benefit available under SSI, or approximately
$446 per month in 1994.[14] There is a resource limit of $2,000 in each month
for the individual. In determining whether the resource limit has been met,
certain items are excluded from consideration such as a home, household
goods, personal effects, and an automobile whose value does not exceed an
amount set by the SSA.[15]

The income of a parent who resides with a child is deemed to be available to the child who is applying for SSI. If the child's parents are working
poor, the child is likely to be eligible for benefits. Children of middle-class
parents are unlikely to receive benefits.[16]

Under SSI or SSDI a person with AIDS who is categorically eligible and
who meets the income and resource standards, if applying for SSI, is presumptively eligible to receive benefits for up to 6 months while a formal
evaluation and a final determination of her claim takes place.[17] The determination of presumptive disability is made on the basis of information
provided by the individual or a member of the individual's family and on
observations made by staff of the SSA. Any benefit that is paid based on
presumptive eligibility must be repaid within six months by proportionate
reductions from future payments.[18]

Evaluation Process Whether or not an adult is eligible for disability
benefits is determined through a five-step evaluation process. The child's
eligibility is determined on the basis of the first three steps.

Steps 1 and 2 require a determination of: (1) whether or not the adult
or older child is presently working or the younger child is engaged in age-
appropriate substantial gainful activity (an affirmative answer disqualifies
the individual) and, if not, (2) whether or not the applicant's impairment(s)
is severe enough to limit significantly her ability to perform basic work- or

school-related activities (if not, she is disqualified.)[19] At step 3 evidence in an applicant's medical file describing her symptoms, signs of illness, and laboratory findings is compared with disability listings.[20] The listed conditions refer to severe conditions, and if there is a match, the applicant is designated disabled and eligible for benefits. Thus, for example, a woman who is seropositive and has *Pneumocystis carinii* pneumonia (PCP) or cervical cancer will be deemed eligible.

Despite the requirement that the medical condition of the person applying for benefits be compared with listed conditions, the SSA did not publish a list of conditions until 1993, after S. P., as she was identified in court papers, sued the Department of Health and Human Services (HHS).[21] S. P. was HIV-positive. She had been hospitalized seven times and was suffering from a "variety of gynecological illnesses including pelvic inflammatory disease, cervical and/or ovarian cancer and pneumonia, yeast infections, urinary tract infections, diarrhea and vomiting."[22] Benefits had been denied her because her condition did not meet the definition of HIV-related disabling conditions.

S. P. argued that the definition of HIV-disability was linked to conditions and illnesses experienced by gay men. The definition, she argued, had been developed by the Centers for Disease Control (CDC) for surveillance purposes and did not take account of conditions common to women and children.[23] Eventually, S. P. was found disabled. Her legacy was the 1993 publication of the listings covering HIV and AIDS and the success that others would have in claiming benefits based on the newly issued listings, which take into account clinical manifestations common to women, including invasive cervical cancer, pulmonary tuberculosis, and recurrent bacterial pneumonia.[24]

Returning to step 3 and assuming that the applicant's condition does not match a listed condition, the question becomes "Is there equivalence between her condition and a listed condition?" Equivalence may be medical or functional. Medical equivalence is found when her condition: (1) matches a listed condition without all of the signs, symptoms, and laboratory findings associated with the listed condition; or (2) does not match a listed condition, but she has the signs, symptoms, and laboratory findings associated with a listed condition; or (3) consists of a combination of impairments that provide the necessary signs, symptoms, and laboratory findings.[25]

Functional equivalence assumes that there is no match between the condition of the applicant and a listed condition and asks "Is her ability to function limited as if her condition were medically equivalent?" Attention turns to issues such as "fatigue and pain . . . [and] frequency and duration of illness [and the] impact of treatment including side effects."[26]

For the adult whose eligibility cannot be finalized at step 3, the inquiry continues, asking whether she is able to do work that she has done in the past (step 4) and, if not, whether she is able to engage in any other substantial gainful activity given her age, education, and work experience (step 5).[27] These steps are a "vocational analysis," and benefits will be denied if the answer to either inquiry is affirmative.

Before the 1996 modifications to the SSI program, a child's application was subject to a fourth step referred to as an Individual Functional Assessment (IFA).[28] An IFA was conceptually comparable to the vocational analysis conducted for adults. An IFA asked whether the child was able to engage in normal everyday activities of living, such as ". . . speaking, walking, washing, dressing and . . . going to school, etc."[29] A child whose impairment significantly reduced her ability to engage in everyday activities, to acquire the skills necessary to assume an adult role, or to "grow, develop, or mature physically, mentally or emotionally and thus to attain developmental milestones"[30] was judged to have an impairment and passed the IFA test. Under the 1996 program modifications IFAs will no longer be conducted.

PART II. MEDICAL CARE

Introduction

Access to medical care requires access to physicians' offices, clinics, and hospitals and the means to pay for needed services. As discussed in chapter 2, section 504 of the Vocational Rehabilitation Act (VRA) and Titles II and III of the Americans with Disabilities Act (ADA) preclude disability-based discrimination in the provision of services, including medical services. Hospitals that receive federal funds under either the Medicare or Medicaid program are recipients of federal funds as defined in the VRA and may be sued for failure to provide medical care to a person with HIV or AIDS.[31] Also, because medical practitioners in private practice operate places of public accommodation, they cannot refuse to provide medical services to people with HIV or AIDS nor can people with either condition be routinely referred to providers for medical service.[32]

While the VRA and the ADA provide important legal protections, neither provides financial aid to the person seeking medical care. Access to medical care requires either independent means, employment-based insurance, or insurance through public programs such as Medicaid or Medicare or programs operated by the Veterans Administration or the Indian Health Service.[33] Some medical services for women with HIV or AIDS are available through programs that are funded under The Maternal and Child Health Service Act[34] or through the Ryan White CARE Act.[35] Thirty-one states, using state and private funding, operate programs for children who are not Medicaid-eligible and who have no other health care coverage.[36]

Access to adequate medical care is unavailable to many Americans, approximately 37 million of whom, including 9.3 million children, are uninsured at any point in time.[37] Of uninsured children, roughly 2.3 million are Medicaid-eligible but are not enrolled either because their parents are not aware of their eligibility or because they experience problems in applying for coverage.[38] Uninsured people tend to be "poor, young, unmarried, uneducated, rural, of color, part-time or self-employed."[39]

Individuals with HIV or AIDS who can afford private insurance may have difficulty obtaining coverage because a majority of insurance companies have expressed a preference not to insure people with either condition.[40] By requiring and using an HIV-test as a basis for denying coverage, insurance companies force the health care costs of the epidemic onto the public sector.[41] In one-half of the states private insurance is available through "risk pools," where insurance companies share responsibility for providing coverage for uninsurable individuals, but cost is a major drawback. Despite statutorily imposed price caps, premiums are often 125 to 200 percent higher than private insurance rates, with yearly premiums estimated to be in excess of $8,000.[42]

Caps on employment-based health insurance which limit the benefits available to those with HIV and AIDS add to the public burden. Title I of the ADA prevents an employer from discriminating against a person with a disability in the "terms, conditions and privileges" of employment. Resorting to Title I, employees with AIDS may be able to prevent benefits caps from being applied. However, the employee claiming discrimination must show that the employer's actions in modifying a benefit plan are a "subterfuge used to evade the purposes" of the act.[43]

Three of four suits filed in 1993 in which persons with AIDS challenged insurance caps as disability-based discrimination have been resolved.[44] They resulted in: (1) the removal of a lifetime benefits cap for AIDS and its related illnesses (set at $50,000 compared to $500,000 for other conditions); (2) a $1 million damage award to be set aside to pay the health care claims of union members with AIDS; and (3) a provision for extended medical coverage for people with AIDS. In 1996, a federal district court in Texas held that an employer who failed to provide health insurance to an employee with AIDS would be in violation of the ADA unless the employer could establish that providing medical coverage would cause an undue hardship. Cost would not suffice to establish an undue hardship unless it brought the employer close to the brink of "financial ruin."[45]

A number of issues related to health care for people with HIV and AIDS are covered in the following pages. These include: (1) physicians' attitudes toward providing care; (2) litigation against physicians for refusing to provide care; (3) health care issues affecting women; and (4) the Medicaid program and the benefits it provides.

Physicians' Attitudes to Treating People with HIV and AIDS

Both physicians and nurses have expressed a preference not to treat people with HIV and AIDS, but the attitudes of physicians have been explored more extensively than that of nurses.[46] The reasons doctors give are mixed and include, not necessarily in the following order: (1) homophobia; (2) a desire not to treat intravenous drug users; and (3) fear of contagion. Some physicians say they lack knowledge to treat patients with HIV and AIDS and they express a desire for educational programs dealing with diagnosis and treatment.[47]

In 1988 and 1989, three surveys were conducted in which medical personnel were asked about matters concerning the treatment of people with HIV and AIDS. Link et al. (1988) surveyed 258 interns and residents in New York City hospitals that served large numbers of AIDS patients. One-half said that they were "mildly, moderately, or extremely resentful of having to take care of AIDS patients,"[48] 25 percent reported that they would not care for patients with AIDS if they had the choice, and an equal percentage said that choosing not to do so would not be unethical. Forty-one percent of medical students polled by Imperato and colleagues[49] (1988) said that physicians should be able to terminate services to patients who develop AIDS if they are able to receive care elsewhere. Forty-eight percent were of the opinion that physicians should be able to decline to serve new patients with AIDS. In a report in a 1989 issue of the *American Family Physician*, states that one-half of 4,000 physicians surveyed reported that they had a right not to treat people with AIDS and 15 percent said they would refuse to do so.[50]

But negative attitudes do not necessarily result in a refusal to provide treatment. Gerbert and her colleagues (1991)[51] report that three-quarters of the 1,121 primary care physicians who responded to their survey had treated at least one person with HIV or AIDS, over two-thirds stated that they had a responsibility to treat people with either condition, but one-half said that they would not do so if they had a choice. Forty-two percent of those responding said that people with HIV and AIDS were welcome in their practice.

Over 3,000 medical residents in the United States ($n = 1,745$), Canada ($n = 685$), and France ($n = 694$) were surveyed by Shapiro and his colleagues (1992);[52] most respondents acknowledged an ethical obligation to treat people with HIV and AIDS. The percentage strongly agreeing that refusal to treat was unethical varied, however, with 87 percent of Canadians, 64 percent of French, and 56 percent of Americans taking this position. Four percent of the medical residents from France, 14 percent from Canada, and 23 percent from the United States said they would not provide care for AIDS patients if they had a choice. In addition, all of the respondents reported that they knew of surgeons who had refused to provide care for at least one patient with HIV or AIDS. Eight percent of the French doctors, 13 percent of Canadian doctors, and 39 percent of American doctors reported that they themselves had refused to provide such care.

Levin and her colleagues (1995) asked whether physicians were willing to provide treatment, including cardiac surgery, dialysis, and resuscitation, for infants (1) with no known risk for HIV; (2) whose mothers were HIV-positive but the infant's risk unknown; and (3) known to be infected.[53] Questionnaires were sent to 1,508 members of the American Academy of Pediatrics Perinatal Medical Section, and 951 responses were received (63 percent). For each of these treatments—resuscitation, dialysis, or cardiac surgery—between 85 percent and 98 percent of respondents would treat infants with no known HIV-risk, between 53 percent and 93 percent would treat when the mother was HIV-positive and the infant's status unknown, and between 22 percent and 50 percent would treat an infant known to be HIV-positive. The respondents' age, gender, and year of graduation from medical school did not affect the responses.

Litigation Against Physicians for Refusal to Provide Treatment

The Council on Ethical and Judicial Affairs of the American Medical Association takes the position that "a physician may not ethically refuse to treat a patient whose condition is within the physician's current realm of competence solely because the patient is seropositive."[54] The need of the AMA to restate a basic tenet of medical ethics is no doubt due to the expressed desire of some physicians not to treat those with HIV or AIDS and in response to suits filed against physicians who allegedly refused to treat patients because of their HIV-status or because of the physician's perception that the patient had HIV or AIDS.

Because the prohibitions in the VRA apply only to entities that receive federal funds, Carol Doe's lawsuit against a physician (filed in 1988 before the ADA was passed) alleging failure to provide prenatal care because she was HIV-positive was dismissed. The court held that the physician could not be sued under the VRA because as an employee of the hospital he was not in a position to accept or reject federal funds.[55] In 1995, Sidney Abbott had better luck than Ms. Doe when she sued a dentist under the ADA for refusing to provide office-based dental services. Because the ADA covers service providers, whether or not they receive federal funds, the court ruled in Ms. Abbott's favor by finding that the dentist had discriminated against her in violation of the ADA.[56]

Under the ADA, referring a patient for medical services solely because of her or his disability and withholding medical treatment from a person because of perception of disability are illegal discrimination. Thus a federal district court in Louisiana found that a dentist had engaged in illegal discrimination when he referred a patient with HIV for a routine dental cleaning,[57] and a federal court in Delaware found that hospital personnel discriminated illegally by failing to "dismantle" a discriminatory plan of treatment that was developed because a patient was presumed to have AIDS because he demonstrated a "gay affect."[58]

Medical Care for Women with HIV and AIDS

Two topics are germane to consideration of health care for women with HIV and AIDS. The first concerns the historical pattern of excluding women from experimental trials for new drugs. The second involves the diagnosis of HIV or AIDS in women. The subject of children's involvement in drug trials is dealt with in the next chapter.

Women and Clinical Drug Trials   The National Institute of Allergy and Infectious Diseases (NIAID) located within the National Institutes of Health (NIH) conducts most clinical trials to develop drug therapies for AIDS and its related illnesses. NIAID conducts its research program mainly through the AIDS Clinical Trial Groups (ACTG), which operates in more then fifty medical centers and universities around the country, and through the Terry Beirn Clinical Research program, which involves seventeen community-based research groups in thirteen cities.[59]

Throughout the early 1990s, men were the primary focus of AIDS research, treatment, and prevention programs. Women were either excluded from or underrepresented in trials of drugs to treat HIV and AIDS. Responsibility for excluding women from drug trials can be traced to guidelines for the clinical evaluation of drugs that were issued in 1977 by the United States Public Health Service (PHS) and that excluded "women of childbearing potential."[60] In addition, women were excluded because it was assumed: (1) that the "natural history" of HIV in women and men was the same and precluded the need to study how women would respond to trial medications in their own right;[61] and (2) that those with a history of drug abuse would not be compliant with treatment regimes. There are data, however, showing no significant difference in rates of compliance with the conditions imposed on participants in drug trials when intravenous drug users are compared to non–drug users.[62]

Natural history studies seek: (1) to describe the course of infection, including the complications that occur and the frequency of their occurrence; (2) to identify predictors of adverse outcomes; (3) to increase the chances for early diagnosis; and (4) to compile information which describes the characteristics of members of at-risk groups who do not become infected. Failure to conduct such studies and the exclusion of women from research protocols prevent the specific medical issues confronting women with HIV and AIDS from being addressed. As a result, the question "Do medications affect women differently from men?" is not answered.

Gender-specific effects would need to take into account the benefits as well as the limitations of different medications, because it is known, for example, that certain treatments for HIV-disease have "potentially debilitating side effects, limited efficacy, and a tendency to produce resistance."[63] In addition, access to research trials may equal access to primary medical care,[64] because such trials may include physical examinations, treatment by medical personnel who are familiar with a woman's health history, regular immune system monitoring, and compassionate treatment not found in the hectic world of emergency room care on which many poor people, especially women, must rely.[65]

In 1993, Congress directed the Secretary of Health and Human Services to develop a plan for inclusion of women (including pregnant women), infants, and children with HIV and AIDS in studies sponsored or conducted by the NIH that address the safety and efficacy of vaccines for the treatment and prevention of HIV-infection.[66] In 1994, the PHS changed its policy by making clear that henceforth applicants for clinical research grants would be required to include women and minorities in study groups. The assumption that women needed protection in the form of exclusionary rules gave way to recognizing that women had a right to choose whether or not to participate in drug trials, based on informed consent, where women would be apprised of risks that might be involved in the treatments or procedures to be employed including the risks that might extend to "the embryo or fetus," if the woman who chose to become a participant became pregnant.[67]

The PHS announced its new policy by promulgating regulations in July of 1994. In addition to requiring that researchers include women in experimental trials, the new regulations required also that evaluation of clinical data be gender-specific so that the effects on women could be culled out from the general conclusions of any study.[68] The effect of the new regulations can be seen in policy changes affecting other governmental agencies. For example, provisions in the Veterans Health Programs Extension Act of 1994 direct the Veterans Administration to "ensure that clinical research conducted or supported by the VA includes women and minorities as subjects, and encourages the expansion of VA medical research relating to the health of women veterans."[69]

The Diagnosis of HIV and AIDS in Women To understand the concern that is addressed in this section, it is important to distinguish a diagnosis of AIDS, based on an opportunistic infection such as *Pneumocystis carinii* pneumonia (PCP), which is "the most common AIDS-defining diagnosis for women and men in the United States,"[70] from a recommendation that a patient be tested for HIV, based on symptoms not specific to the disease.

The difficulty confronting women begins with the fact that less is known about the natural history and progress of HIV-disease in women than in men. In its 1988 report, the Presidential Commission on the Human Immunodeficiency Virus Epidemic commented on the fact that research has focused exclusively on homosexual men and intravenous drug users with the result that little is known about the course of HIV in women. Consequently, diagnosis of AIDS in women may be late or less accurate.[71]

In 1992, the House of Representatives held hearings on HIV- disease and women because many women were developing AIDS and serious illnesses associated with AIDS, and were dying from AIDS. The need to understand the natural history of the disease in women was reiterated and the fact that natural history studies initiated by NIAID did not include comprehensive studies of women was acknowledged.[72] Between 1990 and 1992, no more than 37 percent of funds spent for natural history studies were devoted to issues related to women.[73] The paucity of data on women was highlighted further by Charney and Morgan (1992) in their report in which they reviewed nineteen articles about people with HIV which contained information on almost 5,000 men but only 423 women. Data analysis by gender was often not included in these reports.[74]

Gynecological problems may be the most frequent early symptom of HIV in women.[75] However, physicians lacking such knowledge or not expecting to see symptoms of HIV in the women they treat may fail to recommend HIV-testing and cause women to go undiagnosed and untreated until they are in the later stages of HIV-disease. Failure to diagnose may explain in part what Hellinger (1993) refers to as the "considerable [body of] evidence that women who are diagnosed with HIV exhibit a higher rate of serious infections than do men at entry into the health care system."[76] Because of misdiagnosis, women die without having AIDS,[77] meaning that some contract, suffer from, and die from AIDS before a diagnosis is made. Prophylactic treatment for PCP, which has been found to reduce the overall incidence of HIV-disease and to render it "an uncommon cause of death"[78] could have been provided with proper diagnosis.

In 1993, the Office of Research on Women's Health was established in the NIH. Its mandate is limited, however, to the development of policy to strengthen and enhance research concerning women's health issues and to ensure that research that is conducted by the NIH reflects adequately concerns that bear on the health of women. This office has no power to enforce its recommendations.[79] At the same time, provisions were made to create a National Data System and Clearinghouse on Women's Health[80] to collect and disseminate information regarding research on this subject.

The Office of AIDS Research (OAR) was established in 1988 within the NIH to plan, coordinate, and evaluate all AIDS research, including clinical trials of treatments and therapies for women, infants, and children and to "establish a budget for AIDS research for all AIDS activities of the agencies of the National Institutes of Health."[81] Opposition from Republican members of the House had prevented the OAR from exercising the authority granted to it by statute.[82] However, the federal budget for fiscal year 1997 restored most if not all of the OAR's statutory authority.[83]

Medicaid

The Medicaid program, Title XIX of the Social Security Act, is a needs-based entitlement program for poor people who are categorically eligible due to age, disability, or membership in a family with dependent children.[84] Medicaid is operated in a joint state-federal partnership. It is the major source for health care coverage for women and children who are dependent on publicly supported health care.[85] Federal funds are provided to the states to defray the costs of providing benefits and of administering the program. The federal share is based on a state's per capita income and varies from approximately 50 to 80 percent of program costs.

Reliance on Medicaid has increased as a result of people losing employment-based health insurance. This trade-off has affected the percentage of the adult nonelderly population receiving Medicaid, which increased from 8.5 to 12.4 percent between 1988 and 1992,[86] and the percentage of children receiving Medicaid, which increased between 1989 and 1993 from approximately 14 to 20 percent of U.S. children.[87]

Medicaid is the greatest single payer for health care for people with HIV, between 40 and 50 percent of whom are served by this program, with approximately 62 percent of people with "full-blown" AIDS covered by Medicaid.[88] Thus, Green and Arno (1990) coined the term the "Medicaidization" of AIDS[89] to refer to the trend during the 1980s away from private insurance to Medicaid.

Eligibility   Before the AFDC program was terminated in 1996, eligibility for Medicaid was automatic for those who participated in the AFDC program, for children in foster care who were eligible for AFDC when they entered foster care, and for children who were eligible to receive adoption subsidies. Under the new law, states must continue Medicaid coverage for those who were or would have been eligible for AFDC as of July 16, 1996, as if the AFDC program were still in effect.[90] In almost all states, recipients of SSI are automatically eligible for Medicaid benefits. Those not automatically eligible must, in addition to meeting categorical requirements, satisfy income and resource standards, which vary state-to-state but which are, for the most part, linked to the monthly income limits of the SSI program.[91]

States may extend Medicaid coverage to the "medically needy," who are individuals whose income is too great to qualify them for cash assistance but not sufficient to cover their medical expenses, and to pregnant women and infants in families whose income is up to 185 percent of the federal poverty level.[92] States must provide Medicaid coverage for pregnant women and children up to 6 years of age in families with incomes under 133 percent of the federal poverty level[93] and for children 6 to 10 years of age in families with incomes at or below the federal poverty level. By the year 2002, states must provide coverage for all children up to age 19 whose family income is less then 100 percent of the poverty level.[94]

Reimbursement Rates for Medical Care   Reimbursements to health care facilities often cover only 60 to 70 percent of the costs of treating a person with AIDS.[95] In 1990, Medicaid reimbursements to physicians in San Francisco averaged 33 percent of what was paid by private insurance companies, and in New York, 15 percent. The difference in rates for office visits is striking. Private insurance pays on average $84, compared to $11 paid by Medicaid.[96]

Low reimbursement rates jeopardize access to office-based primary care.[97] For example, some physicians in New York City report that low rates of reimbursement cause them: (1) to limit the number of Medicaid patients they treat; (2) to limit treatment of AIDS patients to those with private insurance or with the ability to pay for services rendered; or (3) to forgo payment for services rendered to AIDS patients because the rate of reimbursement is so low that it is not worth the time it takes to complete the paperwork.[98] Low rates of Medicaid reimbursement also affect treatments received. Bennett and his colleagues (1995)[99] report that black and Hispanic patients covered by Medicaid are less likely to receive prophylaxis for PCP than are black and Hispanic patients entitled to treatment at a Veterans Administration Hospital and that black and Hispanic patients covered by Medicaid have a lower survival rate than black and Hispanic patients covered by other forms of insurance.

Reliance on hospital emergency rooms or "Medicaid mills,"[100] where patients may not benefit from advanced and ongoing treatments, is a by-product of low reimbursement rates. Reliance on emergency room care may result in the undertreatment or nontreatment of poor and minority women because a number of hospitals that serve poor and minority communities are at risk of closing[101] because of policies that restrict hospital admissions, and because of "dumping," which occurs when a hospital refuses to treat an uninsured person despite prohibitions in federal law.[102] Women lacking health insurance are less likely to receive timely and adequate prenatal care, which increases the risks that their children will be born prematurely, suffer from low birth weight, have serious illnesses, and be born with a handicap.[103]

Lack of primary care physicians has been cited as causal to the difficulties that women face in obtaining disability benefits. As reported in Congressional testimony, it is "very difficult to get the forms filled out accurately because you've seen different people every time you've gone to the clinic."[104]

Additional consequences of reliance on emergency room care include increased hospitalizations, inability to gain access to regular ambulatory care in a timely manner, worse health for those served, and increased health care costs. These problems are likely to increase as AIDS becomes more and more a chronic illness and requires the kind of routine medical care provided by primary care physicians.[105] With the rapid increase in new treatments and changing standards of care for patients with AIDS, survival is improved when people with HIV and AIDS are treated by physicians with experience in this area and at hospitals that have experience in treating people with AIDS.[106]

Health care is compromised further because the number of inpatient hospital days per year that are subject to reimbursement by Medicaid is limited. For example, in 1988, people with AIDS averaged 28.4 inpatient hospital days per year, which exceeded either the absolute number of days covered by Medicaid in four states or the number of days covered absent prior approval.[107] Anecdotal evidence from New York and California suggests that the costs of caring for people with AIDS is shifting from inpatient hospital care to outpatient care because of new drug therapies, with a saving of approximately $8,000 per patient per year.[108]

The total lifetime cost of providing medical care to a person with AIDS is estimated to be $115,000, about $50,000 of which is spent prior to an AIDS diagnosis.[109] The average yearly cost for adults with AIDS is approximately $32,508, compared to $37,928 for cases of pediatric AIDS.[110]

To the extent that primary medical care including immune system monitoring is routinely available, people with AIDS require fewer hospitalizations and the cost of care is more similar to the costs associated with providing care for a "moderately expensive, chronic illness than it is to the costs associated with a catastrophically expensive, fatal illness."[111] AIDS care consumes less than 1 percent of the total U. S. health care budget,[112] and even the most "dire scenario" deems it unlikely that AIDS-related health care costs will exceed 2 percent of the health care budget.[113] But given that Medicaid is a federal–state cost-sharing program, the costs are borne disproportionately by a small number of states with the greatest number of AIDS cases.

Services Provided   Federal law identifies a minimum service package which the states must provide to all who are eligible for Medicaid assistance. Mandated are: (1) inpatient hospital care, exclusive of service in an institution for mental illness; (2) outpatient hospital services; (3) other laboratory and x-ray services; (4) physicians' services; and (5) Early Periodic Screening, Diagnostic and Testing Services (EPSDT) for young people under the age of 21.[114]

Prescription drug coverage is not mandated by the Medicaid program but is provided by all states.[115] In addition, the AIDS Drug Reimbursement program, which is authorized under the Ryan White CARE Act, provides funds to assist people with HIV in acquiring needed medications.[116] Prescription drug coverage under the Medicaid program is generally limited as to the number of refills a person may obtain and the total costs of prescription drugs for which states will pay.[117] AIDS medications are very expensive. In 1996, the estimated cost of prescription drugs was between $12,000 and $18,000 per year and some states have signaled their intention to limit the availability of medications for people with AIDS by setting a ceiling on the absolute number of people to be served by drug reimbursement programs; by capping the funds that are available for each individual served; and by excluding from coverage the more costly AIDS-related medications such as protease inhibitors.[118] The high cost of many drugs is protected under the Orphan Drug Act of 1983 through which the federal government offers incentives to drug companies to develop "orphan products"—defined as "drugs, biologics, medical devices and foods for medical purposes which are indicated for a rare disease or condition, i.e. with a prevalence, not incidence, of fewer that 200,000 people in the United States,"[119] such that the market is not sufficient to make its development profitable.

States may, at their option, provide additional medical services and receive federal financial assistance. A variety of options are identified in federal statutes, such as rural health clinics, home health care services, private duty nursing services, clinic services, dental services, and physical therapy.[120]

The Medicare program, Title XVIII of the Social Security Act,[121] is designed to meet the medical needs of retired persons. Medicare will cover certain AIDS-related medical costs for persons under the age of retirement who have been recipients of SSDI for two years. Medicare's role in paying for AIDS-related services has been small because of the two-year waiting requirement and the fact that median survival time for people with AIDS in 1993 was twenty-five months. However, survival time is increasing. In the mid-1980s, average survival time was approximately nine months.[122] If length of survival continues to increase, the role played by Medicare in paying for the costs of treating people with HIV and AIDS could increase.

Medicaid Waivers for People with AIDS   In 1981, Congress authorized the Department of Health and Human Services to grant Medicaid waivers to the states allowing them to sidestep certain Medicaid requirements and to provide special services when doing so would promote cost-effectiveness and efficiency, be cost-neutral, and prevent hospitalization.[123]

Waivers are meant to benefit individuals, including people with AIDS, who might avoid hospitalization with home- or community-based services. These include: (1) case management services; (2) homemaker services; (3) home health aide services; (4) personal care services; (5) adult day health services; (6) habilitation services; (7) respite care services; and (8) day treatment or "other partial hospitalization services, psychosocial rehabilitation services and clinic services."[124]

In addition, states may apply for waivers to benefit children under 5 who at birth tested positive for HIV or who were born drug-dependent,[125] if services, including "nursing care, respite care, physician services, prescription drugs, medical devices, transportation . . . and other services,"[126] would avoid hospitalizations and if the newborn is eligible for aid under the Title IV-E federal foster care program (chapter 4).

PART III. SOCIAL SERVICES AND HOUSING

Three federal policies and the services each makes available to women and children with HIV and AIDS are covered in this section. The policies are the Ryan White Comprehensive AIDS Resources Emergency Act (CARE Act), the Housing Opportunities for People with AIDS Act (HOPWA), and the Alcohol, Drug Abuse and Mental Health Administration Reorganization Act (ADAMHA). Before reviewing these policies and the benefits they provide, it is important to place federal efforts on behalf of people with HIV and AIDS in the proper historical context. This context takes account of the fact that volunteer organizations formed at the community or grassroots level provided almost all of the services that were available to people struggling with HIV-infection for the first decade of the epidemic.

The Grassroots Movement

Social services in the United States are typically provided by public agencies and by not-for-profit agencies who receive financial support from public funds and private donors. Deviations from this approach to providing services may occur when the group to whom services are directed is marginalized (as with gay men in the early days of the epidemic) or when the issue is marginalized (as with domestic violence).[127] In such cases, grassroots groups may step in when government fails to act.

The vacuum created by the absence of federal leadership in the first decade of the epidemic (chapter 1) was filled initially by gay men and lesbians whose grassroots activities resulted in the organization and funding of groups to provide a host of services to people with AIDS.[128] Services included hot lines and newsletters to disseminate what little information was available about the newly emerging disease and assistance with daily household chores and self-care activities to help people with HIV and AIDS remain in their own homes when they became too ill to care for themselves. In addition to groups formed to disseminate information and to provide services, others were organized to further research, including the Kaposi's Sarcomo Education & Research Foundation (later the AIDS Foundation), the AIDS Medical Foundation, and the American Foundation for AIDS Research (AMFAR).[129]

From these early beginnings a movement of community-based social service organizations formed to provide services to people with AIDS that would by the end of the decade number 600.[130] In 1994, the National AIDS Clearinghouse had a list of 18,401 AIDS service organizations in the United States.[131] The value of the labor of volunteers in the mid-1980s was estimated at $1.2 million.[132] According to the National Research Council of the National Academy of Sciences, the "annual cost of caring for persons with AIDS in San Francisco [dropped] from $150,000 to $40,000 [due to the] contributions of volunteers."[133]

By the mid-1980s many groups that were providing assistance to people with HIV and AIDS were likely to be receiving some federal or state funds. By the end of the first decade, services were being provided to a broad spectrum of people that reflected the changing demographics of the epidemic. In 1994, for example, the Gay Men's Health Crisis, Inc., the first multiservice AIDS organization in the United States, reported that 22.5 percent of the 5,000 clients it served were heterosexual, up from 9 percent in 1987, that increasing numbers of its new clients were women, and that 48 percent of all new clients in 1991 were black or Latino.[134]

Today, the numerous organizations providing services to people with HIV and AIDS vary in their programmatic focus and reflect the diverse needs of the people served. Some groups target specific needs by providing: hospice care, meals, legal services, mental health services for children whose parents are HIV-positive, primary pediatric care, residential care for women and children, temporary foster care for children with a parent who is hospitalized, residential care for lesbian/gay youth with HIV or at high risk, and intensive home-based services to enable children to remain in their own homes while their mothers receive drug treatment services.

Other programs are broad based, offering a variety of services under the umbrella of a single organization. Multiservice programs may be staffed by medical, legal, social work and other mental health professionals, working in the community where the person or family resides to provide an array of services including: (1) case management services to help clients identify their needs, plan for meeting identified needs, and obtain assistance when services are not provided by the umbrella agency; (2) coordinating and monitoring services to avoid duplication and to ensure that client needs are being met; (3) information and referral services and education through community outreach programs; and (4) services to help women gain access to drug treatment programs and to relocate their families out of drug-intensive neighborhoods.[135]

Ryan White CARE Act

In August of 1990, almost ten years after the first cases of AIDS were diagnosed, when approximately 140,000 cases had been reported to the CDC and the number of Americans estimated to be HIV-positive was close to 1 million, the federal government passed the first comprehensive legislation to deal with the epidemic. Under provisions in the CARE Act, grants were made available to the states to assist them in their efforts to help people with HIV and AIDS. CARE Act funds have increased each year from more than $200 million in fiscal year 1991 to more then $738 million for fiscal year 1996.[136] The federal budget for fiscal year 1997 contained a proposed increase of $239 million, much of which was to be allocated to the AIDS Drug Reimbursement Program.[137]

The CARE Act provides financial aid to geographic areas that have the greatest number of AIDS cases as well as to states and to public or private entities to develop, organize, coordinate, and operate systems to deliver services to individuals and families. The act consists of four titles.*

Title I: CARE Act Emergency Relief Grant Program   Under Title I, funds are made available to cities or counties that have been hardest hit by the epidemic. Eligible municipalities are those with a population of 500,000 or more who have reported more than 2,000 confirmed AIDS cases to the CDC in the five years preceding the grant application.[138]

Funds are directed to the municipalities' chief elected official, who must create a health services planning council. Council members include representatives of provider groups (i.e., those providing health, mental health, and social services), individuals with HIV and AIDS, and members of the communities affected by the epidemic. Council membership is to reflect the demographics of the epidemic in the area covered by the council. In selecting members, Congress has directed that special attention be paid to "disproportionately affected and historically underserved groups and subpopulations."[139] Councils are charged with developing comprehensive plans for the organization and delivery of health services, and they allocate funds according to the priorities they establish. Funds may be granted to public or not-for-profit groups, such as hospitals, community-based organizations (including hospices and health centers), and ambulatory care facilities, to provide health and support services on an outpatient basis. Services may include case management, substance abuse treatment, mental health treatment, and prophylactic treatment for opportunistic infections. Funds may be used to provide inpatient services if their purpose is to prevent further unnecessary hospitalization or to expedite hospital discharge.[140]

---

*Provisions in the CARE Act that deal with confidentiality, testing, and partner notification are covered in chapter 5.

Title II: CARE Act Grants Under Title II, funds are provided to the states without restrictions based on the number of AIDS cases or incidence in the population, thus making CARE Act funding available for services in small cities and rural areas whose caseload does not satisfy the eligibility requirements of Title I. Improving the "quality, availability and organization of health care and support services for individuals and families with HIV and AIDS disease" is the general purpose of Title II.[141] Grants may be used to establish and operate HIV-care consortia, which are associations of one or more public providers and one or more nonprofit providers of service who organize to plan, develop, and deliver services. Services are to be delivered through consortia, where possible, or through purchase contracts with organizations that are not part of a consortium. Services may include outpatient health and mental health services and support services, such as home health and hospice care, attendant care, homemaker services, day or respite care, benefits advocacy, transportation, nutritional services, referrals for housing, and foster care and adoption services. Title II provides also for a variety of medical services to prevent hospitalization, including the provision of durable medical equipment, day treatment or other partial hospitalization services, home-based drug therapy programs (including prescription drugs administered as part of therapy), routine diagnostic testing, and, where appropriate, mental health, developmental, and rehabilitation services.

Title II grants may be used to provide financial assistance to eligible low-income individuals to maintain their health insurance. The AIDS Drug Reimbursement Program, which provides financial assistance to procure medications to treat HIV, is part of Title II.[142] Because of the high cost of medications for people with AIDS, $52 million dollars of the $738 million appropriated for the CARE Act in fiscal year 1996 is set aside for reimbursement for AIDS drugs.[143]

Title III: CARE Act Early Intervention Services Title III funds are available for early intervention services, including referrals for health services and referrals to programs offering experimental treatments; counseling and testing for HIV; and clinical, diagnostic, and therapeutic services. Services are to be provided on an outpatient basis, and 50 percent of funds must go to primary health care centers and migrant health centers that serve the homeless.[144] Counseling that accompanies HIV-testing must include information about the benefits of testing, early diagnosis, and treatment as well as ways to prevent exposure to and transmission of HIV. Those counseled must be told that medical information is confidential, that anonymous counseling and testing are available, and that they must be given information on their rights to protection against illegal discrimination.

Title IV: Grants for Coordinated Services and Access to Research for Women, Infants, Children, and Youth Through Title IV, grants are made available to providers of primary health care so that women, infants, children, and youth will have the opportunity to participate in research which has the potential for producing clinical benefits. Grantees must provide outpatient health care to women and their families and must include case management services, transportation services, child-care services, and other support services needed to enable women and their families to participate in research programs. Programs must also make referrals for inpatient hospital services, substance abuse treatment, and other needed support services.[145] Grantees must agree that by the end of the second year of a grant, the number of women and youngsters participating in research projects will be "significant."[146]

Special Project of National Significance   Grants may be made in any fiscal year to projects of national significance.[147] These are projects serving people with HIV and AIDS that have a potential for replication and may include projects which: (1) increase the number of health care facilities that serve low-income individuals and families; (2) provide drug abuse and health care services; (3) support respite care services in minority communities to facilitate participation in family-based care networks; and (4) provide health care and support services to underserved populations such as minorities, including Native Americans, people in rural areas, the homeless, and prisoners.

Priorities for Women, Infants, Children, and Youth   In addition to the provisions in Title IV, services for women, infants, children, and youth are required through provisions contained in Titles I and II. Under these Titles, grantees must provide health and support services to women and their families, including treatments to prevent perinatal transmission of HIV.[148] The percentage of funds allocated to services for women and their families must equal the percentage of women with families with AIDS in the grant area.[149]

The 1996 reauthorization of the CARE Act contains provisions for training providers of health care in ways to prevent perinatal HIV-transmission and ways to prevent and treat opportunistic infections.[150]

Use of CARE Act Funds   CARE Act funds have been used for a variety of purposes geared primarily to enable people with HIV and AIDS to remain in their communities by avoiding unnecessary hospitalizations and by receiving help with rent payments. In 1995, the House of Representatives, hearing testimony on the subject of reauthorization of the CARE Act, was told that funds were used: (1) in Houston, to provide free dental care, day treatment, and nutrition services; (2) in Dallas, to refurbish and upgrade housing to create homes for people with AIDS; (3) in Atlanta, to prepare and deliver meals to people at home; (4) in Florida, Hawaii, Minnesota, and Wisconsin, to pay the health insurance premiums of people with AIDS; (5) in Denver, to expand the capacity to provide primary care services, including an AIDS-specific clinic and on-site pharmacy at a local hospital; (6) in Utah, to develop a system of community health centers; and (7) in Missouri, to provide primary health care through a network of 116 primary care physicians who served people living in rural areas including those with no health insurance. In addition, primary health care services have been supported by CARE Act funds in Baltimore, Denver, Los Angeles, Maryland, and South Carolina.[151] In New York, CARE Act funds have been used for outreach programs which have informed over 5,000 Native Americans of services available to them.[152] Twenty-six states used Title IV funds to develop health-related services specifically for women, youth, infants, and children and to provide for developed services through 199 clinical sites.[153]

A significant percentage of CARE Act funds are used to provide health care services that are not covered by Medicaid and to serve people not eligible for Medicaid. For example, in fiscal year 1991, 91 percent of the $77.5 million that was granted under Title II was used for medical and support services, drug reimbursement, home and community-based care programs, and health insurance. The remaining monies were used for planning, evaluation, and program administration.[154]

Serving people in their own homes reduced the average length of hospital stays in Massachusetts from 11.8 days to 9.4 days (at the same time that the average length of stay for all other diagnoses increased) and in Miami from 14 days in 1991 to 8.4 days in 1994.[155] South Carolina reported a significant reduction in the use of hospital emergency room visits after CARE Act funds were used to open a primary care clinic. It was staffed with nurses and physicians trained in the provision of services to people with HIV and AIDS and offered these services to people without Medicaid or other private health insurance.

The Housing Opportunities for Persons with AIDS Act

Lack of adequate housing is an ongoing problem for people with, HIV and AIDS, and federal funding to address this problem is inadequate, according to the Presidential Advisory Council on HIV and AIDS.[156] Funds that are available for housing are provided through the Housing Opportunities for Persons with AIDS Act (HOPWA).[157] Grants may be made to states and localities for the purpose of devising long-term comprehensive strategies to meet the housing needs of people with AIDS and their families.

HOPWA grants may be used to: (1) provide information about housing; (2) coordinate efforts to expand housing; (3) purchase, lease, renovate, repair, or convert housing; (4) provide short-term shelter; (5) provide short-term financial aid to pay rent for homeless people or to prevent homelessness; and (6) provide support services including health, mental health, substance abuse treatment and counseling, day care, and nutritional services. Funds may also be used to develop single-room-occupancy dwellings and to provide low-cost community-based residential alternatives to institutional care.[158]

In 1994, $140.4 million was awarded under HOPWA. The largest share of funds went to rental assistance programs (17 percent, $24.4 million), with programs that provide supportive services receiving $23.1 million (16.5 percent) followed closely by programs to rehabilitate, repair, and convert housing (16.2 percent, $22.7 million). Programs to make short-term payments to prevent homelessness and acquisition programs received approximately

12 percent each ($16.7 million and $17.2 million, short-term payments and acquisitions, respectively).[159]

Congress authorized the allocation of $171 million for fiscal year 1995. However, continuing resolutions provided for only 44 percent of the authorization. As of February 1996, $68,332 had been awarded to seventy-six grantees.[160] In that same month, $7 million became available to fund initiatives for multiply-diagnosed homeless people with HIV and AIDS and for others with chronic alcoholism, drug abuse problems, or serious mental illness.[161] This special initiative was a cooperative effort under HOPWA and the CARE Act's Projects of Special Significance. Projects of particular interest were those that would support the development and evaluation of programs to integrate medical, substance abuse, and mental health services in residential facilities or home health care agencies.

The Alcohol, Drug Abuse, and Mental Health Administration Reorganization Act

The Problem Between 61 and 71 percent of women with HIV contracted the disease through their own drug use or through sexual contact with an IVDU.[162] Treatment programs for substance abusers fall short of the demand for both women and men, but the problem is especially acute for women.[163] A 1989 study of seventy-eight drug treatment programs in New York City, which represented 95 percent of the city's programs, found that more than 50 percent of them refused to treat pregnant women and almost 90 percent refused to treat pregnant women whose addiction was to crack cocaine and who were recipients of Medicaid.[164] The picture is not better elsewhere. Testifying before Congress in 1990, the former governor of Florida reported that 75 percent of women seeking drug assistance in that state are denied help.[165] In 1991, in California and Washington D. C., no more than 20 percent of drug treatment programs served women.[166]

A variety of reasons are offered to explain why women are turned away from drug treatment programs, including the general proposition that programs were developed to treat male addicts and were not prepared to treat women, who, until the 1980s and the emergence of crack cocaine, did not represent a significant percentage of drug addicts. Specific reasons for not serving women included the lack of medical facilities or funds to provide medical services to treat pregnant women and the lack of child-care resources for women with children.[167]

In 1993, a group of substance abusing women sued a New York City hospital by alleging unlawful sex discrimination when the hospital refused to admit them to its drug detoxification program.[168] New York's high court rejected the hospital's defense that lack of equipment and staff to render obstetrical care, not gender bias, explained its failure to treat substance abusing pregnant women. The court ruled that the hospital's policy was discriminatory because it singled out a class of women defined by their pregnancy and treated them differently than others.

Lack of drug treatment facilities and a failure to accommodate the needs of women who abuse drugs are one side of the problem. The other side stems from the fact that pregnant women may avoid drug treatment programs because they fear that their substance abuse will be reported to child protective services when their baby is born and that they will lose custody of their child. (See chapter 4.) In 1990, Connecticut was considering a bill that would have mandated such reporting when a newborn tested positive for drugs. Testimony at legislative hearings captures the concern of some women: "The word on the street is that if you . . . want to keep [your] babies . . . conceal [your] drug use at all costs, even if it means forgoing prenatal care, or delivering . . . at home."[169]

The Alcohol, Drug Abuse and Mental Health Administration Reorganization Act (ADAMHA) was passed in 1992. Congress authorized block grants to the states to enable them to provide a variety of services to individuals who abuse alcohol and drugs.[170] The authorization requires grantee states whose rate of HIV-infection is ten or more cases per 100,000 to carry out one or more projects through which early intervention services (including pretest counseling, HIV-testing, and testing to diagnose the extent of immune system deficiency) are provided and to determine appropriate therapeutic measures at sites where substance abuse treatment is provided.[171] Congress expressed its concern about the problems confronting pregnant women who abused drugs and the consequences of such abuse on newborns in the following ways:

The Center for Substance Abuse Treatment was authorized to award grants to establish: (1) outreach services to pregnant and postpartum women and their infants,[172] including projects for women at risk of HIV-infection, in order to prevent exposure to HIV and to encourage drug treatment;[173] (2) outpatient treatment for pregnant and postpartum women including[174] demonstration projects to provide substance abuse treatment to women with dependent children;[175] and (3) residential treatment programs for drug abusing women and their minor children.[176] Programs must offer, among other things, pediatric health care services, child care while the mother is receiving services, counseling regarding HIV and AIDS, and services to plan for discharge from a residential program and reentry into the community.[177] Programs are to be operated at locations that are accessible to low-income women and services are to be provided in the "language and cultural context that is most appropriate."[178]

States receiving grants must give preference in admissions for treatment to pregnant women who use intravenous drugs followed by pregnant women using nonintravenous drugs[179] who are seeking treatment or who are referred for treatment if they would benefit from assistance. In addition, they must allocate at least 10 percent of funds received to programs that serve pregnant women and their dependent children.[180] Outreach efforts to publicize the availability of drug treatment services, including the fact that preference is given to drug abusing women, are required.[181]

Referrals to the appropriate state agency or official are mandated when the capacity of a treatment facility exceeds the demand for service by pregnant women. States are to maintain and continually update a system to monitor treatment capacity with mechanisms in place for matching the needs of unserved women with treatment facilities that have the capacity to serve them. If there is no treatment facility that is able to admit the woman, interim services must be made available which include referrals for prenatal care, available no later than forty-eight hours after the woman seeks the treatment services.[182]

Recognizing the problems that women have faced in gaining access to drug treatment programs, a number of states have: (1) enacted statutes that provide for treatment for substance abusing women;[183] (2) established research and demonstration programs to assist substance abusing women;[184] (3) permitted any grants that are made to be used for programs or services to assist substance abusing women;[185] (4) expanded pilot programs within a state;[186] (5) guaranteed or enhanced access for women to programs funded by the state,[187] including nondrug related programs that offer nutritional counseling, pediatric care, parenting classes, and child care;[188] and (6) established model programs. These model programs are to help women reduce or eliminate their dependency on drugs or alcohol;[189] to help women at risk of having their children placed in foster care retain their children at home by making services available, including drug treatment and relocation services to help a family move out of a neighborhood where drug use is intensive;[190] and to help women obtain pediatric care, drug treatment, and child development services in a "one-stop-shopping" format where a case manager, acting as a liaison with the state Department of Social Services, assists the mother in obtaining needed services.[191]

Finally, the ADAMHA requires appointment of an Associate Administrator for Women's Services who is charged with identifying women's needs through data-gathering and consultation with an advisory committee and with reporting annually to the Administrator of the Substance Abuse and Mental Health Services Administration.[192]

PART IV. SUMMARY

Cash assistance, medical services, and social services are available to people with HIV and AIDS through a variety of federal programs, including the Supplemental Security Income (SSI) and Social Security Disability Insurance (SSDI) programs, Medicaid, the CARE Act, HOPWA, and ADAMHA. Eligibility for disability-based income assistance is available only for the woman who is HIV-positive and whose physical condition precludes her participation in the labor force, or for her child who is HIV-positive whose condition precludes participating in ordinary everyday activities such as caring for herself or going to school.

The subject of medical care and HIV embraces several distinct topics. First are issues of access to hospitals and clinics, which take account of the closing of hospitals that serve economically poor urban communities and of access to physicians who are willing to provide needed services. There are issues of cost of service and issues that are unique to women because they stem from the failure of the medical community to study the course of HIV in women and to include women in drug trials.

A number of physicians express a preference not to serve those with HIV, but attitudes aside, a great many physicians do provide needed care. Moreover, the provisions in the Americans with Disabilities Act and the Vocational Rehabilitation Act have been successfully invoked by women and men with HIV to ensure that discriminatory practices do not block access to needed care.

Earlier in this chapter, I reported that Medicaid serves between 40 and 50 percent of people with HIV and makes it the greatest single payer for health care for people with HIV-disease. Approximately 62 percent of people with "full-blown" AIDS are covered by Medicaid. Low reimbursement rates paid by the Medicaid program may result in a reluctance of physicians to provide treatment and a paucity of primary care medical facilities in low-income neighborhoods. Consequently, poor women and children rely on hospital emergency rooms and "Medicaid mills" for whatever primary care they receive. Not only does this reliance create a situation where women and children lack primary care physicians who are knowledgeable about their condition and who assume responsibility for routine medical care including ongoing immune-system monitoring, but it places women and children in a position where they may be treated by physicians and in facilities that lack experience in treating HIV and AIDS.

Some women and children who gain access to experimental drug trials may be fortunate, insofar as involvement in drug trials provides access to primary care services. Such coincidence and advantage support the suggestion that poor women and their children do not have routine access to advanced treatments, and in comparison to individuals who have access to experienced primary care physicians and facilities, those who must rely on alternative sources of care may experience worse health, an increase in hospitalizations, and earlier death.

Attention to medical issues of concern to women include the difficulties that women have faced in gaining access to experimental drug trials and problems in receiving accurate diagnosis due to the failure of the scientific community to study the natural history of HIV in women. From the beginning of the AIDS epidemic until 1993, when Congress ordered the Department of Health and Human Services to involve women in drug trials, systematic exclusion of women was the norm. Adverse consequences of this exclusion and neglect include a failure to learn about the natural course of HIV and AIDS in women, hence a failure to develop diagnostic criteria that would allow physicians to detect early signs of HIV-disease, failure to learn whether or not the effects of experimental drugs are the same for women as for men, and finally, the loss to women of the primary health care services, including routine medical care and immune-system monitoring, which are ancillary benefits for those participating in drug trials.

Equally if not more devastating to women's health is the failure of physicians to diagnose correctly HIV-disease, which was the result of not learning about the natural history of HIV in women. The consequences to women ranged from loss of financial benefits to failure to diagnose and treat HIV-infection in women. Benefits were lost because the Social Security Administration did not consider symptoms common to women in the determination of disability.

Building on a grassroots social service movement begun in the early years of the epidemic, the federal government made a commitment to assist people with HIV and AIDS in 1990 with passage by Congress of the Ryan White CARE Act. Under the CARE Act's provisions, funds are made available to cities and states to provide a wide array of services. Available funds have been used for diverse purposes, ranging from the provision of meals to people who are home-bound to providing an array of community-based and home-based medical services and payment for needed medical equipment. The availability of CARE Act funds for outpatient care adds to the availability of such funds through Medicaid waivers and complements the inpatient care provided through the Medicaid program.

The ability to utilize CARE Act funds for community-based and home-based medical care may be critical for maintaining a satisfactory quality of life for people with HIV who are able to reside in their own homes. In turn, the reductions in hospitalizations and hospital days resulting from these services produce savings for other government programs. Provisions in the CARE Act are directed at the needs of women and children by provisions that allocate funds specifically to meet their needs.

The Housing Opportunities for People with AIDS Act (HOPWA) focuses on providing housing opportunities for people with HIV. HOPWA funds may be used to prevent homelessness by providing assistance in making rent payments, by rehabilitating existing housing stock to create single-room dwellings, and by funding of ancillary services for the treatment of medical, substance abuse, and mental health problems.

Because a significant number of women contract the HIV through drug use and because drug treatment programs have typically excluded women, Congress acted in 1992 to make drug treatment more readily available to women when it reorganized the Alcohol, Drug Abuse and Mental Health Administration and authorized the use of grants for outreach services, outpatient services, residential treatment programs for women with children, and demonstration projects to devise ways of serving drug abusing women with children. Revisions made to the law in 1992 require states to give preference to women in admission to drug treatment programs, to develop and implement a data system that can be used to match women who need treatment with facilities providing needed treatment, and to make available interim services within forty-eight hours of a request for treatment if a treatment facility is not available.

CHAPTER 4

The Care of Children and the Child Welfare System

INTRODUCTION

Approximately 80 percent of women with HIV are of childbearing age, 75 percent have children, 50 percent have more than one child,[1] and most are single parents.[2] Due to their own health or the health of their children they will at some time, and perhaps more than once, need assistance with child care. The need to make long-range plans for the future living arrangements of a child is a reality that most women with HIV will confront.

The child-care assistance that a single woman with HIV may need includes: (1) short-term respite from the daily rigors of child care, (2) full-time, temporary care, in or out of the family home, when she is too ill to provide daily care, and (3) permanent care if she cannot or will not provide full-time child care or if she predeceases her child. An estimated 125,000 to 150,000 children will be orphaned by the AIDS epidemic in the 1990s.[3]

This chapter is divided into three parts. Part I begins by addressing the question "Who is providing care in families where the mother and/or child has HIV or AIDS?" Planning options for the HIV-infected parent are also reviewed. These include legal options that are available for the mother who wishes to elect her child's guardian before her death.

A number of women with HIV, or those whose child has HIV, will become involved with the child welfare system. Their involvement is the subject of Part II. Each state operates a child welfare system to protect children from abuse or neglect and to provide homes for those whose parents cannot or will not care for them. In the context of addressing how the state fulfills its obligation to act *in loco parentis* (literally, in the place of the parent), a number of issues are addressed. These issues are the state's responsibility to help a mother maintain her children in their own home, medical decision making for children in state custody (including testing for HIV), and long-range planning for a child's living arrangements. Part III summarizes the material in Parts I and II.

PART I. CHILD CARE AND LONG-RANGE PLANNING

Who Is Caring for the Children?

There is no national data collection system to which one may turn to answer the question "Who is providing care for children in families where the mother and/or child has HIV?" Available data come from separate studies conducted at different times, in different locations, with different methodologies.[4] From these studies we learn that between 45 and 56 percent of children are cared for by their biological mother; 27 to 33 percent are in foster care; 10 to 16 percent are in the care of relatives; and 7 to 10 percent are in other unspecified care arrangements.[5] The only study reporting data on two-parent families informs us that 15 percent of children are cared for by both parents.[6]

Data on the relationship between HIV and the need for foster care placement show widely divergent patterns. The most common estimate is that 27 to 33 percent of the children are in foster care, as reported above, but state-by-state variations are extreme and are not explained by rates of infection in the population. For example, since the late 1990s, Florida, New York, and the District of Columbia have consistently had high rates of infection exceeding 20 cases per 100,000 population, the highest per-capita rates of infection reported by the Centers for Disease Control (CDC). However, there is significant variation across these jurisdictions in the percentage of children in foster care, with approximately 1 percent in Florida, 8 percent in the District of Columbia, and 41 percent in New York. Colorado with a relatively low rate of infection (12 cases per 100,000 population) reports that 23 percent of children whose mothers have HIV are in foster care settings.[7]

Caldwell and colleagues (1992), reporting data from the CDC's Pediatric Spectrum of Disease Project, which conducts surveillance of pediatric AIDS cases in six geographic areas, state that children whose mothers use intravenous drugs (IVDU) are more likely than others to be living with an alternative care giver. Maternal drug use may be the most important factor determining whether or not a child lives with a biological parent.[8]

A number of children live in kinship care arrangements. Kinship care refers to full-time child care provided by a relative. Because the arrangement may be based on an informal agreement between a child's biological mother and a family member or on a formal state-sanctioned agreement, the exact number of children living in kinship care is not known. A caretaker who is a relative may be eligible to receive financial support under the Temporary Assistance for Needy Families Block Grant [formerly, Aid to Families with Dependent Children (AFDC): see chapter 7],[9] which provides financial assistance to dependent children and their adult caretakers to help maintain children in their own homes or in the home of a relative.

A relative who chooses to become a licensed foster parent may be eligible for a higher rate of reimbursement than a nonlicensed relative.[10] In addition to being licensed as a foster parent, receipt of the higher rate requires that the child be eligible for federal support of her foster care placement. Eligible children are those: (1) who would have been eligible for financial assistance under the AFDC program as it existed on June 1, 1995 (except that a child who was abandoned before a determination of eligibility could be made may receive federal support);[11] (2) who were removed from their parent or custodian pursuant to a judicial determination that removal was necessary to protect the child; (3) who are placed in the legal custody of the state; and (4) who are placed in a licensed home. If the child is not eligible for federal support of her foster care placement, the cost of maintaining her in foster care is borne entirely by the state, which need not pay relatives the same rate as nonrelated foster parents.[12]

Grandparents have become key care givers for their grandchildren for a number of reasons, including the rising incidence of HIV and AIDS.[13] Schable and others (1995), from their study of 541 HIV-infected women living in ten states, report that grandparents are second only to the child's biological mother as primary caregivers.[14] A Congressional effort in 1993 to enact legislation that would have made children being raised by their grandparents eligible for financial benefits based on the child's dependency on a recipient of Social Security was not successful.[15]

A significant number of children in foster care are in kinship care arrangements. In New York, 42 percent of the 45,500 children in care are in such homes; and in Illinois, 8,000 out of 18,000 children (44 percent) are placed with relatives.[16]

Factors that Affect Planning Options for the Parent Who Is HIV-Positive

Women with AIDS who are raising their children report that their most pressing legal concern is "Who will care for my children when I die?"[17] This section begins with a brief discussion of issues that affect a mother's options in planning for her child. Next, the weight that courts assign to a custodian's HIV-status in making custody decisions is discussed. Then an approach to assisting HIV-positive women to plan for their children is summarized. Options that allow women to exercise some control over their child's future custodial arrangements are the last topic discussed.

Whether or not a woman is able to exercise any of the planning options that are reviewed below depends on certain conditions. First, she must have legal custody of her child. A woman whose child has been removed from her care with a transfer of legal custody to the state may participate in decision making for her child's future, but she cannot act autonomously in making plans. Second, if the child's father is alive and has participated in raising his child, the mother's wishes cannot, per se, eliminate him as a potential source for child care.[18] Additionally, the exercise of any legal option requires access to legal services, which for many women with HIV must be such free legal services as are available through AIDS-service organizations, law school clinics, and legal aid societies. Finally, judges are the final arbiters of child custody decisions. Whether or not the person a mother nominates as custodian of her child will be appointed will be decided by a judge who, with few exceptions, has a great deal of latitude to make decisions in the best interests of the child.[19]

"Best interests" is an ambiguous concept that is applied in one of two ways. In some states, judges' decisions may rely on personal or social judgments.[20] The court may consider as relevant to a custody decision any behavior or condition of the proposed guardian without addressing whether the factors considered are harmful to the child. Thus if a mother elects as a custodian her lesbian partner or an unrelated adult with a history of drug or alcohol use, the court may not honor her wishes regardless of the relationship between the elected custodian and the child.[21] In other states, judges take into account the behavior of the proposed custodian only to the extent that it affects the child. Here, custody is not as a rule denied solely because a court finds the designated custodian's behavior or condition distasteful without evidence that the behavior of concern is harmful to the child.

The custodial rights of an HIV-positive biological parent, foster parent, and adoptive parent have been challenged by a noncustodial parent or other relative, who argued that the children were at risk of infection from the parent with HIV.[22] In *Steven L. v. Dawn L.*[23] a biological father petitioned for a change of custody when his former wife tested HIV-positive. The court denied his request. Acknowledging that exposure to a contagious disease would not be in a child's best interest, the court was persuaded by uncontested expert testimony that HIV is not easily transmitted and by evidence showing that the mother exercised proper care and control of her child. Infection with HIV is not, by itself, grounds for a change in custody, the court ruled. The mother's condition had not impaired her ability to parent, there was no reason to believe that her condition would do so in the near future, and the child's physical or psychological well-being was not threatened by it. In *Newton v. Riley*, an appellate court in Kentucky, when asked whether the biological mother's decision to live with a man who was HIV-positive constituted grounds to remove the child from her care and place him with his father, answered in the negative.[24]

Another case involved an effort by a state child welfare agency. The agency sought to remove a child from the care of his foster parents, who were preparing to adopt him, after it learned that the foster mother was HIV-infected.[25] The appellate court denied the request because the child was not at risk and because remaining in the foster home was in the child's best interest. However, in another case, on a finding that both adoptive parents were HIV-positive, a court ruled that it was in the child's best interests to permit the biological mother to withdraw her consent to adoption.[26]

Programs to Help the HIV-Positive Mother Plan for Her Child   Special programs in New York and Illinois assist the HIV-positive mother to plan for her child's future.[27] These programs seek to prevent the emergency placement of children through timely planning with the mother when she is well and to ensure that children will have permanent placements when their mothers die. While there are differences in how each program operates, the goals of the Second Family Program in Chicago are similar to those of the Early Permanency Planning Project in New York. Program goals are "to increase access to information referral and counseling for HIV-infected parents; to increase the number of HIV-affected children in permanent placements at their parents' death; and to increase awareness of HIV-affected families' permanency planning needs."[28]

The Chicago program recruits and trains families for the children if placement with relatives is not possible. To ease the child's transition into a new home the child's biological parents are encouraged to develop a relationship with the new family who will, if the situation requires, assume some responsibility for the child when the mother's health deteriorates.

Parents participating in the New York program sign a voluntary placement agreement so the child can enter foster care when the parent finds such change necessary. The Chicago program arranges for transfer of legal custody through either a guardianship or adoption arrangement. If legal custody is transferred while the parent is still alive, "a voluntary open relationship is maintained to preserve the child's relationship with birth parents."[29]

Both the New York and Chicago programs provide referrals for legal services and both provide support services to the biological mother.

Legal Planning Options

Power of Attorney   A woman may execute a power of attorney designating another to act on her behalf or on behalf of her child. A "durable power of attorney" is a special form of power of attorney where the conferred authority begins when the person executing the document becomes incompetent. All states and the District of Columbia have statutes covering powers of attorney, but statutes differ in the powers that can be delegated.

Banks (1993), discussing family law matters for people with HIV and AIDS, cautions that a power of attorney may be a weak approach to fulfilling a woman's wishes for her child, because it may not be recognized as valid by schools, medical providers, or the courts.[30] For example, an Arizona appellate court held that the fact that the child's biological mother had executed a power of attorney granting custody of her child to her own mother did not prevent a juvenile court from exercising its authority to declare the child a dependent of the court.[31]

In *McGuffin v. Overton,* a biological mother in Michigan executed a power of attorney in which she delegated parental authority to the women with whom she had been living for eight years and named her as the guardian of her children in her will. The state Court of Appeals would not honor the mother's wishes against the custody claim of the never-married biological father until the mother's will went through probate and a decision affirming or denying her choice of guardian was made.[32] Until then, the court held, the mother's partner could not challenge the biological father's petition.

However, courts do not always decide against the mother's nominee. Courts in Kansas have ruled that a mother may transfer custody of her child to another through a power of attorney and that she may revoke the granted power unless there are exceptional circumstances showing her to be unfit.[33] In 1989, a Florida court set aside an adoption by the grandparents of a 10-year-old in favor of the mother's former partner, who had been the child's de facto parent.[34] In reaching its decision, the court considered the fact that the grandparents had, after their daughter's death, executed a power of attorney in which they granted all of their authority for custody and control of their granddaughter to the woman with whom their daughter had lived.

Guardianship by Appointment in a Will   A parent may, in her will, designate another to become guardian of her child, but a court need not honor her wishes. A judge who concludes that placement with the person designated by the mother is not in the child's best interest is free to place the child elsewhere.

The peace of mind that a single parent may derive from use of her will to designate her child's guardian will depend on several factors. If the person chosen is unrelated, she or he is considered a "legal stranger" to the child.[35] If a related adult disputes the mother's will, the mother's designee may not be able to contest the claims made by the suitable related adult. The court ruling in *McGuffin*, favoring the never-married biological father, illustrates this point and highlights another limitation of guardianship by appointment in a will. In *McGuffin*, the court said that its ruling would have no bearing on the right of the mother's partner to appeal its custody decision should she be appointed guardian under the terms of her partner's will. The problem lies in recognizing that the court may place the child in whatever home it deems best while awaiting the ruling of a probate court. The time taken to probate the will and then to appeal the unfavorable decision may count against the mother's nominee. Since the child has been placed with the father during this time, the court is likely to consider the effects on the child of removing her from his home. Stated otherwise, if the parties contesting custody are equally qualified to care for the child, the person who has most recently been providing daily child care may win out, because a court is likely to consider it detrimental to the child's best interest to remove her from the home where she has been living.

Adoption or Guardianship While the Parent Is Alive   Four planning options fall under this general heading. First, a parent may petition the court to have another legal guardian of her child appointed while she is alive. The drawback to this option is that the mother must witness the termination of her own rights without any guarantee that the court will appoint as guardian the person of her choice. On the positive side, the mother who successfully pursues her claim will be assured before her death that her child will be cared for by the person of her choice. Before a woman voluntarily transfers her legal custody to another person, she should consider what role, if any, she wishes to continue to have in her child's life and she should negotiate for ongoing involvement if she wishes to be involved. New York and other states permit "open-adoptions" in which the parties agree on a role that the biological parent will play after the adoption, including such provisions as ongoing visitation with the child.[36]

The second and third options involve adoption by a person to whom the mother is legally married or by her unmarried partner. The second option is available in all states, while the third, referred to as a "second-parent adoption," is possible in five states and the District of Columbia.[37] Second-parent adoptions provide an option for the unmarried parent who is in a stable relationship with an adult to exercise control in planning for her child. The parent who exercises either of these two options has the security of knowing that her child will be cared for by a person of her choosing, since the adoptive parent will have presumptive custody of the child when the biological parent dies. The child has the advantages that follow from continuity in caretaking, such as ongoing involvement with extended family members, friends, and community.

The fourth option is "standby guardianship." Standby guardianship provides a means whereby a parent who is likely to die or become incompetent within a period of time specified in statute may designate another to assume legal responsibility for her child. Legal responsibility transfers when the mother becomes incapacitated, at her consent, or at her death.[38] Since a court approves or denies a standby guardianship petition while the mother is alive, this strategy has the advantage of informing her of whether or not her choice of guardian will be honored. If not, she has the option of selecting another person to act as guardian.

The AIDS epidemic, coupled with the uncertainty involved in using traditional approaches to designating a guardian through power of attorney or a will, has prompted passage of standby guardianship legislation in several states.[39] However, a 1993 effort to amend federal law to require states to enact standby guardianship laws failed.[40]

The New York Standby Guardianship law will illustrate the purpose and operation of state statutes. In New York a standby guardian is a person designated by a parent or legal guardian and appointed by the court, (1) when a parent or legal guardian documents that she is likely to die or become incapacitated within two years and petitions the court to approve the appointment of her selected guardian, or (2) when the seriously ill parent or legal guardian who is not able to petition the court designates a standby guardian in a written document which she or her representative must sign. A guardian's authority becomes effective on the consent, incapacity, or death of the parent or legal guardian. The only New York court to consider the proper standard for deciding whether to honor a parent's designation of standby guardian held that although it is within the court's discretion to disapprove the parent's choice if it is in the child's best interests to do so, there is a strong presumption that the choice made by a competent parent will advance the best interests of the child. The court's discretion to disapprove the parent's choice is limited to situations where the court clearly and convincingly believes that appointing the person chosen by the parent would not promote the best interests of the child.[41]

PART II. CHILD WELFARE SYSTEM

Since the majority of women with HIV are poor, purchasing needed child-care services is not a viable option, at least in the long run. Thus women who do not have family or friends to whom they can turn for help with child care will depend on services provided by state or not-for-profit child welfare agencies. Some women may request needed assistance; others will come into contact with a child welfare agency on an involuntary basis, because they have become the subject of a report of child abuse or neglect.

All states operate a child welfare system for the purposes of: (1) protecting children from abuse and neglect; (2) preventing placement of children in foster care; (3) providing foster home care to children whose parents cannot or will not provide for them; and (4) providing permanent homes through adoption or other means for children who cannot be returned to their own homes. Under provisions in the Americans with Disabilities Act (ADA) or the Vocational Rehabilitation Act (VRA), children with HIV or AIDS are entitled to participate in and receive the benefits of services, programs, or activities of a public or private child welfare agency. Several lawsuits have been filed charging state child welfare agencies with discrimination against HIV-positive children. These suits have alleged that children have been denied access to agency programs based on their HIV-status or placed in a group home not equipped to provide needed medical services and without informing the group home that the youth placed in its care was HIV-positive.[42]

In the following discussion, two federal statutes, the Child Abuse Prevention and Treatment Act (CAPTA) and the Adoption Assistance and Child Welfare Act (AACWA) are reviewed. A number of topics are covered, including: (1) child protection laws as they affect a mother with HIV; (2) state responsibility to assist a parent to maintain her child in her own care; and (3) state responsibility to provide medical care for children in state custody, including whether the state can and should test a child for HIV, and, if so, whether the state should disclose information regarding a child's HIV-status to foster and adoptive parents; and (4) planning options for the child with HIV.

Child Abuse Prevention and Treatment Act

In 1974, Congress passed the Child Abuse Prevention and Treatment Act (CAPTA).[43] Federal assistance for dealing with child abuse is available to states that have enacted legislation which provides: (1) for accepting and investigating reports of known or suspected child abuse; (2) for protecting children if abuse or neglect is found; (3) for maintaining the confidentiality of records concerning child abuse and neglect; (4) for appointing a *guardian ad litem* to represent the child in any court proceedings; (5) for educating the public about child abuse and neglect; and (6) for immunizing from suit persons who report in good faith. In 1984, Congress amended the CAPTA to require states to provide for reporting of abuse or neglect of children in state custody perpetrated by foster parents or caretakers in group homes, residential settings, and institutions,[44] and to report as neglect the withholding of medical treatment from disabled infants with life-threatening conditions.[45]

All states have child abuse reporting laws that mandate that professionals who come into contact with children, including social service, medical, psychiatric, psychological, educational, day care, and law enforcement personnel, report known or suspected child abuse and neglect to a designated state agency. Twenty-two states accept reports from any person. In 1993, approximately 2.3 million children were the subject of reports of possible abuse or neglect and 1 million reports were substantiated.[46]

Child abuse reporting laws may affect families with HIV or AIDS if a newborn or older child is abandoned in a hospital, if a child is born with a positive toxicology for drugs or with evidence of maternal use of alcohol during pregnancy, or for matters independent of a parent's HIV-status or use of drugs or alcohol.

Abandoned Babies and the Abandoned Infants Act   In 1988, in response to the problem of infants and young children being abandoned in hospitals, Congress passed the Abandoned Infants Act (AIA).[47] The AIA is concerned with "boarder babies," so called because they literally board at hospitals. In addition to newborns, boarder babies include infants and young children who have been cleared for hospital discharge but who remain in hospitals because there is no home to which they can be discharged. Under the AIA, federal funds are made available to state and not-for-profit agencies that give priority to serving abandoned infants and children who are HIV-positive or who have been perinatally exposed to HIV or to unsafe drugs. Projects are funded to demonstrate ways: (1) to identify and address the needs of these infants and young children; (2) to prevent parents from abandoning their children, including providing services to the family to remedy conditions that increase the likelihood of abandonment; (3) to recruit, train, and retain foster families for abandoned infants and young children; (4) to operate respite care programs for families, including foster families; (5) to recruit and train health and social services personnel to work with all families and with residential programs that care for or serve abandoned infants and young children; and (6) when necessary, to permit the child to reside in foster care.[48]

In March of 1994, it was estimated that 22,000 babies were abandoned at birth and were living in hospitals,[49] an unspecified number of whom were HIV-positive.[50] Hospitals initiate state intervention on behalf of an abandoned child by making a report to the state agency that is designated to receive reports of child abuse or neglect. The state agency commences an investigation that will have as a goal both locating the mother or father or other family member who may assume responsibility for the child and simultaneously planning for placement of the child in a safe environment when she or he is ready for hospital discharge. The outcome of the investigation will depend on a number of factors. If the parent who abandoned the child comes forward, the child may be released to her care with services offered by a social welfare agency; or the child may be released to another family member. Absent either of these options, the state will place the child in a foster care setting when she or he is ready for hospital discharge.

Babies Born with a Positive Toxicology for Drugs In chapter 3, the difficulties that women experience in obtaining treatment for substance abuse were discussed, as was the concern harbored by some women who use drugs that they will lose their newborns if their substance abuse becomes known. This concern stems from the fact that in addition to reporting when a child is abandoned in a hospital, a number of states include prenatal exposure to drugs or alcohol in their definition of child abuse and neglect. Thus if a newborn tests positive for drugs or is born with a birth defect suggestive of maternal alcohol use, such as congenital heart disease, cleft lip and palate, low birth weight, and small head circumference, the mandatory reporting requirements of state law are triggered.[51] Because the conditions that suggest maternal alcohol use are also found in newborns whose mothers do not use alcohol during pregnancy, further evidence may be required to corroborate a hypothesis that these birth defects are related to alcohol consumption.[52]

If state law does not mandate reporting under the conditions just described, case law can be found that supports the proposition that evidence of prenatal exposure to a controlled substance is sufficient to charge a mother with abuse or neglect or to find the child neglected.[53]

However, evidence of use of controlled substances during pregnancy will not necessarily result in finding a mother neglectful. For example, the Appellate Division of the New York Supreme Court ruled that an allegation of abuse or neglect will not be sustained absent proof of repeated prenatal drug use from which an inference of postnatal drug use and danger to a child may be drawn (*In the Matter of Alfredo S.*).[54] Moreover, a mother has the chance at trial to show that her use of drugs during her pregnancy does not establish her lack of fitness to parent.[55] Even if neglect is established, it does not follow that a child will be removed from her or his mother's care.[56] One family court judge in New York ruled that prenatal drug use alone without evidence of neglect by the mother after the child's birth or without evidence that the mother is drug addicted or a regular user is not enough to sustain an allegation of neglect much less to deprive the mother of custody of her child.[57]

In addition to initiating civil proceedings that might result in charging a mother with abuse or neglect, hospital reports that a newborn was drug addicted at birth have been the basis for lodging criminal charges against women for "delivery" of a controlled substance to a minor. Until July of 1996, no state court had been willing to find evidence of a positive toxicology for drugs at birth sufficient to sustain criminal charges. In the summer of 1996, the Supreme Court of South Carolina, based on its determination that a viable fetus is a "person" under state law, sustained the criminal conviction of Cornelia Whitner. Ms. Whitner, whose child tested positive for cocaine at birth, was sentenced to eight years in prison for ingesting cocaine in her third trimester of pregnancy.[58]

In addition to reports of abuse or neglect that are triggered when a parent abandons a child in a hospital or when there is evidence of maternal drug or alcohol use, a family that is coping with HIV may be the subject of a report of child abuse or neglect for reasons unrelated to the presence of HIV. Stated otherwise, an HIV-positive parent may neglect or abuse a child for reasons that do not directly implicate the parent's HIV-status.

The Outcome of a Child Abuse Investigation   Federal law requires that the states protect the child who is abused or neglected, but CAPTA is mainly procedural. Its mandates are concerned with ensuring that states have in place mechanisms to receive and investigate reports of child abuse and neglect. It does not mandate services for families found to have abused or neglected their children, although state and not-for-profit agencies may apply for federal grants to develop and implement research and demonstration programs to test new methods for working with families who abuse or neglect their children.[59] Services to allow children to remain in their own homes are discussed below when the AACWA, which does require such services, is reviewed.[60]

Possible outcomes of a child abuse investigation include: (1) emergency removal of a child from its own home and placement in a protective environment when the evidence suggests a risk of serious harm, or (2) in a nonemergency situation, a determination of whether or not there is credible evidence of abuse or neglect as a predicate to further decision making. If there is not sufficient evidence to sustain an allegation of abuse or neglect in court, parents may be offered services on a voluntary basis. If parents refuse services, the case will be closed. But the fact that an allegation is sustained or sustainable does not mean that the family will receive services. In 1986, the last year for which data are available, the American Humane Association reported that only 45 percent of sustained cases were opened to an agency so that services could be provided.[61]

The Adoption Assistance and Child Welfare Act

In 1980, the Adoption Assistance and Child Welfare Act (AACWA) was signed into law.[62] The objectives of the AACWA are twofold: (1) to prevent the removal of children from their own homes, and (2) to facilitate the placement of children who enter substitute care in permanent family homes, either by reuniting them with their families of origin or through placement in adoptive homes. Federal funds are available to the states to develop and implement programs to achieve the objectives of the AACWA. The AACWA has two main titles: Title IV-E, an open-ended entitlement program under which the federal government contributes to the costs of maintaining certain children in foster care, and Title IV-B, the Child Welfare Services program, which is subject to annual appropriations. We begin with Title IV-B.

Title IV-B Child Welfare Services As the health of an HIV-infected mother deteriorates, her ability to maintain her child at home may depend upon her capacity to obtain services from a child welfare agency, especially if she does not have family or friends who can help her with child care. A range of services may be helpful, including those of homemakers, visiting nurses, and part-time child-care services. Services are critical not only to the mother but to the child who may otherwise have to experience episodes of foster care placement each time the mother's health limits her ability to provide full-time care.

Congress's intent that the states have services available to prevent the unnecessary placement of children in out-of-home care is evident in several ways.

First, the statement of purpose to the Title IV-B Child Welfare Services program says that the availability of federal funding is to encourage and enable the states to "develop and establish, or expand, and to operate a program of family preservation services and community-based family support services" so that placement of children in foster care can be avoided.[63]

Second, to emphasize its commitment to family preservation, Congress amended the Title IV-B program in 1992 with the Family Preservation Act, which made funds available to the states, beginning in fiscal year 1994, to develop and implement, or expand programs to preserve families.[64]

Third, the "reasonable efforts" requirement of the AACWA is further evidence of Congress's intent to prevent removal of children from their own homes. This provision of the law requires a judicial determination in writing on a case-by-case basis that reasonable efforts were made to maintain children in their own homes and to return home children who are removed. The required judicial determination is a condition for the states to claim federal reimbursement to defray the costs of maintaining a child in foster care under Title IV-E of the Social Security Act.[65]

The good intentions that are expressed in the law are offset by underfunding and ambiguous statutory language. When the AACWA was enacted, it included a penalty for states that failed to have in place preventive and family reunification programs. However, this mandate was linked to federal funding. Under current law, the mandate does not "kick in" until Congress appropriates $325 million for two consecutive years to the Child Welfare Services program, which it has never done.[66] The use of Title IV-B funds for services to preserve the family unit is permissive. Title IV-B monies may be allocated to family reunification and adoption programs rather than to programs to prevent placement, and the 1992 Family Preservation Amendments do not alter this kind of permissive allocation.[67]

Also, "reasonable efforts" is not defined in federal statutes or regulations and the Supreme Court has said that the AACWA provides no guidance for how to "measure" this statutory provision.[68] State statutes are equally ambiguous, by defining reasonable efforts vaguely as "the exercise of ordinary diligence and care," as "due diligence," or as "reasonable diligence."[69]

Federal regulations require that each state identify the preplacement preventive and reunification services that exist to help children and families.[70] Federal law suggests an array of services, including: (1) twenty-four hour emergency caretaker and homemaker services; (2) day care; (3) crisis counseling; (4) individual and family counseling; (5) emergency shelters; (6) procedures for gaining access to emergency financial assistance; (7) temporary child care to provide respite to families; (8) postadoption services; and (9) other services, such as home-based family services, self-help groups, services to unmarried parents, provision of or arrangements for mental health, drug and alcohol abuse counseling, vocational counseling, and vocational rehabilitation.[71]

A number of states have codified their obligation to provide preventive and family preservation services, but determining who is eligible to receive services is difficult because of vague statutory language. For example, eligibility may be restricted to those situations where it is "possible and appropriate" to protect the child from separation, or by language requiring a determination that the child is "at risk," at "immediate risk," at "imminent risk," in "imminent danger," or at "actual and imminent risk" of "out-of-home placement."[72]

Florida limits family preservation services by limiting the cost of serving a child in her own home to that of out-of-home care;[73] and New York will not grant authority to a social worker to provide preventive services without official approval (e.g., city or county commissioner) and confirmation that a child will enter foster care without preventive services.[74]

The difficulty with these various qualifications is that they rest on the assumption that risk of placement can be reliably assessed and families referred for service on the basis of agreed upon professional standards. However, studies do not support the suggestion that strategies to assess risk and prevent placement can be applied in a reliable manner.[75]

Title IV-E Foster Care   Foster care refers to the full-time care of a child provided outside of the child's home by a person or persons licensed by the state. The child's caretaker, who may be related or unrelated to the child, receives a cash grant from the state to defray the costs of providing for the child's needs.

Title IV-E is an entitlement program. States that participate in the Transitional Assistance to Needy Families program (TANF, formerly AFDC) must certify that they will operate a foster care and adoption assistance program and that children in either program will be eligible for medical coverage under the Medicaid program.[76]

Federal funds are made available to the states to defray the costs of maintaining eligible children in foster care. Eligible children are those: (1) who would have been eligible for financial assistance under the AFDC program as it existed on June 1, 1995, including children who were abandoned before a determination of eligibility could be made; (2) who were removed from their parent or custodian pursuant to a judicial determination that reasonable efforts were made to prevent removal of the child from her or his home; (3) who are placed in the legal custody of the state; and (4) who are placed in a licensed home. Approximately one-half of children in foster care are supported by federal funds.

There are approximately 500,000 children in foster care in the United States.[77] These children enter foster care for various reasons and under different circumstances including: (1) death of a parent; (2) abandonment; (3) a determination of neglect or abuse; or (4) a parent's request for a voluntarily placement.

State Responsibility for Children in Foster Care   Once a child is placed in foster care, the state assumes responsibility for the child's physical safety, medical needs, and future planning. Written case plans, required by the AACWA, provide a framework for the state to describe how it will meet its responsibilities to the child and her parent.[78] Among other things, a written plan must describe the type of home or institution where the child will be placed and a discussion of the appropriateness of the placement. The plan must describe also the services that are to be provided to the parents, child, and foster parents in order: (1) to improve the conditions in the parent's home, thus facilitating the child's return home; (2) to place the child in an alternative permanent home; and (3) to address the needs of the child while in foster care.[79] To ensure compliance with planning provisions, plan reviews are required every six months with a mandatory review by the court at eighteen months.[80]

The exact number of children in foster care who are HIV- positive or diagnosed with AIDS is not known; nor is it known how many children are in foster care because a parent has AIDS and is too ill to provide care or because a parent has died of AIDS. From the results of a national survey of state agencies that are responsible for providing foster care, Cohen and her colleagues (1994) report that 1,149 HIV-positive children entered care in 1991.[81] The CDC reports that between 125,000 and 150,000 children and youth will be made motherless by HIV in the decade of the 1990s.[82]

Caring for children with HIV and AIDS poses a number of challenges for child welfare agencies. Agencies must find homes for children likely to become seriously ill and die; and they must provide services to the child and her or his parent who may also be terminally ill. When a parent develops full-blown AIDS, it is not likely that she will resume full-time child care, but she may wish to play an ongoing role in caring for her child. In addition, agencies must plan for those children who are not ill but who will become orphans of the AIDS epidemic. They must also train their staff in regard to special laws dealing with matters of confidentiality as it relates to disclosure of HIV- and AIDS- related information and they must educate their staff about legal issues concerning HIV-testing of children in state custody.

The Child Welfare League of America recommends that agencies develop specific policies to address issues that arise from the AIDS epidemic.[83] Whether or not states have developed such policies was addressed in two national surveys: one was conducted in late 1989 and early 1990 with a follow-up in early 1992,[84] the other in 1991.[85] Both surveys covered all fifty states, the District of Columbia, and the territories and asked whether policies had been developed regarding the care of children with HIV. The combined results of these studies reveal that forty states had developed policies. From information provided by twenty-one states we learn that states that developed HIV-related policies were motivated to do so because of the need to clarify issues including: (1) confidentiality; (2) HIV-testing; (3) training of providers and foster families; (4) universal precautions to reduce risk of transmission of HIV; (5) identification of high-risk behaviors; (6) legal issues; and (7) planning for permanent placement for children.

Recruiting Foster Parents   To find foster homes for children with HIV, seven states mandate special recruitment efforts and twenty-nine states provide special training for foster parents in matters relating to HIV. Special licenses for fostering children with HIV are required in forty-six states.[86] Incentives for those willing to foster a child with HIV, including higher rates of payment and special services, may be provided. In New York, for example, in late 1990, foster parents caring for a child with HIV received $1,281 per child per month compared to $400 to $500 per month for other foster children. The foster parent must provide for all of the child's needs out of these funds with the exception of medical needs, which are paid for by the Medicaid program.[87] Supplemental services provided to foster parents in forty-six states include special medical assistance for supplies and equipment, counseling services, and transportation services.[88]

Fostering children with HIV may create special problems once the child becomes symptomatic, including obtaining extensive medical service, providing for special hygiene in the home, and coping with the prejudice that may be demonstrated against the infected child or the family as a whole.[89] Because of these problems, the Child Welfare League cautions agencies that the urgent need to recruit foster parents should not result in a lessening of standards. Screening of applicants to care for children with HIV should consider, among other factors: (1) the applicant's demonstrated ability to cope with serious illness; (2) whether or not the applicant has the time to devote to the needs of an HIV-infected child; (3) whether or not the applicant has an undue fear of transmission through casual contact; (4) whether or not the applicant has other adults to whom she or he may turn for emotional support; and (5) the effects on other family members of having an HIV-infected child in the household.[90]

Health and Developmental Problems of Children in Foster Care

Children who enter foster care in general, when compared with children from the same socioeconomic background, suffer from a variety of health problems.[91] In 1995, the United States General Accounting Office (GAO) reported that the health of foster care children as a group is worse than that of homeless children and children who live in the poorest sections of urban areas. The GAO estimated that 78 percent of young foster children in California, New York, and Pennsylvania were at high risk for HIV due to parental use of drugs but estimated that no more than 9 percent of children in foster care are tested for HIV.[92]

Once in care, many children receive substandard medical services.[93] According to the GAO, and based on its study of cases in California, New York, and Pennsylvania, approximately 12 percent of young foster children receive no regular health care, 34 percent are not immunized, and 32 percent had identified health care needs that were not being met. Moreover, the comprehensive medical examinations and follow-up treatment that are available to Medicaid-eligible children through Early and Periodic Screening, Diagnosis, and Treatment (EPSDT) are provided to no more then 1 percent of children in foster care. EPSDT services offer protections for a child's general health, provide access to other health-related services, and may be critical for the HIV-infected child who needs routine ongoing health care monitoring.[94]

Rendon and his colleagues (1989),[95] describing the health problems of thirty children cared for at the Leake and Watts Children's Home in New York State, the first foster care program for children with AIDS in the United States, report that all of the children were hospitalized at some time "with an average stay of 17 months" and many required emergency medical care. They also found, as did Popola and her colleagues (1994)[96] in their study of ninety HIV-positive children age 5 to 14, behavior problems, emotional problems, low to average intelligence, developmental delays, and the need for special education as characteristics of pediatric AIDS.

Other findings underscore how serious are the needs of HIV-positive children in foster care. For example, Cohen and her colleagues (1994)[97] report that there is an association between a mother's drug use during pregnancy and the health of children born HIV-positive. One-half of 148 HIV-positive children whose mothers used drugs during pregnancy were low birth weight and shorter than average, and 20 percent had head circumference in the lower 5 percent. Of the children who did not seroconvert, 60 percent had neurological deficiencies and 80 percent were developmentally delayed. Of the children who did seroconvert, 30 percent had neurological impairments, and 55 percent were developmentally delayed. Furthermore, as found by Simonds and colleagues, *Pneumocystis carinii* pneumonia (PCP) ranks as the "most common serious opportunistic infection affecting children with perinatally acquired AIDS," regardless of sex, race, region of the country, or maternal risk factors.[98]

Attributing the health problems of children with perinatally acquired HIV to HIV alone is difficult, because the illnesses that these children are born with may be attributable to maternal use of drugs and/or alcohol during pregnancy, to the lack of prenatal care, and to the general poor health that is associated with poverty.[99] Premature births are a confounding factor.[100] A study conducted by Gay and her colleagues (1995) casts some light on these complex health issues. They compared 130 perinatally HIV-infected infants to a group of noninfected infants, excluding infants born to women who acknowledged illicit drug use and those born prematurely. Using standardized tests, evaluations were conducted during the first two years of life. The authors report that the mental and motor development of the HIV-infected infants were significantly delayed relative to the comparison group.[101]

In the mid-1980s, the CDC reported that children diagnosed with AIDS in the first year of life survived an average of nine months after diagnosis with 75 percent dying within two years.[102] By the early 1990s, the pattern of progression from diagnosis to illness to death had changed with some children surviving their first decade of life with few or no symptoms. Research reported by Crossley (1993),[103] Popola et al. (1994),[104] Heymann (1995),[105] and Barnhart and colleagues (1996)[106] indicates that significant numbers of children with perinatally acquired AIDS are now surviving beyond age 5. The evidence is that these youngsters may enjoy years of active, relatively unimpaired life if provided with aggressive medical treatment.

The assumption that AIDS in adults is always fatal has been challenged and, as time passes, so may the assumptions regarding fatality in children.[107] It is clear that, at least for some, infection with HIV results in a pattern of illness that is chronic in nature and this will pose increasing challenges for the day-to-day care of children.

Medical Decision Making for Children in Foster Care   Biological parents have a right to the care, custody, and control of their children. This right is fundamental, with its roots in the Fourteenth Amendment to the United States Constitution.[108] The rights accorded to parents include the right to make medical decisions for their children, but this right is subject to numerous exceptions, such as a minor's right to be tested for sexually transmitted diseases, including HIV, to receive necessary treatment without parental consent,[109] and to terminate a pregnancy without parental consent.[110] In addition, the state may under certain circumstances override a parent's medical choices when intervention is deemed necessary to safeguard a child.[111]

There is only one reported case where a court ordered medical treatment for a child with HIV whose mother refused to allow treatment because she did not believe that the child was infected.[112] However, there is a long line of cases that stand for the proposition that courts will overrule parental decision making when a child's life is threatened because of a parent's refusal to allow necessary medical care even when the parent's objection is based on religious grounds.[113]

A parent's rights vis-à-vis her child are linked to the parent's custodial status. When the state intervenes in family life, the question "What is the balance of rights between parent and child?" is reformulated to ask "What is the balance of rights between the parent, the state, and the child?" The details of this new balance will depend on state law, which, within limits set by the Supreme Court,[114] governs in matters of child custody and on whether legal custody remains with a biological parent or is transferred to the state. If a child enters foster care on a voluntary basis, the child's biological parent may retain legal custody with physical custody transferring to the state. In other situations, the juvenile or family court will transfer legal custody to a state authority. As legal custodian the state is obliged to provide medical care to a child and has a duty to make medical decisions, but the state's decision-making power is generally circumscribed by state statute. For example, in Florida and Pennsylvania the person with legal custody may make "ordinary medical decisions";[115] in Arizona, Idaho, and New Hampshire the right to make medical decisions is expressly made subject to the residual rights and responsibilities of the child's biological parent if the parent's rights have not been terminated;[116] and Georgia and Michigan empower "any person standing *in loco parentis*" to consent to medical treatment for a child.[117]

When the subject of medical decision making turns from day-to-day medical care to testing for HIV or to a child's participation in experimental drug trials, a series of ethical concerns arise that are not present with other medical decisions. These concerns highlight different issues, including the possibility of stigma associated with a diagnosis of HIV. The question also arises as to what are the benefits of being tested and to whom do benefits accrue?

Ethical Issues in the Testing of Children   Testing for HIV raises a number of concerns about informed consent of the person to be tested, confidentiality of medical records, and access to treatment. These topics are covered in depth in the next chapter where the rights of adult women are reviewed, but several issues should be raised at this point. When consideration is given to ordering a person to undergo an HIV test, one must ask "Who are the involved parties?" and "What is to be gained by ordering the test?" Since the great majority of children with HIV became infected in utero, testing a newborn is testing the mother. Many argue against mandatory testing on this basis alone, since it would violate the mother's right to privacy.[118]

This argument has ethical force when: (1) the involved parties are the mother and the child only; and (2) there is no gain for the newborn in the form of medical treatment. Also, if a medical gain is denied to people because of lack of health insurance, any argument that testing should be mandatory loses its moral authority. An argument for testing of newborns for the purpose of providing treatment must take into account the fact that 70 to 75 percent of newborns will seroconvert by their 18th month. Since certain HIV-treatments are toxic and few interventions are totally benign, treating all HIV-infected newborns to benefit 30 percent of them could cause medical problems for the remaining 70 percent.

If available treatments were more helpful than harmful, it would be difficult to argue that a woman's right to privacy overrides the child's right to the degree of good health that she or he would experience through treatment. As between the mother's right to privacy and the child's right to have access to beneficial medical care both the law and ethical norms may shift the balance subordinating the mother's right not to have her child tested to the child's right to treatment that may improve her or his health.

When a child is placed in state custody, medical treatment remains a consideration, but other issues emerge. The state must undertake long-range planning which includes both monetary and nonmonetary issues. As earlier noted, the foster home rate, separate from the costs of medical care, is higher for children with HIV than for others. A state must budget for these costs, in addition to the medical costs of treatment. Account must also be taken of selecting a suitable placement for the child and whether foster or adoptive parents have a right to know the child's health status. In fact, the child has an interest in her caretaker's knowing her health status so that her caretaker is alert to early warning signs of needed medical care and so that the child will not require re-placement should the uninformed caretaker be unwilling to provide care for a chronically ill child. And, as we shall discuss further on, a child with HIV who is adopted may, if her or his HIV-status is unknown at the time of adoption, be denied an adoption subsidy.

A discussion of issues regarding testing of children and access to medical care would be incomplete without considering the participation of children in experimental drug trials. Children who are least likely to be enrolled in clinical trials are those who live in poverty and in the most "severe socially disadvantaged environments."[119] The situation is no different for children in foster care who are unlikely to be enrolled in drug trials. According to the Committee on AIDS Research of the National Research Council, both New York and Florida, whose per capita rate of AIDS is among the highest in the country, have not allowed children to participate in drug trials,[120] although there are some data to suggest that New York has changed its position.[121] The concerns that arise from failure to include children in drug trials are not dissimilar to the concerns, discussed in chapter 3, that arise when women are excluded. These concerns involve such questions as "Do medications affect children differently than they do adults?" For example, the long-term consequences of fetal and neonatal zidovudine (ZDV) use are not known.[122] Also, as noted in chapter 3, for many people access to research trials may be a major route of access to primary care, since the health of those in drug trials is routinely monitored.

Federal regulations provide for the participation of children in drug trials without consent of the child's parent or guardian if an Institutional Review Board determines that a particular research protocol is suitable for a population. The regulations make specific reference to neglected and abused children, for whom parental consent may not be reasonable if appropriate mechanisms are in place to ensure that the child's interests are protected.[123] The regulations do not specify any particular protective mechanism, although decision making by a team including the child's foster parent, a health care worker, an HIV-infected individual, and a lay-advocate has been recommended in the literature.[124] Some states have policies that permit the enrollment of foster children in clinical trials, while others decide whether to permit participation on a case-by-case basis.[125]

State Law on Testing of Children   The conditions under which a child in state custody may be tested for HIV differ state-by state. Statutes provide for testing: (1) with informed consent and permission of a parent or legal guardian;[126] (2) when authorized by a state official;[127] or (3) based solely on the request of a minor,[128] with some states qualifying the minor's right by permitting or requiring a medical provider to inform the minor's parent or legal guardian.[129]

Whether children in state custody should be tested for HIV has been addressed by the American Academy of Pediatrics. It takes the position that "widespread testing of all infants and children awaiting adoption or foster placement is not warranted,"[130] but targeted testing, for example, of children "born in high seroprevalence areas or in high-risk situations," is.[131] The difficulty with this suggestion is that rather than resting on the characteristics of an individual case, such as a child born with a positive toxicology for cocaine, the criterion rests on group membership and may easily become testing of all children of African descent, all Spanish-surnamed children, or all poor children. In hospitals serving poor and/or minority communities such a suggestion may result in the testing of all children.

The suggestion that a child might become infected with HIV through sexual abuse has raised anew the issue of mandatory testing. When the abuse is rape, the American Academy of Pediatrics recommends testing.[132] Although seroprevalence studies for sexually transmitted diseases (STDs) have been conducted with teenagers and adults who receive services from STD clinics, drug abuse treatment centers, and health clinics, none have been conducted for antibodies for HIV when children are known or suspected of being victims of sexual abuse; and data on this subject are sparse.[133] From a survey of professionals involved with helping child victims of sexual abuse, Gellert (1993) reports that of approximately 5,600 HIV-antibody tests involving more than 113,000 sex abuse assessments, twenty-eight children for whom sexual abuse was the only known route of transmission were infected and thirteen children who had other known risk factors were infected.[134]

Disclosure of HIV-Information for Children in Foster Care   Eligibility to receive federal funding under the Ryan White CARE Act requires states to have statutes guaranteeing the confidentiality of HIV-status. (See chapter 5.)[135] Foster and adoptive parents are among those to whom confidential information may be released.[136] For example, Illinois mandates that information about test results or information about any HIV-infection be provided to a child's temporary caretaker;[137] and Wisconsin provides for disclosure of HIV-test results to "an agency preparing a . . . permanency plan for a child in a foster home, group home or institution . . . and disclosure by the agency to the child's foster parent or operator of the group home or institution."[138]

Child welfare agencies with information regarding a youngster's HIV-status may be liable to adoptive parents for failure to disclose information. While legal cases on this issue have not dealt directly with HIV, the principle has been established in several states that adoptive parents may sue an adoption agency for failure to disclose information regarding a child's physical or mental health known to the agency at the time of the adoption. For example, in *Roe v. Catholic Charities of Springfield*,[139] an appellate court in Illinois ruled that two families could sue an adoption agency for fraud for failure to disclose information about the physical and emotional health of adopted children. In this case both families had applied to adopt "normal, healthy" children and to this end had become foster parents of children with a potential for future adoption. The record reveals that the agency told each family that their foster child was "normal in . . . physical and mental condition as well as level of development . . . and that the adoptive parents would incur no unusual or extraordinary medical expense for the child's care and treatment. In addition the agency was said to have reported that they had no information regarding the children's background."[140] Despite these assurances, the agencies knew that the children had problems including a history of psychiatric and psychological treatment for violent behavior and that they were retarded "intellectually, socially and emotionally."[141]

Planning Options for Children in Foster Care   Federal law charges the states with planning for the future living arrangements of children in foster care. The preferred planning options give preference to children being raised by their own parents or in the home of a relative. For children who cannot be returned to their own homes, creating a legally binding relationship between the child and her or his new family takes precedence, thus placing adoption and legal guardianship next in the planning hierarchy. Planned long-term foster care, which, with exceptions discussed below, is least preferred because it lacks the legal safeguards of other options and does not hold out the promise of stability in placement for a child.

With the exception of the child voluntarily placed because a parent requires hospitalization or is experiencing a temporary crisis and has no one to whom she can turn for help with child care, the majority of parents whose children enter out-of-home placement do so because of family problems which must to some extent be ameliorated before a child returns home. The difficulties parents confront may be of a relatively minor nature, where knowledge or skill deficits are causal to child neglect, or they may be quite serious, involving mental illness or substance abuse.

The fact that a family member has HIV or AIDS and that a child has been placed in foster care does not, per se, make that family different from others when it comes to answering the question "What is the appropriate long-term plan for the child?" For example, the parent with HIV or AIDS may be no different from a parent with other serious illnesses where, given assistance at home, for example, with respite care services, homemaker services, visiting nurse services, or day care, she will be able to raise her child. Or, a mother with HIV or AIDS may also abuse drugs or have emotional problems and, for the latter and not the former reasons, be deemed unsuitable as a parent and an agency may undertake to place the child in an adoptive home. Such a decision may be made because the parent, like others who abuse controlled substances, fails to involve herself in programs whose goal is the reduction or elimination of her drug or alcohol problem.

There is, however, another scenario that requires more creative planning options. The concern here is for the parent who has HIV or AIDS, who experiences episodic bouts of illness, who cannot provide day-to-day care, but whose role in the life of her child should be preserved to the extent possible while ensuring the child the greatest attainable degree of stability and continuity.

Some states, by statute, provide planning options for children in foster care that may be suitable for the single parent with AIDS. First, open adoptions where a parent relinquishes her legal rights contingent on a prior negotiated plan for her ongoing involvement with her child is an option, as is transferring legal guardianship to another adult with a defined, ongoing role for the parent. These options provide for the mother's continuing involvement in her child's life and they allow her to know that her child is in a permanent living arrangement before her death.

Other planning options provide for alternative custodial arrangements without terminating parental rights. For example, Florida statutes provide for long-term custody by a related or unrelated adult when sanctioned by a juvenile court, if return home or adoption are not in the child's best interest.[142] The court-appointed custodian has the right to physical custody of the child and the assurance that the relationship will continue, unless she requests its termination or evidence shows that a material change in circumstances necessitates a change of custody. Because the custodian is granted all of the rights of a natural parent, the child has the security of knowing that her arrangement is permanent and the custodial parents may undertake to raise the child as a permanent family member without concern that a social service agency will be looking over their shoulder. The drawback to this arrangement is that there is no guarantee that the family accepting legal custody of the child will continue to receive financial support and medical coverage.

Adoption

When a child is adopted, all rights and responsibilities that existed between the child and her or his natural parents are terminated and transferred to the adoptive parents. Thus the legal relationship that results is similar to the legal relationship between a child and her or his biological parents. Because of the presumed permanency of adoption, it is generally the plan of choice for children who cannot be reunited with their families of origin. Two federal policies have implications for adoptions.

The Adoption Opportunities Act   The Adoption Opportunities Act (AOA)is a discretionary grant program that provides funds to the states to enable them to remove barriers to the adoption of special-needs children.[143] A special-needs child is one who cannot or should not be returned to her or his own home and who, because of "ethnic background, age, or membership in a minority or sibling group, or the presence of factors such as medical conditions or physical, mental, or emotional handicaps," cannot be adopted without financial assistance to adoptive parents.[144] A child known to have HIV or one who has developed AIDS fits within the definition of special needs.

Examples of the problems sought to be eliminated by the AOA include: (1) barriers created by differences in state laws, which made the adoptive placement of a child across state lines difficult; and (2) the absence of mechanisms for states to exchange information about persons seeking to adopt and about children who are available for adoption. The Interstate Compact on the Placement of Children (ICPC) addresses the first problem. The ICPC creates a framework for the sending states and the receiving states to negotiate an agreement for assessing the appropriateness of the proposed placement, for exchanging information, for establishing procedures to ensure proper judicial supervision, and for assigning responsibility for financial, medical, and social services. The National Adoption Information Exchange addresses the second problem. It provides for listing applicants waiting to adopt, information regarding the type of child they are willing to adopt, and children awaiting adoption; and it facilitates matching children with parents.

Adoption Subsidies   Under Title IV-E of the AACWA,[145] the federal government provides funds to the states to reimburse them for part of the costs of subsidizing the adoption of a special-needs child, and these states may provide Medicaid coverage for children receiving adoption subsidies.[146] Children eligible to benefit from this program are those who meet the definition of special-needs child reported above and who were receiving or were eligible to receive payments under the AFDC program as it existed on June 1, 1995, or under the SSI program, or the Title IV-E foster care payments maintenance program. A child who is HIV-positive but asymptomatic and whose HIV-status is unknown at the time she or he is adopted will not, absent another basis for classifying her or him as special needs, qualify for an adoption subsidy.

The amount of subsidy and services to be provided to the child and her or his adoptive parents and assurances that the agreement will remain in effect should the adoptive parents move to another state, are spelled out in an adoption assistance agreement, which is entered into between the adoptive parents and the state in which the child resides.[147] Federal law stipulates that the amount of subsidy paid by the state cannot exceed the foster care maintenance payment that would have been made if the child had remained in a foster home.[148]

PART III. SUMMARY

The great majority of women with HIV have children. Absent family or friends to whom they can turn for help with child care, most will turn to public and not-for-profit child care agencies for help in caring for their children as their health deteriorates. Compounding the day-to-day child-care difficulties that women with HIV must confront is the fact that some are caring for children who are also HIV-infected.

Mothers provide full-time care in approximately one-half of the families where they and possibly their children are HIV-positive. Ten to fifteen percent of children from such families live with relatives and 10 percent live in unspecified living arrangements. The percentage of children in foster care hovers around 28 percent with significant state-by-state variation, ranging from a low of 1 percent in Florida to a high of 41 percent in New York. Children whose mothers use drugs are more likely to be cared for by an alternative care giver.

A woman with HIV who wishes to plan for her child's future living arrangements has a number of options, including: (1) executing a power of attorney which authorizes another to make decisions for her child; (2) designating in her will another person as guardian; or (3) transferring legal custody to another adult during her lifetime. Adoption by a married spouse is an option in all states; and in some states adoption by the mother's unmarried partner and standby guardianship are available choices.

Because states grant to judges who make child custody decisions the authority to make such decisions in the best interests of the child, a woman has no guarantee that a judge will honor her choice. Thus if the mother nominates as a guardian a person who has no legal relationship to her child or if her nominee has a record of alcohol or drug abuse, a judge may not grant custody to the elected person. Adoption by a spouse, second-parent adoption, and standby guardianship are approved or not approved by a court while a woman is living and are, therefore, the only planning options that allow her to know whether or not her choice will be honored.

All states operate a child welfare system for the purpose of protecting abused and neglected children and to provide homes for children whose parents cannot or will not care for them. Women with HIV or AIDS encounter the child welfare system under various circumstances, some of which bear no relation to their HIV-status. For example, any woman who uses non-prescription drugs during the latter stages of her pregnancy, regardless of her HIV-status, runs the risk of giving birth to a newborn who will test positive for drugs. Likewise, a woman who uses alcohol to excess during her pregnancy may give birth to a child with a birth defect that suggests maternal alcohol use. In either situation, a woman may find herself the subject of a report of child abuse or neglect.

Because many women with HIV are poor, they may have little choice but to turn to a state's child welfare system for help with temporary or full-time child care as their health deteriorates. For the woman who does not have family or friends to whom she can turn for help, public or voluntary child-care agencies may be her only choice.

Federal law requires states to have programs for providing services to prevent the unnecessary placement of children in foster care and to enable those in foster care to return to their own homes. While prevention-of-place-ment programs could provide invaluable aid to a woman with HIV or AIDS, neither federal nor state laws create any legal entitlement to prevention services.

HIV poses a number of challenges to state child welfare systems, in-cluding the fact that an unknown percentage of the estimated 100,000 to 150,000 children who will be orphaned by the AIDS epidemic by the year 2000 will require care by the state. Some, but not all of these children, will have HIV. In addition to AIDS orphans, some children with HIV will re-quire state care because their parents abandon them in hospitals.

State child welfare agencies are meeting the challenges posed by the AIDS epidemic in various ways, including: (1) developing policies which address HIV-specific issues, such as confidentiality, testing, involvement of children in clinical drug trials, and other legal matters; (2) mandating special efforts to recruit foster homes and special training for foster par-ents; and (3) developing planning options that permit ongoing contact be-tween a child and her or his biological parent who is too ill to provide full-time child care but who wishes to retain a role in the child's life. Finally, children with HIV and AIDS will qualify as special-needs children for pur-poses of adoption if their HIV-status is known at the time that an adop-tion takes place.

CHAPTER 5

Confidentiality, Testing, and Reproductive Choice

INTRODUCTION

The majority of states, the District of Columbia, and certain of the territories (hereafter the states) have laws addressing confidentiality that apply specifically to HIV and AIDS, and there are federal statutes on this subject. These laws were passed to encourage people to be tested by providing assurances of privacy and to quell the concern that existing confidentiality laws did not offer sufficient protection.

This chapter begins with a review of issues that gave rise to laws addressing confidentiality and testing for HIV and AIDS (Part I). In Part II the legal framework that has emerged at the federal level and in the states to govern testing and confidentiality is reviewed as are the common elements of state confidentiality statutes. Many of the topics addressed in this chapter affect men as well as women, but there are a series of issues, covered in Part III, that affect women only, including pressure to be tested before becoming pregnant; if a woman is pregnant and not sure of her HIV-status, testing may be urged; and if a woman is HIV-positive she may be pressured to elect abortion over childbirth. The chapter is summarized in Part IV.

Confidentiality of HIV-related information and testing for HIV are governed primarily, but not exclusively, by the laws of the states. It is beyond the scope of this chapter to provide a comprehensive review of the positions taken by each state. The material in the following pages contains examples drawn from different states, including illustrations from case law showing how the courts interpret statutory provisions.

PART I. TESTING AND CONFIDENTIALITY

The Issues

Infection with HIV is presumed to be fatal,[1] and stemming its spread is in the public interest. Since there is neither a vaccine nor a cure, this interest is best served when people who are HIV-positive abstain from engaging in those behaviors most likely to transmit the virus (chapter 1). Learning about one's HIV-status may be a crucial first step in modifying behavior. For this reason, both voluntary testing and mandatory testing of those at risk have been advocated as public health measures.[2]

Advocates for testing argue that the information that is provided by an HIV-test is crucial if a woman is: (1) to protect herself from exposure to situations that create risk because her immune system is compromised; (2) to protect others by avoiding the types of contact implicated in transmission of the virus; (3) to notify others with whom she has had contact of their exposure; (4) to make informed reproductive decisions including whether to continue or terminate a pregnancy; (5) to decide whether or not to breast-feed; and (6) to avail herself of early treatment, including monitoring of immune system function.

Testing may be anonymous or confidential. Anonymous testing occurs when the woman who is tested is identified only by a number, in contrast to confidential testing where the woman's identity is known but is not to be divulged. Opposition to testing procedures that identify the person tested by name stems from the concern that information will not remain confidential and takes account of the adverse consequences that may follow from disclosure of test results. As stated by Senator Bennett of Utah:

> In the hospital, most patients are unaware that their records are accessible to almost any health care provider walking into their room or almost any hospital employee with a computer who can gain access to the hospital's computer system. [Many] doctors and nurses . . . refuse to be treated in the hospital where they practice . . . because they know that their colleagues will know why they are in the hospital and know they are being treated.[3]

Adverse consequences that may follow from disclosure of one's HIV-status include: (1) the possibility of state intervention to influence the behavior and the reproductive choices that are made by a woman who is pregnant; (2) fear of quarantine; (3) fear of discriminatory treatment in receipt of medical care, in the workplace, in educational settings, and in obtaining and maintaining housing; and (4) the possibility of losing child custody. For women, concern about discrimination in its various forms may be compounded by fear that their children will be targeted for discriminatory treatment and by their already-experienced discrimination because of their gender, race, or sexual orientation.[4]

Their fears are not groundless. For example, a homeless woman seeking admission to a shelter in New York reported to shelter officials that she had no known health problems, only to learn that information had been entered into the shelter's computer system, after a previous stay, that identified her as HIV-positive.[5] In another situation, a test for HIV was performed on an incarcerated woman without her informed consent.[6] In that case, the woman, who was hearing impaired, did not know that she was being tested for HIV, because the person assigned to explain her rights could not communicate effectively in American Sign Language.[7] Violations of confidentiality have been documented. These include "faxing" patient records from hospital to hospital, posting the names of HIV-positive patients on a laboratory bulletin board, allowing news media into a clinic waiting room, disclosure by a police officer in casual conversation with the neighbors of a woman whose husband was HIV-infected, and opening of a state's HIV-registry to state officials so all health care workers with HIV could be identified and their patients notified.[8] In April of 1996, a suit was filed to prevent federal auditors, engaged in an audit of a federally funded program, from obtaining records of people with AIDS.[9]

Moreover, American history is replete with examples of state-sanctioned mistreatment of the poor and of minorities. Examples include: (1) in 1900, a quarantine during a bubonic plague epidemic that was selectively enforced against 10,000 Chinese people in San Francisco;[10] (2) in the Cold War era, the unauthorized use by the federal government of human subjects in radiation experiments;[11] (3) from 1932 to 1972, the Tuskegee experiments in which more than 400 black men with syphilis were denied treatment so the United States Public Health Service could study the natural history of the disease;[12] (4) up to the mid-1940s, the forced sterilizations of the "socially inadequate classes (the insane, blind, deaf and dependent, including orphans, and people with syphilis, leprosy and epilepsy)";[13] (5) in the early 1970s, the sterilization of between 100,000 and 150,000 poor people, primarily women under threat that their welfare benefits would be terminated;[14] (6) in the 1960s, experiments at a chronic disease hospital that involved the injection of live cancer cells into elderly patients;[15] (7) in the 1970s, in direct contradiction of guidelines issued by a state board of health, the identification and segregation of retarded children, but not nonretarded children, who were carriers of the Hepatitis B virus;[16] and (8) in the 1980s, in studies testing ways to prevent breast cancer, failure to identify to subjects risk of death as a consequence of their participation.[17]

In the early years of the AIDS epidemic, when public policy was being formulated, a consensus developed among politicians, public health officials, and gay and lesbian activists that confidentiality was key to any prevention and treatment strategy that relied on the cooperation of those likely to be infected. In addition, public health officials knew that the cooperation of gay men, who in the early 1980s comprised the great majority of people with HIV and AIDS, would be central to efforts to test experimental treatments and that assurances of confidentiality were key to obtaining their cooperation.[18] With these concerns in mind, approximately two-thirds of the states enacted legislation addressing confidentiality of HIV-related information after acknowledging that existing laws and standards of professional conduct were not sufficient to quiet the concern that test results might be disclosed without the consent of the person tested. The purpose of newly enacted laws, as stated in the preamble to Florida statutes, was to "promote the informed, voluntary, and confidential use of tests designed to reveal the HIV,"[19] or, as stated in New York law, to protect the individual from "the risk of discrimination and the harm to [her or his] interests in privacy"[20] that might result from unauthorized disclosure of HIV-related information.

PART II. TESTING AND CONFIDENTIALITY: THE LEGAL FRAMEWORK

Testing

Requiring a woman to submit to an HIV-test or to unwanted medical treatment implicates her Fourth Amendment right to be free of unreasonable search and seizure and her Fourteenth Amendment right to privacy. However, the fact that an intrusion is unwanted does not render it per se unconstitutional. Whether a particular state action will pass or fail constitutional muster depends on the balance the courts strike between the loss of autonomy and privacy that is caused by the intrusion against the benefit of permitting the act.

There are numerous examples of state action overriding a woman's constitutional rights in the area of medical intervention. Prenatal or newborn screening for a variety of conditions such as syphilis and Hepatitis B is conducted in all states and mandated in some;[21] parents cannot refuse to have their children vaccinated even on religious grounds;[22] and courts have sanctioned cesarean sections and blood transfusions despite the objections of pregnant women.

In 1957 and again in 1989, the Supreme Court set standards for involuntary blood testing which the Court sanctioned if the procedure employed is not "shocking to the conscience."[23] Thus drawing blood from an unconscious prisoner to determine if he was intoxicated was sanctioned, since blood testing is routine in our everyday lives, but pumping the stomach of a person suspected of swallowing narcotics was not, because it is "shocking to the conscience," since the procedure is not commonly experienced.[24] The Court held that mandated testing of certain railroad employees for drugs and alcohol passes constitutional muster, in part because the government's interest in safety outweighs the minimal expectation of privacy held by the employees.[25]

Courts have held that mandatory HIV-testing is permissible in different contexts and with different groups. The State Department may require HIV-tests for foreign service employees, since their HIV-status may pose severe problems on foreign assignments where health and sanitary conditions are hazardous.[26] Mandatory HIV-testing of firefighters is also permissible.[27] As was the case with railroad employees, firefighters have a low expectation of privacy, and their fitness for duty is reasonably related to the purpose for which a test is ordered.

The federal government tests active duty and reserve military personnel for HIV as it does[28] aliens (including applicants for visas, exchange students, and people applying for refugee status),[29] federal prisoners,[30] and applicants for the Job Corps.[31] Between 1987 and 1995, the Centers for Disease Control (CDC) worked with the health departments in a majority of states to conduct blinded HIV-testing of newborns, using blood drawn from the newborn for general medical screening. Congress, through provisions in the Ryan White CARE Act, has made funds available to the states to develop programs to test state prisoners[32] and to test civilians who would give informed consent, receive counseling, and be assured of confidentiality.[33] Congress, in the 1996 reauthorization of the CARE Act, established a requirement that the states implement the CDC's recommendations that all pregnant women be offered voluntary HIV-testing and counseling about HIV-disease.[34] Grants are authorized to help the states in this effort. The CARE Act requires an evaluation of the states' efforts to reduce perinatal HIV-transmission and requires mandatory testing in states that do not have mandatory testing programs by the year 2000 if those states fail to demonstrate either: (1) that a 50 percent reduction in perinatally caused new AIDS cases has occurred, or (2) that at least 95 percent of women who have received at least two prenatal visits have been tested for HIV.[35]

If courts determine that the risk of transmission of the HIV is low, they show less tolerance for mandatory testing programs. The Eighth Circuit Court of Appeals found that a county health service agency policy requiring certain employees to submit to mandatory testing for HIV and for Hepatitis B violated the Fourth Amendment rights of employees, since the risk of transmission was minuscule.[36]

Justifications for Testing: Contact Tracing and Partner Notification   Contact tracing and partner notification occur when individuals with a communicable or contagious disease (index patients) by themselves or with assistance identify, locate, and notify those with whom they have had the type of contact through which HIV might be transmitted that they have been exposed. Partner notification may occur through patient referral or referral by a medical provider. With the former, the individual with HIV informs directly those who may have been placed at risk. Health department or medical personnel may help the index patient by instructing her in ways of making contact with and in developing skills for informing others. When provider referral is chosen, the index patient makes available to the provider information needed to make contact with those who may have been placed at risk.

Partner notification has been a central public health strategy since the mid-1940s when it was implemented for syphilis control after penicillin became generally available. Partner notification has been used in the control of other sexually transmitted diseases (STDs) and has been shown to be effective, but costly, in controlling flare-ups of infections and in targeting high-risk populations.[37]

The Law on Contact Tracing and Partner Notification   The CARE Act requires states to provide partner notification services but does not mandate notification with this exception: a state must make a good faith effort to notify the spouse of an HIV-positive person that she or he may have been exposed to HIV and should be tested.[38] Otherwise, requirements for notification are left to the discretion of the public health officials of each state.[39] Funds for counseling, testing, and partner notification are available to the states through the CDC, and all of the states offer counseling about the importance of notifying partners and other risk-reducing strategies.

Most states have approached contact tracing and partner notification with caution, lest those at risk avoid testing for fear of being pressured to identify their contacts. In New York, for example, the state Commissioner of Public Health chose not to classify HIV as a communicable or sexually transmitted disease in order to exempt HIV from the reporting and contact tracing provisions of the law, which are triggered whenever a sexually transmitted disease is diagnosed. New York's high court upheld the commissioner's decision when challenged by four medical societies.[40]

Some states do mandate contact tracing and partner notification. South Carolina requires notification to the extent that funds are available;[41] Utah requires contact tracing;[42] Iowa permits the index patient's identity to be revealed to the extent necessary to protect a third party from transmission;[43] and North Carolina mandates that all HIV-positive individuals notify their partners.[44]

Common elements of state statutes addressing partner notification and satisfying the CARE Act requirement for partner notification are: (1) required counseling of the person with HIV, which includes urging the individual to contact directly those who may be at risk; (2) permission for a medical provider or public health official to notify contacts if, after counseling, the provider or official reasonably believes or has good cause to believe that the contact will not be made; (3) confidentiality for the index patient; (4) assurance that the physician or public health official is not under a legal duty to notify; and (5) immunity from liability for notifying or for failure to notify.[45]

The Pros and Cons of Contact Tracing and Partner Notification
The arguments favoring contact tracing and partner notification are the same arguments made to support the suggestion that an individual be tested. They focus on the need for the information provided by a test to protect oneself and others and to make informed reproductive decisions. According to estimates made by the CDC, twenty new infections can be avoided for every one hundred HIV-infected persons identified. The resulting net saving is $20 per $1 invested.[46]

A review of several studies of contact tracing in various states precedes the arguments against the use of this strategy.

Consideration of contact tracing and partner notification as public health strategies gives rise to several questions: What percentage of partners are located? What do people identified through contact tracing think of receiving notice of their exposure? Of those located, what percentage agree to be tested? Do the data suggest the superiority of either provider referral or patient referral? Data to answer these questions are limited, but suggest that between 50 percent[47] and 81 percent of partners are located[48] and between 47 percent[49] and 100 percent of located partners agree to be tested.[50]

In South Carolina in 1988, all of the sexual contacts of a single HIV-infected man from the two years preceding his identification were traced. Tracing was limited to contacts who resided in one rural county. Sixty-four in-county residents who had contact with the index patient or with his contacts were identified and sixty-three agreed to be tested. Twelve were seropositive. Eight of these men, including the index patient, were followed-up at six months. Three of the eight reported no sexual contacts in the follow-up period and five reported a decreased number of contacts relative to the prenotification period.[51]

In 1990, in another study in South Carolina, 202 individuals were asked what they thought about having been notified. Of the 132 (65 percent) responding to this inquiry,[52] 87 percent said that the health department was correct to notify them and 92 percent said that notification should continue. Responses did not vary by the gender, race, sexual orientation, or drug-use pattern of the person notified.

A study conducted in North Carolina compared provider referral to partner referral, and found the former superior with 50 percent of identified partners contacted compared to 10 percent in the patient referral group.[53] But caution must be exercised in interpreting the low rate of contact in the patient referral group, because only notified people who came to the public health department for testing were counted as successful contacts.[54] Since about 40 percent of all HIV-testing occurs in the private sector, many people may have been tested elsewhere and would not be counted for purposes of this study. Moreover, since North Carolina mandates that HIV-positive people notify their contacts with a possible fine or imprisonment as sanctions for failure to do so,[55] it would not be surprising to learn that some notified people would elect not to be tested and that some North Carolinians have elected to travel to the few counties in the state that provide anonymous testing.[56]

Alternative hypotheses for the low rate of contacts by the patient contact group include a lack of resources (e.g., telephone, transportation), physical limitations associated with HIV-infection, fear of domestic violence that data show is associated with partner notification (women were more likely than men to agree to participate in the North Carolina study), and fear that a relationship might end if partners were notified.[57]

According to Marks and his colleagues (1992), the available data suggest that between 7 and 52 percent of those who are HIV-positive will notify their partners on their own.[58] Reporting the results of a study of 111 men, these researchers state that the number of past sexual partners was the strongest predictor of effort to notify, with an inverse relationship between efforts and number of partners. Their data showed a nonsignificant association between the availability of social supports and the likelihood of contacting past partners, but those who discussed this issue with family, friends, professional counselors, or others in support groups were most likely to make contact.

At present, the effectiveness of partner notification programs to control HIV is not known. Partner notification for patients with Hepatitis B, whose epidemiology is similar to that of HIV, has proven difficult because of the prolonged incubation period, the large number of anonymous sex partners, and the inaccessibility of the intravenous drug-using population.[59]

Opponents of contact tracing argue that people at risk may avoid testing and counseling if public health officials are aggressive in pressing an infected person to identify others.[60] Thus a concerted effort at contact tracing may produce the opposite of the desired results; and some opponents of contact tracing allege that the South Carolina study had such an effect, by noting that the number of people tested was cut in half when the state began taking names.[61] Critics view the study as labor-intensive and expensive. Its cost, exclusive of follow-up, was $6,500 and resulted in the investigation of only one HIV-infected man. If the investigators had tried to identify all contacts for a longer time period (five years, for example), the costs would have been even higher. Moreover, if efforts were made to contact all sexual and needle-sharing partners in major cities, the costs would eclipse the costs of all other prevention and education activities. In certain areas where high-risk groups congregate, individual tracing could result in identification of whole communities.[62]

Cautioning against any single approach to partner notification, the CDC highlights the importance of balancing a public health department's available resources against the numbers of people who test positive for HIV to set strategy. Development and evaluation of different approaches to partner notification that are applicable to different "clinical and sociocultural settings in both areas with high and low HIV- seroprevalence rates,"[63] are encouraged. In San Francisco, for example, which has a high seroprevalence rate, provider referral for all partners of gay men was seen as cost prohibitive. However, the San Francisco Health Department did use partner notification for heterosexual sex partners of people with AIDS. The San Francisco experience illustrates the use of targeted notification, which may be especially important for women of childbearing age who may not know that they are at risk of HIV-infection because they are not aware of their partner's sexual or drug-using history.

With the advent of home HIV-testing and the anonymity that it provides, the issue of partner notification will be left to individual discretion.[64]

Justification for Testing: Treatment and Prevention   In the late 1980s, health professionals, convinced that Zidovudine (ZDV, aka AZT) would delay the onset of AIDS symptoms, urged testing, contact tracing, and early treatment for members of high-risk groups.[65] But ZDV proved disappointing in long-term studies, which showed that it had limited benefits lasting a limited time.[66] At a meeting at the National Institutes of

Health in 1993, experts reviewed findings from the Concorde study, the longest study of the effects of ZDV on early HIV-infection. Based on data showing that the drug had not fulfilled its promise as an early treatment, new guidelines were set that counseled against treatment with the drug for early HIV-infection, long before symptoms of full-fledged AIDS develop.[67]

Concerns about the efficacy of ZDV as a preventive drug were echoed in three studies reported in 1995 that examined the effects of the drug on different populations. In the first reported study, ZDV was administered to 839 infants and young people age 3 months to 18 years. ZDV, alone, was so ineffective in preventing the progression of the HIV that this arm of the research was brought to a premature halt although the study groups where children received ZDV in combination with other drugs was continued.[68] According to a second study that was reported by Volberding and his colleagues (1995),[69] asymptomatic adults whose CD4 count exceeds 500 do not benefit from taking ZDV. The researchers assigned approximately equal numbers of 1,637 subjects, 90 percent of whom were white gay males, to a placebo group and to two experimental groups. Each experimental group received different dosages of ZDV. Based on a six-and-one-half year follow-up, the conclusion was reached that treatment with ZDV for asymptomatic adults did not defer the onset of AIDS nor did it prolong survival.

In the third study, Chaisson et al. (1995)[70] asked whether demographic variables including gender, race, age, method of contracting HIV, income, and education were associated with survival. They report no differences in survival rate in a sample of 1,372 seropositive patients that could be attributed to any of the demographic variables studied. Thirty percent of the patients were women, 77 percent were black, and 21 percent were white. The median age of study participants was 34 years, with a range of 17 to 72 years. Poor rates of survival were associated with taking ZDV in the early stages of HIV-infection, with CD4 cell counts of less than 350, older age, and unemployment. Discussing their findings in relation to earlier studies showing that homosexual men and whites survived longer than women, blacks, and intravenous drug users (IVDUs), the authors conclude that inadequate medical care, not gender, race, or IVDU, explain different rates of survival.

Women taking ZDV have reported side effects including headaches, nausea, vomiting, and anemia; and for some there is the possibility of developing a resistance to the drug.[71] These and other side effects experienced by women and men, including bone marrow suppression and muscle inflammation, further limit the use of this medication with adults and children.[72] The reported rate of birth defects among infants whose mothers took ZDV during their first trimester is one for every forty-six live births, a figure that does not differ from the proportion of birth defects in the general population. The CDC refers to this finding as preliminary, due to small sample size, "differential reporting of pregnancy outcomes, losses to follow-up, and underreporting."[73]

The hope that medical science would yield discoveries to improve the health of people with HIV received a boost in July of 1996 when data were reported that combinations of new drugs were effective in suppressing the amount of HIV in the blood of infected people to quantities that could not be detected for long periods of time.[74] The reported data came from two studies that involved small numbers of patients, data was not analyzed by gender, children were not among those studied, and subsequent reports indicate that the new drug combinations do not have lasting effects for between 10 and 30 percent of people.[75] There are unanswered questions regarding new treatment protocols that include: (1) when to begin treatment; (2) what side effects may emerge over time; (3) will treatment gains be sustained over time; and (4) will the HIV mutate in response to new drugs and become resistant as it has in the past. Nevertheless, the findings add to the hope that HIV-disease will become a manageable chronic illness, controllable if not curable, through medication.

Unanswered questions support the recommendation that case-by-case decision making, rather then blanket rules, be the norm.[76] There is no evidence that any of the new drugs function prophylactically. The most effective way to use the new drugs has not been determined,[77] and, no doubt due to the failure of ZDV to live up to its early promise, experts suggest caution in predicting the long-range effects of new drug therapies until they are subject to long-term studies with large numbers of patients. Considering side effects, the development of drug resistance over time, and uncertainty as to when to begin treatment, arguments for testing that rest solely on early drug treatment do not stand up to close scrutiny.

An individual who is at risk for HIV may be urged to take a test for reasons unrelated to early drug treatment. Several examples illustrate the importance of testing for and knowing one's HIV-status. Testing is recommended for anyone with an STD because STDs are seen as facilitating transmission of HIV.[78] Women who are HIV-positive have been advised to have a Pap smear "twice during the first year after diagnosis and once a year thereafter if the previous results are normal." Women are also advised to have regular gynecological exams because of the many cervical abnormalities which are associated with HIV. For HIV-positive children, routine immunizations have to be adjusted because those ordinarily given may be harmful to a child whose immune system is compromised.[79] Little is known about the testing practices of adolescents. The limited data that are available indicate that adolescents who are at risk are not routinely tested. Ignorant of their HIV-status, many adolescents do not seek medical care until their immune systems are severely compromised.[80] In addition, guidelines for preventing opportunistic infections, issued by the CDC in July 1995, serve as a reminder of the risks that confront people who are HIV- positive in everyday situations because their immune systems are compromised. Practical recommendations contained in these guidelines include, among others, avoiding exposure to young animals and avoidance of drinking surface water.[81]

The benefits of prophylactic treatment to prevent the onset of *P carinii* pneumonia (PCP) provides another argument for testing. Hoover and his colleagues (1993) report that new cases of PCP in adults declined after 1988 when PCP prophylaxis became common and that prophylaxis "delays the first AIDS-related illness by 6 to 12 months."[82] Prophylaxis for PCP is recommended when an adult's T-cell count falls below 200[83] and for newborns at 4 to 6 weeks of age or as soon thereafter as their HIV-status is determined.[84] Since more than one-half of all cases of PCP in newborns occur between 3 and 6 months of age, close monitoring in the first months of life is crucial.[85] The fact that approximately 70 percent of newborns seroconvert by 18 months of age was, until recently, a cause for concern that prophylaxis, if given to all, could prove harmful to the majority who are not infected. This concern is alleviated to the extent that new diagnostic techniques (the polymerase chain reaction test), which permit diagnosis of HIV-infection at birth in almost one-half of all cases and by 1 to 3 months of age in 95 percent of cases, are available.[86] However, the test relies on expensive technology and access to it may be limited.[87] Other tests have been developed with a promise of early detection but their efficacy is debated in the medical literature.[88]

There have been no controlled studies of PCP prophylaxis in HIV-infected infants. In an effort to clarify some of the questions that controlled studies might answer, Thea (1996)[89] and his colleagues conducted a retrospective review of hospital records. Their data describe the health of infants released from New York City hospitals. They report that only three cases of PCP were confirmed for seventy children who received primary prophylaxis before 18 months of age compared with twelve cases (28 percent) among forty-two children who did not receive primary prophylaxis at any time before they reached 18 months of age. In mid-1996, Barnhart and colleagues reported data on 2,148 perinatally infected children. Seventy-two percent of the children were "long-term survivors," i.e., living beyond 4 years of age and their survival was attributed, in part, to clinical intervention before the onset of AIDS.[90] Unfortunately, knowledge that a child is at risk for HIV does not guarantee that the child will receive prophylaxis, according to data compiled by Simonds and his colleagues (1995) based on a review of the medical records of 300 children with PCP.[91]

Confidentiality

Protection for confidentiality of medical information is rooted in the common law principle that physicians have a duty not to disclose medical information about their patients and in a patient's constitutionally protected right to privacy.

The right to privacy is explicit in some state constitutions. In the federal Constitution this right is derived mainly from the concept of liberty in the Fourteenth Amendment and from the Ninth Amendment's reservation of rights to the people.[92] The Supreme Court has discussed the right of privacy as embracing two matters: information privacy, which protects the individual against disclosure of personal information and which is implicated directly in disclosure of medical information, and decisional privacy, which is implicated in a woman's right to choose to continue or terminate a pregnancy.[93]

In *Whalen v. Roe*,[94] plaintiffs challenged a New York statute that created a centralized databank for storing personal identifying information on individuals receiving prescriptions for drugs such as opium, cocaine, and amphetamines. The Supreme Court said that the Fourteenth Amendment confers on the individual an "interest in avoiding disclosure of personal matters,"[95] but the Court held that the patient-identification system was a reasonable exercise of state power and that there was no evidence to sustain the allegation that the plaintiffs' constitutional rights to privacy were threatened. Several federal circuit courts have interpreted *Whalen* to find that an individual has a constitutionally protected right to privacy in her medical records.[96] The Court of Appeals for the Second Circuit held that the constitutional right enumerated in *Whalen* extends to persons who are HIV-infected who "clearly possess a constitutional right to privacy regarding their condition."[97] In contrast, a federal district court in Virginia, after acknowledging the existence of authority to support a claim that the federal Constitution protects an individual's personal privacy in her medical history, held that the scope of this right was not so clear as to find against an army supervisor for disclosing a civilian employee's HIV-status.[98]

There is no single federal statute that requires patient consent as a condition for release of information in a medical record, although the Medical Records Confidentiality Act, introduced in Congress in 1995, purports to do so.[99]

Statutes that protect information and that govern its release are found in various federal laws and in state law. At the federal level, protection is found in the Federal Privacy Act,[100] which protects individual privacy with regard to information systems maintained by federal agencies, and in statutes which contain provisions affecting specific types of disclosures, and in case law. The Americans with Disabilities Act (ADA) protects against disclosure of medical information that is acquired in the course of a preemployment medical examination by requiring that an employer maintain such information on separate forms in a separate medical file and treat the information as confidential.[101] The CARE Act[102] contains provisions for confidential reporting of HIV-information to government officials for surveillance purposes. Under the Violence Against Women Act,[103] victims of sex crimes that may involve the transmission of an STD including HIV may obtain information regarding the HIV-status of their assailants by pursuing an order in a federal court requiring a defendant to submit to blood tests.[104] The Victim's Compensation Assistance Act[105] provides for anonymous and confidential testing for HIV at government expense. Finally, federal law governing the Veterans Health Administration contains provisions for confidentiality of medical records but limits the protection by providing for disclosure of HIV-related information to federal or state officials if other laws provide for disclosure. Since, as discussed further on, a number of state laws provide for disclosure of otherwise confidential information, this proviso offers a point of entry for state officials to gain confidential records.[106]

Common Elements of State Confidentiality Statutes   Confidentiality laws typically preclude testing for HIV without the informed consent of the person to be tested. Many states provide for anonymous testing as further protection. To ensure that the person to be tested understands the right to privacy, some states require that confidentiality rules and/or the right to take an anonymous test be explained prior to testing.[107]

Informed consent generally requires a written statement, signed by the person to be tested, that she has been told that her participation is voluntary, that her consent may be withdrawn, that she has been informed that she may receive an anonymous test, and that she has been informed of: (1) the purpose of the test, its meaning, and the benefits of early diagnosis; (2) the procedures followed in conducting the test; and (3) the law regarding the confidentiality of information including any provisions in the law that permit disclosure to others.[108]

Further protection against unwarranted testing is found in statutes requiring: (1) that consent forms for HIV-testing not simply be a part of a general medical consent form, unless the general form expressly states that a test for HIV may be carried out, and (2) that a physician who orders such a test must certify that informed consent was received.[109] Also, states may: (1) require written consent for each release of HIV-related information, including the release of medical records that contain the results of an HIV-test; (2) require specification of the purpose of the release, identification of the person or persons to whom the information may be released, and the period of time during which the release is in effect; and (3) preclude disclosure on the basis of a general authorization for release of medical information.[110]

Other elements common to confidentiality statutes include provisions for civil penalties, generally a fine, for unauthorized disclosure of HIV-related information and provisions for bypassing informed consent procedures that apply to: (1) providing treatment in medical emergencies; (2) conducting research in settings where identity of the individual tested is not known and cannot be determined; (3) testing to determine whether a donated organ contains HIV; and (4) testing pursuant to a court order. Some states have bypass provisions that have the effect of rendering less protection than is implied by use of the concept of informed consent. For example, one state allows a physician to order an HIV-test, if she determines that it is medically indicated;[111] and other states allow testing at the physician's discretion if she is exposed to the body fluids of a person in a manner that would create a risk if the patient were HIV-positive.[112]

All states disclose to the CDC confirmed cases of AIDS without identifying the person diagnosed, and states must have procedures for confidential reporting of test results to state public health officials for statistical and epidemiological analysis as a condition for federal funding under the CARE Act.[113] Precisely what is reported to state officials varies, and the rules in a number of states limit the protections found in confidentiality statutes. Some states require reporting of positive test results with information identifying the tested person but stipulate that results remain confidential;[114] others provide for reporting of demographic information such as age, race, and gender without reporting of names;[115] and others have no specific reporting requirements. Several states, while requiring that the names of all who test positive be reported to state officials, provide also for anonymous testing by permitting the establishment of a specified number of anonymous testing sites across the state.[116] The Illinois Department of Public Health has proposed the creation of a statewide registry which would contain the names of all who test positive for HIV on the assumption that a list of names would improve treatment.[117] Taking the opposite position, the California Medical Association withdrew its support for mandatory named-reporting of people with HIV, because it questioned whether such reporting would further the attainment of its public health goals.[118]

In addition to reporting to state officials, some states allow for reporting to health care providers who are said to need this information for the purpose of diagnosis and treatment,[119] and there is case law to support the proposition that a person who knows that she or he is HIV-positive has a duty to disclose this information prior to having sexual contact, even if precautions are used.[120]

Under provisions of the CARE Act, states must implement procedures for notifying emergency response employees (firefighters, law enforcement officers, paramedics, emergency medical technicians) who believe that they have been exposed to HIV and who request information confirming or denying the possibility of exposure, information on the HIV-status of the person who received emergency medical care.[121]

Disclosure of HIV-Information   Disclosure of otherwise confidential HIV-information is permitted under a variety of circumstances, for example, when disclosure is ordered by a court or when necessary to maintain order and prevent transmission in a prison. There are situations in which the person with HIV may have an affirmative duty to disclose her status. All types of disclosures are not proscribed by statute. While receiving a physical examination, Richard Urbaniak disclosed to a nurse that he had tested positive for HIV.[122] The nurse told a physician who recorded this information in Urbaniak's medical record, which was distributed to others including a number of employees at the patient's insurance company. An appellate court in California held that the confidentiality statute under which Urbaniak brought suit was limited to disclosures of information contained in a medical record describing the results of a blood test and that Urbaniak's self-disclosure to the nurse did not constitute the kind of behavior the statute proscribed. Relying on this decision, an appellate court in Wisconsin held that disclosure of a prisoner's HIV-status by employees of a county jail was not a prohibited disclosure, because they learned of the prisoner's HIV-status from a medical report that the prisoner brought with him to the jail and not from the contents of the prisoner's actual medical record.[123] The prisoner's actual medical record was the only information source covered by the statute. But a disclosure by a physician of a patient's

HIV-status was held to violate New York law because the authorization signed by the patient did not state the nature of the information to be disclosed and was not dated.[124]

As earlier noted, an individual's right to privacy in the contents of her medical records is protected by the Fourteenth Amendment. On this basis, a federal district court in New Jersey concluded that Jane Doe had a protected right to information regarding her husband's HIV-status and that the state had no compelling interest in disclosing this information to a neighbor of the Does'.[125] Ms. Doe had a right to sue for the "harassment, discrimination and humiliation" she and her children suffered after the disclosure. Likewise, a woman in Massachusetts had a right to sue the town of Plymouth and a police officer who allegedly disclosed her HIV-status to others.[126] And a federal district court in New York approved a cash settlement in favor of Mary Doe's children, who alleged that the city's Department of Social Services had improperly disclosed the HIV-status of family members.[127]

Disclosure in Prisons   Disclosure of HIV-information in a prison setting may occur in different ways. For example, segregation of those who are HIV-positive indirectly informs others of their health status, while access to prison records directly informs others.

When issues of disclosure in prisons arise, courts frequently defer to decisions made by prison officials based on their need to maintain discipline and order, which outweighs the prisoner's constitutionally protected right of privacy.[128] Some states, by statute, provide for testing of prisoners without informed consent if the director of a correctional institute can show good cause for requiring the test[129] or if the prisoner has been convicted of a sex crime.[130] Disclosure of a prisoner's HIV-status to prison officials or staff may be permitted in some states: (1) if the person receiving the information is authorized to access the type of record which would contain information on a prisoner's HIV-status;[131] (2) to allow for assigning a prisoner who tests positive to a private cell;[132] (3) to segregate the prisoner likely to engage in behavior that would transmit the virus;[133] or (4) to allow any person, including volunteers at the prison who come into contact with inmates, to take appropriate action to protect the inmate or themselves.[134]

Federal courts have held that segregating HIV-positive prisoners does not violate their constitutional rights,[135] even when, on one occasion, the segregation lasted for nine months. During this period of time, an HIV-positive woman was isolated in a hospital room because prison policy proscribed mixing HIV-positive inmates with those in the general population and because there was no separate facility for HIV-positive women.[136] On the other hand, failure to segregate HIV-positive prisoners does not constitute cruel and unusual punishment in violation of the Eighth Amendment rights of noninfected prisoners with whom they live in the general prison population.[137]

But court decisions involving prisoner rights do not always favor prison administrators. Louise Nolley was an inmate in a New York State correctional facility which had a policy of segregating prisoners who were mentally ill, suicidal, or dangerous to themselves, and of marking with red stickers the records of prisoners with HIV to inform prison personnel that they were in contact with a person infected with a contagious disease.[138] The court held that use of red stickers informed others of Ms. Nolley's status as HIV-positive and was a prohibited disclosure under New York's Public Health Law and the federal Constitution. As to the issue of segregation, however, the court held that it did not constitute a disclosure to the general prison population, since prisoners were segregated for reasons other than their HIV-status, but it did constitute a disclosure to prison personnel because they could observe and discriminate between those segregated for reasons of mental illness from those segregated because of their health status.

Disclosure Under Court Order   Provisions in state law that permit disclosure of protected information and that provide for testing under a court order are common. States receiving federal funds under the CARE Act must have criminal statutes that provide for the prosecution of a person who knows that she or he is HIV-positive and who intentionally transmits the virus.[139] A person asking a court to issue an order to disclose HIV-related information must, as a rule, demonstrate a compelling need or show good cause as to why the court should permit disclosure.[140] It is not uncommon for courts to mandate safeguards prior to disclosure, including requirements that: (1) notice be given to affected parties to allow them to dispute the disclosure; (2) records be sealed; (3) proceedings be conducted *in camera*; and (4) use of fictitious names be permitted.

Courts have permitted testing: (1) of a prison inmate after a guard reported that she was bitten by the inmate;[141] (2) of a woman who bit a sheriff's deputy during a child custody hearing;[142] and (3) of persons against whom criminal charges were lodged for biting police officers,[143] a security guard and store manager,[144] or a mental health worker.[145] Courts have also ordered (1) testing for prosecution of rape[146] or other sexual offenses;[147] (2) disclosure of a physician's HIV-status to former patients and to physicians whom he had assisted in surgery;[148] (3) access by a state health department to all of the medical records of a dentist who died of AIDS for the purpose of undertaking an epidemiological study of the dentist's patients;[149] and (4) disclosure to aid in pretrial discovery when a person has alleged that he or she was infected (a) by a sexual partner who knowingly transmitted HIV;[150] (b) by an inmate whom corrections officers had failed to restrain;[151] and (c) through transfusions with tainted blood.[152] And the courts have found that the Constitution is not offended when a statute provides that any person convicted of unlawful possession of a hypodermic needle,[153] or of prostitution be tested.[154]

Duty to Disclose   Thus far we have considered situations in which disclosure of HIV-information is permitted. Whether there are circumstances that create an obligation to disclose one's HIV-status or to disclose the HIV-status of another is a further dimension of this issue. In chapter 2 we saw that a hospital could require a health care worker to disclose his HIV-status when the inquiry was job-related and consistent with business necessity and that the worker's failure to disclose his HIV-status was sufficient to justify his dismissal. But the Court of Appeals for the Ninth Circuit found that a physician did not have a duty to disclose his HIV-status when the work he performed did not create a risk of transmission if infection-control procedures were followed.[155] And a California appellate court ruled that a physician's duty to his patient was to exercise care when performing medical procedures, not to disclose his HIV-status.[156] The opposite conclusion was reached by the Maryland Court of Appeals, when it found that a surgeon had a duty to warn his patients that he was HIV-positive, because there is a possibility, however remote, of transmitting the virus and because of the seriousness of the harm that could result.[157]

There is case law to support the proposition that a person who knows that she is infected with a sexually transmitted disease (STD) has a duty to warn her sex partners.[158] And a number of states permit, but do not mandate, disclosure of otherwise confidential HIV-related information to medical personnel for the purpose of diagnosis and treatment. Thus a New York court could find in *Ordway v. County of Suffolk*[159] that prison officials did not have a duty to inform a physician of an arrestee's HIV-status prior to surgery and that a physician would not be successful in suing for emotional distress that he claimed to have suffered because he was not informed of the arrestee's HIV-status. However, the fact that statutes are permissive allows a court to reach the opposite conclusion. For example, in *Selby v. Rapping,* it was held that a prisoner could not sue a prison official for disclosing his HIV-status to a physician who was to provide treatment to the prisoner.[160] And in North Carolina, failure to disclose information about a pregnant woman's HIV-status, when disclosure was mandated by hospital policy and permitted by state statute, provided grounds for dismissing a physician from the hospital.[161]

PART III. REPRODUCTIVE CHOICE

In 1973 the Supreme Court in *Roe v. Wade* established a framework which governs a woman's right to choose to continue or terminate a pregnancy.[162] The Court balanced the rights of a pregnant woman against the interest of the state, which exists throughout pregnancy, in protecting a woman's health and that of the fetus. Until the point of fetal viability the state's interest is subordinate to a woman's right to elect to continue or to terminate her pregnancy. The state may erect barriers to abortion as long as the erected barriers do not create an undue burden for the woman seeking to exercise her constitutional rights. Thus a requirement in Pennsylvania law that a woman be given "truthful, nonmisleading information about the nature of the abortion procedure, the attendant health risks and those of childbirth, and the 'probable gestational age' of the fetus" is consistent with the state's interest in potential life. Requiring that a woman receive this information does not amount to a substantial obstacle to the exercising of her constitutional rights. But requiring that a woman sign a form indicating that she has notified her husband of her intention to terminate her pregnancy is a substantial obstacle.[163] After viability, state laws restricting a woman's right to choose, including an outright ban on abortion, will survive constitutional scrutiny, if the law contains exceptions that permit abortion when a woman's life or health are in danger. Health includes psychological as well as physical well-being.[164] If there is a conflict between the health or life of a pregnant woman and that of her fetus, safeguarding the health and life of the woman is primary.[165]

A woman's right to elect abortion does not obligate any unit of government to fund the procedure.[166] Some medical providers refuse to provide abortion services to women who are HIV-positive. Sangree reports that the only provider of abortion services in South Carolina refused to assist two HIV-positive women, unless they agreed to tubal ligations.[167] Gittler and Rennert (1992) discuss a study which found that:

> Two-thirds of the abortion facilities . . . canceled appointments made by allegedly HIV infected women once their infection status was disclosed. Some of the facilities attempted a plausible response, such as their inability to handle that type of procedure. Others changed the vacation schedules of the physicians or quoted inflated prices for abortion services to discourage those seeking care. Still others openly reported their staff refused to care for HIV infected patients.[168]

The following topics are addressed in this section: a discussion of state action against women during their pregnancy is followed by a review of court-ordered medical interventions that are against the wishes of the pregnant woman. Directive counseling is the next topic, after which we revisit the subject of testing for HIV and consider this matter in the context of pregnancy. Constitutional and ethical issues that arise from this review are the last topic.

State Action Against Women for Conduct During Pregnancy

As we saw in chapter 4, supported either by statute or case law, states may charge a woman with neglect if her newborn tests positive for drugs or displays symptoms associated with maternal alcohol use during pregnancy. Charging a woman with child maltreatment for conduct occurring during pregnancy demands the reconciliation of two contradictory positions: first, the Supreme Court has said that a fetus is not a person subject to full legal protection;[169] and second, state laws that provide authority for charging a parent with neglect or abuse if a newborn tests positive for illegal drugs or is born with signs or symptoms that suggest maternal alcohol use during pregnancy concern acts toward living children.

Courts reconcile these positions in different ways. Some start with identifying those situations in which a fetus has been accorded rights. For example, parents may sue for the wrongful death of a fetus, some courts have sustained suits by children for injuries they suffered in utero, and a fetus may have a right to inherit.[170] Whether the right to sue for wrongful death is a "fetal right" or the right of the parent is subject to debate, and inheritance rights attach only if the fetus is born alive. Tort claims brought for injuries in utero are brought by children born alive.

Some courts take as a starting point the statement of the Justices in *Roe* that states have a legitimate interest in potential life and that this interest becomes compelling at the point of fetal viability. Taking this view, courts in Ohio and Michigan[171] argues that *Roe* "compels" a finding that a viable unborn fetus is a child or that *Roe* provides for this finding when it is in the child's best interest. Courts in New York and California bypass altogether the suggestion that a finding of neglect might interfere with a woman's rights under *Roe* by arguing that their decisions rest on protection of a child already born, not on a woman's conduct during her pregnancy. For example, one New York appellate court ruled that the concern in a neglect proceeding was not with a fetus, and the issue did not involve a mother's right to privacy. The concern was with protecting a child that the woman had chosen to carry to term and deliver.[172]

Despite a willingness to sustain charges that prenatal ingestion of drugs or alcohol supports a charge of abuse or neglect, state courts, with the exception of South Carolina, have not been willing to accept the suggestion that criminal charges may be lodged against a pregnant woman for "delivery" of a controlled substance to a newborn. (See chapter 4.) Additional efforts to control a woman's conduct during pregnancy for the sake of the fetus are found in court orders not to become pregnant, to use specific forms of contraception,[173] or to submit to bimonthly blood tests to detect pregnancy.[174] In one case a pregnant woman was incarcerated for forging checks to protect the fetus from harm due to the mother's purchasing drugs to satisfy her addiction.[175]

Court Ordered Medical Treatment

Courts are asked to order medical treatment under different circumstances. Women with HIV and those with an HIV-positive child may be affected by court orders that: (1) seek to override a woman's authority to make medical decisions for her child; (2) force medical treatment on a competent adult for her own sake; and (3) force medical treatment on a competent adult for the sake of a second party.

The first two issues are not difficult to dispose of. The Supreme Court has ruled that a state, acting in its role of *parens patriae*, may order needed medical care for a child.[176] An Alabama Court of Appeals, for example, ordered treatment for an HIV-infected child over the objections of the child's mother, who did not believe that her child was infected.[177] Courts in other states have ordered treatment even when doing so overrides a parent's religious-based objection to treatment.[178]

Ordering medical treatment for a competent adult who refuses treatment affecting only herself presents another matter. The right to privacy found in the federal Constitution and the Fourth Amendment's protection against unreasonable search and seizure, which protect against unwarranted intrusion into a person's body, confer on a competent adult the right to refuse medical treatment,[179] and this right overrides any interest the state may have in ordering treatment.

Court authority to order a pregnant woman to submit to medical care for the sake of an unborn child poses the greatest threat to the privacy of pregnant women. Courts have ordered blood transfusions[180] and one court ordered that the woman undergo a cesarean if needed.[181] In each case the fetus was viable, the woman had decided to carry to term and to deliver, and the orders were justified by the courts based on the state's interest in preserving life.

But an Illinois Appellate Court refused to issue an order for performance of a cesarean, even though the fetus was viable and the decision probably harmful to its survival.[182] The court distinguished its decision from others ordering blood transfusions, because of the intrusiveness of a cesarean compared to a transfusion. The Supreme Judicial Court of Massachusetts vacated an order of a lower court which had ordered a pregnant woman to undergo a surgical procedure which would have enabled her to carry her fetus to term based on a woman's constitutional right to privacy.[183] In a like manner the Appellate Court for the District of Columbia refused to issue an order compelling a pregnant woman, not near term, to submit to a cesarean even though the decision might ultimately be fatal to the child.[184]

In only one case did a court issue an order for a blood transfusion for a "potentially viable" fetus who, for the purpose of the case, was deemed a "human being." The New York court appointed a guardian of the unborn child and sanctioned his use of his medical judgment to do all that was necessary to save the life of the fetus, including the transfusion of blood into the mother.[185]

Directive Counseling

The right to have children is a fundamental liberty protected by the federal Constitution;[186] and directive counseling, where a woman is "urged" to submit to an HIV-test and, if positive, to postpone or terminate pregnancy, threatens that right. The United States Public Health Service has issued guidelines for counseling and testing for HIV that stress nondirective counseling.[187] There is only one reported case involving this issue. In *Doe v. Jamaica Hospital*, a woman with HIV sued a physician under the Vocational Rehabilitation Act. She argued that her rights as a disabled person had been violated when the physician urged her to have an abortion.[188] Other evidence of directive counseling is anecdotal.

Sangree (1993),[189] in her narrative on this subject, says that a person who had done HIV-counseling reported that reimbursement rates for counseling sessions were greater when the women counseled agreed to be tested than when they refused. For this reason counselors

> felt pressure to obtain consent [and] even the most ethical . . . were swayed. [Moreover] because reimbursement was greater when the test

results were positive, women who acknowledged a history of high-risk behavior or who were members of groups with high incidence of HIV infection (i.e. African-American or Latin-American) were even more likely to be pressured to accept testing. One woman was even tested after refusing consent.

An HIV-positive Native-American woman said that she was urged to have an abortion. One of two doctors treating her:

> "strongly recommended" an abortion because her "baby would have AIDS" and "would die within the first year." The other doctor [said], "Who do you think you are to bring a baby into this world only to watch it suffer and die?" The woman . . . refused to have an abortion, and . . . her baby was not infected with HIV.[190]

HIV-Testing, Pregnant Women, and the Protocol 076 Study

Blinded screening of newborns for surveillance purposes was routine until 1995 when the CDC suspended its HIV-survey so that it could revisit its overall strategy for compiling surveillance data.[191] Impetus for this decision came from two sources: (1) the introduction in Congress of legislation which would unblind tests involving newborns, and (2) the results of a controlled study of 477 pregnant women infected with HIV that was reported in late 1994 (Protocol 076 Study, hereafter Protocol Study).[192] In the reported study, half of the women who qualified as participants received ZDV; the other half a placebo. The study participants are described as having mildly symptomatic HIV and, with nineteen exceptions, no prior treatment with antiretroviral drugs. All of the women were between fourteen and thirty-five weeks gestation and had a CD-4 T-cell count greater than 200. Slightly over 8 percent of the babies born to women receiving the experimental drug, compared to 25.5 percent of the babies born to women in the control group, were HIV-infected.

The data from the Protocol Study are likely to reinforce the view of those physicians who think that the use of a state's coercive power on behalf of a fetus is called for.[193] For example, in 1987, Kolder and her colleagues conducted a national survey of obstetricians who head fellowship programs in Maternal-Fetal Medicine in forty-five states and the District of Columbia. Twenty-six of fifty-seven program directors (46 percent) expressed the view that mothers who endanger a fetus by refusing medical advice should be detained in hospitals or elsewhere to ensure compliance with medical orders and 27 (47 percent) thought that court orders should go beyond requiring emergency cesareans to save a fetus to include other procedures (for example, intrauterine transfusions) with the potential to save life. Fifteen of fifty-eight respondents (26 percent) thought that the state should engage in surveillance of women in their last trimester of pregnancy who are outside of the hospital system.[194] Bayer (1994) reports that national surveys indicate that the vast majority of physicians favor mandatory screening of pregnant women, and a number of physicians favor forced intervention to protect the fetus.[195]

Minkoff and Willoughby (1995) identify both positive and negative conclusions that could be drawn from the Protocol Study. First, they note that there are no treatments that, when begun after birth, will save a newborn from an AIDS-related death. However, rather than jumping to the conclusion that this finding justifies mandated testing and forced treatment of pregnant women, they raise a series of questions regarding the study results. For example, will the findings hold true outside of the controlled research setting and is it not possible that failure rates may exceed the 8 percent reported? This conclusion requires recognition of the fact that the population of women served in the real world includes all those excluded from the study because their CD-4 cell counts were too low, their pregnancy too advanced, their exposure to ZDV too prolonged, and their chances greater of carrying resistant strains of the virus. Also, identifying women who are eligible for the treatment regimen requires a degree of precision that may prove difficult, since such identification will rely on patients' recollection, unless a woman has received regular, ongoing medical care with rigorous documentation.[196]

The concerns expressed by Minkoff and Willoughby are echoed by the CDC. Discussing the implications of the Protocol Study for testing and treatment of pregnant women, the CDC cautions against overgeneralizing the study's results, because: (1) perinatal transmission occurred despite drug therapy; (2) knowledge regarding the effectiveness of the treatment program for women with advanced HIV-infection, those who have been taking antiretroviral medications, and women with ZDV-resistant strains of the virus is lacking; (3) the fact that there were no short-term side effects in the study population cannot be taken as a measure of what these effects might be when the use of ZDV becomes more common; (4) there may be long-term risks to a child exposed to ZDV in utero and early infancy; and (5) we do not know whether taking ZDV during pregnancy will affect the drug's efficacy for the woman when it becomes indicated for her own health.[197] Bayer adds to these concerns by asking "Will administering ZDV to pregnant women and newborns pose a risk to the 70 to 80 percent who, while born infected, would seroconvert?"[198] This question is relevant despite the existence of new tests for early detection of HIV-infection in newborns, because the costs of the testing procedures may limit their general use.

In addition to questions regarding who is an appropriate candidate for the treatment regimen described, any suggestion that treatment be imposed on pregnant women must take account of the fact that the women in the study had to take ZDV five times a day during the second and third trimesters of pregnancy, that ZDV was administered intravenously during labor and delivery, and that the drug was given to newborns for the first six to seven weeks of life.[199] Efforts to impose such a regimen would likely fail constitutional scrutiny, would be ethically repugnant, and virtually impossible to enforce.

In July 1995, the CDC issued guidelines recommending that health care providers counsel and encourage pregnant women to be tested for HIV. They recommended that testing be voluntary, based on informed consent, and in keeping with other legal requirements of the state in which the mother lives. Moreover, the provision of prenatal or other health care services should not be made contingent upon a woman's decision whether or not to be tested and women should not be reported to child protective services for any reason related to accepting or rejecting an HIV-test. [200] The American Academy of Pediatrics and the American College of Obstetricians and Gynecologists support the recommendation that testing be voluntary.[201] However, in the fall of 1996, the American Medical Association, based on new data showing a decline in perinatal transmission when pregnant women take ZDV, changed its position to recommend mandatory testing for pregnant women.[202]

The CDC's guidelines do not recommend: (1) mandatory testing; (2) testing for all women or for targeted groups based on identification of group members as being at risk; nor (3) informed refusal, which permits testing absent a signed statement specifically rejecting an HIV-test.[203] The 1996 reauthorization of the CARE Act requires states that do not have mandatory testing programs to implement the CDC guidelines.

There is evidence that women will agree to voluntary testing when counseling is provided regarding the implications of a positive test result. For example, 95 percent of the women counseled at Harlem Hospital agreed to be tested,[204] as did 91 percent of those counseled at Johns Hopkins.[205] Anecdotal evidence from physicians supports the suggestion that 90 percent or more of women accept offers of voluntary testing and counseling.[206] Moreover, while little is known about the numbers of eligible women who receive ZDV treatment during pregnancy,[207] data from a New York City hospital inform us that of forty-nine HIV-infected women who were offered ZDV, thirty-seven (76 percent) accepted the entire course of treatment and one women (2 percent), rejecting treatment for herself, accepted it for her newborn. Nine women (18 percent) refused treatment and two (4 percent) chose to terminate their pregnancies. The women who refused ZDV were those for whom IVDU was their identified risk factor and they were likely to continue the use of illegal drugs during pregnancy.[208] These data support the suggestion that it would be unprincipled to mandate testing without providing the option of voluntary participation based on informed consent.[209]

As to the question "How voluntary is the consent given?" Faden and her colleagues at Johns Hopkins[210] asked 556 women whether they had felt pressured by hospital staff to take an HIV-test. Conceding the difficulties of measuring accurately whether or not consent is voluntary, these authors report that a suggestion that the women felt coerced to consent to testing was not supported by the evidence.

Constitutional Scrutiny

Any effort to mandate testing and treatment of pregnant women and not other groups would likely run afoul of the Equal Protection clause of the Fourteenth Amendment and would probably violate a woman's privacy rights under the Fourteenth Amendment.

The Equal Protection clause precludes discrimination where groups of similarly situated people are treated differently, unless the state can demonstrate a purpose that overrides individual rights. Any program that mandated HIV-testing for pregnant women only would be subject to an equal protection challenge, because the state action would deprive pregnant women (and not any others who are HIV-positive) of their fundamental right to be free from unwanted intrusions into their bodies. Because this right is fundamental, the state would have to demonstrate a compelling interest in forced testing and it would have to show that the objective of testing could not be accomplished in other, less intrusive ways. An effort of the state to justify its actions because of its interest in protection of the fetus is not likely to stand up to close scrutiny because of the equivocal nature of the data from the Protocol Study and because voluntary testing provides a less intrusive means of accomplishing the desired goal.

Considering first the data from the Protocol Study, the treatment regimen was begun in the early stages of pregnancy at which time a woman's right to choose to continue or terminate her pregnancy is paramount to any interest the state may have in protecting a fetus. Even postviability decisions that interfere with a woman's choices will not pass constitutional muster if they subordinate the woman's health to the health of the fetus. The suggestion that treatment may jeopardize a woman's health is not unreasonable. ZDV is known to have toxic side effects, and when a woman's health reaches the point where the benefits of the drug outweigh its toxicity, it is not known whether early administration will reduce later effectiveness.

A state would have difficulty in arguing for mandated treatment because such treatment is in the best interests of the child. First, considering the fact that approximately 70 percent of children will seroconvert, coupled with the known side effects of the drug on adults and our ignorance regarding its long-term effects on infants and young children, a best interests argument is difficult to support. And we must bear in mind that 8 percent of the children whose mothers took ZVD in the Protocol Study tested positive for HIV. For these children, we must ask whether early treatment might render the drug less effective at later stages of the illness. It is wise also to bear in mind that in the late 1980s testing for all people at risk was strongly recommended because early treatment with ZDV was thought to be beneficial. Such benefit proved not to be the case, and several years hence recommendations that are based on findings from the Protocol Study may be called into question.

Regarding the constitutionality of mandatory testing and treatment of pregnant women, it would be unwise to assume that conclusions drawn from the Protocol Study will, ipso facto, apply to the future when new developments in drug therapy may support different arguments for mandatory testing and treatment. Possibly, a drug administered postviability will have the same results as reported in the Protocol Study and be shown to be harmless to the health of a pregnant woman. Under such a scenario, the state's compelling interest in the fetus could trump a woman's right to decline treatment.

PART IV. SUMMARY

Since the start of the AIDS epidemic more than two-thirds of the states have passed laws to safeguard confidential HIV-related information. Protection for such information is found also in federal law, including the Ryan White CARE Act and the Americans with Disabilities Act, and in various provisions of the federal Constitution. This summary is organized by the topics of confidentiality and testing; of contact tracing and partner notification; and of reproductive choice.

Confidentiality and Testing

Confidentiality laws that protect from disclosure HIV- and AIDS-related information were enacted to encourage people to be tested for the presence of the virus. Confidentiality laws that existed in the early 1980s when the first cases of AIDS were diagnosed were not seen as offering sufficient protection against privacy violations and the discriminatory consequences that might follow from unwarranted disclosure of an individual's HIV-status. Concern about disclosure of protected information was justified, whether based on a review of the historical record and the numerous ways in which official bodies have violated the public trust such as the Tuskegee experiments and forced sterilization of poor women, or on a review of contemporary matters such as calls for quarantine of people with HIV, documented instances of discrimination in housing, education, and employment, as well as documented violations of confidentiality.

The knowledge that a test for HIV yields is necessary for making informed decisions that are required: (1) to protect oneself from situations that are health threatening because of a compromised immune system; (2) to protect others by avoiding contacts that are implicated in the transmission of HIV; (3) to choose whether or not to have children or, if pregnant, whether to continue or terminate a pregnancy; and (4) to seek routine medical care including immune system monitoring and prophylactic treatment.

HIV-testing is mandatory in the armed forces and for Job Corps applicants, aliens, and federal prisoners. The federal government makes funds available to the states for mandatory testing of prisoners. Blinded testing of newborns, with surveillance data reported to the CDC, has been supported by federal funds, and federal policy requires that states offer counseling and testing to pregnant women. But by-and-large, testing for HIV and confidentiality of HIV-related information are matters controlled by state law. In general, states prohibit testing for HIV without the informed consent of the person to be tested, but there are exceptions, as when a test is ordered by a court.

State efforts to safeguard privacy are found when: (1) anonymous as well as confidential testing is available, (2) state policy favors voluntary over mandatory testing, and (3) confidentiality laws with penalties for violations exist. While state law may limit disclosure of HIV-related information, there are "gaps" in disclosure rules. These gaps, when considered in light of documented violations of patient confidentiality, are sufficient to raise concern about the degree of protection afforded by current laws. For example, some states require named-reporting to public health officials of all who test positive for HIV, and some permit disclosure to medical providers. A few states allow a medical provider to order a test for HIV without the informed consent of the person tested if the provider has good cause for doing so. Finally, disclosure statutes have been shown to be limited in the protections they offer, because some courts have interpreted them to limit disclosure only to information that is contained in a medical record, thereby providing a window through which a great deal of information may flow without affording statutory protection to the individual.

When the individual's right to privacy is pitted against the state's interest in testing or disclosing test results, the courts seek to balance the rights of the concerned parties. Courts will, as a rule, defer to the judgment of government officials that testing is needed to maintain order in prisons, and the Supreme Court has ruled that testing of people in certain occupations (e.g., firefighters, railroad employees) is justified because taking a blood sample is a minimal intrusion into a person's body and people in certain occupations have a minimum expectation of privacy. Many states will allow testing of those charged with or convicted of crimes where the evidence suggests an intent to transmit HIV.

Contact Tracing and Partner Notification

The CARE Act requires the states to provide for tracing the known contacts of a person who tests positive for HIV and for informing those who are located of their exposure. The CDC provides funds for contact tracing and partner notification programs. However, federal law does not mandate either contact tracing or partner notification. Some state laws do mandate such procedures and impose on the individual who tests positive an obligation to divulge the names of her or his sex or needle sharing partners. However, the majority of states have approached this issue with caution, in part out of a concern that contact tracing and partner notification will cause people to avoid being tested and in part for practical reasons. The latter draws attention to the latency between exposure to HIV and the point in time when a person learns her or his HIV-status. During this interval, which may be a decade or more, an individual may have numerous contacts during which the HIV could be transmitted. The costs of identifying and tracing all of these contacts could eclipse all available prevention funds.

Reproductive Choice

The right of a pregnant woman to choose to continue or terminate her pregnancy is rooted in the federal Constitution. The state has an interest in protecting the woman and her fetus throughout the term of pregnancy, but the state's interest is minimal until the point of fetal viability. Even then, protecting a woman's health and life takes precedence over measures taken on behalf of her fetus.

Some courts have sanctioned coercive intervention on behalf of a fetus. Nevertheless, the general rule is that courts will not interfere with a woman's pregnancy until it is clear that she has chosen to carry to term and deliver. At that point courts justify state intervention for the sake of the child to be born and do not see this intervention as conflicting with either the mother's privacy rights or with the legal position that the fetus is not a person entitled to full constitutional protection. But the law is equally clear that the state may intervene on behalf of a born child regardless of parental objections if necessary to save a child's life even when a parent's objections are rooted in religious convictions.

The intent of Congress that all newborns be tested for HIV and that test results be given to their mothers is clear in the 1996 reauthorization of the CARE Act. Provisions in the 1996 reauthorization require states to implement mandatory testing programs by the year 2000, unless a state is able to show that significant numbers of pregnant women voluntarily agree to be tested. Mandatory testing of newborns is mandatory testing of their mothers. But it is not likely that an argument that this violates a woman's privacy rights would prevail against an argument that testing is in the best interest of a child. There is sufficient legal precedent to justify mandatory testing of newborns. Justification can be found in legal provisions that permit testing of newborns for STDs, that allow for mandatory vaccination of children, and that support the general right of the state to intervene to protect the health and safety of children. Moreover, by giving voluntary testing a chance before mandating HIV-tests, the state is heading off any argument that the federal Constitution requires the least intrusive approach to accomplishing state goals, when an individual's fundamental rights are made subservient to interests that are advanced by the state. Finally, evidence indicating that early intervention on behalf of newborns is critical to their survival provides states a compelling justification for intervention.

Whether any decision that limits a woman's constitutionally protected freedoms is equitable and ethical will ultimately depend on the balance that is struck between the rights of the individual and the obligations of the state. This balancing act is reflected in the discussion of how courts justify intervention in decisions that limit a woman's reproductive choices and her right to make treatment decisions affecting her child's medical needs. But this discussion is incomplete without considering the state's obligation to provide medical services to women and children with HIV and AIDS to offset the intrusion that would result from any mandatory testing program. Whether the state will live up to its part of the bargain—to the obligation that it assumes to provide needed medical care that justifies the intrusion—remains unanswered.

CHAPTER 6

Adolescents and HIV and AIDS: Population Demographics and Prevention Strategies

INTRODUCTION

This chapter is about HIV and AIDS in adolescents and about programs that seek to educate young people about HIV and AIDS. In 1995, the United States invested $1.4 billion in AIDS-related research,[1] yet neither a vaccine to prevent transmission of the virus nor a cure for those already infected seems imminent. In lieu of a vaccine or cure, the United States and most nations of the world have chosen education as the preferred mode for preventing transmission of HIV.[2]

Educational programs advance public health goals when they: (1) inform people about modes of transmission, (2) help people to identify their own risk factors, (3) encourage people to avoid behaviors likely to transmit the virus or to take precautions to reduce the chances of viral transmission, and (4) assist HIV-positive people to identify and develop ways to avoid situations which threaten their health and compromised immune systems. However, developing and implementing educational programs regarding HIV and AIDS have been fraught with difficulties because of a concern that certain avenues of education may produce negative outcomes. For example, opponents claim that sex education or condom distribution programs may encourage young people to engage in sexual behavior they might otherwise avoid or that needle exchange and bleach distribution programs might increase illicit drug use.

This chapter begins with a description of the incidence and prevalence of HIV and AIDS among adolescents, followed by a review of research describing adolescent risk-taking behaviors (Part I). In Part II federal law on the subject of AIDS-related education is described, educational campaigns and programs directed toward adolescents and young adults are reviewed, and data describing program evaluation are presented. The chapter concludes with a summary in Part III.

PART I. THE INCIDENCE AND PREVALENCE OF HIV AND AIDS AMONG ADOLESCENTS

Data describing the incidence and prevalence of HIV and AIDS in young people distinguish pediatric HIV and AIDS, occurring in children less than 13 years of age, from HIV and AIDS in adolescents, who are 13 to 19 years of age. Children with pediatric AIDS are different from adolescents in two respects: First, 90 percent of all pediatric AIDS cases reported through the end of 1995 were caused by in utero transmission of HIV,[3] and second, HIV-disease has, until recently, shown a different pattern of progression in pediatric cases, with the majority of children dying before 2 years of age. (See chapter 4.) Adolescents become infected with HIV in the same manner as adults (see Table 6.1), and the progression of the illness in adolescents is similar to that in adults.

Because it may take ten years or more to progress from infection with HIV to the development of illnesses symptomatic of AIDS, it is assumed that most young people who develop AIDS in their 20s were infected in their adolescence. Thus to understand HIV in adolescents fully, data on young people age 20 to 29 must be considered and are included in this chapter.

Rates of HIV-Infection in Asymptomatic Adolescents

Data describing rates of HIV-infection in adolescents and young adults are available from four sources: (1) from tests conducted for Job Corps applicants;[4] (2) from tests conducted for applicants to the military;[5] (3) from blinded surveys of college students, using blood samples collected for other purposes;[6] and (4) from data compiled by the CDC for general surveillance purposes.

The data from these sources are not directly comparable. The CDC collects data nationwide through anonymous surveys using blood samples collected at sites such as STD clinics, family planning centers, youth detention centers, and hospitals. While the available information is limited to those using the services of these sites, the CDC sample is broader than that of the Job Corps, which consists of youth who participate in this federally funded program for young people who have dropped out of high school and who are socioeconomically disadvantaged. Some applicants for the military and some university students may be demographically similar to those sampled by the CDC but they differ from those in the Job Corps in that those in the military or in college must have a high school diploma or its equivalent and in neither group is access limited to people who are socioeconomically disadvantaged. The university sample differs, if in no other way, than by the choice of those sampled to pursue higher education. Also, a young person who self-identifies as homosexual would be excluded from the military, accepted by the Job Corps, and would presumably be included in data compiled by the CDC and from universities.[7]

A further difference in the data from these sources is that the time periods in which they were collected do not always overlap. Job Corps data describe applicants in the period from 1987 to 1990, military data describe those who applied between 1985 and 1989, the university sample was collected between April of 1988 and February of 1989, and the CDC data used here describe a sample on whom data were gathered between 1990 and 1992.[8]

The rate of seroprevalence among Job Corps applicants was high relative to other groups.* The overall rate of infection per 1,000 applicants was 3.6 compared to a rate of 0.34 per 1,000 for young people applying to the military, a rate of 0.3 reported by Sweeny and her colleagues using data compiled by the CDC, and a rate of 0.2 among university students.

Among applicants to the Job Corps and to the military and the sample of youth described by Sweeny et al., rates of seroprevalence among young women were higher than among young men. Rates were not higher for women in the university sample. The high rates for young women described by Sweeny and colleagues varied by data collection site with the highest rates among those in correctional facilities where the seroprevalence rate among young women was 1.2 per 1,000 compared to 0.2 per 1,000 among men. Young women age 16 to 17 who applied to the Job Corps had rates of infection of 2.3 per 1,000, compared to 1.5 per 1,000 for young men; and among those applying to the military, young women age 17 and 18 had a rate of infection of 0.25 per 1,000, compared to 0.23 per 1,000 among same-age males.

The data in Table 6.1 report method of exposure to HIV by gender and by the age categories of 13 to 19 and 20 to 24 for young people who are asymptomatic. These data describe the cumulative number of cases reported to the CDC at the end of 1995.

Unidentified or unknown risk factors account for 47 percent of cases among adolescent females (age 13 to 19) and 44 percent of cases among young women (age 20 to 24). Where a risk factor has been identified, heterosexual contact with a person at risk for or known to have HIV accounts for the greatest number and percentage of cases. Forty-four percent of adolescent females and 40 percent of young women were exposed to HIV through heterosexual contact.

For males in both age categories, same sex contact accounts for the greatest number and percentage of cases, representing 44 percent of cases

---

* In 1995, the CDC reported that the rate of seroprevalence among Job Corps applicants had remained stable since 1990. "CDC Releases HIV/AIDS Trends," *AIDS Weekly Plus* (December 11, 1995): 10.

TABLE 6.1
Number and Percentage of Asymptomatic Young Women
and Men by Method of Exposure to HIV by Age

Exposure Category	13–19		20–24*		Total
	Female	**Male**	**Female**	**Male**	**Total**
Men with men	—	636 (44%)	—	4,413 (53%)	5,049
IVDU	112 (8%)	78 (5%)	463 (14%)	495 (6%)	1,148
Blood product**	11 (<1%)	116 (8%)	33 (1%)	127 (2%)	287
Heterosexual	605 (44%)	90 (6%)	1,295 (40%)	448 (5%)	2,438
Unknown***	652 (47%)	453 (31%)	1,409 (44%)	2,225 (27%)	4,739
Men with men & IVDU	—	86 (6%)	—	560 (7%)	646
Totals	1,380	1,459	3,200	8,268	14,307

Source: U.S. Department of Health and Human Services, Public Health Service, Centers for Disease Control, *HIV Surveillance Report: U.S. HIV and AIDS Cases Reported Through December 1995* 7 (1995): 33 (hereafter CDC 1995).

*Data by gender for 25 to 29 year olds were not separately reported by the CDC.

**Combines hemophiliacs and recipients of blood transfusions.

***This category includes those with no reported history of exposure by any means of exposure listed in the CDC's hierarchy (see chapter 1). This category includes also those whose exposure history is under investigation, those who would not be interviewed, those who were lost to follow-up, and those for whom no methods of exposure could be identified after investigation. People are reclassified if information becomes available which supports placing them in an exposure category.

among adolescent males age 13 to 19 and 53 percent of cases among young men age 20 to 24. Unidentified or unknown risk factors rank second for adolescent males and young men. Regardless of gender and age, intravenous drug use is directly implicated in the transmission of HIV for a relatively small number of young people, representing at most 14 percent of cases for young women age 20 to 24 compared to 38 percent of cases among women in general (not in Table 6.1; see chapter 1).

As discussed in chapter 1, local departments of health investigate cases that are classified as risk factor unknown or unidentified and reclassify them if risk factors are identified. For women, the majority of reclassified cases are reclassified as exposure through heterosexual contact (66 percent) as are reclassified cases involving men (59 percent). If these figures hold true for the young people described here, the overwhelming majority of females between the ages of 13 and 24 who test positive for HIV-antibodies will have been exposed through heterosexual contact. For young men, same sex contact will remain the primary route of transmission.

Cases of AIDS in Adolescents

As of December 31, 1995, 2,354 adolescents and 92,928 young adults aged 20 to 29 were reported to the CDC as having AIDS (Table 6.2). AIDS among adolescents accounts for less than 1 percent of all cases of AIDS. However, as noted above, a complete picture of the magnitude of the problem of AIDS among adolescents requires that cases of AIDS in 20- to 29-year-olds be taken into account because of the latency between exposure to HIV and de-

TABLE 6.2
Number of Females and Males with AIDS by Race and Age Categories of 13 to 19 and 20 to 29 and Percentage of These Groups by Racial Categories Compared to All Cases of AIDS—As of December 1995

Race	13–19		20–29		Total and Percentage by Race: 13- to 29-Year-Olds	Number and Percentage of Cases: All Ages
	Female	Male	Female	Male		
White	151 (18%)	687 (45%)	4,173 (25%)	37,578 (49%)	42,589 (45%)	243,107 (47%)
Black	537 (65%)	503 (33%)	8,844 (52%)	23,016 (30%)	32,900 (35%)	174,714 (34%)
Hispanic	126 (15%)	311 (20%)	3,709 (22%)	14,572 (19%)	18,718 (20%)	90,031 (18%)
Asian/Pacific Islander	4 (<1%)	18 (1%)	62 (<1%)	521 (<1%)	605 (<1%)	3,555 (<1%)
American Indian/ Alaska Native	1 (<1%)	14 (<1%)	57 (<1%)	276 (<1%)	348 (<1%)	1,333 (<1%)
No Information	1 (<1%)	1 (<1%)	13 (<1%)	107 (<1%)	122 (<%)	745 (<1%)
Total	820 (35%)	1,534 (65%)	16,858 (18%)	76,070 (82%)	95,282	513,485*

Source: CDC, 1995: 16.
*1 case missing.

velopment of AIDS-defining symptoms. The combined total of 95,282 cases of AIDS reported for adolescents and young adults accounts for 19 percent of the 513,485 cases of AIDS that were reported to the CDC by the end of 1995. In early 1996, the National Institutes of Health (NIH) reported that the rate of increase of AIDS cases is greater among young people born in 1960 or later, than it is among older people.[9] Of cases reported by the end of 1994, 45 percent of adolescents and 58 percent of young people age 20 to 29 had died.[10]

The number of young women compared to young men with AIDS by race and age is reported in Table 6.2. Also reported are the cumulative number and percentage of cases by race for those 13 to 29 years of age and the total number of cases of AIDS by race regardless of age as of December 31, 1995. The racial composition for adolescents differs only slightly from all cases: White adolescents account for 45 percent of cases among adolescents, compared to whites as 47 percent of all cases; black adolescents account for 35 percent, compared to blacks as 34 percent of all cases; and Hispanic youth account for 20 percent of cases among adolescents, slightly higher then the 18 percent of all cases of AIDS among Hispanic people. Native Americans, Alaskan Natives, and people whose background is traced to Asian countries account for less then 1 percent of cases in any age group.

Two aspects of the data reported in Table 6.2 are striking. First, the percentage of cases among black women is far in excess of the percentage of cases among black men. Young black women age 13 to 19 account for 65 percent of cases in that age group and for 52 percent of cases among 20- to 29-year-olds compared to young black men who represent 33 percent of cases among 13- to 19-year-olds and 30 percent of cases of those 20 to 29 years of age. The percentages are reversed for whites, where, regardless of age, the percentage of men with AIDS is at or nearly twice that for women, and for Hispanics where the percentage of women is either less than that of men (15 percent compared to 20 percent, female to male 13- to 19-year-olds) or slightly higher (22 percent female compared to 19 percent male, 20- to 29-year-olds). The percentages among other racial or ethnic groups does not exceed 1 percent regardless of age category or gender.

The second striking aspect of these data is that young women age 13 to 19 account for 35 percent of all cases of AIDS in that age group, nearly twice the percentage of cases accounted for by women age 20 to 29, who represent 18 percent of cases in that age group and two-and-one-half times greater than the 14 percent of cases accounted for by women in all age groups. (Not in Table 6.2; see chapter 1.)** In 1994, adolescent women accounted for 43 percent of all cases reported to the CDC, up from 14 percent of cases in 1987.[11]

The data in Table 6.3 describe by gender the means by which those age 13 to 19 and 20 to 24 who have AIDS were exposed to HIV. These data are consistent with the data in Table 6.1, which describe means of exposure for young people who are infected with HIV and asymptomatic. When method of exposure is known, heterosexual contact and IVDU rank first and second for young women 13 to 24 years of age. Heterosexual contact accounts for transmission in 54 percent of cases involving young women 13 to 19 years of age and 51 percent of cases involving young women 20 to 24 years

TABLE 6.3
Number and Percentage of Cases of AIDS by Exposure Category by Age Through December 1995

Exposure Category	13–19		20–24*		Total
	Female	Male	Female	Male	
Men with men	—	501 (33%)	—	9,084 (63%)	9,585 (45%)
IVDU	132 (16%)	97 (6%)	1,430 (31%)	1,803 (13%)	3,462 (16%)
Heterosexual	440 (54%)	38 (2%)	2,338 (51%)	505 (4%)	3,321 (16%)
Blood product	69 (8%)	712 (46%)	117 (3%)	640 (4%)	1,538 (7%)
Unknown**	179 (22%)	109 (7%)	674 (15%)	802 (6%)	1,764 (8%)
Men with men and IVDU	—	77 (5%)	—	1,562 (11%)	1,639 (7%)
Total	820	1,534	4,559	14,396	21,309

Source: CDC, 1995: —
*Data by gender for 25 to 29 year olds were not reported.
**See note to Table 6.1 for an explanation of this category.

**Excluding cases of pediatric AIDS, there were 71,818 cases of AIDS among adolescent and adult women reported to the CDC through the end of 199t. This represents 14 percent of the total of 506,537 cases of AIDS among adolescents and adults reported in this time period. United States Department of Health and Human Services, Public Health Service, Centers for Disease Control and Prevention, *HIV/AIDS Surveillance Report: Year End Edition* 7 (1995). (See CDC 1995: 11–12.)

of age. IVDU is directly implicated in transmission in 16 percent of cases in the young women age 13 to 19 and in 31 percent of cases in women age 20 to 24. No risk factor was reported for 22 percent and 15 percent of 13- to 19-year-olds and 20- to 24-year-olds, respectively. As discussed above, the percentage of cases attributable to heterosexual contact may increase through investigation and reclassification of cases listed as unknown risk factor.

Forty-six percent of AIDS cases among adolescent males are attributed to exposure through contaminated blood products. The high percentage of cases attributed to this method of exposure (compared to 8 percent of cases among asymptomatic adolescent males) is no doubt due to a high percentage of young male hemophiliacs who received contaminated blood products before 1985 when testing of blood products became routine. Sexual contact between men ranks second for young men age 13 to 19 and first for young men age 20 to 24, where it accounts for 63 percent of cases. The percentage of cases attributable to IVDU for males 13 to 24 years of age is markedly less than for females (16 percent female and 6 percent male, 13- to 19-year-olds; 31 percent female and 13 percent male, 20- to 24-year-olds).

Adolescent Risk-Taking Behavior and HIV

With the exception of 13- to 19-year-old males who were exposed to HIV through contaminated blood products, sexual activity is the primary route of exposure for the young women and men described in this chapter. The role played by sexual contact in exposing young people to HIV will likely be greater than shown in the preceding tables when cases are reclassified from "unknown" to known routes of transmission, since reclassification results in identifying sexual contact in a majority of cases.

A high percentage of adolescents are sexually active. Approximately 40 percent of 9th graders; 48 percent of 10th graders, 57 percent of 11th graders, and 72 percent of 12th graders report having had intercourse, according to data reported by the CDC (1992), and 50 percent of all new HIV-infections occur in people under the age of 25.[12] The Committee on Adolescence of the American Academy of Pediatrics estimates that one-half of all adolescents are sexually active by age 17. Multiple partners are not unusual, with 19 percent of high school students reporting four or more partners.[13] Gaiter and Berman (1994) report that approximately 25 percent of young women age 18 and 19 have had six or more sexual partners, with approximately 20 percent of boys of the same age reporting six to ten partners.[14]

Condom use among adolescents is increasing but consistent use of condoms is not the norm. Data compiled by the CDC in its Youth Risk Behavior Surveys describe the sexual behavior of public and private high school students in the fifty states and the District of Columbia. They show that the percentage of students who report using condoms at their last intercourse increased significantly from 46 percent in 1991 to 53 percent in 1993. However, analyzed by subgroups, the data show significant increases are sustained only for young women (38 percent reporting condom use in

1991 compared to 46 percent in 1993) and for blacks (48 percent in 1991 compared to 57 percent in 1993).[15] However, young women whose first sexual experience is with an "older" male (where older is defined as an age difference of 3 to 21 years) may be at greater risk than young women with same age partners because older men are less likely to use condoms and they are more likely than same age men to be HIV-infected because of a more "varied" sexual history.[16]

Using data from the National Survey of Adolescent Males, Sonenstein, Pleck, and Ku (1995) report that between 1979 and 1988 condom use among sexually experienced males more than doubled from a 1979 low of 21 percent to close to 58 percent in 1988.[17] However, consistent use of condoms is low, with 35 percent of young men reporting condom use at each intercourse; and use of condoms peaked with no increase in reported use as shown in a follow-up study conducted by Sonenstein et al., in 1991. Black youth are more likely than white or Hispanic youth to use condoms at their most recent intercourse but less likely than others to use condoms at their first intercourse. For all racial groups, condom use declines with age, from a high of 52 percent of youth age 17-1/2 to 19 years reporting condom use, dropping to 39 percent among 20- to 24-year-olds and to 33 percent among those 25 to 29 years of age. As age increases, young men rely on their female partners to use protection.

A number of factors affect condom use. These include belief systems and number of partners. As is the case with older women, some teens display an "optimism bias" or a general belief that they are at low risk for contracting HIV.[18] Others believe that risk is low if their partners appear healthy, if they exercise care in selection of partners, or because they are in monogamous relationships and believe that their partners are faithful. Young gay men have reported a lack of support from peers for practicing safer sex, and some young women fail to take account of their own and their partners' past relationships and behaviors, reinforcing their belief that they have little cause for concern.[19] Lack of knowledge of their partners' past sexual and drug using history was cited as one factor creating risk of HIV-infection for pregnant Hispanic adolescents whose risk was assessed at a prenatal care clinic in New York City.[20]

Young people who believe that condom use will reduce their chances of contracting HIV are more than twice as likely to use them as their peers who do not hold this belief,[21] but concern about contracting HIV decreases the longer younger people remain sexually active.[22] Thus it is not surprising to learn that condom use decreases as the number of partners increases, with 50 percent of students in grades 7 through 9 with one partner reporting condom use compared to 27 percent with six or more partners.[23] Five hundred seventy-one women, age 18 to 23, enrolled at the University of Michigan, report an increase in risky behaviors as the number of sex partners increases. Sixty-four percent of the women report condom use at their first intercourse but the percentage drops to 49 percentage with their fifth or sixth partner.[24]

The likelihood of condom use is reduced if young men believe that they will be embarrassed when purchasing or using them or that their pleasure will be reduced. Increased use of condoms is associated with a normative belief that men are responsible for using contraception, when they do not associate a woman's pregnancy with their own sense of masculinity; and when they believe that the women with whom they have sexual relations will appreciate their use.[25]

The failure to use condoms consistently coupled with an "immature" biological system puts adolescents at greater risk than adults of contracting sexually transmitted diseases (STDs). The American Academy of Pediatrics (1994) reports that sexually active adolescents have the highest rates of STDs such as gonorrhea, syphilis, and pelvic inflammatory disease than any age group and account for one-third of the STDs reported annually.[26] While in high school, one out of every four adolescents contracts an STD.[27] Between 1960 and 1988, the gonorrhea infection rate for 15- to 19-year-olds increased 170 percent,[28] although by 1993, the trend was to reduced rates of gonorrhea among 15- to 19-year-old females and males.[29]

In Los Angeles, Kipke and her colleagues (1995)[30] interviewed 409 "street youths" recruited from shelters, drop-in settings, and street sites where youth "hang-out." Their sample included young people age 13 to 23, 26 percent of whom were female, with black, Latino, and white youth representing 22 percent, 15 percent, and 52 percent, respectively, and Asian and Native American youth representing 2 percent and 6 percent of those interviewed. The majority of the sample was homeless (72 percent) and heterosexual (62 percent) with 17 percent describing themselves as bisexual and 22 percent as homosexual.

Seventy percent of those interviewed reported that they are sexually active and 43 percent report engaging in "survival sex" (e.g., the exchange of sex for money, food, shelter, or drugs), which exceeds the 26 percent to 30 percent of youth whom others report exchanging sex for survival needs.[31]

In the thirty days preceding the interviews, 52 percent of the young people said that they had one sexual partner, 24 percent reported two to five partners, and 24 percent reported five or more partners. In this respect, these young people are not very different from their peers, and like their peers, those in a relationship, regardless of gender, race, or homeless status, are less likely to use condoms with their primary partners. Young people having sex outside of primary relationships were significantly more likely than those whose sexual activity was confined to a primary relationship to report having been infected with an STD; to have been high on drugs or alcohol at their last sexual encounter; and not to have used a condom during oral, vaginal, and anal intercourse. Young people who report carrying condoms are the group most likely to use them.

PART II. AIDS EDUCATION PROGRAMS

Education about HIV and AIDS is provided in a variety of forms, including: (1) media campaigns directed toward the general public, (2) information provided in response to queries from individuals who call hotlines,

(3) community outreach programs that target specific populations, such as at-risk youth, (4) one-on-one counseling that occurs in the context of HIV-testing and partner notification programs, (5) needle exchange and bleach distribution programs, and (6) lectures and classroom-based instruction. Education is carried out in diverse settings, such as youth centers, public health clinics, physicians' offices, the workplace, educational institutions, juvenile correctional facilities, and on the streets where outreach programs send staff to work with youth and others who do not frequent institutional settings.

Regardless of the medium or the setting, the goal of AIDS-related education is to stem the spread of HIV by causing people not to engage in behaviors implicated in its transmission or by causing people to engage in practices that reduce or eliminate the likelihood of transmission.

The following topics are reviewed next. First, the role of the federal government in funding education programs and in setting rules for use of federal funds is explored and followed by a discussion of the content of education programs for adolescents. Evaluation of education programs is the last topic covered in this section.

Federal Funding and Federal Rules for AIDS Education

Federal funds are available to the states to establish educational programs to prevent or reduce exposure to or transmission of HIV.[32] Funds may be used to develop curriculum materials, to train those who will become "AIDS-educators," to operate education programs for school-aged children, and to conduct public information programs and "activities" related to prevention and diagnosis,[33] including demonstration projects to achieve preventive and diagnostic purposes. Federal law permits the CDC to establish a clearinghouse to provide information regarding AIDS to government officials and the public and mandates that a toll-free number be established, operated, and maintained on a round-the-clock basis to provide information and respond to inquiries from the general public.

Federal law provides guidance for the content of educational programs by directing that (1) educational materials must stress the harmful effects of "promiscuous" sexual activity; stress the positive effects of abstinence, with the condition that funds may not be used to provide education or information that directly promotes or encourages homosexual or heterosexual sexual activity;[34] (2) accurate information is important, but use of material that is "obscene" is forbidden and public service announcements and advertisements must "warn" individuals about activities which place them at risk of infection; and (3) funds may not be used to supply hypodermic needles or syringes for illegal drug use unless the Surgeon General finds needle exchange programs to be effective in reducing drug abuse and transmission of HIV.[35]

The involvement of affected communities in planning educational programs is stressed in federal law. This requirement is found in provisions mandating that programs directed to school-aged children be planned in consultation with local school boards,[36] in provisions for involvement in program planning by community groups, organizations, and individuals toward whom prevention and education efforts are directed, and in provisions for ongoing involvement between recipients of federal monies and members of affected populations and with health care providers.[37]

Educational Programs Directed Toward Adolescents

While adolescents may receive educational messages through any medium, there has been a special emphasis on reaching young people through school-based programs and through outreach programs that target youth in homeless shelters, community centers, gay and lesbian youth centers, and other organizations that serve young people.

AIDS education should begin in kindergarten and continue throughout the school years, according to the CDC, the American Academy of Pediatrics, and the Surgeon General.[38] In 1994, the latest year for which data are available, approximately three-quarters of the states required HIV and AIDS prevention education within the health and education curriculum.[39] All states provide the option for parents to excuse their children from instruction dealing with this subject matter. States that do not require education about HIV and AIDS recommend it.[40] States requiring HIV-prevention education require in-service training for those who teach this subject. However, findings from the 1994 School Health Policies and Programs Study conducted by the CDC in which a nationally representative sample of 502 school districts was surveyed, inform us that only one-third of teachers had received training in the two years preceding the survey, which raises questions about whether students are receiving information describing new methods of preventing HIV-transmission.[41]

Backstrom and Robins (1996) surveyed state legislators who chaired health committees and the chief health officers of all states. Approximately 97 percent of legislative health committee chairs and 100 percent of health officers agreed that AIDS education should be required in public school. However, only 43 percent of legislators and 58 percent of health officers thought that their states should publish explicit sex education material.[42]

In addition to educational programs that deal with HIV and AIDS, approximately 400 high schools and junior high schools operate school-based, health service clinics whose work may contribute to the overall effort to educate young people. The majority of clinics offer family planning services, slightly more than 25 percent provide prescriptions for birth control pills, but less then 20 percent provide condoms.[43]

Program Content   Contentious issues in the area of education regarding HIV and AIDS center around two questions: First, "What should the content of educational programs and messages be?" and second, "Should schools be permitted to distribute condoms to young people?" Parents have sued school districts over these matters. Courts have found that (1) parents may choose whether or not their children will attend sex education classes but do not have a constitutionally protected right to dictate the contents of an AIDS education curriculum;[44] (2) state law may trump parental objections to an AIDS education program, even when the parents' objections are based on First Amendment religious grounds, if the state is able to demonstrate a compelling interest in mandating a particular education program;[45] (3) a local school board cannot dictate that each class session must devote more time to the subject of abstinence than to other ways of avoiding HIV-infection;[46] and (4) a school district may not dispense condoms to unemancipated minors without parental consent or a provision allowing parents to opt out of a condom distribution program.[47] The Parental Rights and Responsibilities Act of 1995, introduced in Congress in 1995, would make it difficult for a state to "interfere with or usurp" parents' rights to control their child's upbringing, including matters that pertain to education and health care of their child except under very narrowly defined circumstances.[48]

Concern about the content of AIDS education messages is not confined to school-based programs but is directed also to the form and content of public information campaigns. In 1994, a federal district court in Massachusetts held that protecting children from advertisements in subway and trolley cars that used "witty sexual innuendos in promoting use of condoms" to prevent the spread of HIV was not sufficiently compelling to justify the limitation on speech that rejection of these ads would involve.[49]

Efforts to restrict the content of AIDS information campaigns to material not offensive to the general public spurred the Gay Men's Health Crisis, Inc. (GMHC), a social service organization in New York City that assists people with HIV and AIDS, to sue the CDC. GMHC alleged that the CDC exceeded its statutory authority when it limited grants for education programs to applicants whose material was not offensive, because the statute proscribed grants only if material was obscene.[50] A federal district court agreed with the GMHC. Congress had expressed its intent that the standard used to evaluate material be an obscenity standard, thus the CDC had exceeded its authority by limiting grants to material that was not offensive. The court found the offensive standard so vague as to provide little if any guidance for people charged with designing educational materials and an actual hindrance to the development of educational materials.

In 1992, an oversight hearing was held by members of Congress who sought answers to the question "Have political considerations influenced policy decisions related to HIV and AIDS prevention programs?"[51] In expressing their dissatisfaction with AIDS education programs, some members of Congress addressed: (1) matters of form by suggesting that failure to utilize television effectively deprives some people of the benefits of educational messages, since hotlines are not accessible to people without telephones and print media are of little or no use to the estimated 70 million Americans who read poorly or not at all; (2) matters of content by charging that the public information campaign of the United States Department of Health and Human Services was "tame" and its messages unclear and ambiguous, informing people that they are at risk from a series of unnamed behaviors;

and (3) matters of availability by citing the failure to provide condoms to teenagers as an option in a comprehensive public health program. Criticism was leveled at the Department of Health and Human Services whose efforts were said to be ineffectual, guided "by judgments of the worth of individuals, by homophobia, and by active contempt for the people most affected by the disease," rather than by a public health agenda which should focus on efforts to present information to guide prevention and behavior change.

Public education campaigns have been criticized for failure to present a candid approach to prevention and for missing the chance to reach great numbers of people with AIDS prevention messages despite data showing that multimedia educational campaigns increase condom use.[52] Singled out for criticism was the CDC's "America Responds to AIDS" campaign, which some members of Congress faulted because the campaign, which made use of print, radio, and television advertisements, failed to make use of ads that had been developed to explain the role of condoms in preventing HIV-transmission and that encouraged condom use. There were no ads that clearly showed the risks of having unprotected sex or sharing dirty needles; and in the view of some representatives the ads contained no prevention messages.[53]

In November 1995, the Department of Health and Human Services announced a new marketing campaign aimed at young people age 18 to 25. Campaign ads were to show young adults who would speak candidly about their lives and who would model protective behaviors and skills, including abstinence and consistent condom use.[54]

Much of the concern regarding HIV and AIDS curricula comes down to a debate about whether educational materials should focus strictly on abstinence or whether knowledge- and skills-based instruction should be included. Concern about curriculum materials that deal with knowledge and skills focus attention on possible negative outcomes, such as hastening the onset of intercourse or increasing the frequency of sexual activity. Available data do not support these concerns. Kirby and his colleagues (1994) reviewed the professional literature from which they identified twenty-three investigations of school-based programs. Programs that cover abstinence, contraception, pregnancy, sexually transmitted diseases, and HIV and AIDS do not increase sexual activity.

> National surveys provide consistent evidence that the programs . . . did not hasten intercourse when they were implemented among older students; [although these studies] provide less consistent evidence about their impact among younger students. [However] . . . studies of specific programs that included instruction on contraception consistently indicated that none of these programs hastened the onset of intercourse. Indeed, all of them either delayed the onset of intercourse or had no effect upon the initiation of intercourse . . . of . . . studies that examined program impact upon frequency of intercourse, none found significant increases in frequency of intercourse, and one found a significant decrease among the relatively small proportion of youths who initiated intercourse after program implementation.[55]

Further confirmation for the proposition that specific and detailed information does not hasten or increase sexual activity comes from Western Europe. Researchers report that a Swiss marketing effort to educate young people about condom use did not increase sexual activity among young people even though the program used very explicit material.[56]

Those who argue for inclusion of knowledge- and skills-based materials take as their starting point the suggestion that effective educational programs must target group-specific needs[57] and they must provide information regarding skills needed to reduce risk, for example, skills for negotiating with a partner for use of condoms.[58] A program that focuses on abstinence takes an all-or-nothing approach where only one educational outcome is valued and leaves vulnerable young people whose behavior does not conform and who may not have access to information about and ways to reduce the specific risks they confront.[59]

Criticism of abstinence-only programs has been consistent. In 1986, Dr. C. Everett Koop, then the United States Surgeon General, said that young people were not receiving vital information regarding sex, sexual practices, and homosexuality and that as a consequence their health and well-being were being jeopardized.[60]

In its 1993 report *Preventing HIV/AIDS in Adolescents*, the National Commission on AIDS reported that only three states, Massachusetts, South Carolina, and New Jersey, made use of curriculum materials that addressed adequately the "cognitive, affective, and skills domains" of HIV-prevention. The report said that educational programs "lack instruction about sexual responsibility and decision making," and they fail to discuss human sexuality in a positive framework. Program instruction on condom use is inadequate and there is an overemphasis on abstinence, the end result of which is that there is no talk of behaviors that define safer sex and there is no discussion of sexual orientation.

In 1994, Blair and Hein, in addition to echoing concerns expressed by the National Commission, reported that programs utilize outdated instructional material because they do not monitor themselves.[61] They found that 90 percent of the states with HIV and AIDS curricula have guidelines for the presentation of information on abstinence, but few have guidelines that address and mandate frank discussion of risk behaviors and methods of transmission of HIV.

In 1994, Klein and her colleagues, discussing sex education curricula, report that abstinence-only curricula contain significant gaps in information and that they are medically inaccurate.[62] They concluded that focusing exclusively on abstinence as the only appropriate choice for young people was "sexist, homophobic, and [reflected] anti-choice biases." According to Klein et al., abstinence-based curricula fail to present a positive view of human sexuality, they do not contain content on safer sex, they set forth the view that women bear total responsibility for regulating sexual behavior because males are "unable to control their sexual impulses," and they assume that all students are heterosexual.

Analysis of data from the CDC's Prevention of HIV in Women and Infants Demonstration Project highights the importance of providing explicit information on effective ways to prevent disease transmission. One hundred seventy-four women age 15 to 34 were asked questions to determine what they knew about the effectiveness of different approaches to preventing the transmission of STDs. Approximately 30 percent of the women thought that the use of birth control pills, surgical sterilization, and devices such as Norplant protected them from STDs.[63]

In 1996, ten years after Dr. Koop issued his warning that the health of young people was in jeopardy due to lack of information, the White House Office of National AIDS Policy, in its report to the president, said that school-based programs overemphasized abstinence and failed to provide enough information to young people on how to prevent HIV-infection and its spread. The report continued by noting that accurate information on modes of transmission should be included in school-based curricula, which should provide information on assessment of personal risk of infection and skills training. In some school districts, educational policies preclude discussion of subjects such as intercourse, homosexuality and bisexuality, and condom use. Because the content of some curriculum materials is homophobic in its design and implementation, many gay and bisexual adolescents are deprived of the information they need to protect themselves.[64]

Evaluation of HIV/AIDS Education Programs

Whether AIDS and HIV educational programs are effective in reducing or eliminating behaviors likely to result in transmission of the virus is addressed in this section as is the question "To the extent that programs report success, what factors are associated with their success?" Before beginning, a caveat regarding the limitations of reported evaluations is in order.

By their nature, questions regarding the effects of risk reduction efforts focus on the most intimate of behaviors, causing researchers to rely on self-report measures as indicators of program outcomes. Stanton and colleagues (1996)[65] suggest that self-report data that are gathered in longitudinal studies can be presumed more reliable than data compiled only once, if the contents of a follow-up report confirm information earlier provided. To question the veracity of self-reports when follow-up data are stable in relation to baseline data, it would be necessary to hypothesize not only that young people are concocting their stories but that they remember their fabrications in the months between baseline and follow-up.

Other measures, changes in rates of STDs among gay men, for example, reflect significant behavioral change. When the temporal relationship between STD reduction and the onset of the HIV-epidemic is considered, reason dictates that there is a connection between behavior change and information regarding routes of HIV-transmission. Nevertheless, conclusions about the efficacy of any particular educational intervention cannot be drawn. For example, because change occurred in gay men who were aware of their HIV-status as well as in gay men who were not aware, such change cannot be linked to educational messages received when individuals present themselves for counseling and testing for HIV.[66]

The literature on evaluation of educational programs links program efficacy to three factors: first, whether the program provides information only or includes also a skills-based component; second, the duration of an educational program; and last, whether the message is targeted to group-specific needs.

Information and Skills   There are data to show that information campaigns directed at the general public and at young people in school settings yield gains in knowledge regarding routes of transmission of HIV,[67] even among elementary school children,[68] and that programs that provide sexually explicit information before adolescents become sexually active have a greater impact on behavior than do programs begun after young people become sexually active.[69] There is little support for the proposition that merely providing information—without more skills development, for example—will result in behavior change.[70] The Congressional Office of Information Technology, from its assessment of AIDS education programs, concluded that an inclusive educational program must provide "information, exploration of values and attitudes, skills building, and access to services, including condom availability."[71]

Likewise, Holtgrave et al. (1995),[72] from their review of HIV-prevention programs, concluded that those offered in school settings that were most likely to delay the start of or reduce the likelihood that young people will engage in high-risk behavior: (1) should provide information on how to avoid becoming infected and how to avoid spreading infection; (2) should help young people develop skills to avoid, cope with, or leave high-risk situations; and (3) should motivate students "through peer presentations and support groups to use their newly acquired, HIV-relevant knowledge and skills."[73]

In a controlled investigation, Walter and Vaughan (1993)[74] assigned 1,201 9th through 11th grade students from four academic schools in New York City to an intervention ($n = 667$) and a comparison ($n = 534$) condition. Approximately 59 percent of the students were female; 37 percent were black, 35 percent Hispanic, and 28 percent "other" (mostly non-Hispanic white or Asian). The sample was divided almost evenly between 9th and 11th graders (48 and 52 percent, respectively). The mean age of the students was 15.7 years, with a range of 12 to 20 years. Students in the intervention group were exposed to six one-hour class sessions with content concerning methods of transmission, ways to assess one's own risk of infection, values clarification, and training in negotiation skills to delay the onset of intercourse, to negotiate condom use, to obtain condoms, and to use them correctly. Outcomes, evaluated at a three-month follow-up with information based on self-report, showed that the intervention had a significant and favorable but modest impact on involvement in sexual intercourse with high-risk partners, monogamy, and the use of condoms. There was no increase in students reporting sexual abstinence. Outcomes did not vary significantly by school or by any demographic characteristic of the students.

Stanton and colleagues (1996) studied the use of various methods of contraception by 383 African-American youth age 9 through 15, approximately 44 percent of whom were young women. All of the young people were participants in a randomized controlled trial of an AIDS prevention education program which sought to increase the use of condoms relative to other less effective methods of contraception for reducing the spread of HIV. Two hundred six youths were assigned to the intervention program, which met once each week for eight weeks, and 177 to a control group. Increased use of condoms was associated with receipt of AIDS education.[75]

An evaluation of an AIDS education program in which 157 black male teenagers in a Philadelphia school received five hours of education likewise reported favorable outcomes, including an increase in knowledge regarding HIV and consistency of condom use, but as with the Walter and Vaughn study, outcomes were not favorable for sexual abstinence. The conclusion that curricula dealing with abstinence neither delay nor reduce the frequency of intercourse is borne out by others.[76]

Further evidence of the importance of skills development in reducing risk taking behaviors comes from a study conducted by DiClemente and Wingood (1995).[77] One hundred twenty-eight African-American women, age 18 to 29, who did not have a history of IVDU and who had not used crack cocaine in the 3 months prior to the study, were randomly assigned to a social skills intervention group ($n = 53$), an HIV-education condition ($n = 35$), or a "delayed HIV-education" group ($n = 40$). The women in the social skills intervention group were exposed to five educational sessions that were conducted by two African-American peer educators. In addition to providing information about HIV and its transmission, sessions emphasized the importance of gender and ethnic pride, consistent condom use, and strategies that women could use to manage risky sexual situations. Training included also engaging in problem-solving exercises where the women applied their newly acquired skills.

Based on self-report at a three-month follow-up, the women in the social skills intervention group, compared to women in the HIV-education group (who were exposed to a two-hour risk-reduction lecture) and those in the "delayed HIV-education" group (for whom there was no intervention until they had completed follow-up interviews at the end of three months), were twice as likely to demonstrate consistent condom use. In addition to limits imposed by self-report data, approximately 22 percent of subjects were lost at follow-up; however, the percentage of participants unavailable for follow-up did not differ across the treatment conditions.

From their review of the effectiveness of school-based programs in reducing risk taking behaviors, Kirby and his colleagues report that programs that postponed the onset of intercourse, increased condom use or use of other types of contraception, or decreased sexual risk taking behavior had six characteristics in common:

> (a) theoretical grounding in social learning or social influence theories, (b) a narrow focus on reducing specific sexual risk-taking behaviors, (c) experiential activities to convey the information on the risks of unprotected sex and how to avoid those risks and to personalize that information, (d) instruction on social influences and pressures, (e) reinforcement of individual values and group norms against unprotected sex that are age and experience appropriate, and (f) activities to increase relevant skills and confidence in those skills.

Program Duration   There is evidence that program duration has an effect on behavior change and that intervention must be sustained if long-term behavior change is to be maintained.[78] HIV-prevention programs in school-based settings lasting twenty to twenty-five hours influence students to delay or reduce risk taking behaviors according to Holtgrave et al.,[79] and information reported by Kirby and others (1991) indicates that reduction in behaviors creating risk in a group of 145 black and Hispanic pregnant teens in New York were observed only after fifteen hours of "intensive individualized intervention."[80]

The fact that counseling in conjunction with testing for HIV is of brief duration may account for the fact that there is little evidence to show that counseling reduces risk taking behaviors.[81] As earlier noted, behavior change among gay men, reflected in reduced incidence of STDs, cannot be linked to testing-associated counseling because incidence decreased among men regardless of whether they knew their HIV-status.

Among heterosexuals, Higgins reports that only among couples where one partner is HIV-positive is there a clear benefit from counseling measured in reductions in risk taking behavior.[82] But Johnson's (1994) report of data from Europe is not consistent with the data reported by Higgins. Of heterosexual couples who received repeated counseling, where one partner was HIV-positive, nearly 50 percent continued to practice unprotected sex throughout a twenty-month follow-up period. Rates of seroconversion were high among couples whose use of condoms was inconsistent with a zero rate of conversion for couples whose use of condoms was consistent.[83]

Choi and Coates (1994) reviewed seventy-seven published studies of HIV-education programs that were implemented worldwide during the past ten years. The reviewed programs that were directed toward a variety of groups, including adolescents, young adults, IVDUs, and gay or bisexual men, were conducted in schools and clinics, and focused on units of different size including the individual, the group, the organization, and the community. Approximately 26 percent of the studies reported long-term behavior change. Maintenance of behavior change was associated with interventions that were continuous and repetitive.[84]

Targeting Groups and Realistic Messages   To suggest that HIV and AIDS educational programs should be targeted at specific groups may seem obvious given the language and cultural diversity of the United States, the variety of groups to be reached whose differences are not based on language or cultural issues, and the probability that different media will have to be utilized if all groups are to be reached. Yet the involvement of affected communities in planning educational programs has not been the norm and was not required by federal policy until the mid-1990s.

In 1992, members of a Congressional committee concluded, among other things, that education messages funded by the federal government should be targeted at specific audiences and should include specific information directed to the audience the message is meant to reach.[85] In 1993, the National Commission on AIDS stressed the importance of developing educational programs that took account of language and cultural difference.[86] However, not until 1994 did the CDC require health departments in the states that administer HIV-prevention programs to convene community councils with members from affected groups to participate in the planning of educational programs.[87]

One of the conclusions reached by Holtgrave and his colleagues from their review of the effectiveness of HIV-prevention programs is that successful programs should be community-level interventions that: (1) are tailored to the audience, sensitive to its culture, and responsive to differences in age, education, gender, geography, sexual orientation, and racial and ethnic difference, as well as to differences in values, beliefs, and norms; (2) take account of developmental differences, e.g., messages designed for junior high school students will probably be rejected by high school students; and (3) use specific and appropriate language that goes beyond simply delivering messages in the language spoken by the audience.[88] Programs will be rejected, they concluded, and deemed "inappropriate, superfluous, and a waste of scarce resources" if they fail to address the prevention needs of the community served.

There is support for the suggestion that HIV-prevention messages should be delivered by members of affected communities and that their content should be appropriate and realistic to the particular lives of those within these communities. DiClemente and Wingood (1995) posit that the effectiveness of their AIDS education program that targeted African-American women may have been due to the use of African-American peer educators.[89] The value of peer educators is supported by the work of Kelly and his colleagues. To reach gay men in small communities they recruited "popular" gay men whom they trained in HIV-prevention methods and methods of message delivery. The men were asked to go back to their communities with the messages and to share the information they had acquired with male patrons of gay bars. Emphasis in the education messages was on behavior change, and the peer educators provided support for modifying sexual risk taking conduct. Changes in behavior were evaluated from responses to pre- and postintervention surveys. There was a 24% decrease from baseline in the "mean percentage of gay men reporting unprotected anal intercourse during the preceding two months . . . with self-reported use of condoms for all anal intercourse . . . increas[ing] by 15 percent."[90] The number of gay men reporting more than one sex partner decreased by 6 percent.[91]

Preliminary analysis of data from a project in Seattle, where female sex workers were recruited to act as peer counselors, shows that the peer counselors were successful in persuading other women not to engage in risky behaviors.[92]

Stevenson and Davis (1994) randomly assigned 121 African-American teenagers to two intervention groups. The first was exposed to a "culturally similar video" (CSV) and the second to a "culturally dissimilar video" (CDV).[93] There was significant improvement in knowledge regarding HIV for the CSV group compared to the CDV group, although there was no group difference in beliefs about prevention. The authors report that the teens in both groups were critical of both the CSV and CDV videos to the extent that neither was wholly realistic. The young people stated that the videos would have a greater impact if they featured someone "living, struggling, and then dying from AIDS."[94]

Education Programs Targeted at Intravenous Drug Users

Earlier in this chapter, I said that IVDU is directly implicated in the transmission of HIV in a relatively small number of cases involving young people under the age of 19. As age increases so does the role of IVDU in transmitting HIV. The percentage of women directly affected by IVDU increases from a low of 16 percent for young women age 13 to 19 to 31 percent for women age 20 to 24 and to 38 percent for women regardless of age. IVDU is directly implicated in a smaller percentage of cases involving young men age 13 to 24. IVDU accounts for 13 percent of cases among men age 20 to 24 compared to 31 percent of cases for women in the same age category.

For IVDUs and homeless youth, outreach programs that provide services in the communities where young people are found may be the only way of getting across educational messages. After a discussion of needle exchange and bleach distribution programs, we will look at the interventions used by several community-based educational programs and their evaluations.

The first needle exchange program (NEP) was established in 1988 in Tacoma, Washington. Since that time, sixty-eight NEPs have been implemented in forty-six cities in twenty-one states.[95] Thirty-three programs are legal (55 percent). The states in which they operate do not require a prescription to purchase a hypodermic syringe or a prescription requirement was waived for the NEP. Nineteen are illegal (32 percent) but tolerated. The state has a prescription-purchase law, but the NEP is formally supported or approved by elected officials. Eight NEPs operate "underground" (13 percent) because they have no legal sanction.

In 1995, the North America Syringe Exchange Network in collaboration with the U. S. Conference of Mayors and Beth Israel Hospital in New

York conducted a survey of NEPs. Sixty of the sixty-eight programs responded. In addition to exchanging needles, NEPs provide (1) condoms ($n =$ 45); (2) HIV-testing and counseling ($n = 23$); (3) tuberculosis testing ($n =$ 12); and (4) primary health care ($n = 10$). Most programs (85 percent) counsel the use of medicinal alcohol to sterilize the injection site; the use of new sterile needles for each injection; the avoidance of used syringes; the use of clean or sterile water to prepare drugs for injection; and the return of used syringes to the NEP for disposal.

In 1995, the National Academy of Sciences reported the results of their review of studies that assessed the impact of NEPs and bleach distribution programs on HIV-transmission.[96] Despite methodological problems in studying NEPs (e.g., lack of random assignment because of technical and ethical problems, high rates of attrition, and self-report bias), the authors concluded that the cumulative weight of the evidence from all studies was a reasonable proxy for methodological rigor.[97]

The academy's review does not contain direct evidence that NEPs reduce the incidence of HIV-infection although the results of a study conducted in New York City and reported in late 1996 suggest that the rate of HIV-infection among partipants in a needle exchange program was significantly less than the rate of infection among nonparticipants.[98] Rather, the academy reviewer reasoned to the conclusion that NEPs reduce the incidence of HIV-infection from data showing that the proportion of contaminated to noncontaminated needles that are in circulation is reduced by needle exchange programs. By increasing the availability of sterile injection equipment and by reducing the availability of contaminated equipment, an important risk factor for transmitting HIV is eliminated from the environment. Support for this inference is found in data showing that needle exchange among a similar population reduced the spread of Hepatitis B and Hepatitis C virus.[99]

Moreover, the academy concluded that there is no "credible" evidence to support the suggestion that NEPs increase drug use among program participants. Nor is there evidence that the availability of sterile injection equipment increases the number of new injection drug users.[100]

In addition to NEPs, community-based outreach programs endeavor to provide education and services to people who are not reached through formal educational programs, including homeless youth and IVDUs.

The CDC's AIDS Community Demonstration Projects (CDPs)[101] target: (1) high-risk youth, defined as those who are not living at home and who are not in school; (2) IVDUs' female sex partners; (3) female prostitutes; (4) IVDUs who are not in treatment programs; and (5) men who have sex with men but who do not identify themselves as gay. Community members provide education by using real stories of successful behavior change by one or more members of the targeted community. The stories are "translated" into HIV-prevention messages. Preliminary analysis shows more routine use of bleach to clean injection equipment and more use of condoms during sexual intercourse by those exposed to the information about prevention than by those not exposed.

The National Institute on Drug Abuse supports the National AIDS Demonstration Research projects (NADR) that serve IVDUs who are not in drug-treatment programs.[102] At twenty-eight sites, participants were randomly assigned to standard or enhanced AIDS education and counseling sessions. Outcomes were reported at a six-month follow-up. Outreach efforts were evaluated for 13,475 IVDUs and their 6,216 sex partners.

Those in the standard intervention group received: (1) information about condoms as well as the distribution of condoms and bleach to clean needles; (2) a single session where individuals were counseled regarding transmission of HIV and given information about strategies to avoid exposure; and (3) an HIV-antibody test including posttest counseling for those who chose to be tested. Enhanced counseling included also (4) individual and group counseling on behavior change strategies, (5) couples counseling; (6) cognitive skills training, (7) social skills training, and (8) networking with peers. Differences between groups were statistically significant with the enhanced intervention group demonstrating reductions in the frequency with which they injected drugs, borrowed injection equipment, used noninjected drugs, and in the number of sex partners.[103]

A different intervention strategy was employed by NADR projects carried out at three sites in Chicago.[104] In the Chicago program, outreach workers (1) are former IVDUs; (2) work with networks of IVDUs, not with individuals; (3) provide general education information and assist network members in assessing their own risk for infection; (4) offer more than one option for managing identified risks by offering (a) access to treatment to stop IVDU, (b) strategies to reduce the sharing of injection equipment, (c) instruction on use of bleach to clean equipment, and (d) materials that can be used to clean needles and syringes and (5) reinforce teaching through repeated encounters with network members.

The projects report positive outcome measured by the number of seroconversions among a population of 641 HIV-negative IVDUs followed over four years. Without the outreach program, it was estimated that 172 of these IVDUs would seroconvert. The actual number of new infections was ninety. The percentage of IVDUs engaging in risky drug behaviors decreased from 100 percent to 14 percent during the study period.

PART IV. SUMMARY AND CONCLUSION

At the end of 1995, young people who are presumed to have contracted AIDS in their adolescence accounted for approximately 19 percent of cases of AIDS in the United States. Adolescent women age 13 to 19 account for 35 percent of AIDS cases among all 13- to 19-year-olds, nearly double the 18 percent of cases among young women age 20 to 29. The majority of cases of AIDS among young women age 13 to 19 and 20 to 29 occur among black women, who account for 65 percent of cases for those 13 to 19 years of age and 52 percent of cases for those 20 to 29 years of age. Blacks are the only racial group where the percentage of women with AIDS is significantly greater than the percentage of cases among males.

Approximately 50 percent of adolescents are sexually active by age 17, and 19 percent of high school students report having multiple sex partners. Condom use among adolescents is increasing, but condoms are used inconsistently and their use decreases as age and number of partners increase. Use of condoms by young people is affected also by a mix of myth and misconception. The myth of invulnerability, not uncommon to young people, mixes with the belief that risk is reduced if one chooses partners who appear healthy and if one believes their relationship to be monogamous and their partner faithful. Failure to take into account one's own sexual and drug using history as well as that of their partners adds to the risks confronting young women and men.

Education is the primary tool used to provide young people with the information and skills they need to protect themselves from infection with HIV. The majority of the states provide for school-based educational programs regarding HIV and AIDS, but there has been considerable disagreement about what young people should be taught in school-based programs. The issue in its simplest terms asks two questions: whether curriculum materials should focus solely on abstinence, and whether curriculum materials should provide information only or focus also on the development of skills. At the core of this debate is the fear that if education is not focused on abstinence, there will be an increase in sexual activity among young people, just as it is feared that needle exchange programs will increase the use of illegal drugs. Criticism of abstinence-based programs has been consistent since 1986, when Dr. C. Everett Koop noted that lack of information was jeopardizing the health of young people.

Program evaluation data point to the importance of skills training if educational programs are meant to affect behavior. From evaluations of HIV and AIDS education programs we have learned that: (1) programs that provide information only have not been shown to affect behavior; (2) programs that combine content on values with information on how to avoid infection and that attend to developing skills needed to avoid, cope with, or leave high-risk situations delay the start of or reduce the likelihood that young people will engage in high-risk behaviors; (3) programs that make use of peer educators and support groups seem to be effective in motivating students to demonstrate their newly acquired knowledge and skills; (4) program effectiveness is linked to duration and intensity with one-shot counseling sessions that are associated with HIV-testing showing little if any effect in modifying behavior; (5) programs that are targeted to specific groups, with content shaped to accommodate differences in age, gender, geography, race, sexual orientation, and language differences are more likely to accomplish their goals than are programs that fail to take account of group differences; and (6) programs that make use of realistic messages that address the experiences of the targeted group are more effective than watered-down versions of reality.

There are no empirical data to support the proposition that young people who receive explicit sex education messages begin sexual activity earlier or have more sexual experiences than those who do not receive such messages. Empirical data yield information regarding the elements of education programs that are most likely to affect behavior. They show that programs should be designed and implemented using what has been shown to be effective because "as each generation . . . come of age, they . . . face an epidemic not unlike the generation before. In every group, by race and gender, there is [a] substantial increase in the rate of infection as individuals enter their late teens and early twenties."[105]

As discussed in chapter 1, more than one-half of AIDS cases that were reported to the CDC in 1995 came from outside of the original centers of the epidemic. The highest proportion of cases of AIDS among adolescents and young adults are being reported in small cities, towns, and rural areas.

Unlike their counterparts who reside in major metropolitan areas where information about HIV and AIDS may be acquired through a variety of formal and informal means, young people in areas of the country that until now have been less directly affected by the epidemic may be those in greatest need of educational programs that take into account the actual behaviors and experiences that young people confront.

CHAPTER 7

Welfare Reform and Its Effects on Women and Children with HIV and AIDS

INTRODUCTION

In chapter 3 the Supplemental Security Income program (SSI) and the Social Security Disability Income program (SSDI) were described. These programs have in common the provision of cash assistance to eligible individuals with disabilities. Some women and children with HIV are asymptomatic carriers of the virus, meaning that they do not have the signs or symptoms associated with AIDS and are not eligible for assistance under a disability-based income maintenance program. However, financial assistance has been available to dependent children and their caretakers without regard to disability through the Aid to Families with Dependent Children program (AFDC).

In March 1996, the rules for eligibility for SSI were changed to disqualify from coverage individuals whose alcohol or drug use was the basis of their disability.[1] The passage of the Personal Responsibility and Work Opportunity Act (hereafter PRA) in the summer of 1996 made further changes to the SSI program and ended the AFDC program.[2]

The question addressed in this concluding chapter is "How will women with HIV and women raising children with HIV be affected by the 1996 welfare reforms?" The material that follows is speculative to a degree, because we do not know how the provisions that modify the SSI program will be interpreted by those charged with developing regulations or by the courts should litigation result, nor do we know how the states will design the welfare programs they must design and implement to replace AFDC.

This chapter describes, first, the major provisions of the Temporary Assistance for Needy Families program (TANF), which replaces the AFDC program. To illustrate how families with HIV may be affected by TANF, I rely on programs that are currently operating under the authority of what are called "AFDC-waivers." AFDC-waiver programs contain many of the provisions that appear in the statute enacting TANF, thus they provide some insight into how states may design and implement their TANF programs, and they highlight areas where problems may exist for women and children with HIV and AIDS. Next, a review of changes to the SSI program is followed by a discussion of how welfare reform may affect the availability of medical services under the Medicaid program. In the conclusion, the issues that are raised in this chapter are discussed and put into context with reference to issues raised in earlier chapters.

Before beginning, please note the following. Welfare reform will have very different effects on citizens of the United States than on individuals and families who are in the United States legally but have not become U.S. citizens.[3] Prior to passage of the PRA, a noncitizen, legally in the United States, was eligible to receive benefits under the AFDC, SSI, or Medicaid programs. With some exceptions,[4] the PRA provides that legal residents who are not citizens will not be eligible for federal benefits until they attain citizenship, except that noncitizens whose work history makes them eligible for benefits for SSDI will retain this entitlement and noncitizens with the HIV or AIDS will be eligible for assistance funded through the Ryan White CARE Act.[5] States may, at their option, provide Medicaid benefits to noncitizens whose residence in the United States is legal; and noncitizens who lose their eligibility for assistance under a federal program may apply for state aid. As of late February 1997, forty states had filed their welfare reform plans with the United States Department of Health and Human Services (HHS). Thirty-six of forty state plans include provisions for providing cash benefits to poor legal immigrants who were in the United States on August 22, 1996—the date that President Clinton signed the welfare reform legislation.[6]

Any person who enters the United States on or after the PRA takes effect will not be eligible for any federal means-tested public benefit for 5 years.[7] Noncitizen beneficiaries of SSI or AFDC at the time the PRA goes into effect will remain eligible for a maximum of one year but are subject to earlier termination based on a review of their eligibility status.

No data have been published that report the number of people who are eligible for financial aid based on their HIV-status who will lose benefits under these new provisions.

PART I. WELFARE REFORM AND THE TEMPORARY ASSISTANCE TO NEEDY FAMILIES BLOCK GRANT

Efforts to reform welfare programs have a long history.[8] Their most recent incarnation began in early 1995 when a debate began both in Congress and between Congress and President Clinton about reform of the welfare system.[9] The 1995–1996 welfare-reform debate was about reducing federal expenditures for welfare and it was about ideology. The latter covered a range of issues including the proper balance of responsibility between the federal government and state governments in establishing policy goals and the proper means of achieving policy goals, and the social responsibility of government for assisting people in need.

Ending the entitlement to AFDC, creating a block grant, and capping available funds were key elements of the Republican-sponsored reform proposals. Block grants are, in theory, less regulated than single-issue legislation such as income support for disabled people under the SSI program.[10] Fewer federal regulations give the states greater flexibility in setting eligibility standards and in day-to-day program operation. In a capped block grant each state knows in advance the amount of money it will receive, and if the number of program applicants exceeds the appropriated funds, assistance is denied or if granted is paid for by the state entirely from its own revenues.[11]

The Temporary Assistance to Needy Families Program

The Temporary Assistance for Needy Families (TANF) Block Grant eliminates the AFDC program. TANF and the AFDC program it replaces share the goal of providing financial support to families for the purpose of allowing children to be raised in their own homes or in the home of relatives.[12] However, TANF goes beyond this statement of purpose to articulate a series of objectives that seek to modify the behavior of current or soon-to-be parents through a series of measures intended to: (1) restore the American family; (2) reduce out-of-wedlock pregnancies; (3) reduce welfare dependency; (4) increase work opportunities for parents; and (5) control welfare spending.[13]

Under the provisions of TANF, each state receives a lump-sum payment from the federal government. The grant amount will be determined by a complex formula that is based on funds that were provided to the states under the AFDC program between 1992 and 1995. TANF, like AFDC, is a federal-state cost-sharing program and states must continue to allocate their own funds at a rate equal to 75 percent of the funds they allocated in 1994 or 80 percent if the state fails to meet the mandatory work requirements established under TANF.[14] States may transfer up to 30 percent of block-grant funds to other programs such as the Title XX Social Service Block Grant through which states fund social services such as child care.[15]

TANF sets guidelines the states must follow in operating their programs. By July 1, 1997, each state was required to submit to the Department of Health and Human Services a plan describing how it will operate its TANF program. States were allowed to implement their new programs before that date, but they were not required to do so. TANF must operate statewide, but states are not required to serve all political subdivisions in a uniform manner. Thus states are allowed to tailor their program to regional needs.[16]

Each state sets its own rules for program eligibility. To discourage people from moving from low-benefit to high-benefit states, residency requirements are allowed where the benefit paid to newcomers would equal the benefit received in the state of prior residence.[17]

TANF participants must engage in work when the state concludes that they are ready to engage in work or when they have received aid for twenty-four months, whichever is earlier.[18] A state may require a recipient to work in less than two years, within thirty or sixty days, for example, or be dropped from the program. "Engaged in work" means involved in an acceptable work activity for at least twenty hours per week in the years 1996 through 1998, twenty-five hours per week in 1999, and thirty hours a week in the year 2000. Women caring for children under 6 years of age need not work for more than twenty hours per week.[19] States may define work to include activities such as: (1) employment in a subsidized or unsubsidized job in the private or the public sector; (2) involvement in a work-experience program, if private sector employment is not available; (3) job search and job readiness assistance; (4) involvement in a community service program; (5) education directly related to employment including vocational education or job-skills training; or (6) secondary school attendance or involvement in a program leading to a certificate of general equivalence.

The percentage of a state's TANF caseload that must work is set by federal rules. Required participation rates range from a low of 25 percent in 1997 to a high of 50 percent in 2002 and thereafter.[20] No one may be a beneficiary of TANF for more than five years except for cases defined by a state as "hardship" cases (see below).[21]

Teenage parents may not participate in TANF unless living with a parent, guardian, or adult relative.[22] Teenagers who have not completed high school or its equivalent may meet their work obligation if they are in high school, in a program leading to an equivalence certificate, or in an educational program that is directly related to employment.[23]

Medical assistance will continue for one year for families who become ineligible for TANF because of increased earnings.[24]

Exceptions to Work Requirements   States may exempt up to 20 percent of their caseload from the five-year time limit for reasons of "hardship,"[25] which the states are free to define. In addition, states may exempt single parents from TANF's work requirements, if the parent is caring for a child under 12 months of age;[26] or if the parent is caring for a child under 6 years of age and is unable to obtain needed child care. Legitimate reasons for not obtaining child care include the: (1) inability to locate appropriate child care within a reasonable distance from the parent's home or place of work, (2) the lack of suitable informal child care by a relative or under other arrangements, or (3) the lack of appropriate and affordable formal child care arrangements.[27]

The capping of TANF funds creates an incentive for states to reduce costs, because any costs that exceed the cap must be paid entirely from state revenues. States may reduce costs by: (1) reducing the amount of benefits paid; (2) imposing restrictive eligibility standards to limit the number of program participants; (3) defining disability to require all but the most severely disabled to work; (4) defining hardship to exclude the "unworthy" poor, i.e., those deemed responsible for their situation; and (4) requiring recipients to go to work within months of entering a TANF program. For states that reduce their welfare caseload TANF contains a bonus by lessening the state's obligation to put people to work.[28] Since the cost of putting people to work is high because of state-supported day care, subsidized jobs, and job training, states may choose to reduce their welfare caseload by imposing restrictive eligibility standards and restrictive definitions of disability.

The likelihood that all TANF participants who are required to work will find jobs is not great. In July 1996, the Congressional Budget Office (CBO) reported that most states would not be able to meet the work requirements imposed by welfare reform proposals.[29] This conclusion is supported by a General Accounting Office (GAO) study (1995) of the Job Opportunities and Basic Skills Training Program (JOBS), which was part of the AFDC program.[30] Maximum monthly enrollment in work-related activities under the JOBS program did not exceed 13 percent despite the promise of child care and a rich array of services.[31] The GAO concluded that inability to locate a sufficient number of child-care slots was a major factor in limiting participation rates. Any state that considers imposing work requirements on women whose children have HIV or AIDS should note that states reported great difficulty in finding child care for infants and children with special needs, including those created by illness.[32]

AFDC Waivers   Since 1962, states have been able to request "waivers" from the regulations that the Social Security Act imposed on the AFDC program.[33] Waivers allow states to implement experimental, pilot, or demonstration projects that promote the purposes of the Social Security Act and that are cost neutral.

Waiver programs are important despite the new law creating TANF. First, as designed by the states, some waiver programs share TANF goals, such as time-limited assistance and residency requirements, and thus illustrate the kinds of programs states may implement under TANF. Second, states that have received waivers are allowed to continue the programs they have implemented. If there are conflicts between state law governing waiver programs and federal law governing TANF, state law will control program operations.[34] For example, family caps under which grants do not increase for children born to women already receiving cash assistance, or where grants increase at a fraction of the increase in a nonwaiver program, are not a part of TANF but are permissible under AFDC-waivers. Waivers are "good" for five to eleven years from their time of issuance, therefore some state waiver programs could remain in effect into the next century. Finally, states may continue to request waivers, which if approved by July 1, 1997, allow the state to operate a waiver program under its own rules and bypass the TANF mandated provisions.[35] As of November 1995, waivers had been granted to forty-three states, several of which have received multiple waivers and operate more then one pilot program.[36]

Waiver programs have been subject to legal challenge. A federal court sanctioned New Jersey's implementation of a family cap, which eliminated the customary benefit increase for a child born after a family was receiving AFDC.[37] The Supreme Court of Wisconsin upheld a sixty-day residency requirement[38] which the court ruled was not as "onerous" as a one-year requirement that was found unconstitutional by the United States Supreme Court in 1969 because it impinged on a citizen's right to travel.[39] In contrast, a federal court in California, relying on the 1969 Supreme Court decision, enjoined the state from implementing a residency requirement that would have limited benefits for newcomers to the state for a twelve-month period of time to the amount they had been receiving in their state of prior residence.[40]

Waiver Programs and Disability   A major concern for women with HIV and AIDS is what provisions the states will make for women who are disabled and for women caring for a disabled child. The JOBS program exempted parents who were too "ill or incapacitated" to participate in work activities. Women with symptomatic HIV were exempted, because anyone who satisfied the eligibility requirements for assistance under the SSI or SSDI programs was deemed to be incapacitated for purposes of the JOBS program.[41]

While it may seem unlikely that a state would mandate participation in a work program for disabled women under penalty of losing some or all of their cash benefits, California contemplated such a mandate in its Assistance Payments Demonstration Project (APDP). A group of women challenged the state on behalf of their children and themselves, and the Circuit Court of Appeals for the Ninth Circuit enjoined California from implementing its waiver-approved program. The court said the idea of imposing a work-incentive benefits cut on women whose disabilities would preclude their involvement in a work program was "absurd." In addition, the court admonished the state for failure to provide exemptions for women unable to find work and for those who could not obtain child care.[42]

Other states have structured their waiver programs to take into account parental disability, by exempting from participation those who are disabled, incapacitated, impaired, ill, or injured, or by providing good cause exemptions to excuse women who are not able to work.[43] Some waiver programs do not mandate participation by a parent who is a full-time caretaker of a disabled-dependent person[44] as well as parents whose need for child care cannot be met.[45] Women with AIDS are protected by these provisions as long as the states continue their waiver programs, or if in implementing TANF they adopt the definition of disability that is used to determine eligibility for benefits under federal programs.[46] (See chapter 3.)

Welfare Reform and Women with HIV in Their Families—A Likely Scenario   The question to which we now turn is "How would a woman who is HIV-positive, or whose child is HIV-positive, fare under a specific welfare-reform proposal?" To try to answer this question, a welfare-reform proposal submitted for federal approval by the state of Wisconsin in May 1996 will be used for purposes of illustration. There are sufficient similarities between the provisions in the Wisconsin initiative and the PRA to make this exercise fruitful.

Some general observations provide a starting point. The program that Wisconsin proposes to implement is called "Wisconsin Works."[47] Three program provisions would make it difficult for any woman who is managing her own or her child's HIV to survive in the state of Wisconsin. First, there is a sixty-day in-state residency requirement as a condition for program eligibility, including eligibility for medical services. While a woman who chooses to move to Wisconsin may be able to manage for sixty days without cash assistance she would be at great risk if during the waiting period she or her child required medical care, which, except for emergency care, would not be available.[48] Second, young mothers under the age of 18 are not eligible for cash assistance. Medical care is available if a young woman resides with her custodial parent or parents and their income is at or below 165 percent of the federal poverty level. Medical coverage is available also for the minor mother who is in state-supervised foster care under a court order.

The third provision of concern is the time-limited nature of the program, which is similar to that under TANF. Wisconsin Works limits receipt of aid to sixty months, although the sixty months need not be consecutive. As HIV-disease takes on the characteristics of a chronic illness and extends the period of financial or medical dependency, a woman with symptomatic HIV could find herself too disabled to work yet no longer eligible for state aid. The Wisconsin statute provides that the sixty-month time limit may be extended for "unusual circumstances," but the state has deferred to a later time specifying what these circumstances may be.[49] Likewise, the five-year time limit set by the TANF program does not apply to cases exempted for reasons of hardship, but how states will define hardship remains to be seen.

For women who participate in Wisconsin Works, eligibility for health care continues beyond the time limit for financial aid. The state's statute provides that eligibility for health care is for twelve consecutive months or until the adult recipient has employment-based health care coverage, whichever takes longer.[50] In addition, medical coverage is available for the working poor (those whose income is at or below 165 percent of the federal poverty level) thus increasing the universe of those eligible for state-sponsored medical insurance.

Turning to more concrete examples and specific effects, the following can be said. A woman who is HIV-positive but asymptomatic and who has a child who is HIV-positive and in good health would be expected to participate in a work program. Child-care subsidies are available to women with dependent children who are less than 10 years of age.[51]

If a woman is receiving SSI she is not eligible to participate in Wisconsin Works, but the state would pay a stipend of $77 per month for each of her dependents. This stipend would be subject to the five-year time limit.[52] Health insurance for women receiving SSI would be available through the Medicaid program not the Wisconsin Works program.

As to the HIV-positive woman who is physically unable to participate in the work force in an ongoing manner, but whose disability is not severe enough to qualify her for SSI, and the woman who must remain at home to care for a child with HIV, the following provisions apply if HIV-disease is defined by the state as an "incapacitating" condition. Wisconsin Works provides that a woman whom the states deems to be "incapacitated" for at least sixty days, who is needed in the home due to the disability of another, or who cannot participate in a regular job program will participate in the Transitional Placement Program (TPP).[53] Women in the TPP receive a monthly stipend that is equal to 70 percent of the minimum wage. Participants must be involved in a work activity. Work activities include participation in training or education programs, in volunteer work, or in counseling, physical rehabilitation, or alcohol and drug abuse assessment and rehabilitation programs. Involvement in a TPP is limited to two years, but this limit is subject to an extension under circumstances that are not spelled out in the statute.

Supplemental Security Income

Congress modified the SSI program in two ways: first, coverage is denied to anyone whose disability is based solely on the use of alcohol or drugs; and second, procedural changes were made in the way in which eligibility for children is determined.

Alcohol and Drug Abuse as a Basis for Disability   Until March 1996, an income-eligible woman for whom alcohol or drug addiction was a contributing material factor to her disability was eligible to receive cash benefits under the SSI program for 3 years if she participated in treatment when appropriate treatment was available. Federal law required that her cash grant be paid to a third party who was expected to manage her benefits. In most states, eligibility for SSI confers an automatic grant of Medicaid coverage.

In March 1996, federal law changed, ending SSI and SSDI benefits for people for whom alcoholism or drug addiction is a contributing material factor to their disability, lest individuals with drug or alcohol problems be rewarded for their failure to work.[54] Congress's concern that the availability of an SSI grant "rewarded" alcohol or drug use was reinforced by a 1994 GAO report documenting that for the great majority of drug or alcohol abusers treatment was either not occurring or could not be determined.[55] Moreover, the purpose of the third-party payee provision was being subverted, because the third party was most likely a relative or friend who presumably could be pressured to turn over funds.[56]

The law is silent on the subject of continuing Medicaid coverage for people whose disability is based on use of alcohol or drugs. Presumably, loss of SSI or SSDI would require separate application for medical assistance and would leave the disqualified applicant uninsured for some period of time.

As of December 1995, 38 percent of women with the HIV acquired their infection through intravenous drug use (IVDU).[57] For these women this change in the law raises two concerns. First, if a woman's disability claim is based solely on her alcohol or drug addiction, she will lose benefits under the new legislation, although benefits would be continued if her medical record lists an AIDS-defining condition as a secondary condition.[58] But some women who contracted HIV while receiving SSI for an alcohol- or drug-related disability may not have updated their medical records and they will lose benefits. Moreover, regulations do not require the recording of secondary conditions. Thus, an HIV-positive woman who relied on her alcohol- or drug-related disability and did not disclose her HIV-status will lose her benefits. Failure to update medical records or to record a secondary condition will not preclude reapplication for benefits but may result in a loss of income for the period of time it takes to create the necessary record.

The second concern that arises is that it is possible that the statutory language that precludes eligibility if alcoholism or drug addiction is a contributing material factor to an applicant's disability could be interpreted to deem ineligible anyone whose HIV was contracted through IVDU. Stated otherwise, when a woman applies for benefits based on an HIV-related disability, it is not impossible to imagine an argument that but for her IVDU she would not be HIV-positive. Her use of intravenous drugs could be construed as a contributing material factor to her disability, and benefits could be disallowed.

Childhood Disability   As discussed in chapter 3, the 1996 amendments to the SSI program ended the use of Individualized Functional Assessments (IFAs) for children and for the first time defined childhood disability.

IFAs were used when a child's medical condition was not among those on the list of medical conditions used by the Social Security Administration to determine eligibility for SSI. If conducting an IFA resulted in a determination that a child's impairment seriously limited her ability to undertake age-appropriate activities, she was deemed eligible to receive benefits. In late 1996 it was estimated that in the early months of 1997 approximately 300,000 children would be notified of the SSA's intention to review their cases.[59]

Congress eliminated the IFAs because of a concern that children with modest conditions or impairments were receiving cash assistance and that children whose eligibility was based on maladaptive behavior (defined as behavior that is destructive to oneself, others, property, or animals) were being coached by their parents to "fake" mental impairments. The Congressional Budget Office (CBO) estimates that approximately one-half of the children who qualified for benefits under an IFA, and approximately 21 percent of all children receiving benefits, or some 200,000 children would, be deemed ineligible with changes to the law.[60]

It is not likely that the changes to the SSI program will affect a child with AIDS. As discussed in chapter 3, a person with AIDS who meets categorical and income requirements is eligible for SSI benefits, and the law would not exclude children whose conditions were the same as those of eligible adults. At risk are children who may display symptoms of HIV-infection that are unique to children, creating a situation similar to that faced by women before the listings were changed to reflect conditions only they experience (see chapter 3).

Under current law, a child not eligible for SSI benefits might be eligible for financial assistance under the TANF program. However, it cannot be assumed that this conclusion is correct, since states have yet to establish eligibility criteria for TANF programs. It is also worth noting that the cap on TANF funds could create a situation where a child or an adult who is otherwise eligible for benefits will not receive benefits once the fiscal cap is reached.

Medicaid

The Medicaid Transformation Act of 1995 ("Medigrant") sought to end the entitlement to Medicaid coverage and to create a block-grant program.[61] This effort failed, and under the reform measures creating the TANF program states must continue Medicaid coverage for those who were or would have been eligible for AFDC as of July 16, 1996, as if the AFDC program were still in effect.[62] In most states Medicaid coverage is automatic for recipients of SSI.

States are under pressure to contain the costs of providing medical care. States can limit program costs in different ways, including limiting program growth by changing the rules for eligibility and limiting the services available to provide no more than is mandated by federal law. Requiring Medicaid recipients to enroll in managed-care programs is another approach that states may try in an effort to control program costs. Medicaid waivers, discussed briefly in chapter 3, allow states to mandate participation in managed care medical programs. We turn now to the subject of managed care and to the implications that moving Medicaid recipients into such programs may have for women and children with HIV and AIDS.

Managed Care   Moving Medicaid recipients away from fee-for-service medical plans, which reimburse providers for the costs of all or almost all of the rendered services, into managed care plans is the most frequently discussed approach to reducing Medicaid spending, although it is questionable whether managed care programs can affect savings over and above those already achieved by the low reimbursement rates paid by Medicaid.[63]

The concept of managed care covers an array of programs having in common only the use of a "gatekeeper" who controls access to specialized services. Otherwise, programs run the gamut from those that are "capitated," where providers are paid a fixed sum for all rendered services, to primary care case management models (PCCM), in which each rendered service is paid for.[64] Any fixed-rate payment plan offers cost-control incentives not found in fee-for-service programs, since the provider in a fixed-rate plan suffers a monetary loss if cost of service exceeds the fixed rate of payment.

A transition from fee-for-service to fixed-rate payment systems has a number of ramifications for women with HIV and AIDS. First, the costs for caring for people without health insurance are covered in part by state and local taxes and in part by "fee shifting," where some of the costs for caring for the uninsured are shifted to the insured.[65] Fixed-rate payment systems prevent cost shifting. Thus providers cannot generate revenue to serve people who lack insurance. Closing of hospitals, particularly those in urban areas that serve economically depressed communities and are used by poor people for primary health care, has been attributed to the shift to managed care.[66]

There is evidence that health care programs that reimburse on a fixed-rate schedule discourage hospitals from admitting people with AIDS.[67] Yet hospital-based care is necessary when community-based care is not available. For example, a single-state study by the GAO of hospital use of inpatient and outpatient care found that women with HIV had limited access to community-based residential care programs, including community-based medically managed day care.[68] Consequently, hospitals had to provide more costly inpatient care for longer periods of time until community facilities were found to which patients could be transferred.[69]

Questions have been raised as to whether managed care programs can supply the specialized care required by people with HIV and other serious illnesses, unless these programs reimburse providers on a fee-for-service basis or provide special capitation rates for those with HIV. People with AIDS have been critical of managed care programs, which they claim do not meet their needs, in part, due to low reimbursement rates.[70] A women's advocacy group in New York reported that 95 percent of the managed care programs they contacted could not make referrals to primary care physicians with experience in treating people with HIV and AIDS.[71]

Discussion

This book is being written at a time when there is reason for optimism and reason for concern for women with HIV and AIDS. Confidence that government will sustain and support its efforts on behalf of people with HIV and AIDS and provide service to greater numbers of people is found in the fact that the Ryan White CARE Act has been reauthorized and funds, including funds to purchase needed medications, have increased. Congress has directed the Secretary of Health and Human Services to develop a plan to ensure that women (including pregnant women), infants, and children are included in studies sponsored or conducted by the National Institutes of Health that address medical issues of concern to women with HIV. Provisions in the 1996 reauthorization of the CARE Act provide for grants for health and support services for women, infants, and children and seek to ensure their inclusion in research programs. Grants made by the Center for Substance Abuse Treatment require preferential treatment for pregnant women who are using drugs. Further reason for hope is to be found in the research reported in the summer of 1996 revealing that new drug combinations were effective in suppressing the amount of HIV in the blood of infected people. These data add to the belief that AIDS may become a manageable chronic illness rather than a terminal condition.

However, reason demands that optimism be balanced by reflection on the historical record and with consideration to the discussion of policy changes reviewed in this chapter. The discrimination experienced by people with AIDS has been documented at a number of points in this text. The fear that discriminatory attitudes will translate into outright denial of benefits, limited benefits, or denial of treatment is not without a basis in fact. For the first decade of the epidemic, many women with AIDS were deemed ineligible for assistance because their physical problems did not match the established profile of AIDS defining illnesses, the natural history of HIV-disease in women went unexplored, and poor women have had and continue to have difficulty gaining access to primary medical care, to drug treatment programs, and to experimental drug trials. Compounding these problems are the documented instances of physicians refusing to treat people with HIV and the willingness of some physicians to withhold treatment from infants known to be HIV-positive.

These facts are sufficient in themselves to question whether government will appropriate the resources that will be required to provide new drug therapies to all who might benefit from them and to question the continued commitment of government to assist women and children in need. This concern has special resonance in a political climate that views as legitimate expressly incorporating behavior change goals into social policy and where punishing people for nonconforming behavior by withholding financial and medical benefits that are essential to survival is considered legitimate.

It would be naive to assume that the life-threatening nature of HIV will prevent the imposition of behavior-based restrictions on women who are considered to be "at fault" for contracting the disease, even though their children will bear part of the consequences of a parent's loss of financial assistance.[72] It is important to bear in mind that: (1) believing that some people immigrate to the United States to collect public assistance,[73] the federal government has terminated financial aid to almost all legally admitted noncitizens without regard to the fact that many are taxpayers, that approximately one-quarter of those applying for SSI were in the United States more then three years before applying for aid, and that 26 percent of immigrants receiving SSI are 75 years of age or older;[74] (2) believing that parents coach their children to misbehave in order to collect SSI benefits, even though a government report showed the lack of evidence to support this contention,[75] the federal government has changed the rules for determining SSI eligibility to eliminate a significant number of child beneficiaries; and (3) believing that the benefits of receiving an AFDC check enter into a teenager's calculations when she decides to become a mother, despite the lack of evidence for this proposition, the federal government has terminated cash assistance for young women who do not live with an adult.[76]

The Urban Institute (1996) estimates that federal spending on social welfare programs will be reduced by $16 billion due to welfare reform legislation that was passed in 1996.[77] Approximately 1 million families will lose all assistance under cuts made by the TANF program alone.[78] As noted above, many people who lose federal benefits will turn to the states for financial assistance. This shift will increase competition within states for limited funds and will pit the elderly against children and people with AIDS against people coping with other life-threatening illnesses. Funding shortages will also increase competition across programs. For example, it is reasonable to conclude that the demand for foster care will increase as noncitizen immigrants, women under the age of 18 who do not live with an adult, and those who exceed the five-year time limit imposed by TANF are no longer able to care for their children. Any increased demand for foster care caused by such factors will come on top of the caseload growth that is likely to result if estimates of the number of children who will be orphaned by the AIDS epidemic are accurate.

The gains made by people with HIV and AIDS, especially in the first decade of the epidemic, came about mainly through grassroots activities. "Ordinary" people, including people with HIV, and professionals from medicine, social work, and the law, stepped in to fill a breach created by a government unwilling to deal with people with HIV-disease. These people, together with a small group of politicians, introduced and fought for legislation that would assist people with HIV and AIDS.

Activities undertaken by people with HIV and by others acting on their behalf include: (1) raising funds so that social, medical, food, and housing services could be provided; (2) raising funds so that research could be conducted; (3) demonstrating and protesting for changes in the way government approves of and makes available experimental drugs; (4) lobbying for legislation beneficial to people with HIV; and (5) litigating to gain access to benefits that were denied and to put an end to discriminatory treatment in education, housing, employment, and receipt of medical care.

A statutory framework and a body of case law upholding the right of people with HIV to be treated fairly and in a humane manner have emerged, and women and children with AIDS have access to federal and state medical and financial aid programs. But as the contents of this chapter suggest, statutory protections can be undermined and provisions taken for granted, such as the benefits that were provided through the AFDC program for over a half century, can be lost. Ensuring that the current definitions of disability found in civil rights statutes and benefit-conferring statutes continue to control decisions affecting the rights of people with HIV and AIDS is crucial as is working to guarantee that programs such as TANF take into account the needs of and limitations of women with HIV and women raising children with HIV.

Welfare reform reflects a tension between a desire to help those deemed most worthy of government assistance and a desire to use social policy as a tool to change the behavior of people who are seen as responsible for their problems. Legislation to reform the social welfare system does not specifically target women with HIV and AIDS nor does it provide any assurance of ongoing support for them. For example, federal law makes no provision for exempting disabled women and women who are caring for disabled children from TANF's work requirements. Women with HIV, relative to others with HIV-disease, may suffer disproportionately. This conclusion is supported by the historical record, which is replete with examples of inattention to the needs of women who are HIV-positive, and by the fact that many HIV-positive women are single parents who because they are poor rely on the programs directly affected by welfare reform. The advances that have been made in advocacy, programs, and law to protect people with AIDS have not always directly focused on women with AIDS, but these efforts can be directed toward the particular needs of women.

N O T E S

CHAPTER 1

1. The first Congressional appropriation specifically for AIDS was made in 1982 when $2 million was appropriated to the Centers for Disease Control. (In 1981, $5.5 million had been diverted to AIDS research from other sources. See 136 *Cong. Rec.* S18139-01 October, 25 1990.) In 1982, the Congressional Research Service reported that the National Institutes of Health's research budget for Toxic Shock syndrome amounted to $36,100 per death and for Legionnaire's disease, $34,841 per death. By contrast, the NIH spent about $3,225 per AIDS death in fiscal 1981 and $8,991 in fiscal 1982. Cited in Shilts, Randy, *Politics, People and the AIDS Epidemic: And the Band Played On*, (New York: St. Martin's Press, 1987): 186.

2. Levine, Arnold J., et al. *Report of the NIH AIDS Research Program Evaluation Working Group of the Office of AIDS Research Advisory Council*, Washington, D.C.: National Institutes of Health (1996).

3. "The Federal Response to the AIDS Epidemic: Information and Public Education," Hearings held before a subcommittee of the Committee on Government Operations of the House of Representatives (March 16, 1987), cited in, United States House of Representatives, "The Politics of AIDS Prevention: Science Takes a Time Out," 102d Cong., 1st Sess. Rep. No. 102-1047 (1992); United States House of Representatives, Subcommittee on Human Resources and Intergovernmental Relations, "AIDS Treatment and Care: Who Cares?" 101st Cong., 2d Sess. Rep. No. 674 (1994).

4. "AIDS Treatment and Care," note 3.

5. Testimony of Dr. Donald Francis reported in "The Politics of AIDS Prevention," note 3.

6. Testimony of Senator Lautenberg, reported in the 136 *Cong. Rec.* S12534-05 (August 4, 1990).

7. Testimony before the Subcommittee on Health and the Environment, Committee on Energy and Commerce, United States House of Representatives (February 27, 1990) cited in "AIDS Treatment and Care," note 3.

8. "AIDS Treatment and Care," note 3.

9. 136 *Cong. Rec.* S15038-01 (October 12, 1990).

10. Ibid. S15082. Four hundred scientists were asked whether funds for AIDS research were: (1) helpful in advancing science in areas beyond HIV-disease; (2) about the right amount; or (3) disproportionate to other needs. The report in the Congressional Record states that 148 scientists responded. The information reported is limited to the following. Fifty percent said that research into HIV and AIDS contributed substantially to other basic sciences and to the development of knowledge in areas such as neurology and oncology. An equal percentage expressed the opinion that federal spending for AIDS and HIV research was about right, with nearly one-third expressing the opinion that spending was too low. Opinion was about equally divided on the question of whether too much funding for research was being diverted to AIDS from other fields.

11. Backstrom, Charles, and Robins, Leonard, "State AIDS Policy Making: Perspective of Legislative Health Committee Chairs," *AIDS and Public Policy Journal* 10 (1995): 238–248.

12. Brandt, Alan M., "AIDS in Historical Perspective," in Pierce, Christine, and VanDeVeer, Donald (Eds.) *AIDS: Ethics and Public Policy*, (Belmont, CA: Wadsworth Publishing Company, 1988): 31–38.

13. Ibid. 33.

14. Ibid.

15. Lawrence, Jill, "Mother of Arcadia AIDS Family Recounts Rejection, Persecution," *N.Y. Times*, Sect. A, Col. 3 (September 11, 1987): 16.

16. [Editorial], "White House Inhospitality," *N.Y. Times*, Sect. A, Col. 1 (June 16, 1995): 26.

17. "Masons Renege on Camp Offer to Children with H.I.V." *N.Y. Times*, Metro, Col. 1 (August 12, 1995): 23, 25. A new camp was found and funds were donated to cover the cost of entertaining the children.

18. Brandt, note 12: 33, 35; Kurth, Ann, "An Overview of Women and HIV Disease," in Kurth, Ann (Ed.) *Until the Cure: Caring for Women with HIV,* (New Haven: Yale University Press, 1993): Ch. 1.

19. *Association of Relatives & Friends of AIDS Patients v. Regulations & Permits Administration*, 740 F Supp 95 (D.Puerto Rico, 1990).

20. Closen, Michael J., Bobinski, Mary Anne, Herman, Donald H. J., et al., "Criminalization of an Epidemic: HIV-AIDS and Criminal Exposure Laws," *Arkansas Law Review* 46 (1994): 921–983. States receiving federal funds under the Ryan White CARE Act must ensure that their criminal laws provide for the prose-

cution of a person who intentionally transmits HIV but federal law does not require states to adopt new laws. (See chapter 5.)

21. [Editor] "Relationship of Syphilis to Drug Use and Prostitution—Connecticut and Philadelphia, Pennsylvania; Morbidity and Mortality Weekly Report; Column," *Journal of the American Medical Association* 261 (1989): 353.

22. United States Department of Health and Human Service, Public Health Service, Centers for Disease Control and Prevention, *HIV/AIDS Surveillance Report: Year End Edition*, 7 (1995): 10 (hereafter 1995 *Year End Report*).

23. Blendon, Robert J., Donelan, Karen, and Knox, Richard A., "Public Opinion and AIDS: Lessons for the Second Decade; Public Opinion and Health Care," *Journal of the American Medical Association* 267 (1992): 981.

24. Blendon, Robert J., and Donelan, Karen, "Discrimination Against People with AIDS: The Public's Perspective," *New England Journal of Medicine* 319 (1988): 1022–1026.

25. Clemo, Lorrie, "The Stigmatization of AIDS in Infants and Children in the United States," *AIDS Education & Prevention* 41 (1992): 308–318.

26. United States House of Representatives, "The Americans with Disabilities Act of 1990." 101st Cong., 2d Sess., House Rep. No. 485, Part II, (1990), codified at 42 U.S.C.C.A.N. 303.

27. Shipp, E. R., "Concern Over Spread of AIDS Generates a Spate of New Laws Nationwide," *N.Y. Times*, Sect. A, Col. 1 (October 26, 1985): 30.

28. 131 *Cong. Rec.* H8006-04 (October 2, 1985).

29. Closen, Bobinski, and Herman, note 20: Fn8.

30. States may quarantine individuals to protect the health and safety of the general public as long as the actions taken do not violate the federal Constitution. *Jacobson v. Com. of Massachusetts,* 197 U.S. 11 (1905). See "Poll Indicates Majority Favor Quarantine for AIDS," *N.Y. Times* (December 20, 1985) A24, Col. 1; "Judge in AIDS Hearing Asks About Quarantine for Adults," *N.Y. Times* (October 1, 1985) Metro, Col. 7: 7 (A State Supreme Court justice expressed incredulity that the City Health Department does not quarantine adults with advanced cases of AIDS.); Trafford, Abigail, Witkin, Gordon, et al., "The Politics of AIDS—A Tale of Two States," *U.S. News & World Report*, November 18, 1985: 70 (Texas health commissioner proposes that AIDS patients be quarantined from the general public, and according to Houston's former mayor, one way to deal with AIDS is to "shoot the queers."); Lewin, Tamar, "Rights of Citizens and Society Raise Legal Muddle on AIDS," *N.Y. Times* (October 14, 1987) Sect. A, Col. 1: 1 (Senator Jesse Helms and Pat Robertson have suggested that quarantine may become necessary for people with AIDS.); Purdham, Todd S., "Despite Protests, Dinkins Chooses Indiana Official as Health Chief," *N.Y. Times* (January 20, 1990) Sect 1, Col. 4: 1 (A news report was issued this week suggesting that Dr. Woodrow Myers, the newly appointed New York City Health Commissioner, would not rule out quarantining AIDS carriers.)

31. Bayer, Ronald, "Public Health Policy and the AIDS Epidemic: An End to HIV Exceptionalism?" *New England Journal of Medicine* 324 (1991): 1500–1504.

32. "Quarantine Lifted on AIDS Case, But the Boy Involved Is Confined," *N.Y. Times* (June 17, 1987) Metro, Col. 4: 9; Annas, George J., "Detention Of HIV-Positive Haitians at Guantanamo—Human Rights and Medical Care," *New England Journal of Medicine* 329 (1993): 589–592.

33. These issues, with the exception of voiding of marriages, are reviewed in subsequent chapters. On voiding marriages, see *T.E.P. and K.J.C. v. Leavit,* 840 F. Supp. 110 (D. Utah, 1993).

34. *Year End Surveillance Report,* note 22: 39.

35. The CDC stopped using as an exposure category "born in Pattern II countries," which is a World Health Organization classification that includes countries where heterosexual contact is thought to be the main mode of transmission. Those previously classified as born in Pattern II countries are now classified by the exposure categories listed in the text. See United States Department of Health and Human Services, Public Health Service, Centers for Disease Control and Prevention, *AIDS Public Information Data Set,* (Washington, D.C.: December 1994).

36. Female-to-female transmission can follow from exposure to cervical and vaginal secretions. See American Medical Association Council on Scientific Affairs, "Health Care Needs of Gay Men and Lesbians in the United States," *Journal of the American Medical Association,* 275 (1996): 1354.

37. White, Jocelyn C., and Levinson, Wendy, "Lesbian Health Care: What a Primary Care Physician Needs to Know," *Western Journal of Medicine* 162 (1995): 463.

38. Brookmeyer, Ron, and Gail, Mitchell, H., *AIDS Epidemiology: A Quantitative Approach,* (New York: Oxford University Press, 1994).

39. *Public Health Reports* 105 (1990). See also Brookmeyer and Gail, note 38.

40. Onorato, Ida M., Grinn, Marta, and Dondero, Timothy J., "Applications of Data from the CDC Family of Surveys," *Public Health Reports* 109 (1994): 204–211.

41. "The Politics of AIDS Prevention," note 3.

42. United States Department of Health and Human Services, Public Health Service, "Update: Mortality Attributable to HIV Infection Among Persons Aged 25–44 Years—United States, 1994," *Morbidity and Mortality Weekly Report* 45 (1996): 121–125.

43. Onorato, Grinn, and Dondero, note 40.

44. Hurley, Peter, and Pinder, Glenn, "Ethics, Social Forces, and Politics in AIDS-Related Research: Experience in Planning and Implementing a Household HIV Seroprevalence Survey," *Milbank Quarterly* 70 (1992): 605.

45. *Year End Surveillance Report,* note 22: 10, 16, and 29.

46. Ibid.

47. United States Department of Health and Human Services, Public Health Service, "First 500,000 AIDS Cases—United States, 1995," *Morbidity and Mortality Weekly Report* 44 (1995): 849. See also *Year End Surveillance Report,* note 22: 5.

48. In 1993, the definition of reportable cases expanded to include all HIV-infected people with "severe immunosuppression" defined to include those whose T-cell count was less than 200, people with "pulmonary tuberculosis, recurrent pneumonia or invasive cervical cancer." Fifty-four percent of the cases reported in 1993 were due to the expanded definition. (United States Department of Health and Human Services, Public Health Service, *Morbidity and Mortality Weekly Report* 43 (1994): 160.

49. Karon, J. M., Rosenberg, P. S., Mcquillan, G., et al., "Prevalence of HIV Infection in the United States, 1984 to 1992," *Journal of the American Medical Association 276*, (1996): 126–31.

50. *Year End Surveillance Report*, note 22: 10, 12.

51. United States Department of Health and Human Services, Public Health Service, Centers for Disease Control and Prevention, "Update: AIDS Among Women—United States, 1994," *Morbidity and Mortality Weekly Report* 44 (1995): 81.

52. Scarlet, Gabriella, "Pediatric HIV Infection," *Lancet* 348 (1996): 863–868.

53. *Year End Surveillance Report*, note 22.

54. Ibid.

55. "Update: Mortality Attributable to HIV Infection," note 42; Fahs, Marianne C., Waite, Douglas, Sesholtz, Marilyn, et al., "Results of the ACSUS for Pediatric AIDS Patients: Utilization of Services, Functional Status, and Social Severity; AIDS Costs and Service Utilization Survey," *Health Services Research* 29 (1994): 5. ACSUS, the AIDS Cost and Services Utilization Survey, was conducted by the United States Public Health Services to compile longitudinal data describing utilization of medical services by people with HIV.

56. "Update," note 55.

57. El-Bassel, Nabila, Ivanoff, Andre, Schilling, Robert F., et al., "Preventing HIV/AIDS in Drug Abusing Incarcerated Women Through Skills Building and Social Support Enhancement: Preliminary Outcomes," *Social Work Research* 19 (1995): 131–141. Data reported between 1989 and 1992 showed that the rate of HIV-infection among incarcerated women was higher than among incarcerated men. See Polonsky, Sara, Kerr, Sandra, Harris, Benita, et al., "HIV Prevention in Prisons and Jails: Obstacles and Opportunities," *Public Health Reports* 109 (1994): 615.

58. Forsyth, Brian W. C., "A Pandemic Out of Control: The Epidemiology of AIDS," in Geballe, Shelley, Gruendel, Janice, and Andiman, Warren, *Forgotten Children of the AIDS Epidemic,* (New Haven: Yale University Press, 1995): Ch. 1.

59. Frascino, Robert J., "Changing Face of HIV/AIDS Care—Mother-Fetal and Maternal-Child HIV Transmission," *Western Journal of Medicine* 163 (1995).

60. Ibid.

61. *Year End Surveillance Report*, note 22.

62. United States Department of Health and Human Services, Public Health Service, Centers for Disease Control and Prevention, "AIDS Among Children—United States, 1996" *Morbidity and Mortality Weekly Report,* 45 (1996).

63. Guinan, Mary E., "Artificial Insemination by Donor: Safety and Secrecy." Editorial, *Journal of the American Medical Association* 273 (1995): 890.

64. There has never been a randomized trial from which the likelihood of risk of transmission through breast-feeding could be determined. Newborns whose mothers develop primary infections while nursing may be at greater risk because of the high viral burden carried by the mother. See Committee on Pediatric AIDS, 1995 to 1996, "Human Milk, Breastfeeding, and Transmission of Human Immunodeficiency Virus in the United States," *Pediatrics* 96 (1995): 977–979. See also Heymann, David L., "AIDS: Mother to Child," *World Health* 40 (1995): 31.

65. On invasive surgical procedures and risk from sexually transmitted diseases, see McCarthy, Michael, "Can HIV-1 Transmission Be Prevented During Pregnancy and Labor?" *Lancet* 348 (1996): 1021; on risk through unprotected sex during pregnancy, see Centers for Disease Control, *AIDS Daily Summary* (September 27, 1996) discussing a report made by Dr. Pamela B. Matheson and her colleagues from the New York City Department of Health.

66. [Editor] "Heterosexual Transmission of Acquired Immunodeficiency Syndrome and Human Immunodeficiency Virus Infection—United States; Morbidity and Mortality Weekly Report; Column," *Journal of the American Medical Association* 262 (1989): 463.

67. Anastos, Kathryn, and Vermund, Sten, "Epidemiology and Natural History," in Kurth, Ann (Ed.) *Until the Cure: Caring for Women with HIV,* (New Haven: Yale University Press, 1993): Ch 11; European Study Group on Heterosexual Transmission of HIV, "Comparison of Female to Male and Male to Female Transmission of HIV in 563 Stable Couples," *British Medical Journal* 304 (1992): 809.

68. Davis, Susan F., Byers, Robert H., Lindegren, Mary Lou, et al., "Prevalence and Incidence of Vertically Acquired HIV Infection in the United States," *Journal of the American Medical Association* 274 (1995): 952; Heymann, note 64.

69. Davis, Byers, and Lindegren, note 68: 92.

70. *Year End Surveillance Report*, note 22: 12.

71. Ibid. 39.

72. This category includes people exposed through "HIV-infected blood, body fluids, or concentrated virus in health care, laboratory, or household settings," one person who intentionally inoculated himself with contaminated blood and twenty-nine young people exposed in utero who were not diagnosed until after age 13. *Year End Surveillance Report*, note 22: 26.

73. United States Department of Health and Human Services, Public Health Service, Centers for Disease Control and Prevention, *HIV/AIDS Surveillance Reports for 1987 through 1992* (1992).

74. Commission on Behavioral and Social Sciences and Education, National Research Council, *Preventing HIV Transmission: The Role of Sterile Needles and Bleach*, (Washington, D.C.: National Academy Press, 1995): 33.

75. United States House of Representatives, "Ryan White CARE Act Amendments of 1995", 104th Cong., 1st Sess. Rep. No. 245 (1995).

76. United States Department of Health and Human Services, Public Health Services, Centers for Disease Control and Prevention, *Morbidity and Mortality Weekly Report* 44 (1995): 849.

77. Ibid.

78. "Update: AIDS Among Women," note 51.

CHAPTER 2

1. 29 U.S.C.S. §701 *et seq.* (Law. Co-Op. 1995).

2. 42 U.S.C.S. §12101 *et seq.* (Law. Co-Op. 1995).

3. 42 U.S.C.S. §3601 *et seq.* (Law. Co-Op. 1995).

4. See United States Justice Department, "Application of Section 504 of the Rehabilitation Act to HIV-Infected Individuals," (1988) (Individuals with HIV are disabled because of a substantial limitation to procreation and intimate sexual relationships.) The legislative history of the ADA makes clear Congress's intent to include those with HIV in the definition of disability. (H.R. Rep. No. 485(II), 101st Cong., 2d Sess. 1990; 1990 U.S.C.C.A.N. §303) and appendix to 29 CFR §1630.2(j) (HIV infection is an impairment which is inherently substantially limiting.) [Report 485, titled "The Americans with Disabilities Act of 1990" was issued in four parts, numbered I through IV and reprinted at 1990 U.S.C.C.A.N. §§267 (Part I), 303 (Part II), 445 (Part III) and 512 (Part IV). These reports are hereafter referred to as Rep. No. 485(I), (II), (III) or (IV).] Efforts to exclude "any current impairment that consists of an infectious, contagious or communicable disease whether or not such disease causes a physical or mental impairment during the period of contagion" from the definition of handicap, which effort was directed at excluding people with HIV from coverage under the FHA, were defeated. ("Fair Housing Amendments Act of 1988," 100th Cong., 2d Sess. 1988, House Rep. No. 711, 1988 U.S.C.C.A.N. 2173 (hereafter Rep. No. 711).

5. 20 U.S.C.S. §1400 *et seq.* (Law. Co-Op. 1995).

6. 42 U.S.C.S. §3604(2)(A) through (C) (Law. Co-Op. 1995). On protection for foster parents, see *Gorski v Troy*, 929 F.2d 1183 (7th Cir., 1991).

7. 42 U.S.C.S. §§3602(b) & 3604(a)-(d) (Law. Co-Op. 1995).

8. 42 U.S.C.S. §3604 (Law. Co-Op. 1995).

9. 42 U.S.C.S. §3617 (Law. Co-Op. 1995).

10. 42 U.S.C.S. §3607 (Law. Co-Op. 1995) covers noncommercial buildings, private clubs, and elder housing. 42 U.S.C.S. §3603(b)(1) (Law. Co-Op. 1995) covers single-family housing sold or rented by an owner. For a case decided on the latter exemption, see *Hogar Agua y Vida en el Desierto v. Suarez-Medina*, 829 F.Supp. 19 (D.Puerto Rico, 1993) vacated by 36 F.3d 177 at 177 (1st Cir., 1994).

11. 42 U.S.C.S. §3604(f)(3)((C)(i)-(iii) (Law. Co-Op. 1995).

12. 42 U.S.C.S. §3604(f)(9) (Law. Co-Op. 1995).

13. 42 U.S.C.A. §12101 *et seq.* (Law. Co-Op. 1995).

14. 42 U.S.C.S. §12117 (Law. Co-Op. 1995).

15. Title IV covers telecommunications services and requires relay services for hearing- and speech-impaired individuals. This Title amends the Communications Act of 1934, 47 U.S.C.S. §201 (Law. Co-Op. 1995). Other Titles, and the protections they include are: Title V, miscellaneous provisions: (a) the Act is not to be construed to apply a lesser standard than the Rehabilitation Act of 1973 and it does not preempt other laws providing greater or equal protection to the disabled (§501); (b) states are not immune for violations of the ADA (§502); and (c) employers are liable for retaliation against an individual who opposes an unlawful employment practice (§503). The provisions in §504 require the issuance of guidelines to ensure that buildings, facilities, rail passenger cars, and vehicles are accessible to individuals with disabilities. Attorneys' fees are provided for in §505. Technical assistance to help employers understand their responsibilities under the act are provided for in §506, and §507 provides for gathering information on problems that confront disabled people in utilizing wilderness areas. Section 509 makes the rights and protections of the act applicable to Congress; §513 supports the use of alternative means of dispute resolution; while §514 provides for severability if any provision of the ADA is found to be unconstitutional. §§508, 510, 511, and 512 identify groups not covered by the law; see note 74 and accompanying text.

16. 42 U.S.C.A. §12201(a) (Law. Co-Op. 1995).

17. 42 U.S.C.S. §12111 (Law. Co-Op. 1995).

18. 29 U.S.C.S. §793(a) (Law. Co-Op. 1995); 41 C.F.R. 60.741.4.

19. Rep. No. 485(III), note 4.

20. Ibid.

21. 42 U.S.C.S. §12111(5)(A) (Law. Co-Op. 1995).

22. 42 U.S.C.S. §12112(a) (Law. Co-Op. 1995).

23. *Cain v. Hyatt*, 734 F.Supp. 671 (E.D. Pa., 1990).

24. N.Y. Executive Law, §292(5) (McKinney 1995).

25. 42 U.S.C.A. §12111(8) (Law. Co-Op. 1995), 29 C.F.R. §1630.2(m) (1995).

26. *Southeastern Community College v. Davis*, 442 U.S. 397 at 406 (1979).

27. 42 U.S.C. §12111(8) (Law. Co-Op. 1995). Factors considered in determining whether or not a function is essential include the employer's judgment and written job descriptions that were prepared before advertising for or interviewing job applicants, the amount of time spent performing the function; (29 C.F.R. §1630.2(n)(3)(iii); the consequences of not requiring the incumbent to perform the function (29 C.F.R. §1630.2(n)(3)(iv); applicable collective bargaining agreements (29 C.F.R. §1630.2(n)(3)(v)); the work experience of past incumbents in the job (29 C.F.R. §1630.2(n)(3)(vi); and the work experience of current incumbents in similar jobs (29 C.F.R. §1630.2(n)(3)(vii).

28. 42 U.S.C.S. §12111(9)(A)(B); 29 C.F.R. 1630.2 §(o)(i)-(iii) (Law. Co-Op. 1995).

29. 42 U.S.C.S. §12112(b)(1)-(7) (Law. Co-Op. 1995).

30. 42 U.S.C.S. §12112(b)(1)-(7) (Law. Co-Op. 1995).

31. 29 U.S.C.S. §706 (8)(D) (Law. Co-Op. 1995).

32. 42 U.S.C.S. §12132 (Law. Co-Op. 1995).

33. 42 U.S.C.S. 12131(2) (Law. Co-Op. 1995).

34. 42 U.S.C.S. §12131(1)(A)-(C) (Law. Co-Op. 1995).

35. 42 U.S.C.S. §12131(2) (Law. Co-Op. 1995).

36. 42 U.S.C.S. §12141(2) (Law. Co-Op. 1995).

37. 49 U.S.C.S. §1374(c) (Law. Co-Op. 1995).

38. 42 U.S.C.S. §12142 (a)-(c) (Law. Co-Op. 1995).

39. 42 U.S.C.S. §12143(c)(4) (Law. Co-Op. 1995).

40. 42 U.S.C.S. §12141(1) (Law. Co-Op. 1995).

41. 42 U.S.C.S. §12182 (Law. Co-Op. 1995).

42. 42 U.S.C.S. §12181 (Law. Co-Op. 1995). Owner-occupied buildings with no more than five rooms for rent are excepted. Ibid., §(7)(A).

43. 42 U.S.C.S. §12182(b)(2)(A)(iv) (Law. Co-Op. 1995).

44. 42 U.S.C.S. §12181(9) (Law. Co-Op. 1995).

45. Rep. No. 485(III), see note 4.

46. 42 U.S.C.S. §12181(9)(A)-(D) (Law. Co-Op. 1995).

47. *Pennsylvania Association for Retarded Children v. Commonwealth of Pennsylvania*, 334 F. Supp. 1257 (E.D.Pa., 1971); *Mills v. District of Columbia*, 348 F. Supp. 866 (D.C.D.C., 1972).

48. The Individuals with Disabilities in Education Act is found at 20 U.S.C.S. §1400 *et seq.* (Law. Co-Op. 1995). The requirement for educating handicapped children in the same setting as nonhandicapped children is found at 20 U.S.C.S. §1412(5)(B) (Law. Co-Op. 1995) and 45 C.F.R. §84.34.

49. 45 C.F.R. §84.31

50. *Martinez v. School Board of Hillsborough County*, 675 F.Supp. 1574, (M.D.Fla., 1987), 692 F.Supp. 1293, (M.D.Fla., 1988) Vacated, 861 F.2d 1502, (11th Cir., 1988), on remand, 711 F.Supp. 1066, (M.D.Fla., 1989).

51. *Smith v. Robinson*, 468 U.S. 992 at 1017 (1984).

52. Children with disabilities include those "with mental retardation, hearing impairments including deafness, speech or language impairments, visual impairments including blindness, serious emotional disturbance, orthopedic impairments, autism, traumatic brain injury, other health impairments, or specific learning disabilities." 20 U.S.C.S. §1401(1)(i) (Law. Co-Op. 1995). Chronic or acute health problems included in "other health impairments"

refers to conditions such as a heart condition, tuberculosis, rheumatic fever, nephritis, asthma, sickle cell anemia, hemophilia, epilepsy, lead poisoning, leukemia, or diabetes that adversely affect a child's educational performance. 34 C.F.R. 300.7(b)(8).

53. *District 27 Community School Board v. Board of Education*, 130 Misc.2d 398 (N.Y.Sup., 1986). See also *Doe v. Belleville Public Schools District,* 672 F. Supp. 342 at 345 (S.D.Ill., 1987) (AIDS is not covered by the EAHCA. A child with AIDS could become eligible for its protection if he developed chronic or acute health problems which adversely affect his school performance.); *Robertson v. Granite City Community Unit School District,* 684 F. Supp. 1002 at 1005 (S.D.Ill., 1988) (The EAHCA applies to AIDS only if the child's physical condition adversely affects her educational performance.)

54. *Martinez v. Hillsborough*, note 50. The child in this case was mentally retarded in addition to having AIDS. Her retardation, alone, qualified her for protection under the EAHCA.

55. *District 27 Community School Board*, at 414, note 53.

56. *School Board of Nassau County v. Arline*, 480 U.S. 273 (1987).

57. *Reynolds v. Brock*, 815 F.2d 571, (9th Cir., 1987), aff'd 985 F.2d 470 (9th Cir., 1993), rehearing denied, 994 F.2d 690 (9th Cir., 1993).

58. *Johnston v. Morrison, Inc.,* 849 F.Supp. 777 (N.D.Ala., 1994).

59. *Norcross v. Sneed*, 573 F.Supp. 533 (W.D.Ark., 1983), aff'd 755 F.2d 113 (8th Cir., 1985).

60. *Ross v. Beaumont Hospital*, 687 F.Supp. 1115 (E.D.Mich., 1988).

61. *D'Amico v. New York State Board of Law Examiners,* 813 F.Supp. 217 (W.D.N.Y., 1993).

62. *Tsetseranoe v. Tech Prototype,* 893 F.Supp. 109 (D.N.H., 1995).

63. *Finley v. Giacobbe*, 827 F. Supp. 215 (S.D.N.Y., 1993).

64. Gittler, Josephine, and Renner, Sharon, "Symposium: HIV Infection Among Women of Reproductive Age, Children, and Adolescents: HIV Infection Among Women and Children and Antidiscrimination Laws: An Overview," *Iowa Law Review* 77 (1992): 1321.

65. United States Department of Health and Human Services, Public Health Service, Centers for Disease Control, *Morbidity and Mortality Weekly Report* 42 (1993): 870.

66. Overall, 34 percent of U. S. employers have dealt with cases involving employees perceived to have AIDS or diagnosed with HIV or AIDS. More then 67 percent of companies employing between 2,500 and 5,000 employees report having employed at least one HIV-positive employee. Klein, Jeffrey S., "With More Businesses Having to Accommodate HIV-Positive Employees, Companies Need Guidelines to Address Federal Disability Law and Privacy Rights," *National Law Journal* B5, col. 1 (1994).

67. 42 U.S.C.S. §12101(a)(1) (Law. Co-Op. 1995).

68. The definition of disability in the ADA appears at 42 U.S.C.S. §12102(2)(A)-(C) (Law. Co-Op. 1995). For the VRA, see 29 U.S.C.A. §706(8)(b), and for the FHA, see 42 USCS § 3602 (Law. Co-Op. 1995). Congress declined to create a definitive list of the conditions, diseases, or infections that might constitute physical or mental impairments (Rep. No. 485(II), see note 4), but guidance can be found in federal regulations that identify a variety of conditions, diseases, and disorders covered by the law [29 C.F.R. §1630.2 (h)(1) and (2) defines physical or mental impairment as: (1) Any physiological disorder, or condition, cosmetic disfigurement, or anatomical loss affecting one or more of the following body systems: neurological, musculoskeletal, special sense organs, respiratory (including speech organs), cardiovascular, reproductive, digestive, genito-urinary, hemic and lymphatic, skin, and endocrine; or (2) Any mental or psychological disorder, such as mental retardation, organic brain syndrome, emotional or mental illness, and specific learning disabilities.]

69. 45 C.F.R. §84.3(j)(2)(iii) (West 1996).

70. 29 C.F.R. §1630.2(l)(1) thru (3) (1995).

71. 42 U.S.C.S. §3607(3)(B)(4) (Law. Co-Op. 1994).

72. Rep. No. 711, note 4.

73. Ibid.

74. 42 U.S.C.S. §12211 (Law. Co-Op. 1995).

75. The VRA and Title I of the ADA use the phrase "otherwise qualified." Title II of the ADA drops the adjective "otherwise" extending its protection to the "qualified" individual with a disability and Title III uses neither "otherwise qualified" nor "qualified." Definitions in the ADA state that the term "qualified individual with a disability" is derived from regulation for implementing the VRA. The referred to regulations delete the adjective "otherwise," referring to the "qualified handicapped person " (45 C.F.R. 84.3(k) or they state that the phrase "qualified handicapped person is synonymous with "otherwise" qualified handicapped person (7 C.F.R. 15b.3(n)). The IDEA uses the phrase "qualified" without any modifier (45 C.F.R. §84.3(k)(2)-(4)). The FHA does not use the term "otherwise qualified." However, Congress's intent to codify this provision is discussed in the report of the House Judiciary Committee on the Fair Housing Amendments of 1988 (H.R. Rep. No. 711, note 4). The committee stated its intention that the otherwise qualified standard articulated by the Supreme Court in *Arline* be applied in the context of housing.

76. Rep. No. 711, note 4: Fn 77.

77. *School Board of Nassau County v. Arline*, note 56.

78. Ibid. 288.

79. 840 F.2d 701, (9th Cir., 1988).

80. Ibid. 705.

81. Ibid. 707.

82. Ibid. 708.

83. 42 U.S.C.S. §12112(d)(4)(A) (Law. Co-Op. 1995).

84. 42 U.S.C.S. §12112(3)(A)(B) (Law. Co-Op. 1995) An employment entrance exam is permitted if: (1) all entering employees are subjected to the examination regardless of disability; (2) information obtained about the applicant's medical condition or history is collected and maintained on separate forms and in separate medical files and is treated as a confidential medical record, except that: (a) supervisors and managers may be informed regarding necessary restrictions on the work or duties of the employee and necessary accommodations; (b) first aid and safety personnel may be informed if the disability might require emergency treatment; and (c) government officials investigating compliance with the law have access to relevant information on request.

85. 42 U.S.C.S. §12112(4)(A) (Law. Co-Op. 1995).

86. *Doe v. Kohn Nast & Graf, P.C.*, 866 F.Supp. 190 (E.D.Pa., 1994).

87. *Doe v. City of Chicago*, 883 F. Supp. 1126 (N.D.Ill., 1994).

88. *Leckelt v. Board of Commissioners of Hospital District No. 1*, 714 F.Supp. 1377 (E.D.La., 1989) aff'd 909 F.2d 820 (5th Cir., 1990).

89. *Smith v. Dovenmuehle Mortgage, Inc.,* 859 F.Supp. 1138 (N.D. Ill., 1994)

90. *McNemar v. Disney Stores,* 1995 WL 390051 (E.D.Pa., 1995)aff'd 91 F.3d 610 (3rd. Cir., 1996).

91. *Martinez*, note 50: 1071.

92. Courts in the following cases made an express finding that children with HIV were otherwise qualified: *Thomas v. Atascadero Unified School District*, 662 F. Supp. 376 at 381 (C.D. Cal., 1986); *Robertson v. Granite City*, note 53; *Doe v. Dolton Elementary School District No. 148*, 694 F. Supp. 440 at 440 (N.D.Ill., 1988); *Martinez v. School Board of Hillsborough County*, note 50. That children with HIV are otherwise qualified can be inferred from *Ray v. School District of DeSoto County*, 666 F. Supp. 1524 at 1524 (M.D.Fla., 1987); *Phipps v. Saddleback Valley Unified School District*, 204 Cal.App.3d 1110 at 1110 (Cal.App. 4 Dist., 1988); *District 27 Community School Board*, note 53.

93. Medical opinion has been consistent in concluding that risk of HIV-transmission is low; See *Chalk,* note 79: 705–706 (Based on the testimony of five experts plus 100 articles from medical journals including a report of the Surgeon General of the United States, finding that there was no "significant risk of transmission"); *Raytheon Co. v. Fair Employment & Housing Commission*, 212 Cal. App.3d 1242 at 1251 (Cal.App. 2 Dist., 1989) (All the considerable medical information collected established that AIDS was not transmissible in the workplace.); *Doe v. District of Columbia,* 769 F.Supp. 559 at 563 (D.D.C., 1992) (Based on the uncontroverted testimony of plaintiff's experts we find that the ability to perform as a firefighter is unaffected by plaintiff's asymptomatic HIV-positivity.); *Doe v. Dolton*, note 92, *Ray v. School District*, note 92 (All of the experts agree that there is no significant risk of transmission of AIDS in the classroom setting.); *Martinez*, note 50 (The doctor has changed his position, acknowledging that his earlier testimony that the child posed a danger to others was mainly for his comfort.); District 27, note 53 (The only

expert to conclude children with AIDS should not be allowed in school was not an epidemiologist, had done no research on the issue of HIV-transmission, and conceded his lack of familiarity with the findings derived from the studies of family members and health care workers.)

94. *Ray v. School District*, note 92: 1536.

95. *Doe v. Dolton*, note 92: 445.

96. *Martinez,* note 50.

97. Ibid.

98. See note 75 for a discussion of the phrase "otherwise qualified" as it is used in the VRA, ADA, FHA, and IDEA.

99. *United States v. University Hospital,* 729 F.2d 144 (2d Cir., 1984).

100. Ibid. 157.

101. *Glanz v. Vernick,* 750 F. Supp. 39 (D.Mass., 1990), 756 F. Supp. 632 (D.Mass., 1991); *Woolfolk v. Duncan,* 872 F.Supp. 1381 (E.D.Pa., 1995); *Toney v. U.S. Healthcare, Inc.,* 838 F.Supp. 201 (E.D.Pa., 1993), 870 F.Supp. 357 (E.D.Pa., 1994) aff'd, 37 F.3d 1489 (3rd Cir., 1994).

102. *Glanz v. Vernick,* 1990 at 45-46.

103. *In the Matter of Baby "K,"* 832 F. Supp. 1022 at 1028 (E.D.Va., 1993), aff'd 16 F.3d 590 (4th Cir., 1994), *cert* denied, 115 S.Ct. 91 (1994).

104. *Woolfolk,* note 100.

105. Ibid. 1389.

106. For the ADA, see 42 U.S.C.S. §12111(9)(A)(B) (Law. Co-Op. 1995). For the VRA, see 45 C.F.R. §84.3(k)(1). For the FHA, see §3604(f)(3)(B) (Law. Co-Op. 1995).

107. *Phipps v. Saddleback,* note 92.

108. *White v. Western School Corp.,* IP 85-1192-C, slip Op., (S.D.Ind., 1985).

109. *Robertson v. Granite City,* note 53.

110. *Ray v. School District,* note 92.

111. *Martinez,* note 50.

112. See notes 92 through 97 and accompanying text.

113. *Bradley v. University of Texas A & M Medical Center,* 3 F.3d 922 at 924 (5th Cir., 1993); *Mauro v. Borgess Medical Center,* 886 F.Supp. 1349 at 1352-1353 (W.D.Mich., 1995).

114. *Scoles v. Mercy Health Corporation,* 887 F.Supp. 765 (E.D.Pa., 1994).

115. *Doe v. Washington University,* 780 F.Supp. 628 (E.D.Mo., 1991).

116. *Doe v. University of Maryland,* 50 F.3d 1261 (4th Cir., 1995).

117. *Cain v. Hyatt,* note 23.

118. Ibid. 683. A person with HIV may be eligible for leave under the provisions of the Family and Medical Leave Act of 1993, which permits eligible employees to take medical leave of up to twelve weeks in a twelve-month period when their health renders them unable to work (29 U.S.C.S. §2601 (Law. Co-Op. 1994). The act applies to employers with fifty or more employees (29 C.F.R. §825.102) and defines an eligible employee as one who worked for at least 1,250 hours during the twelve months immediately preceding the start of the leave period (29 C.F.R. §825.110 (a)(1) & (2)).

119. Rep. No. 711, note 4; 42 U.S.C.S. §3604(f)(3)(A)(B) (Law. Co-Op. 1995).

120. See note 26.

121. Ibid. 409.

122. Ibid. 410.

123. Ibid. 398.

124. See note 115.

125. Ibid. 630.

126. Ibid. 633.

127. 42 U.S.C.S. §§12113(a)(2) and (c)(1) (Law. Co-Op. 1995).

128. 29 C.F.R. §1630.

129. 42 U.S.C.S. §12111(10) (Law. Co-Op. 1995); 29 C.F.R. §1630.2 (p)(1) & (p)(2)(i) through (iv).

130. 567 F. Supp. 369 (E.D. Pa., 1983).

131. 29 U.S.C.A. §706 (8)(D) (West 1994); 42 U.S.C.S § 3604(f)(9) (Law. Co-Op. 1995); 29 C.F.R. §1630.3(r).

132. The CDC investigated the allegation that Dr. David Acer, a Florida dentist, had infected six of his patients. United States Department of Health and Human Services, Public Health Service, Centers for Disease Control, "Investigations of Persons Treated by HIV-Infected Health-Care Workers in the United States," *Morbidity and Mortality Weekly Report* (1993) 841. In early 1994 questions arose about the veracity of the stories told by the six patients. One was reported to have "consorted with a prostitute," another, who claimed to have been treated by Dr. Acer was, in fact, treated by a hygienist in his office and never saw Acer, and another patient is reported to have had risk factors other than her visits to Dr. Acer. According to a *New York Times* article, CDC investigators made it clear that they did not find the story of the latter patient wholly credible and "that the patient believes there would be serious negative impact if her mother believed she participated in any risky behaviors" (Stephen Barr, "What If the Dentist Didn't Do It?" (*N.Y. Times*, April 16, 1994, at 1, 21, col. 1). On June 26, 1994, Frank Rich, reporting on a *60 Minutes* television program said to be based on information obtained through the Freedom of Information Act, said that "there is now strong reason to suspect that Dr. Acer was the innocent victim of both a witch hunt and an inadequate investigation by the CDC. A sworn videotaped deposition and

a gynecological exam reveal that one of the dentist's . . . patients . . . though publicly declaring herself virginal, had a history of both sexual activity and venereal infection" (Frank Rich, *N.Y. Times*, "The Gay Card," 4, 17 col. 1).

133. Nichols, Ronald L., "Percutaneous Injuries During Operation: Who Is at Risk for What?" *Journal of the American Medical Association* 267 (June 1992): 2938.

134. Panlilio, Adelisa L., Shapiro, Craig N., Schable, Charles A., et al., "Serosurvey of Human Immunodeficiency Virus; Hepatitis B Virus, and Hepatitis C Virus Infection Among Hospital-Based Surgeons," *Journal of the American College of Surgeons* 180 (1995): 16–24.

135. See, generally, United States Department of Health and Human Services, Public Health Service, Centers for Disease Control, "Recommendations for Preventing Transmission of Human Immunodeficiency Virus and Hepatitis B Virus to Patients During Exposure-Prone Invasive Procedures," *Morbidity and Mortality Weekly Report* 1 (1991); American Academy of Pediatrics, Task Force on Pediatric AIDS, "Pediatric Guidelines for Infection Control of Human Immunodeficiency Virus (Acquired Immunodeficiency Virus) in Hospitals, Medical Offices, Schools, and Other Settings," *Pediatrics* 82 (1988): 801–807; American Academy of Pediatrics, Task Force on Pediatric AIDS, "Guidelines for Human Immunodeficiency Virus (HIV)-Infected Children and Their Foster Families," *Pediatrics* 89 (1992); American Academy of Pediatrics, Task Force on Pediatric AIDS, "Infants and Children with Acquired Immunodeficiency Syndrome: Placement in Adoption and Foster Care," *Pediatrics* 83 (1989); Task Force on Children and HIV Infection, *Report of the CWLA Task Force on Children and HIV Infection: Initial Guidelines*, (Washington, D.C.: Child Welfare League of America, no date).

136. Katsiyannis, Antonis, "Policy Issues in School Attendance of Children with AIDS: A National Survey," *Journal of Special Education* 26 (1992): 219-226.

137. 42 U.S.C.A. §12113(d)(1)(B) (West 1994); 57 FR 40917 (1992).

138. Centers for Disease Control, note 135. The Ninth Circuit Court of Appeals adopted this reasoning in finding that the health of a physician who performed physical examinations for the FBI was irrelevant to the FBI's concern about risk to its employees. When risk of transmission is remote as it is in conducting physician examinations the pertinent inquiry is whether the infection control procedures followed by the hospital are sufficient to ensure that those examined are not placed at risk, not whether an examining physician has HIV or AIDS. *Doe v. Attorney General of the United States*, 814 F.Supp. 844 (N.D.Cal., 1992). On remand from the 9th Circuit for findings on the merits (941 F.2d 780 9th Cir., 1991) rev'd, 62 F.3d 1424, unpublished disposition, 1995 WL 392178 (1995), *cert* granted for redetermination of damages award, 1996 WL 341602 (1996).

139. *Doe v. University of Maryland*, note 116: 1263.

140. American Academy, "Pediatric Guidelines," note 135.

141. Ibid.

142. Ibid.

143. House Rep. No. 711, note 4.

144. Summers, Patrick F., "Comment: Civil Rights: Persons Infected with HIV: Stewart B. McKinney Foundation v. Town Plan & Zoning Commission: Forcing the AIDS Community to Live a Prophylactic Existence," *Oklahoma Law Review* 46 (1993): 531.

145. Zolopa, Andrew R., Hahn, Judith A., Gorter, Robert, et al., "HIV and Tuberculosis Infection in San Francisco's Homeless Adults: Prevalence and Risk Factors in a Representative Sample," *Journal of the American Medical Association* 272 (1994): 455.

146. *Baxter v. Belleville*, 720 F Supp 720 (S.D.Ill., 1989); *Stewart B. McKinney Foundation, Inc. v. Town Plan & Zoning Commission*, 790 F Supp 1197 (D.Conn., 1992); *Association of Relatives & Friends of AIDS Patients v. Regulations & Permits Administration*, 740 F Supp 95 (D.Puerto Rico, 1995); *Support Ministries for Persons with AIDS, Inc. v. Village of Waterford*, 808 F. Supp. 120 (N.D.N.Y., 1992).

147. *Baxter v. Belleville*, note 146: 732.

148. *Support Ministries for Persons with AIDS*, note 146: 122–123.

149. *Support Ministries for Persons with AIDS*, note 146: 123–124.

150. Ibid. 124–126.

151. Ibid. 134

152. Note 93.

153. The assumption that HIV is always fatal is challenged by data describing long-term survivors (i.e., people with HIV-infection who do not develop AIDS-related symptoms). See Giuseppe Pantaleo, Stefano Menzo, Mauro Vaccarezza, et al., "Studies in Subjects with Long-Term Nonprogressive Human Immunodeficiency Virus Infection," *New England Journal of Medicine* 332 (1995): 209–216; Yunzhen Cao, Limo Qin, Linqi Zhang, et al., "Virologic and Immunologic Characterization of Long-Term Survivors of Human Immunodeficiency Virus Type 1 Infection," *New England Journal of Medicine* 332 (1995): 201–208. Lawrence K. Altman, "Long-Term Survivors May Hold Key Clues to Puzzle of AIDS," *N.Y. Times*, (1995) Section C, p. 1.

In the fall of 1996, based on a study of approximately 2,000 HIV-positive people, researchers from the National Cancer Institute identified a gene which, if inherited from both parents, provides almost complete protection from HIV and if inherited from one parent can extend survival time for up to three years. United States Department of Health and Human Services, Public Health Service, Centers for Disease Control, *AIDS Daily Summary*, (September 27, 1996).

154. *Doe v. University of Maryland*, note 116: 1266.

155. See also *Scoles v. Mercy Health Corporation*, note 114. Scoles's surgical privileges were suspended after he disclosed his HIV-status to colleagues. His privileges were reinstated with the proviso that he inform his patients of his HIV-status before performing any invasive procedure. Nevertheless, he sued

the hospital, alleging that their concerns about liability and an unreasonable fear of AIDS motivated their actions. He claimed also that he did not pose a significant risk to his patients. The court rejected Scoles's defense, because he had not proven that he did not pose a risk to his patients and because the chance of transmission would exist as long as Scoles performed surgery and the harm is a fatal disease. The court's reasoning is flawed in two respects: first, it is impossible to prove conclusively that no risk exists and the Supreme Court did not set such a requirement in *Arline* (see note 78 and accompanying text). Second, each surgical procedure is an independent event and the suggestion that risk is increased simply because the event is repeated is not logical.

156. *Raytheon Co. v. Fair Employment & Housing Commission*, note 93.

157. Ibid. 1252.

158. Note 93.

159. Ibid. 569.

160. Ibid. See also *Roe v. District of Columbia*, 842 F. Supp. 563 (D.D.C., 1993) dismissed as moot, 25 F.3d 1115 (D.C. Cir., 1994. *Roe* concerned a firefighter's claim that he had been "wrongfully denied [the] opportunity to perform mouth-to-mouth resuscitation because of [his] handicap, consisting of his being a carrier for the Hepatitis B virus" (Ibid. 563). The district court, discussing employment decisions that are based on fear of contagion by persons with the hepatitis B virus and by those with HIV found the "nature of the risk . . . and the probabilities [that] the disease will be transmitted" (Ibid. 569) to be so remote as to require finding for Roe.

161. The Centers for Disease Control reports that the kind of nonsexual person-to-person contact that generally occurs among workers and clients or consumers in the workplace does not pose a risk of transmission of HIV. United States Department of Health and Human Services, Public Health Service, Centers for Disease Control, *Recommendations for Preventing Transmission of Infection with Human T-Lymphotropic Virus Type III/Lymphadenopathy-Associated Virus in the Workplace, Morbidity and Mortality Weekly Report 34* (1985): 682.

162. A person who is denied medical services in an emergency has recourse under the Emergency Medical Treatment and Active Labor Act, 42 U.S.C.S. §1395dd (Law. Co-Op. 1996).

163. *The City of Cleburne v. Cleburne Living Center,* 473 U.S. 432, 105 S.Ct. 3249 (1985).

164. Ibid. 3258–3260.

CHAPTER 3

1. Schable, Barbara, Diaz, Theresa, Chu, Susan Y., et al., "Who Are the Primary Caretakers of Children Born to HIV-Infected Mothers? Results from a Multistate Surveillance Project," *Pediatrics* 95 (1995): 511–515.

2. 42 U.S.C.S. §401 *et seq.* (Law. Co-Op. 1995).

3. 42 U.S.C.S. §1381 *et seq.* (Law. Co-Op. 1995).

4. Regulations for determining medical equivalence for adults are found at 20 C.F.R. §416.926 and for children at §416.926(a).

5. The definition of disability for Title XVI is found at 42 U.S.C.S. §1382c(a)(3)(B) (Law. Co-Op. 1995); and for Title II at 42 U.S.C.S. §423(d)(1)(A)(B) (Law. Co-Op. 1995).

6. 142 *Cong. Rec.* H8829 (July 30, 1996). The definition of disability for the SSI and SSDI programs has been the same. The 1996 welfare reform legislation refers to the definition of childhood disability with reference to the SSI program. It is reasonable to conclude that this definition will apply also to the SSDI program.

7. 42 U.S.C.S. §414(a)(2) (Law. Co-Op. 1995).

8. 42 U.S.C.S. §402(d)(1) (Law. Co-Op. 1995).

9. 42 U.S.C.S. 423(d)(1)(A) (Law. Co-Op. 1995).

10. 42 U.S.C.S. §402(e)(B)(ii) (Law. Co-Op. 1995).

11. 42 U.S.C.S. §416(d)(e)(f) (Law. Co-Op. 1995).

12. 42 U.S.C.S. §423(c)(1)(B)(i) and (ii) (Law. Co-Op. 1995).

13. 20 C.F.R. 416.974(b)(3)(vii).

14. 42 U.S.C.S. §1382(a)(1)(A) and (c)(1) (Law. Co-Op. 1995).

15. 42 U.S.C.S. §1382b(1) through (4) (Law. Co-Op. 1995).

16. McCormick, Harvey L., *Social Security Claims and Procedures: Part VI. Supplemental Security Income Act*, (St. Paul: West Publishing Co., 4th ed., 1995 Pocket Part).

17. 42 U.S.C.S. §1383(a)(4)(A)(B) (Law. Co-Op. 1995).

18. 142 *Cong. Rec.* H8829 (July 30, 1996).

19. If an applicant claims more than one impairment, the determination of eligibility is made on the basis of the combined effects of the claimed impairments. (20 C.F.R. 416.924(b) [for children] and 42 U.S.C.S. §1382c(a)(3)(F) [for adults].)

20. See 20 C.F.R. 416.924(b). A listing of child impairments is found at 20 C.F.R. pt. 404, subpt. P, App. 1 (pt. B) (1993); adult impairments are found in pt. A.

21. McGovern, Theresa M., "S. P. v. Sullivan: The Effort to Broaden the Social Security Administration's Definition of AIDS," *Fordham Urban Law Journal* 21 (1994): 1083.

22. Ibid.

23. The SSA argued that as early as 1983 it had instructed its staff to conduct disability evaluations on a case-by-case basis and that evaluations were not to be limited by the CDC's surveillance definition (20 C.F.R. Part 404). The

Third Circuit Court of Appeals found this claim lacking in merit, because the SSA's guidelines consisted of internal, "subregulatory materials," [*Rosetti v. Shalala*, 12 F.3d 1216 at 1219 at 1220 (3rd Cir., 1993)] and that it "could and did change its rules and policies for handling HIV- and AIDS-based claims as it saw fit."

24. See *Anderson v. Shalala*, 1993 WL 289203 (D.Kan., 1993) on remand from the Tenth Circuit for reevaluation of claims based on the July 1993 listings (34 F.3d 1076, 1994); *Cohen v. Chater*, 1995 WL 405028 (E.D.N.Y., 1995) (Mr. Cohen has documented his HIV-infection and has been denied benefits without consideration of the new listings).

25. McCormick, note 16.

26. Boskey, Jill A., and Malvey, Thomas J., "HIV Disability Claims: A Reference for the Advocate," *Social Security Reporting Service* 46 (1994): 5.

27. 20 C.F.R. 416.920(e)-(f); 20 C.F.R. §1520(e)-(f).

28. In 1990, the Supreme Court, in *Sullivan v. Zebly* (110 S. Ct. 885) held that a child's rights were violated when her claim was denied based on a determination at step 3 without considering additional factors. The Court established the requirement that an IFA be conducted. Congress overturned this provision in 1996 (see note 6).

29. *Sullivan v. Zebly*, note 28: 896.

30. 20 C.F.R. 416.924(a)(1)(2).

31. *Glanz v. Vernick*, 756 F.Supp. 632 at 636 (D.Mass., 1991).

32. *United States v. Morvant*, 898 F.Supp. 1157 (E.D.La., 1995).

33. The Medicaid program is found at 42 U.S.C.S. §1396, *et seq.* (Law. Co-Op. 1995); Medicare at 42 U.S.C.S. §1395, *et seq.* (Law. Co-Op. 1995); Indian Health Services at 25 U.S.C.S. §1603, *et seq.* (Law. Co-Op. 1995); and Veterans Administration Programs at 38 U.S.C.S. §301, *et seq.* (Law. Co-Op. 1995).

34. 42 U.S.C.S. §701 *et seq.* (1995).

35. 42 U.S.C.S. §300ff *et seq.* (Law. Co-Op. 1996).

36. United States General Accounting Office, *Health Insurance for Children— State and Private Programs Create New Strategies to Insure Children*, Rep. No. 96-35 (1996).

37. The number of uninsured children is reported in: United States General Accounting Office, *Health Insurance for Children—Many Remain Uninsured Despite Medicaid Expansion* Rep. No. 95-175 (July 19, 1995). The number of uninsured Americans is reported in: Commission on Behavioral and Social Sciences, National Research Council, *The Social Impact of AIDS in the United States*, (Washington, D.C.: National Academy Press, 1993): 46. The meaning of the figure of 37 million uninsured has been debated. The National Research Council reports that six months was the median period of uninsurance and that 70 percent of all periods end within nine months. Therefore, some critics imply that the situation is not as bad as the figure of 37 million implies. [See Swartz, Katherine, "Dynamics of People without Health Insurance: Don't

Let the Numbers Fool You; Caring for the Uninsured and Underinsured," *Journal of the American Medical Association* 271 (1994):64.] Swartz, one of the authors of the study that produced the six-month figure, makes several points about how her data have been used: (1) to say that half of all uninsured spells end within six months is the same as saying that one-half last longer (approximately 28 percent exceed one year and 15 to 18 percent exceed two years); (2) data gathered at a single point in time (on the first day of the month, for example) exclude those whose spell of uninsurance has just ended and those whose spell is about to begin. Because an average spell may last six months does not support the conclusion that one-half of the people counted on a specific day will regain their insurance within that time period; (3) the problem of uninsurance that confronts "repeaters," those who will experience episodic periods of uninsurance, effectively being uninsured "most of the time," gets lost when the six-month average is applied; and (4) the data she and her colleagues used in their study were gathered in a period of time when the economy was recovering from a recession and unemployment was falling, in short, a period of time when the number of Americans covered by employment-based insurance plans may have been at its best.

38. See "Health Insurance for Children—Many Remain Uninsured," note 37.

39. Bradford, William A., Jr., Zavos, Michele A., et al., "The AIDS Epidemic and Health Care Reform," *John Marshall Law Review* 27 (1994): 279.

40. Three hundred twenty-five insurance companies responding to a 1985 survey report that AIDS is an "uninsurable" condition. Ninety-nine percent considered people with Aids-Related Complex (ARC; which refers to a constellation of factors, such as repeated fevers, unexplained weight loss, and swollen lymph nodes, found in some people with HIV) to be uninsurable and 95 percent say that they would refuse to insure any person who tested positive for HIV (Ozawa, Martha N., Auslander, Wendy F., and Slonim-Nevo, Vered, "Problems in Financing the Care of AIDS Patients," *Social Work* 38 (1993): 373). There is evidence that private insurance companies have discriminated against people with HIV by "red-lining" certain areas of a city known to have a heavy concentration of gay people and by denying insurance to people based on occupational category [See, Isbell, Michael T., "AIDS and Access to Care: Lessons for Health Care Reformers," *Cornell Journal of Law & Public Policy* 3 (1993): 7].

41. See CA-HLTH-ANN, §199.21 & California Insurance Code §799.10 (West 1994); CO-ST-ANN §10-3-1104.5 (West 1995); CT-ST-ANN §19a-586 (West 1995); FL-ST-ANN §627.429 (West 1994); GA-ST-ANN §31-22-9.2(f) (West 1995); IL-ST-ANN §50/3(c) (West 1995); IA-ST-ANN §505.16(1) (West 1995); ME-ST-ANN §19203-A (West 1995). Applicants for health insurance must report preexisting conditions, such as a positive HIV-test, under penalty of losing benefits. Courts are unlikely to hold an insurance company liable to reimburse medical providers if the insured misrepresented her medical condition at the time of applying for insurance [Draper, Jane M., "Annotation: Rescission or Cancellation of Insurance Policy for Insured's Misrepresentation or Concealment of Information Concerning Human Immunodeficiency Virus (HIV), Acquired Immunodeficiency Syndrome (AIDS), or Related Health Problems, 15 *A.L.R.5th* 92 (1995)].

42. See Bradford and Zavos, note 39; Isbell, note 40. The Consolidated Omnibus Reconciliation Act of 1985 (COBRA) requires employers with twenty or more workers to permit workers to continue, at their own expense, their health insurance for eighteen months following termination of employment at a cost not to exceed 2 percent of the group insurance premium. In addition, thirty-six states have statutory provisions that permit a person to convert group insurance to individual insurance plans. Some who cannot afford risk pools may, because of the COBRA cap, be able to maintain private insurance, limited, however, to the eighteen months specified in the statute (42 U.S.C.S. §300ff-25(a)(1) (Law. Co-Op. 1995).

43. 42 U.S.C.S. §12201(c) (Law. Co-Op. 1995). 42 U.S.C.S. §12112(a) (Law. Co-Op. 1995). Before passage of the ADA, an employee's claim that lowering his medical benefits violated federal law was not successful. *McGann v. H & H Music Co.,* 742 F.Supp. 392 (S.D.Tx., 1990) aff'd 946 F.2d 401 (5th Cir., 1991), *cert* denied, 506 U.S. 981.

44. Rulings have been issued in: *Estate of Mark Kadinger v. International Brotherhood of Electrical Workers, Local 110,* Civil Action No. 3-93-159, 1993 U.S. Dist. Lexis 18982 (MN. Dist. Ct. December 21, 1993); *EEOC v. Mason Tenders,* No. 93-3865 (S.D.N.Y., 1995); *and Doe v. Laborer's District Council,* cited in Bradford, note 39: Fn. 213. *Carparts Distribution Center, Inc. v. Automotive Wholesaler's Association of New England,* 826 F. Supp. 583 (D.N.H., 1993) vacated and remanded, 37 F.3d 12 (1st Cir., 1994) is unresolved at the time of this writing.

45. *Anderson v. Mayer,* Lexis 4736 (E.D.Tx., 1996): 44–47.

46. Buchanan, Robert J., and Colby, David, "Medicaid Policies for the Physicians' Services Provided to Medicaid Recipients with AIDS," *AIDS and Public Policy Journal* 11 (1996): 47–60.

47. See Sadovsky, Richard, "HIV-Infected Patients: A Primary Care Challenge," *American Family Physician* 40 (1989): 121; No author, "Physicians' Attitudes Toward HIV-Infected Patients; Tips from Other Journals," *American Family Physician* 47 (1993): 491.

48. Link, R. N., Feingold, A. R., Charap, M. H., et al., "Concerns of Medical and Pediatric House Officers About Acquiring AIDS from Their Patients," *American Journal of Public Health* (1988): 455–459.

49. Imperato, P. J., Feldman, J. G., Nayeri, K., DeHovitz, L., "For Patients with AIDS in a High Incidence Area," *New York State Journal of Medicine* 88 (1988): 223–227.

50. No author, "Medical Student Attitudes Toward AIDS Patients," *American Family Physician* 40 (1989): 236.

51. Gerbert, Barbara, Maguire, Bryan T., Bleecker, Thomas, et al., "Primary Care Physicians and AIDS: Attitudinal and Structural Barriers to Care," *Journal of the American Medical Association* 266 (1991): 2837.

52. No author, "U.S. Doctors More Reluctant to Treat AIDS Patients; Compared with French & Canadian Physicians; VIII International Conference on AIDS," *AIDS Weekly* (1992).

53. Levin, Betty Wolder, Krantz, David H., et al., "The Treatment of Non-HIV-Related Conditions in Newborns at Risk for HIV: A Survey of Neonatologists," *American Journal of Public Health* 85 (1995): 1507–1513.

54. Council on Ethical and Judicial Affairs Report, "Ethical Issues Involved in the Growing AIDS Crisis," *Journal of the American Medical Association* 259 (1988): 1360.

55. *Doe v. Jamaica Hospital*, 608 N.Y.S.2d 518 (N.Y. A.D., 1994). Although filed in 1988, this ruling is the first published decision in this case.

56. *Abbott v. Bragdon*, 912 F.Supp. 580 (D.Me., 1995).

57. *Morvant*, note 32. *D.B. v. Bloom*, 896 F.Supp. 166 (D.N.J., 1995) (Dentist's claim that patient required specialized care was a pretext for discrimination. No special skills are required to treat a patient who is HIV-positive).

58. *Miller v. Spicer*, 822 F. Supp. 158 (D.Del., 1993). A surgeon refused to operate on a lacerated tendon, claiming that he did not perform the surgery. He would later admit to having performed the surgery "thousands of times." Ibid. 161.

59. On NIAID clinical trials, see *Women and HIV Disease: Falling Through the Cracks* 102d Cong., 2d Sess., Rep. No. 1086 (1991): 70–82. On the Terry Beirn program, see 42 U.S.C.A. §300cc-13 (West 1996). NIAID also conducts a program to test new treatments through the Division of AIDS Treatment Research Initiative. In 1992, only forty-nine subjects were enrolled compared to over 5,000 in the Terry Beirn program and over 20,000 in the ACTG.

60. "Guidelines for the Study and Evaluation of Gender Differences in the Clinical Evaluation of Drugs," 58 F.R. 139 39406 (July 21, 1993).

61. Bobinski, Mary Anne, "Women and HIV: A Gender-Based Analysis of a Disease and Its Legal Regulation," *Texas Journal of Women and the Law* (1994): 3–56.

62. Broers, Barbara, Morabia, Alfredo, and Hirschel, Bernard, "A Cohort Study of Drug Users' Compliance with Zidovudine Treatment," *Archives of Internal Medicine* 154 (1994): 1121 (Comparing 151 intravenous drug users (IDUs) with 162 others. To the extent that IDUs did not comply, homelessness and the presence of a psychiatric diagnosis were correlated with noncompliance). See also, Samuels, J. E., Hendrix, J., and Hilton, M., "Zidovudine Therapy in an Inner-City Population; Journal Review," *AIDS Alert* 5 (1990): 219; Wartenberg, Alan A., " 'Into Whatever Houses I Enter': HIV and Injecting Drug Use." Editorial, *Journal of the American Medical Association* 271 (1994): 151.

63. Johnston, Margaret I., and Hoth, Daniel F., "Present Status and Future Prospects for HIV Therapies," *Science* 260 (1993): 1286–1287.

64. Long, Iris L., "A Community Advocate's View of Clinical Research," in Kurth, Ann (Ed.) *Until the Cure: Caring for Women with HIV,* (New Haven: Yale University Press, 1993): Ch. 8.

65. Mohr, Penny E., "Patterns of Health Care Use Among HIV-Infected Adults: Preliminary Results," *ACSUS Report* 3 (1994): 3.

66. "National Institutes of Health Revitalization Act of 1993," (June 10, 1993)
    P.L. 103-43, codified at 107 Stat. 200 (June 10, 1993); 42 U.S.C.S. §300cc-
    41(a)(1) (Law. Co-Op. 1995).

67. 59 F.R. 156, 41769 (August 15, 1994).

68. 42 U.S.C.S. §298a-2 (Law. Co-Op. 1995); 42 U.S.C.S. §300cc-41 (Law. Co-Op.
    1995).

69. "Veterans' Health Program Extension Act of 1994," 103rd Cong., 2d Sess. Rep.
    No. 3313, P.L. 103-452, codified at 108 Stat. 4783 (1994).

70. Anastos, Kathryn, and Vermund, Sten, "Epidemiology and Natural History,"
    in Kurth, Ann (Ed.), note 64: Ch. 11.

71. Presidential Commission on the Human Immunodeficiency Virus Epidemic,
    "Report of Presidential Commission on the Human Immunodeficiency Virus
    Epidemic: Submitted to the President of the United States," (Washington,
    D.C.: The Commission, June 24, 1988).

72. "Women and HIV Disease," note 59.

73. Ibid. 113.

74. Cited in Anastos, note 70: 162.

75. Ibid. 157.

76. Hellinger, Fred J., "The Use of Health Services by Women with HIV Infec-
    tion," *Health Services Research* 28 (1993): 543.

77. "Women and HIV Disease," note 59: 1–2.

78. Gallant, Joel E., McAvinue, Sharon M., Moore, Richard D., et al., "The Im-
    pact of Prophylaxis on Outcome and Resource Utilization in Pneumocystis
    Carinii Pneumonia," *Chest* 107 (1995): 1018.

79. 42 U.S.C.S. §287d (Law. Co-Op. 1995).

80. 42 U.S.C.S. §287d-1 (Law. Co-Op. 1995).

81. "NIH Revitalization Act," note 66.

82. Presidential Advisory Council on HIV/AIDS, *Progress Report: Implementation
    of Advisory Council Recommendations*, (Washington, D.C.: 1996): 6. Available
    from the White House Office on AIDS. When the federal budget was passed
    for fiscal year 1995–1996, Congress hinted at the possibility that the authority
    of the OAR might change in 1997, but did not say what this change might
    be. See 142 *Cong. Rec.* H4187-01 (April 30, 1996).

83. United States House of Representatives, "Making Appropriations for the De-
    partment of Defense for the Fiscal Year Ending Sepetember 30, 1997, and for
    Other Purposes," 104th Cong., 2nd Sess. Rep. No. 863 (September 28,1996).

84. 42 U.S.C.S. §1396 *et seq.* (Law. Co-Op. 1995).

85. English, Abigail, "Pediatric HIV Infection and Perinatal Drug or Alcohol Ex-
    posure: Legal Issues and Legal Advocacy," in Barth, Richard P., Pietrzak,
    Jeanne, and Ramler, Malia (Eds.) *Families Living with Drugs and HIV: In-
    tervention and Treatment Strategies,* (New York: Guilford Press, 1993):Ch. 13.

86. No author, "Access/Quality/Cost Health Insurance: Study Shows Major Shifts in Coverage," *American Health Line* 4 (1996).

87. "Health Insurance for Children—Many Remain Uninsured," note 37.

88. United States House of Representatives, Subcommittee on Human Resources and Intergovernmental Relations, *AIDS Treatment and Care: Who Cares?* 101st Cong., 2d Sess. Rep. No. 674 (1994); Buchanan, Robert J., "Medicaid Policies for the Nursing Facility Care Provided to Medicaid Recipients with AIDS," *AIDS and Public Policy Journal* 10 (1995): 94.

89. Green, Jesse, and Arno, Peter S., "The 'Medicaidization' of AIDS: Trends in the Financing of HIV-Related Medical Care," *Journal of the American Medical Association* 264 (1990): 1261.

90. Personal Responsibility and Work Opportunities Act of 1996, P.L. 104-193, codified at 110 Stat. 2105 (1996).

91. Bradford and Zavos, note 39.

92. 42 U.S.C.S. §1396(a)(viii) (Law. Co-Op. 1995).

93. *Omnibus Budget Reconciliation Act of 1989*, P.L. 101-239 codified at 103 Stat. 2106 (1989).

94. *Omnibus Budget Reconciliation Act of 1990*, P.L. 101-508, 104 Stat 1388 (November 5, 1990).

95. Green and Arno, note 89.

96. Ibid.

97. Buchanan and Colby, note 46.

98. "AIDS Treatment and Care," note 88.

99. Bennett, Charles L., Horner, Ronnie D., Weinstein, Robert A., et al., "Racial Differences in Care Among Hospitalized Patients with Pneumocystis Carinii Pneumonia in Chicago, New York, Los Angeles, Miami, and Raleigh-Durham," *Archives of Internal Medicine* 155 (1995): 1586.

100. Medicaid mills are "small clinics that provide primary care. Forty percent of the physicians working in New York's Medicaid mills are not listed in the N.Y. State Medical Directory; many are not board certified. In general the "mills" provide a very low level of care to poor persons who have few options." "AIDS Treatment and Care," note 88: Fn 150. See also Williams, Robert M., "The Costs of Visits to Emergency Departments," *New England Journal of Medicine* 334 (1996): 642–646.

101. See Lado, Marianne L. Engelman, "Breaking the Barriers of Access to Health Care: A Discussion of the Role of Civil Rights Litigation and the Relationship Between Burdens of Proof and the Experience of Denial," *Brooklyn Law Review* 60 (1994): 239.

102. The Emergency Medical Treatment and Active Labor Act (EMTALA) 42 U.S.C.S. §1395dd (Law. Co-Op. 1995) provides that hospitals with emergency departments that receive federal funds cannot transfer patients without a series of safeguards including medical screenings and stabilizing treatments.

103. "Health Insurance for Children—Many Remain Uninsured," note 37.

104. "Women and HIV Disease," note 59: 20–27.

105. Fleishman, John A., Hsia, David C., and Hellinger, Fred J., "Correlates of Medical Service Utilization Among People with HIV Infection," *Health Services Research* 29 (1994): 527.

106. Volberding, Paul A., "Improving the Outcomes of Care for Patients with Humanimmunodeficiency virus Infection," *New England Journal of Medicine* 334 (1996): 729–731.

107. Buchanan, Robert J., Kircher, Fred G., "Medicaid Policies for AIDS-Related Hospital Care; Health Care Needs of Vulnerable Populations," *Health Care Financing Review* 15 (1994): 33.

108. United States Department of Health and Human Services, Public Health Service, Centers for Disease Control, *AIDS Daily Summary*, (October 10, 1996).

109. Hellinger, Fred J., "The Lifetime Cost of Treating a Person with HIV," *Journal of the American Medical Association* 270 (1993): 474.

110. Hsia, David C., Fleishman, John A., et al., "Pediatric Human Immunodeficiency Virus Infection: Recent Evidence on the Utilization and Costs of Health Services, " *Archives of Pediatrics & Adolescent Medicine* 149 (1995): 489.

111. Hellinger, note 109.

112. "AIDS Treatment and Care," note 88.

113. National Commission on AIDS, "America Living with AIDS," cited in Isbell, note 40: Fn 36.

114. 42 U.S.C.S. §1396(a)(1)(2)(3)(4B) and (5) (Law. Co-Op. 1995). State plans must include assurances that all under the age of 21 who are eligible for medical assistance will be informed that EPSDT services are available, and about the need for age-appropriate immunizations against vaccine-preventable diseases (42 USC 1396a(a)(43)(A) (Law. Co-Op. 1995).

115. Holahan, John, Coughlin, Teresa, Liu, Korbin, et al., *Cutting Medicaid Spending in Response to Budget Caps,* (Washington, D.C.: The Urban Institute, 1995): 8.

116. See the discussion of Title II of the CARE Act, this chapter.

117. The state of Missouri limited coverage for AZT to persons with certain diagnosis and under certain conditions. The Eighth Circuit Court of Appeals found the state in violation of Medicaid regulations. The state "may not arbitrarily deny or reduce the am)unt, duration, or scope of a required service . . . to an otherwise eligible recipient solely because of the diagnoses, type of illness or condition." [*Weaver v. Reagen*, 701 F.Supp. 717 (W.D.Mo., 1988) Aff'd, 886 F.2d 194 at 197-198 (1989).]

118. "AIDS: New Drug Therapies Unaffordable for Majority Infected with HIV," *BNA Health Care Daily*, (February 5, 1996). Pear, Robert, "Expense Means Many Can't Get Drugs for AIDS" *N.Y. Times* (February 16, 1997) A1.

119. 21 U.S.C.S. 360ee (Law. Co-Op. 1995); 59 F.R. 156 No. 41769.

120. 42 U.S.C.S. §1396d(2)(B); 1396d(7)-(11) (Law. Co-Op. 1995).

121. 42 U.S.C.S. §1395 *et seq.* (Law. Co-Op. 1995).

122. Buchanan and Kircher, note 107.

123. 42 U.S.C.S. §1396n(b) (Law. Co-Op. 1995); 42 C.F.R §441.300; 42 C.F.R. §440.180(b)(1)-(8).

124. 42 C.F.R. §440.180(b)(1)-(8).

125. 42 U.S.C.S. §1396n(e) (Law. Co-Op. 1995).

126. 42 C.F.R. §440.180.

127. Domestic violence was a marginalized issue, not tackled by government, for different reasons. A man's prerogative to "use violence to manage his household," was legally protected in the nineteenth century and has been socially sanctioned in the twentieth century. [See Special Issue, "Legal Responses to Domestic Violence: New State and Federal Responses to Domestic Violence," *Harvard Law Review* 106 (1993: 1528).] It would be the late 1970s before a woman who was battered by her husband would have any legal recourse beyond obtaining an injunction. Thus what came to be called the Battered Women's Movement began as a grassroots activity where women developed shelters and programs to help victims of domestic violence. Writing in 1995, Schneider says there has been "little government or private funding to support [the movement]. Until very recently, there was virtually no government support for work on domestic violence at the federal level." (See, generally, Schneider, Elizabeth M., "Symposium on Reconceptualizing Violence Against Women by Intimate Partners: Critical Issues: Epilogue: Making Reconceptualization of Violence Against Women Real," *Albany Law Review* 58 (1995): 1245.)

128. Funds were raised at gay bars, parties, and auctions. Special events were held such as the Madison Square Garden Circus at which $250,000 was raised for the GMHC [Shilts, Randy, *And the Band Played On,* (New York: St. Martin's Press, 1987):282]; "AIDS Walks" occur annually in a number of cities, raising large sums of money ($5 million was raised in one afternoon in New York City, *N.Y. Times,* May 20, 1996, B3); and benefits, such as the annual fashion benefit for AIDS Project Los Angeles ($600,000 in one afternoon, *The Advocate,* Issue 635, August 10, 1993:43) and concerts (AmFAR raised $1 million at a 1994 concert, *The Advocate,* Issue 680, May 2, 1995:27). Between 1991 and 1995, the Elizabeth Taylor Foundation had given more than $3 million to AIDS causes (*The Advocate,* Issue 691, October 3, 1995:12); and in 1995, David Geffin donated $4 million to the GMHC ($2.5 million) and the God's Love We Deliver food program ($1.5 million) (*The Advocate,* Issue 690, September 19, 1995:12).

Discussing fundraising, the National Research Council (note 41: 170) reports that mainline charities and foundations were reluctant to become involved in AIDS issues because of the associated stigma. The exception was the Robert Woods Johnson Foundation, which, as of 1993, had given more than $20 million for AIDS-related purposes and whose leadership drew in other foundations which, to date, together with corporations, have donated approximately $120 million.

129. See Shilts, note 128; Burkett, Elinor, *The Gravest Show on Earth: America in the Age of AIDS,* (New York: Houghton Mifflin, 1995).

130. National Research Council, note 37: 160.

131. Burkett, note 129: 145.

132. Arno, Peter S., "The Non-Profit Sector's Response to the AIDS Epidemic: Community-Based Services in San Francisco," *American Journal of Public Health* 76 (1986): 1325–1330.

133. Ibid.

134. *The Advocate* (April 19, 1994) Issue 653: 31; *The Advocate* (February 25, 1992) Issue 597: 44.

135. See Levine, Carol (Ed.) *Orphans of the HIV Epidemic,* (New York: United Hospital Fund, 1993); Sokal-Gutierrez, Karen, Vaughn-Edmonds, Holly, and Villarreal, Sylvia, "Health Care Services for Children and Families," in Barth et al., note 85: Ch. 6; Anderson, Gary R. (Ed.) *Courage to Care: Responding to the Crisis of Children with AIDS,* (Washington, D.C.: Child Welfare League of America, 1990): Ch. 4; Scott, Deborah E., Hu, Dale J., Hanson, Celine I., et al., "Case Management of HIV-Infected Children in Missouri" *Public Health Reports* 110 (1995): 355–356; Siegel, Galia, "Ventures into the Unprecedented: The Challenge of Integrating Women's Drug Treatment, Family Preservation and HIV Services," *Georgetown Journal on Fighting Poverty* 1 (1993): 104; Indyk, Debbie, Belville, Renate, Lachapelle, Sister Susanne, et al., "A Community-Based Approach to HIV Case Management: Systematizing the Unmanageable," *Social Work* 38 (1993): 380; Caldwell, M. Blake, Mascola, Laurene, Smith, Walter, et al., "Biologic, Foster, and Adoptive Parents: Care Givers of Children Exposed Perinatally to Human Immunodeficiency Virus in the United States," *Pediatrics* 90 (1992): 603–607.

136. United States Department of Health and Human Services, Health Resources and Services Administration, *AIDS Funding History—FY 1986–FY 1997,* (Washington, D.C.: 1996). Between 1986 and 1991 (the first full year of funding under the CARE Act), federal funds were available to the states under grant programs such as the AIDS Service Demonstration Grants, Formula Grants for Home Health, Drug Reimbursements, and Community Health Care Service for AIDS. These programs were incorporated into the CARE Act. President Clinton's budget proposal for FY 1997 contained a request of more than $830 million for the CARE Act. The CARE Act is found at 42 U.S.C.S. 300ff *et seq.* (Law. Co-Op. 1996).

137. 104th Cong., 2d Sess. 142 *Cong. Rec.* S11911 (September 30, 1996).

138. 42 U.S.C.S. §§300ff-11 to -18 (Law. Co-Op. 1996).

139. 42 U.S.C.S. §300ff-12(b) (Law. Co-Op. 1996).

140. 42 U.S.C.S. §300ff-14(b)(A)(B) (Law. Co-Op. 1996).

141. 42 U.S.C.S. §§300ff-21 to 30 (Law. Co-Op. 1996).

142. 42 U.S.C.S. §300ff-(25)-(26) (Law. Co-Op. 1996).

143. 142 *Cong. Rec.* S 4161, Vol. 142(55) "1996 Balanced Budget Downpayment Act—Conference Report," (Thursday, April 25, 1996).

144. Ryan White Care Reauthorization Act of 1996, 104th Cong., 1st Sess. S. 641 (1996) Part C-Early Intervention Services, codified at 42 U.S.C.A. §300ff-51(b) & 52(a) (Law. Co-Op. 1996). See also Conference Committee Report to accompany S. 641, 104th Cong. 2d Sess. Rep. No. 545 (1996).

145. 42 U.S.C.S. §300ff-71 (Law. Co-Op. 1996).

146. Ibid.

147. Ibid. §300ff-101.

148. The treatments referred to are discussed in chapter 5, where the Protocol 076 studies, which report a significant decrease in perinatal transmission of HIV, are reviewed.

149. See Committee Report to accompany S. 641, note 141 and 42 U.S.C.S. §300ff-14 (Law. Co-Op. 1996).

150. 42 U.S.C.S. 300ff-28(e) (Law. Co-Op. 1996).

151. See "Aids Funding" Testimony of the AIDS Action Council, before the House of Representatives, Subcommittee on Health and Environment of the Committee on Commerce, (April 5, 1995); "Ryan White Care Act Amendments of 1995," 104th Cong., 1st Sess. Hse. Rep. No. 104-245, (September 14, 1995); Report to the Chairman, Committee on Labor and Human Resources, *Ryan White Care Act: Access to Services by Minorities, Women, and Substance Abusers,* (Washington, D.C.: General Accounting Office, January 1995).

152. American Indian Community House HIV/AIDS Project News, New York (1996): 21.

153. See "AIDS Funding," note 151.

154. McKinney, Martha M., Wieland, Melanie K., Bowen, G. Stephen, et al., "States' Responses to Title II of the Ryan White CARE Act; Ryan White Comprehensive AIDS Resources Emergency Act of 1992," *Public Health Reports* 108 (1993): 4.

155. Care Act Amendments of 1995, note 151.

156. Presidential Advisory Council on HIV/AIDS, *Report Three, April 26, 1996, Continued Steps for Presidential Action,* (Washington, D.C. 1996): 3. Available through the White House Office on AIDS).

157. The program is authorized by the AIDS Housing Opportunity Act (AOHA) of 1992 (42 USCS §12901 *et seq.* (1995).

158. 42 U.S.C.S. §12906 *et seq.* (Law. Co-Op. 1995).

159. Office of HIV/AIDS Housing, United States Department of Housing and Urban Development, *HOPWA Formula Programs:1994 Summary,* August 1995.

160. "Authorizations to Date—FY 1996 HOPWA Formula Allocations," February 8, 1996. Document provided to the author by the United States Department of Housing and Urban Development.

161. 7664 FR Vol 61(40) (February 28, 1996).

162. Commission on Behavioral and Social Sciences and Education, National Research Council, *Preventing HIV Transmission: The Role of Sterile Needles and Bleach,* (Washington, D.C.: National Academy Press, 1995).

163. Golden, Megan R., "When Pregnancy Discrimination Is Gender Discrimination: The Constitutionality of Excluding Pregnant Women from Drug Treatment Programs," *New York University Law Review* 66 (1991): 1832; Zuckerman, Barry, "Developmental Considerations for Drug- and AIDS-Affected Infants," in Barth, Pietrzak, and Ramler, note 85: Ch.3.

164. Golden, note 163: 19.

165. "Women and HIV Disease," note 59: 49.

166. Ibid.

167. Golden, note 163.

168. *Elaine W. v. Joint Diseases North General Hospital,* 613 N.E.2d 523 at 525 (N.Y., 1993).

169. *In re Valerie D.*, 595 A.2d 922 (Conn.App., 1991), *cert* granted, 600 A.2d 1029 (Conn., 1991), rev'd 613 A.2d 748 (Conn., 1992).

170. "ADAMHA Reorganization Act of 1991," 102d Cong., 1st Sess. S. Rep. No. 102-131 (July 30, 1991) at 1992 U.S.C.C.A.N. 277. 42 U.S.C.S. §300x *et seq.* (Law. Co-Op. 1995).

171. 42 U.S.C.A. §300x-24(b)(1)(A) through (C)(2) (West, 1996); 45 C.F.R. §96.121.

172. 42 U.S.C.A. §290bb(b)(2) 1995 (West 1996).

173. 42 U.S.C.A. §290bb-3(6) & §290bb-33 (West 1996).

174. Ibid. §290bb-2.

175. Ibid. §290bb-3(b)(1).

176. Ibid. §290bb-1.

177. Ibid. §290-bb-1(d)(1)-(11).

178. Ibid. 290bb-1(h)(1)(2).

179. 45 C.F.R. §96.131. Next in order are injecting drug users following by all others.

180. 42 U.S.C.A. §300x-22(a)(A)(B) (West 1996).

181. Ibid.

182. 45 C.F.R. §96.131.

183. MD-ST-ANN §8-403.1 (West 1995); CO-ST-ANN §25-1-212 (West 1995); LA-ST-ANN §46:2505 (West 1994); MN-ST-ANN §254A.17 (West 1994); PA-ST-ANN §553 (Purdon 1994).

184. AZ-ST-ANN §36-2903 (West 1995); CT-ST-ANN §19a-7e (West 1994).

185. WI-ST-ANN §46.86 (West 1995); NY-Mental Hygiene Law §19.09, 19.15.

186. CA-HLTH & S §11757.59 (West 1994).

187. Illinois uses the term "guarantee" (IL-ST-ANN §301/35-5 (West 1995)) and Virginia, "enhance" (VA-ST-ANN §2.1-51.15:1 West 1995)).

188. CA-ST-ANN §11757.59 (West 1994); CO-ST-ANN §25-1-212 *et seq.* (West 1995).

189. Swenson, Victoria J., and Crabbe, Cheryl, "Pregnant Substance Abusers: A Problem That Won't Go Away," *Saint Mary's Law Journal* 25 (1994): 623.

190. Caldwell et al., note 135.

191. Zuckerman, note 163: 53; Hofkosh, Dena, Pringle, Janice L., Wald, Holly P., et al., "Early Interactions Between Drug-Involved Mothers and Infants: Within-Group Differences." *Archives of Pediatrics & Adolescent Medicine* 149 (1995): 665.

192. 42 U.S.C.A. §290aa(f) (West 1996).

CHAPTER 4

1. Forsyth, Brian W. C., "A Pandemic Out of Control: The Epidemiology of AIDS," in Geballe, Shelley, Gruendel, Janice, and Andiman, Warren, *Forgotten Children of the AIDS Epidemic,* (New Haven: Yale University Press, 1995): Ch. 1; Schable, Barbara, Diaz, Theresa, Chu, Susan Y., et al., "Who Are the Primary Caretakers of Children Born to HIV-Infected Mothers? Results from a Multistate Surveillance Project," *Pediatrics* 95 (1995): 511–515; Michaels, David, and Levine, Carol, "Estimates of the Number of Motherless Youth Orphaned by AIDS in the United States," *Journal of the American Medical Association* 268 (1992): 3456.

2. Provisional Committee on Pediatric AIDS, American Academy of Pediatrics, "Perinatal Human Immunodeficiency Virus Testing," *Pediatrics* 95 (1995): 303–307.

3. Caldwell, Flemming, and Oxtoby, cited in United States Department of Health and Human Services, Public Health Service, Centers for Disease Control, "Update: Mortality Attributable to HIV Infection Among Persons Aged 25–44 Years—United States, 1994," *Morbidity and Mortality Weekly Report* 45 (1996): 3.

4. Caldwell, M. Blake, Mascola, Laurene, Smith, Walter, et al., "Biologic, Foster, and Adoptive Parents: Care Givers of Children Exposed Perinatally to Human Immunodeficiency Virus in the United States," *Pediatrics* 90 (1992): 603–607; Schable et al., note 1; Nicholas, Stephen W., and Abrams, Elaine J., "The 'Silent' Legacy of AIDS: Children Who Survive Their Parents and Siblings." Editorial, *Journal of the American Medical Association* 268 (1992): 3478.

5. See Schable et al., note 1; Caldwell et al., note 4; and Nicholas and Abrams, note 4.

6. Schable et al., note 1.

7. See Schable et al., note 1; Caldwell et al., note 4; Nicholas and Abrams, note 4; Hopkins, Karen M., "Emerging Patterns of Services and Case Finding for Children with HIV Infection," *Mental Retardation* 27 (1989): 219–221, cited

in Weimer, Deborah, "Beyond Parens Patriae: Assuring Timely, Informed, Compassionate Decisionmaking for HIV-Positive Children in Foster Care," *University of Miami Law Review* 46 (1991): FN 1; Per-capita rates of infection are reported in: United States Department of Health and Human Services, Public Health Service, Centers for Disease Control, *HIV/AIDS Surveillance Reports* (1992).

8. Caldwell et al., note 4.

9. "Conference Report on H.R. 3734, Personal Responsibility and Work Opportunity Reconciliation Act of 1996," 104th Cong., 2d Sess. H. Rep. 725, 142 *Cong. Rec.* H8829 (July 30, 1996).

10. *Miller v. Youakim*, 440 U.S. 125 (1979).

11. 42 U.S.C.S. §672 as amended, August 4, 1996.

12. *King v. McMahon*, 186 Cal.App.3d 648 (Cal.App. 1 Dist., 1986); *Lipscomb v. Simmons,* 962 F.2d 1374 (9th Cir., 1992).

13. Senator Mark Hatfield, "Grandparents Back in the Parenting Business," 139 *Cong. Rec.* S16534-01 (1993).

14. Schable et. al., note 1: 25.

15. United States Senate, *Grandparents Raising Grandchildren Assistance Act of 1993* 103rd Cong., 1st Sess. S. Bill 1016 (1993).

16. Killackey, Elizabeth, "Kinship Foster Care," *Family Law Quarterly* 26 (1992): 211.

17. Smith, James Monroe, "Legal Issues Confronting Families Affected by HIV," *John Marshall Law Review* (1991): 543–569; Isbell, Michael T., *HIV & Family Law: A Survey,* (New York: Lambda Legal Defense and Education Fund, 1992): 16.

18. *Stanley v. Illinois*, 405 U.S. 645 (1972) (An unmarried biological father who participates in raising his children is not presumptively an unfit custodian).

19. Some states have sought to limit judicial discretion by adopting the Uniform Marriage and Divorce Act (9A U.L.A. 561 (1987), which identifies factors to be considered by the decision maker in resolving custody disputes between a child's parents.

20. Stein, Theodore J., "Child Custody and Visitation: The Rights of Lesbian and Gay Parents," *Social Service Review*, 70(1996): 435–450.

21. Stein, Theodore J., "The Custodial & Visitation Rights of Parents Who Are HIV Positive or Diagnosed with Acquired Immune Deficiency Syndrome," *AIDS and Public Policy Journal* 9 (1994): 122–129.

22. Stein, notes 20 and 21.

23. 148 Misc.2d 779 at 779 (N.Y.Fam. Ct., 1990).

24. 899 S.W.2d 509 (Ky.App., 1995).

25. *In the Interest of John T.*, 538 N.W.2d 761 (Neb.App., 1995).

26. *Matter of Adoption of Johnson,* 612 N.E.2d 569 (Ind.App. 1 Dist., 1993). The final decision is reported in *Bell v. A.R.H.,* 654 N.E.2d 29 at 34, (Ind.App., 1995).

27. Prince, Regina J., "The Child Welfare Administration's Early Permanency Planning Project," in Levine, Carol (Ed.) *Orphans of the HIV Epidemic,* (New York: United Hospital Fund, 1993): 115; Robinson, Robert P., Monk, Elizabeth, Coon, Linda, et al., "Social Catastrophe: Orphaned by AIDS; Children of Parents with AIDS," *Journal of the American Medical Association* 269 (1993): 1942.

28. Robinson et al., note 27: 1942.

29. Robinson et al., note 27: 1942.

30. Banks, Taunya L., "Reproduction and Parenting," in Burris, S., Dalton, H. L., et al., *AIDS Law Today,* (New Haven: Yale University Press, 1993): 226.

31. *In the Matter of the Appeal in Maricopa County Juvenile Action,* 845 P.2d 1129 (Ariz.App. Div.1, 1993).

32. *McGuffin v. Overton,* 542 N.W.2d 288 (Mich.App., 1995).

33. *Matter of Guardianship of Williams,* 869 P.2d 661 (Kan., 1994).

34. *In re Pearlman,* No. 87-24926 DA (Fla. 17th Cir.Ct., 1989).

35. *Adoption of Tammy,* 619 N.E.2d 315 (Mass., 1993).

36. Social Service Law, §383-c (McKinney 1994).

37. See *Adoption of Tammy,* note 35; *In re M.M.D.,* 662 A.2d 837 (D.C.App., 1995); *Adoption of B.L.V.B.,* 628 A.2d 1271 (Vt., 1993); *In the Matter of Jacob,* 660 N.E.2d 397 (N.Y., 1995); *In re Petition of K.M.,* 653 N.E.2d 888 (Ill.App. 1 Dist., 1995); *In the Matter of the Adoption of Two Children by H.N.R.,* 666 A.2d 535 (N.J.Super.A.D., 1995). CF, *In the Interest of Angel Lace M.,* 516 N.W.2d 678 (Wis., 1994) [Wisconsin statutes do not permit second-parent adoptions because the unmarried partner is neither the husband or wife of the biological parent (at 507) and the child is not available for adoption because her biological parent's rights have not been terminated). A dissenting justice argued that the state's adoption statutes should be liberally construed to permit the adoption, since it was clearly in the child's best interests ("everyone [including the child's biological father] agrees that the adoption is in Angel's best interest" at 523, 525, which was the basis for decisions favoring second-parent adoptions in other jurisdictions.

38. Turano, Margaret Valentine, *Supplementary Practice Commentaries (1994) to New York's Surrogate's Court Procedure Act,* Chapter 59-A, Article 17, Guardians and Custodians (McKinney 1995).

39. CA STA §S45a-624(e)(West 1994); FL STA §744.304 (West 1994); ILL STA §1-2.23 (West 1995); MD EST & TRSTS §13-903 (West 1994); M.C.L.A. §330.1640 (West 1994); N.J.S.A. §3B:12-68 (West 1994); WI STA §880.36 (West 1995); W.S.A. §880.36 (West 1995). Standby guardianship statutes do not always apply to a person with AIDS. See VA STA §37.1-128.2 (provides for appointment of a standby guardian for the mentally ill or mentally retarded). An Illinois court held that common-law jurisdiction would permit a

state court to craft standby guardianship as a remedy. *In re Estates of Herrod,* 254 Ill.App.3d 1061 (Ill.App. 1 Dist., 1993).

40. "Standby Guardianship Act," 103rd Cong., 1st Sess. H.R. 1354 (1993).

41. *In the Matter of Guardianship of Rene O.C.,* 606 N.Y.S.2d 872 (N.Y.Sur., 1993).

42. Four class actions have been filed by children in state custody, one of which was dismissed because none of the named plaintiffs met the statutory definition of disability (*Jeanine B. by Blondis v. Thompson,* 877 F.Supp. 1268 (E.D.Wi., 1995). Three suits are in litigation [*Baby Neal v. Casey,* 821 F.Supp. 320 (E.D.Pa., 1993), denial of class certification rev'd and remanded 43 F.3d 48 (3rd Cir., 1994); *Eric L. v. Harry Bird,* 848 F.Supp. 303 (D.N.H., 1994); *Marisol v. Giuliani,* 95 Civ. 10533, Lexis 8420 (S.D.N.Y., 1996) (Motion for class certification granted)].

43. 42 U.S.C.S. §5101 *et seq.* (Law. Co-Op. 1995).

44. 42 U.S.C.S. §51013(1) (Law. Co-Op. 1995).

45. 42 U.S.C.S. §5106a(b)(10) (Law. Co-Op. 1995).

46. United States General Accounting Office, Rep. GAO/HEHS 95-208, *Child Welfare — Complex Needs Strain Capacity to Provide Services,* (Washington, D.C.: 1995).

47. The Abandoned Infants Act (P.L. 100-505, 1988, as amended P.L. 102-236 (1991) 105 Stat. 1812-1816) amends the Adoption Assistance and Child Welfare Act.

48. Ibid.

49. Testimony of Senator Patrick Leahy before the Senate Agriculture Committee Hearings on the Better Nutrition and Health for Children Act of 1993, Federal Document Clearing House, 1994 WL 224552 (1994).

50. "Abandoned Infants Act," note 47.

51. See, for example, FLA. STAT. ANN. §415.503(10)(a)(2) (West 1994) (Harm to a child . . . may occur when a parent inflicts injury . . . including physical dependency of a newborn infant upon controlled substances); See also UT-ST-ANN §62A-4a-404 (West 1995); MA-ST-ANN CH. 119 §51A (West 1995); IN-ST-ANN §31-6-4-3.1(a) (West 1995); IL-ST-ANN, CH. 705 ACT 405 §2-3(1) (West 1995); MINN-ST-ANN, CH. 626 §556(2) (West 1995); KY-ST-ANN, §214.160 (West 1995); OK-ST-ANN, CH. 71 §7103 (West 1995).

52. Aase, Jon M., "Clinical Recognition of FAS: Difficulties of Detection and Diagnosis; Fetal Alcohol Syndrome; Includes Bibliography; Special Issue: Alcohol-Related Birth Defects," *Alcohol Health & Research World* 18 (1994): 5.

53. See, for example, *In re Stefanel Tyesha C.,* 556 N.Y.S.2d 280 (N.Y.A.D., 1 Dept., 1990). Appeal dismissed, 565 N.E.2d 1267 (N.Y., 1990); *In re Dustin T.,* 93 Md.App. 726 at 732, (Md.App., 1992) *cert* denied 620 A.2d 350 (Md., 1993) (A mother's prenatal conduct may be evidence of neglect.); *In re Troy D.,* 215 Cal.App.3d 889 at 897, (Cal.App. 4 Dist., 1989), review denied (1990) (Jurisdiction may be exercised because Troy was born under the influence of a dangerous drug.); *In the Matter of Baby X,* 293 N.W.2d 736 at 739 (Mich.App., 1980) (When a newborn is suffering from narcotics withdrawal

the mother's prenatal treatment can be considered evidence of neglect.); *In re Ruiz*, 500 N.E.2d 935 (Ohio Com. Pl., 1986) (When a newborn shows evidence of narcotics withdrawal, the child may be considered neglected.)

54. 568 N.Y.S.2d 123 at 126 (N.Y.A.D., 1991).

55. *In re Stefanel Tyesha C.,* note 53: 283.

56. Ibid.

57. *In the Matter of Sharon Fletcher*, 533 N.Y.S.2d 241 (N.Y.Fam.Ct., 1988).

58. *Whitner v. State*, 1996 WL 393164 (S.C., 1996) (Two justices dissented, finding that a fetus is not a person under state law). Courts have refused to sustain criminal charges against mothers whose children tested positive for cocaine at birth in the following cases: *Johnson v. State*, 578 So.2d 419 (Fla. App. 5 Dist., 1991) rev'd, 602 So.2d 1288 (Fla., 1992); *State v. Gray*, 584 N.E.2d 710 (Ohio, 1992); *State v. Luster*, 419 S.E.2d 32 (Ga.App., 1992); *cert.* denied (1992); *Jackson v. State*, 833 S.W.2d 220 (Tex.App. 14 Dist., 1992); *People v. Hardy*, 471 N.W.2d 619 (Mich., 1991); *Reyes v. People*, 141 Cal.Rptr. 912 (Cal.App. 4 Dist., 1977); *People v. Encoe*, 885 P.2d 596 (Nev., 1994); *Reinesto v. State*, 894 P.2d 733 (Ariz.App. Div. 1, 1995); *Commonwealth v. Pellegrini*, 608 N.E.2d 717 (Mass., 1993).

59. 42 U.S.C.S. §5106(a)(1) & §5116 (Law. Co-Op. 1995).

60. 42 U.S.C.S. §629a(B) (Law. Co-Op. 1995).

61. American Association for Protecting Children, *Highlights of Official Child Neglect and Reporting Laws, 1986*, (Denver: American Humane Association, 1988).

62. 42 U.S.C. §620 *et seq.* (Law. Co-Op. 1995).

63. 42 U.S.C.S. §625(a)(1) and §629(a) (Law. Co-Op. 1995).

64. United States House of Representatives, "Family Preservation Act of 1992" H.R. Rep. No. 684I, 102d Cong. 2d Sess. (July 22, 1992) (hereafter Preservation Act), Codified at 42 U.S.C.S. §629 (Law. Co-Op. 1995).

65. 42 U.S.C.S. §671(a)(15) (Law. Co-Op. 1995).

66. The amount specified in 1980 was $266 million for 2 consecutive years. Appropriated funds never reached this amount but came close in 1989 when approximately $246 million was appropriated, at which time Congress upped the ante to $325 million (42 U.S.C.S. §627(b) (Law. Co-Op. 1995). The Child Welfare Services program is found at 42 U.S.C.S. §620 and the funding mandate applies only to Part I. Funds appropriated for Part II, the Family Preservation Amendments, do not count toward triggering the mandate.

67. 42 U.S.C.S. §629a(A)(i)(ii) (Law. Co-Op. 1995).

68. *Suter v. Artist*, 112 S.Ct. 1360 at 1368 (1992).

69. See, for example, KY-ST-ANN §620.020(9) (West 1994); MN-ST-ANN §260.012(b); MO-ST-ANN §211.183(2).

70. 45 C.F.R. §1357.15(e).

71. Ibid. §(e)(2).

72. AR-ST-ANN §s9-16-106 (West 1994); KY-ST-ANN §200.590 (West 1995); LA-ST-ANN §46:287.6 (West 1994); WA-ST-ANN §74.14C.005 (West 1994); FL-ST-ANN §415.515; Consolidated Laws of NY §409-a; CA WEL & INST §16500.5 (West 1994); IN-ST-ANN §12-14-25.5-2 (West 1995); IA-ST-ANN §232.102 (West 1994); NJ-ST-ANN §30:4C-76 (West 1994); NC-ST-ANN §143B-150.6 (West 1994); TN-ST-ANN §37-3-602 (West 1995); PA-ST-ANN §62 (Purdon 1994); NM-ST-ANN §32A-17-3 (West 1994); UT-ST-ANN §62A-4a-103 (West 1994).

73. FL-ST-ANN §415.522 (West 1995).

74. Social Service Law §409-a (McKinney 1994).

75. Lindsey, Duncan, *The Welfare of Children,* (New York: Oxford University Press, 1994): 117.

76. United States Congress, *Personal Responsibility and Work Opportunity Reconciliation Act of 1996 — Conference Report on H.R.* 3734 "Part A — Block Grants for States for Temporary Assistance for Needy Families, §402(B)(3), 104th Cong., 2d Sess. 142 *Cong.Rec.* H8829-02 (Tuesday, July 30, 1996).

77. Lindsey, note 75: 66.

78. 42 U.S.C.S. §675(5)(A) (Law. Co-Op. 1995).

79. 42 U.S.C.S. §675(1) (Law. Co-Op. 1995).

80. 42 U.S.C.S. §675(5)(B)(C) (Law. Co-Op. 1995).

81. Cohen, Felissa L., and Faan, Wendy M., "Foster Care of HIV-Positive Children in the United States," *Public Health Reports* 109 (1994): 60–67.

82. "Update," note 3.

83. Child Welfare League of America, Task Force on Children and HIV Infection, Subcommittee on Family Foster Care, *Meeting the Challenge of HIV Infection in Family Foster Care,* (Washington, D.C.: 1991): 15.

84. English, Abigail, "The HIV-AIDS Epidemic and the Child Welfare System: Protecting the Rights of Infants, Young Children, and Adolescents," *Iowa Law Review* 77 (1992): 1509.

85. Cohen and Faan, note 81.

86. Ibid.

87. Commission on Behavioral and Social Sciences, National Research Council, *The Social Impact of AIDS in the United States*, (Washington, D.C.: National Academy Press, 1993): 46.

88. Cohen and Faan, note 81.

89. Groze, Victor, McMillen, J. Curtis, and Haines-Simeon, Mark, "Families Who Foster Children with HIV: A Pilot Study," *Child and Adolescent Social Work Journal* 10 (1993): 67–87.

90. "Meeting the Challenge," note 83.

91. Schor, E. L., et al., Committee on Early Childhood, Adoption, and Dependent Care, 1993 to 1994, "Health Care of Children in Foster Care," *Pediatrics* 93 (1994): 335–338.

92. United States General Accounting Office, Rep. GAO/HEHS 95-114, *Foster Care—Health Needs of Many Young Children Are Unknown and Unmet*, (Washington, D.C.: 1995).

93. Ibid. See *LaShawn A. v. Dixon*, 762 F.Supp. 959, 971 and 974 (D.D.C., 1991). Child and Family Services has consistently failed to provide appropriate medical services to children.

94. "Foster Care—Health Needs," note 92.

95. Rendon, Mario, Gurdin, Phyllis, et al., "Foster Care for Children with AIDS: A Psychosocial Perspective," *Child Psychiatry and Human Development* 19 (1989): 256.

96. Popola, Pamela, Alvarez, Mayra, and Cohen, Herbert J., "Developmental and Service Needs of School-Age Children with Human Immunodeficiency Virus Infection: A Descriptive Study," *Pediatrics* 94 (1994): 914–918.

97. Cohen and Faan, note 81: 12.

98. Simonds, R. J., Oxtoby, M. J., Caldwell, M. B., et al., "Pneumocystis Carinii Pneumonia Among U.S. Children with Perinatally Acquired HIV Infection," *Journal of the American Medical Association* 270 (1993): 470. See also Groze, Victor, Haines-Simeon, Mark, and Barth, Richard P., "Barriers in Permanency Planning for Medically Fragile Children: Drug Affected Children and HIV Infected Children," *Child and Adolescent Social Work Journal* 11 (1994): 63–85.

99. Likewise unraveling the effects of limited health care and environmental factors on the health problems of children born with a positive toxicology for drugs is difficult. The evidence that children who demonstrate symptoms of drug withdrawal at birth suffer long-term consequences is equivocal. See Zuckerman, Barry, "Developmental Considerations for Drug- and AIDS-Affected Infants," in Barth, Richard P., Pietrzak, Jeanne, and Ramler, Malia (Eds.) *Families Living with Drugs and HIV: Intervention and Treatment Strategies,* (New York: Guilford Press, 1993): 37 (Only 25 percent of the weight loss of low birth weight infants of mothers using cocaine during pregnancy can be attributed to cocaine use. The remainder is caused by factors such as cigarette smoking, poor nutrition, and marijuana use); Chasnoff and colleagues, "Cocaine Use in Pregnancy," *New England Journal of Medicine* 313 (1988): 666–669 (No significant differences in the number of physical anomalies between drug-exposed and non-drug-exposed infants); Day, Nancy L., and Richardson, Gale A., "Comparative Teratogenicity of Alcohol and Other Drugs: Prenatal Exposure to Alcohol or Other Drugs Can Impair Physical, Intellectual, and Behavioral Development," *Alcohol Health & Research World* 18 (1994): 42 (Most prospective studies do not report a relationship between prenatal exposure to cocaine and physical defects); Hofkosh, Dena, Pringle, Janice L., Wald, Holly P., et al., "Early Interactions Between Drug-Involved Mothers and Infants: Within-Group Differences," *Archives of Pediatrics & Adolescent Medicine* 149 (1995): 665 (Studies controlling for the effects of tobacco, alcohol, poor nutrition, lack of prenatal care, and psychosocial stressors confirm a small, independent effect of prenatal cocaine exposure on birth weight, length, and head circumference with no significant differences between groups of cocaine-exposed and non-exposed infants on global assessments of neurodevelopment. A study of 144 mothers who abused cocaine and their infants showed that mean developmental scores at 1 year of age were

within the average range for this group of substance-exposed infants whose mothers were receiving follow-up and support services. Standard developmental assessments do not support earlier claims of devastating neurodevelopmental difficulties among infants exposed to cocaine); Bopp, James, Jr., Gardner, Deborah Hall, "AIDS Babies, Crack Babies: Challenges to the Law," *Issues in Law & Medicine* 7 (1991): 3 (Caution is suggested in assuming that early developmental problems will linger. Some studies indicate that cocaine-exposed infants "catch-up" developmentally when they are raised in a nurturing environment); Chiriboga, Claudia A., Vibbert, Martha, Malouf, Renee, et al., "Neurological Correlates of Fetal Cocaine Exposure: Transient Hypertonia of Infancy and Early Childhood," *Pediatrics* 96 (1995): 1070–1077 (Cocaine-exposed infants demonstrated pathological muscle tone which resolved by 24 months. The developmental scores of cocaine-positive compared to cocaine-negative infants were the same at all ages. It is important to distinguish the effects of alcohol use during pregnancy from the use of drugs such as cocaine or heroin. Some children whose mothers use alcohol during their pregnancy will develop Fetal Alcohol Syndrome [FAS]); Day and Richardson, above (Studies of children with FAS report developmental problems such as children being small for their age and evidencing mental impairment but nonetheless displaying "a range of growth and intellectual abilities from normal to severely retarded . . . higher rates of behavioral problems, delayed motor and speech development and hearing impairments." As these children mature, many of the problems identified early remain with them and are compounded by school problems including difficulties concentrating, and attention and behavioral problems. As with drug use, Day and Richardson caution that environmental factors confound reported outcomes and much of the data are derived from case studies and suffer from the methodological problems inherent in data based on a clinical population and one where controls are lacking).

100. Pinkney, Deborah S., "Motherless Child; The AIDS Epidemic Is Creating the Largest Orphan Crisis Since the Influenza Outbreak of 1918; How Can Physicians Help?" *American Medical News* 37 (1994): 13: Cites Jennifer F. Havens, Medical Director, Pediatric Psychiatric Clinic, Columbia-Presbyterian Medical Center.

101. Gay, Caryl L., Armstrong, F. Daniel, Cohen, Donna, et al., "The Effects of HIV on Cognitive and Motor Development in Children Born to HIV-Seropositive Women with No Reported Drug Use: Birth to 24 Months," *Pediatrics* 96 (1995): 1078–1082 (Both groups were delayed relative to the group on which the test was standardized. The authors state that one of the two tests was language-biased).

102. Bopp and Gardner, note 99.

103. Crossley, Mary A., "Of Diagnoses and Discrimination: Discriminatory Nontreatment of Infants with HIV Infection," *Columbia Law Review* 93 (1993): 1581.

104. Popola, Alvarez, and Cohen, note 96.

105. Heymann, David L., "AIDS: Mother to Child," *World Health* 48 (1995): 31.

106. Barnhart, Huiman X., Caldwell, M. Blake, Thomas, Pauline, "Natural History of Human Immunodeficiency Virus Disease in Perinatally Infected Chil-

dren: An Analysis from the Pediatric Spectrum of Disease Project," *Pediatrics* 97 (1996): 710–716.

107. Pantaleo, Giuseppe, Menzo, Stefano, Vaccarezza, Mauro, et al., "Studies in Subjects with Long-Term Nonprogressive Human Immunodeficiency Virus Infection," *New England Journal of Medicine* 332 (1995): 209–216; Cao, Yunzhen, Qin, Limo, Zhang, Linqi, et al., "Virologic and Immunologic Characterization of Long-Term Survivors of Human Immunodeficiency Virus Type 1 Infection," *New England Journal of Medicine* 332 (1995): 201–208; Clotet, B., Ruiz, L., Ibanez, A., et al., "Long-Term Survivors of Human Immunodeficiency Virus Type 1 Infection," *New England Journal of Medicine* 332 (1995): 1646–1648.

108. *Santosky v. Kramer,* 455 U.S. 745 at 745 (1982).

109. States permitting a minor, usually defined as one at least 12 years of age, to be tested and treated for sexually transmitted diseases and for HIV without parental consent include: AL-ST-ANN §22-11A-19 (West 1995); AZ-ST-ANN §44-133.01 (West 1994); CA-ST-ANN §6926 (Deering 1995); DE-ST-ANN §708, §1202(f) (West 1994); AR-ST-ANN §20-16-508 (a)(1) (West 1994); CO-ST-ANN §13-22-102 (West 1995); OH-ST §3701.242 (Baldwin 1995); NM-ST-ANN §24-2B-3 (West 1995); NY-ST-ANN §2780(5) (McKinney 1995).

110. *Planned Parenthood of Southeastern Pennsylvania v. Casey,* 112 S.Ct. 2791 (1992).

111. Rampino, Kenneth J., "Annotation: Power of Court or Other Public Agency to Order Medical Treatment Over Parental Religious Objections for Child Whose Life Is Not Immediately Endangered," 52 *A.L.R.3d* 1118. (Law. Co-Op. 1995); Williams, John C., "Annotation: Power of Court or Other Public Agency to Order Medical Treatment for Child Over Parental Objections Not Based on Religious Grounds," *97 A.L.R.3d 421* (Law. Co-Op. 1995).

112. *A.D.H. v. State Department of Human Resources,* 640 So.2d 969 (ALA.Civ.App., 1994).

113. See note 111.

114. *Wisconsin v. Yoder*, 406 U.S. 205 at 233 (1972) Limiting parental authority to make medical decisions "even when linked to a free exercise claim . . . if it appears that [the] decisions will jeopardize the health or safety of the child, or have a potential for significant social burdens."

115. FL-ST-ANN §39.01(29) West 1994; 42 Pa. C.S.A. §6357 (West 1995).

116. AZ-ST-ANN §8-531 (West 1995); NH-ST-ANN §169-C:3 (Butterworth 1994); ID-ST-ANN §16-2002 (West 1995).

117. GA-ST-ANN §31-9-2 (West 1995); MI-ST-ANN §400.66h (West 1995).

118. See, generally, Waysdorf, Susan L., "Families in the AIDS Crisis: Access, Equality, Empowerment, and the Role of Kinship Caregivers," *Texas Journal of Women and the Law* 3 (1994).

119. Fahs, Marianne C., Waite, Douglas, Sesholtz, Marilyn, et al., "Results of the ACSUS for Pediatric AIDS Patients: Utilization of Services, Functional Status, and Social Severity; AIDS Costs and Service Utilization Survey," *Health Services Research* 29 (1994): 549.

120. "The Social Impact of AIDS," note 87: 218–219.

121. McNutt, Briar, "The Under-Enrollment of HIV-Infected Foster Children in Clinical Trials and Protocols and the Need for Corrective State Action," *American Journal of Law & Medicine* 20 (1994): 231.

122. Frascino, Robert J., "Changing Face of HIV/AIDS Care— Mother-Fetal and Maternal-Child HIV Transmission," *Western Journal of Medicine* 163 (1995): 368.

123. 45 C.F.R. §46.408(c) 1995.

124. Weimer, note 7: 379.

125. McNutt, note 121.

126. ND-ST-ANN §23-07.5-02 (West 1995); NM-ST-ANN §24-2B-3 (West 1995); WI-ST-ANN §252.15(2)(b) (West 1995).

127. RH-ST-ANN §23-6-14 (West 1995); IL-ST-ANN §5/5 (West 1995); CA-ST-ANN §199.27(a)(2) (West 1994); NC-ST-ANN §130A-148(h) (West 1995); OH-ST-ANN §3701.242(E)(5) (Baldwin 1995); CT-ST-ANN §19a-582 (West 1994); CO-ST-ANN §25-4-1405(6) (West 1995); GA-ST-ANN §31-22-9.2 (West 1995).

128. See notes 108 and 109 and accompanying text.

129. CO-ST-ANN §25-4-1405(6) (West 1995); IA-ST-ANN §141.22(6) (West 1994); MI-ST-ANN §333.5127(1) (West 1995).

130. Plotkin, Stanley A., Cooper, Louis Z., Evans, Hugh E., et al., "American Academy of Pediatrics: Task Force on Pediatrics AIDS Infants and Children with Acquired Immunodeficiency Syndrome: Placement in Adoption and Foster Care," *Pediatrics* 83 (1989): 609–612.

131. Plotkin, Stanley A., Cooper, Louis Z., Evans, Hugh E., et al., "Task Force on Pediatric AIDS: Guidelines for Human Immunodeficiency Virus (HIV)-Infected Children and Their Foster Families," *Pediatrics* 89 (1992): 681–683.

132. Gellert, George A., Berkowitz, Carol D., et al., "Testing the Sexually Abused Child for the HIV Antibody: Issues for the Social Worker," *Social Work* 38 (1993): 389–394.

133. Gutman, Laura T., Herman-Giddens, Marcia E., and McKinney, Ross E., "Pediatric Acquired Immunodeficiency Syndrome Barriers to Recognizing the Role of Child Sexual Abuse," *American Journal of Diseases of Children*, Special Issue (1993): 775.

134. Gellert, George A., Durfee, Michael J., Berkowitz, Carol D., et al., "Situational and Sociodemographic Characteristics of Children Infected with Human Immunodeficiency Virus from Pediatric Sexual Abuse," *Pediatrics* 91 (1993): 39–44.

135. 42 U.S.C.S. §300ff-61 *et seq*. (Law. Co-Op. 1995).

136. See, for example: NY-ST-ANN §2782(1)(h) (McKinney 1995); ND-ST-ANN §23-07.5-05(1)(a) (Butterworth 1995); KY-ST-ANN §214.625(5)(C)(9) (Butterworth 1995); LA-ST-ANN §40:1300.14(B)(7) (West 1994); MO-ST-ANN §191.6561(1)(C) (Vernon 1994); FL-ST-ANN §381.004(3)(f)(11) (West 1994).

137. IL-ST-ANN §5/5 (West 1995).

138. WI-ST-ANN §252.15 (West 1995 Pocket Part) §§40, 41.

139. 588 N.E.2d 354 (Ill.App., 1992).

140. Ibid. 356.

141. Ibid. Adoption agencies have been sued for fraud in the following cases: *Burr v. Board of Commissioners*, 491 N.E.2d 1101 (Ohio, 1986); *Michael J. v. County of Los Angeles Department of Adoptions*, 247 Cal.Rptr. 504 (Cal.App. 2 Dist., 1988); *County Department of Public Welfare v. Morningstar*, 151 N.E.2d 150 (Ind.App., 1958); *Mallette v. Children's Friend and Service,* 661 A.2d 67 (R.I., 1995); *Allen v. Allen*, 330 P.2d 151 (Or., 1958); *In re Welfare of Alle*, 230 N.W.2d 574 (Minn., 1975); *Mohr v. Commonwealth,* 653 N.E.2d 1104 (Mass., 1995); *Juman v. Louise Wise Services,* 620 N.Y.S.2d 371 (N.Y.A.D., 1995); *Vaughn v. North Carolina Department of Human Resources*, 252 S.E.2d 792 (N.C., 1979).

142. FL-ST-ANN §39.01(63) (West 1995). The following also provide for the transfer of permanent or legal custody to a relative or nonrelative foster parent, or other suitable person who is able to provide long-term care. MO-ST-ANN §211.477(3)(2) (Vernon 1994); MT-ST-ANN §41-3-1014(4)(d) (West 1993); SD-ST-ANN §26-8A (West 1995).

143. 42 U.S.C.S. §5111 *et seq.* (Law. Co-Op. 1995).

144. 42 U.S.C.S. §673(c)(1)(2) (Law. Co-Op. 1995).

145. 42 U.S.C.S. §673 *et seq.* (Law. Co-Op. 1995).

146. 42 C.F.R. §435.308(b)(2) (Law. Co-Op. 1995).

147. 42 U.S.C.S. §675(3) (Law. Co-Op. 1995).

148. 42 U.S.C.S. §673 *et seq.* (Law. Co-Op. 1995).

CHAPTER 5

1. See chapter 2, note 153.

2. Bayer, Ronald, "Ethical Challenges Posed by Zidovudine Treatment to Reduce Vertical Transmission of HIV," *New England Journal of Medicine* 331 (1994): 1223–1225; Hoffman, Christopher A., Munson, Ronald, Thea, Donald M., et al., "Ethical Issues in the Use of Zidovudine to Reduce Vertical Transmission of HIV," *New England Journal of Medicine* 332 (1995): 891–892.

3. 141 *Cong. Rec.* S15576 (October 24, 1995).

4. On influencing behavioral choices, see reproductive decision making, this chapter; on employment, housing, and educational discrimination, see chapter 2; on physicians' attitudes, see chapter 3; and on child custody, see chapter 4. On quarantine, see "Poll Indicates Majority Favor Quarantine for AIDS," *N.Y. Times* (December 20, 1985): A 24, Col. 1 (A *Los Angeles Times* poll found that most Americans favor the quarantine of AIDS patients. Some would support using tattoos to mark those with the deadly disorder); "Judge in AIDS Hearing Asks About Quarantine for Adults," *N.Y. Times* (October 1, 1985) B7, Col. 6 (A State Supreme Court justice expressed incredulity that the City Health Department does not quarantine adults with advanced cases of AIDS);

Traffor, Abigail, Witkin, Gordon, et al., "The Politics of AIDS—A Tale of Two States," *U.S. News & World Report* (November 18, 1985): 70 (Texas health commissioner proposes that AIDS patients be quarantined and according to Houston's former Mayor, one way to deal with AIDS is to "shoot the queers"); Lewin, Tamar, "Rights of Citizens and Society Raise Legal Muddle on AIDS," *N.Y. Times* (October 14, 1987) A1, Col. 1 (Senator Jesse Helms and Pat Robertson, the former television evangelist, say that quarantine may become necessary for people with AIDS); "Quarantine Lifted on AIDS Case, But the Boy Involved Is Confined," *N.Y. Times* (June 17, 1987) B9, Col. 4 (14-year-old boy who is HIV-positive was quarantined and confined to a mental ward); Purdham, Todd S., "Despite Protests, Dinkins Chooses Indiana Official as Health Chief," *N.Y. Times* (January 20, 1990) Sect. 1, Col. 1 (Dr. Woodrow Myers, New York City's new Health Commissioner, would not rule out quarantining AIDS carriers); "Many Nations Pass Laws Against Those Afflicted with AIDS," *N.Y. Times* (July 28, 1988) B2 Col. 6 (At least fifty criminal prosecutions of people with HIV have occurred and numerous states are calling for quarantine, isolation, or criminal prosecution); Smothers, Ronald, "3 Judges Exclude AIDS Defendants," *N.Y. Times* (December 14, 1988) A21, Col. 1 (Three Alabama judges require defendants with AIDS to enter their guilty pleas and receive their sentences by telephone because the judge fears being infected with the AIDS virus. Referring to reports from the Surgeon General and the CDC that AIDS can't be casually spread, he said, "Call me paranoid if you want to, but they haven't proved it to me yet"); Lambert, Bruce, "With Few Tested, AIDS Debate Erupts," *N.Y. Times* (July 23, 1989) 1 28, Col. 4 (The CDC is urging all states to record cases of infected people with mild or no symptoms. The agency would not take a position on the listing of names).

5. *Rescue Mission Alliance v. Mercado*, 637 N.Y.S.2d 580 (N.Y.A.D. 4 Dept., 1996).

6. Gostin, Lawrence O., "The AIDS Litigation Project: A National Review of Court and Human Rights Commission Decisions, Part I: The Social Impact of AIDS," *Journal of the American Medical Association* 263 (1990): 1961.

7. *Clarkson v. Coughlin*, 898 F.Supp. 1019 (S.D.N.Y., 1995).

8. See *Cong. Rec.*, note 3; Gostin, note 6; [Editorial], "Maintaining Confidentiality," *Lancet* 346 (1995); *Doe v. Borough of Barrington*, 729 F. Supp. 376 (N.J., 1990); Doughty, Roger, "The Confidentiality of HIV-Related Information: Responding to the Resurgence of Aggressive Public Health Interventions in the AIDS Epidemic," *California Law Review* 82 (1994): 113; "CDC Makes Plans to Evaluate State HIV Testing Programs," *AIDS Alert* 8 (1993): 71.

9. Lewin, Tamar, "Lawsuit Seeks to Bar U.S. from Access to AIDS Files," *N.Y. Times* (April 3, 1996) A 13.

10. *Jew Ho v. Williamson*, 103 F. 10 (N.D.Cal., 1900).

11. United States General Accounting Office, *Scientific Research — Continued Vigilance Critical to Protecting Human Subjects*, Rep. No. 96-72 (1996).

12. Commission on Behavioral and Social Sciences, National Research Council, *The Social Impact of AIDS in the United States*, (Washington, D.C.: National Academy Press, 1993): 87.

13. Sangree, Suzanne, "Control of Childbearing by HIV-Positive Women: Some Responses to Emerging Legal Policies," *Buffalo Law Review* 41 (1993): 320–323.

14. *Relf v. Weinberger*, 372 F. Supp. 1196 at 1199 (D.C.D.C., 1974).

15. *Scientific Research — Continued Vigilance,* note 11.

16. *New York State Association for Retarded Children, Inc. v. Carey*, 466 F. Supp. 479 (E.D.N.Y., 1978), aff'd 612 F.2d 644 (2d Cir., 1979).

17. *Scientific Research — Continued Vigilance,* note 11.

18. See Doughty, note 8: 113; Bayer, Ronald, "AIDS, Public Health, and Civil Liberties: Consensus and Conflict in Policy," in Reamer, Frederic G. (Ed.) *AIDS and Ethics*, (New York: Columbia University Press, 1991): 26–49.

19. FL-ST-ANN §381.004(1) (West 1994).

20. New York Pub. Health Law, §2780, Legislative Intent. Sec. 1 of L.1988, c. 584 February 1, 1989.

21. Acuff, Katherine L., "Prenatal and Newborn Screening: State Legislative Approaches and Current Practice Standards," in Faden, Ruth, Geller, Gail, and Powers, Madison (Eds.) *AIDS, Women and the Next Generation: Towards a Morally Acceptable Public Policy for HIV Testing of Pregnant Women and Newborns,* (New York: Oxford University Press, 1991): Ch. 6.

22. *Prince v. Massachusetts*, 64 S.Ct. 438 (1944).

23. *Breithaupt v. Abram*, 77 S.Ct. 408 (1957).

24. *Rochin v. California*, 72 S.Ct. 205 (1952).

25. *Skinner v. Railway Labor Executives' Association,* 109 S.Ct. 1402 (1989).

26. *Local 1812, American Federation of Government Employees v. United States Dept. of State*, 662 F. Supp. 50 (D.D.C., 1987).

27. *Anonymous Firemen v. City of Willoughby*, 779 F. Supp. 402 (N.D.Ohio, 1991).

28. 32 C.F.R. §58.4(b) (West 1995).

29. 42 C.F.R. §§34.1 and 34.3 (West 1995).

30. 28 C.F.R. §§549.16, 549.18 (West 1995).

31. Gostin, Larry O., "Public Health Strategies for Confronting AIDS: Legislative and Regulatory Policy in the United States," *Journal of the American Medical Association* 261 (1989): 1621–1630.

32. 42 U.S.C.S. §300ff-48 (Law. Co-Op. 1995).

33. 42 U.S.C.S. §§300ff-61 and 300ff-62 (Law. Co-Op. 1995).

34. 42 U.S.C.A. §300ff-33 (West 1996).

35. 104th Cong., 2d Sess. *Ryan White CARE Act Amendments of 1996*, P.L. 104-146, 110 Stat. 1346 at 1370 (May 1996).

36. *Glover v. Eastern Nebraska Community Office of Retardation*, 867 F.2d 461 (8th Cir., 1989) *cert* denied 110 S.Ct. 321 (1989); See also *Barlow v. Ground*, 943 F.2d 1132 (9th Cir., 1991) *cert* denied 112 S. Ct. 2995 (1992) (The risk of HIV-transmission is too remote to justify a warrantless blood test. The evidence will not disappear before a warrant can be obtained).

37. Centers for Disease Control and Prevention, "Partner Notification for Preventing Human Immunodeficiency Virus (HIV) Infection—Colorado, Idaho, South Carolina, Virginia," *Journal of the American Medical Association* 260 (1988): 613–615.

38. 42 U.S.C.A. 300ff-27a (West 1996).

39. 42 U.S.C.A. §300ff-46(b) (West 1996).

40. *New York State Society of Surgeons v. Axelrod,* 572 N.E.2d 605, (N.Y., 1991).

41. SC-ST-ANN §4-29-90 (West 1995).

42. Pavia, Andrew T., Benyo, Mary, et al., "Partner Notification for Control of HIV: Results After 2 Years of a Statewide Program in Utah," *American Journal of Public Health* 83 (1993): 1418–1424.

43. IA-ST §141.6 3(c)(1)(2) (West 1994)

44. Landis, Suzanne E., Schoenbach, Victor J., Weber, David J., et al., "Results of a Randomized Trial of Partner Notification in Cases of HIV Infection in North Carolina," *New England Journal of Medicine* 326 (1992): 101–106.

45. See, for example, CT ST s 19a-582(a)(b) (West 1995); FL-ST §§384.25, 455.2416 (West 1995); CA-Hlth & S §121015 (West 1995); GA-ST §24-9-47(g), (j) (West 1995); MT-ST, 44 A.G. Op. 37 (1992); LA R.S. 40 §1300.14(E)(1) (West 1995); ID-ST-ANN §39-610 (West 1994); HI-ST §325-101 (Michie 1995); IL-ST CH 410 §325/5.5(a) (Smith-Hurd 1995); KS ST §65-6004 (West 1994); KY-ST §311.282 (Baldwin 1994); MD HEALTH GEN §18-337 (Michie-Butterworth 1995); MI-ST-ANN §333.5114a (West 1995); NH-ST-ANN §141-F:9 (West 1994); OH-ST §3701.241 (Baldwin 1995); PA-T 35 P.S. §7609 (Purdon 1995); RI-ST §23-6-17(b)(3) (Michie 1994); TX HEALTH & S §81.051 (Vernon 1995); UT-ST §26-6-3 (Michie-Butterworth 1995); and WV-ST § 16-3C-3 (Michie-Butterworth 1995).

46. Watters, John K., "HIV Test Results, Partner Notification, and Personal Conduct." Commentary, *Lancet* 346 (1995): 326.

47. Vernon, T. M., Jr., "Partner Notification for Preventing Human Immunodeficiency Virus (HIV) Infection—Colorado, Idaho, South Carolina, Virginia," *Journal of the American Medical Association* 260 (1988): 613–615; Landis et al., note 44.

48. Vernon, note 47.

49. Hoffman, Richard E., Spencer, Nancy E., and Miller, Lisa A., "Comparison of Partner Notification at Anonymous and Confidential HIV Test Sites in Colorado," *Journal of Acquired Immune Deficiency Syndromes and Human Retrovirology* 8 (1995): 406–410.

50. Vernon et al., note 47; Pavia et al., note 42.

51. Wykoff, Randolph F., Heath, Clark W., Hollis, Shirley L., et al., "Contact Tracing to Identify Human Immunodeficiency Virus Infection in a Rural Community," *Journal of the American Medical Association* 259 (1988): 3563–3566.

52. Jones, Jeffrey L., Wykoff, Randolph F., Hollis, Shirley L., et al., "Partner Acceptance of Health Department Notification of HIV Exposure, South Carolina," *Journal of the American Medical Association* 264 (1990): 1284.

53. Landis et al., note 44.

54. Ibid.

55. Ibid.

56. Only 18 of North Carolina's 100 counties offer anonymous testing. In the period 1991 to 1993, requests for tests increased 64 percent in counties that offer anonymous testing compared to 44 percent in other counties. Adolescents, African-Americans, and other nonwhites were most likely to seek anonymous testing. See "AIDS Study Links HIV Test Increases to Confidential Protections," *BNA Health Care Daily*, October 25, 1996, citing a study reported in the October issue of the *American Journal of Public Health*.

57. North, Richard L., and Rotherberg, Karen H., "Partner Notification and the Threat of Domestic Violence Against Women with HIV Infection," *New England Journal of Medicine* 329 (1993): 1194–1196; Land, Helen, "AIDS and Women of Color," *Families in Society: The Journal of Contemporary Human Services* (1994): 355–361.

58. Marks, Gary, Richardson, Jean L., Ruiz, Monica S. et al., "HIV-Infected Men's Practices in Notifying Past Sexual Partners of Infection Risk," *Public Health Reports* 107 (1992): 100–105.

59. Vernon, note 47.

60. Gostin, Larry O., "Public Health Strategies for Confronting AIDS; Legislative and Regulatory Policy in the United States," *Journal of the American Medical Association* 261 (1989): 1621–1630; Rutherford, George W.,"Contact Tracing and the Control of Human Immunodeficiency Virus," *Journal of the American Medical Association* 259 (1988): 3609–3610.

61. Lambert, Bruce, "As AIDS Spreads, So Do Warnings for Partners," *N.Y. Times* (May 13, 1990) Sect. 1, Col. 3: 22; Lambert, Bruce, "With Few Tested, AIDS Debate Erupts," *N.Y. Times* (July 23, 1989) Sect. 1, Col. 4: 28.

62. Rutherford, note 60.

63. CDC "Editorial Note," note 37.

64. Leary, Warren E., "F.D.A. Approves Home AIDS Test; Marketing Is to Begin in June," *N.Y. Times* (May 15, 1996) A15, col. 1.

65. "Dr. Joseph & AIDS Testing," *N.Y. Times* (November 16, 1989) A30, Col. 1 (City Health Commissioner urges contact tracing because drugs like AZT can help delay the onset of symptoms); "A Life-Saving AIDS Strategy," *N.Y. Times* (August 20, 1989) Sect. 4, 22, col.1 (Exploiting the effectiveness of AZT in delaying the onset of symptoms requires a major policy shift to more testing).

66. Hamilton, John D., Hartigan, Pamela M., Simberkoff, Michael S., et al., "A Controlled Trial Of Early Versus Late Treatment with Zidovudine in Symptomatic Human Immunodeficiency Virus Infection—Results of the Veterans Affairs Cooperative Study," *New England Journal of Medicine* 326 (1992): 437–443.

67. Altman, Lawrence K., "The Doctor's World; Government Panel on H.I.V Finds the Prospect for Treatment Bleak," *N.Y. Times* (June 29, 1993) Sect. C, col. 3: 1.

68. Altman, Lawrence K., "Children: AIDS Study Finds AZT Ineffective," *N.Y. Times* (February 14, 1995); "News Capsules," *The Blue Sheet* 38 (1995): 12–14.

69. Volberding, Paul A., Lagakos, Stephen W., Grimes, Janet M., et al., "A Comparison of Immediate with Deferred Zidovudine Therapy for Asymptomatic HIV-Infected Adults with CD4 Cell Counts of 500 or More per Cubic Millimeter," *New England Journal of Medicine* 333 (1995): 401–407.

70. Chaisson, Richard E., Keruly, Jeanne C., Moore, Richard D., "Race, Sex, Drug Use, and Progression of Human Immunodeficiency Virus Disease," *New England Journal of Medicine* 333 (1995): 751–756.

71. "Most Physicians Say AZT Benefits Outweigh Fears and Risks for Pregnant Women," *AIDS Alert*, 9 (1994): 53. In early 1997, the National Institutes of Health (NIH), based on data showing that ZDV caused cancer in baby mice, recommended continued use of the drug by HIV-positive pregnant women. The NIH recommended that women be informed of the possible link between the drug and cancer. (See Olivero, O. A., Beland, F. A., Fullerton, N. F., and Poirer, M. C., "Vaginal Epithelial DNA Damage and Expression of Prenoplasaatic Markers in Mice During Chronic Dosing with Tumorigenic Levels of 3'-azido-2',3'-Dideoxythymidine," *Cancer Biotechnology Weekly* (1995); Neergard, L., "Panel Backs Continued Use of AZT in Pregnancy" *Washington Post* (January, 15, 1997) A6.

72. Antoine, Florence S., "Scientists Changing Therapy Outlook for AIDS Patients," *Journal of the National Cancer Institute* 82 (1990): 992–996; Hoover, Donald R., Saah, Alfred J., Bacellar, Helena, et al., "Clinical Manifestations of AIDS in the Era of Pneumocystis Prophylaxis," *New England Journal of Medicine* 329 (1993): 1922–1926; Love, Jamie, and Shearer, William T., "Zidovudine and Didanosine Combination Therapy in Children with Human Immunodeficiency Virus Infection," *Pediatrics* 96 (1995): 407–408; Husson, Robert N., Mueller, Brigitta U., Farley, Maureen, et al., "Zidovudine and Didanosine Combination Therapy in Children with Human Immunodeficiency Virus Infection," *Pediatrics* 93 (1994): 316–322.

73. United States Department of Health and Human Services, Public Health Service, Centers for Disease Control and Prevention, "Birth Outcomes Following Zidovudine Therapy in Pregnant Women; AZT," *Journal of the American Medical Association* 272 (1994): 17.

74. Altman, Lawrence K., "Scientists Display Substantial Gains in AIDS Treatment," *N.Y. Times* (July 12, 1996) A1.

75. United States Department of Health and Human Services, Public Health Service, Centers for Disease Control, *AIDS Daily Summary*, (December 11, 1996).

76. Pinching, Anthony J., "Managing HIV Disease After Delta: Questions Remain About How to Manage Patients Already on Nucleoside Monotherapy; Delta Clinical Trial Compared AZT Monotherapy and Combination Therapy,"

British Medical Journal 312 (1996): 521; Stephenson, Joan, "New Anti-HIV Drugs and Treatment Strategies Buoy AIDS Researchers. Medical News & Perspectives," *Journal of the American Medical Association* 275 (1996): 579; DeNoon, Daniel J., "Best Combination So Far: Indinavir + AZT + ddI: Anti-HIV Drugs," *AIDS Weekly Plus* (January 1996); Voelker, Rebecca, "Several New Drugs Shift Direction of Treatment and Research for HIV/AIDS," *Journal of the American Medical Association* 275 (1996): 89; "AZT Studies Reinforce Benefits of Combination: New Anti-HIV Drug, 3TC, Yields Exciting Results," *Aids Alert* 10 (1995): 11; "Potent New AIDS Drugs Underscore Promise of Combination Therapy; 3TC," *AIDS Alert* 11 (1996): 1; "Hit Hard Early or Delay? New Drugs Cloud Options; Possible Drug Resistance in Protease Inhibitors," *AIDS Alert* 11 (1996): 40.

77. Agency for Health Care Policy and Research Clinical Practice Guidelines, "Managing Early HIV Infection," *American Family Physician* 49 (1994): 801; "An HIV Battle Plan," *Medical Economics Publishing* 58 (1995): 18; Filice, Gregory, and Pomeroy, Claire, "Preventing Secondary Infections Among HIV-Positive Persons," *Public Health Reports* 106 (1991): 503–517; Lipsky, James J., "Antiretroviral Drugs for AIDS," *Lancet* 348 (1996): 800–803.

78. "More Studies Implicate STDs As Risk Factor in HIV Infection; Sexually Transmitted Diseases," *AIDS Alert* 9 (1994): 138.

79. Ploughman, Penelope, "Public Policy versus Private Rights: The Medical, Social, Ethical, and Legal Implications of the Testing of Newborns for HIV," *AIDS and Public Policy Journal* 10 (1994): 182–204.

80. Povinelli, Maryanne, Remafedi, Gary, and Tao, Guoyu, "Trends and Predictors of Human Immunodeficiency Virus Antibody Testing by Homosexual and Bisexual Adolescent Males, 1989–1994," *Archives of Pediatrics & Adolescent Medicine* 150 (1996): 33.

81. Kaplan, Jonathan E., Masur, Henry, et al., "Reducing the Impact of Opportunistic Infections in Patients with HIV Infection: New Guidelines," *Journal of the American Medical Association*, 274 (1995): 347.

82. Hoover et al., note 72.

83. See note 77.

84. United States Department of Health and Human Services, Public Health Service, Centers for Disease Control, "1995 Revised Guidelines for Prophylaxis Against Pneumocystis *carinii* Pneumonia for Children Infected with or Perinatally Exposed to the Human Immunodeficiency Virus," *Morbidity and Mortality Weekly Report* 44 (1995): 1–11.

85. Simonds, R. J., Oxtoby, Margaret J., Caldwell, M. Blake, et al., "Pneumocystis Carinii Pneumonia Among US Children with Perinatally Acquired HIV Infection," *Journal of the American Medical Association* 270 (1993): 470.

86. Provisional Committee on Pediatric AIDS, American Academy of Pediatrics, "Perinatal Human Immunodeficiency Virus Testing; Provisional Committee on Pediatric AIDS," *Pediatrics* 95 (1995): 303–307.

87. Chavkin, Wendy, "Pneumocystis Carinii Pneumonia in Children with Perinatally Acquired HIV Infection." Letter to the Editor, *Journal of the American Medical Association* 271 (1994): 102.

88. Miles, Steven A., Balden, Erin, Magpantay, Larry, et al., "Rapid Serologic Testing with Immune-Complex-Dissociated HIV p24 Antigen for Early Detection of HIV Infection in Neonates," *New England Journal of Medicine* 328 (1993): 297–302; Fauvel, Micheline, Henrard, Denis, Delage, Gilles, et al., "Early Detection of HIV in Neonates," *New England Journal of Medicine* (1993) 329: 60–62 (Arguing that the data presented by Miles et al. do not support the conclusion that their assay is reliable in early detection of HIV).

89. Thea, Donald M., Lambert, Genevieve, Weedon, Jeremy, et al., "Benefit of Primary Prophylaxis Before 18 Months of Age in Reducing the Incidence of Pneumocystis carinii Pneumonia and Early Death in a Cohort of 112 Human Immunodeficiency Virus-infected Infants," *Pediatrics* 97 (1996): 59–64.

90. Barnhart, Huiman X, Caldwell, M. Blake; Thomas, Pauline, et al., "Natural History of Human Immunodeficiency Virus Disease in Perinatally Infected Children: An Analysis from the Pediatric Spectrum of Disease Project," *Pediatrics 97 (*1996): 710–716.

91. Simonds, R. J., Lindegren, Mary Lou, Thomas, Polly, et al., "Prophylaxis Against Pneumocystis *carinii* Pneumonia Among Children with Perinatally Acquired Human Immunodeficiency Virus Infection in the United States," *New England Journal of Medicine* 332 (1995): 786–790.

92. Privacy protections are found also in the First Amendment (government is limited in its ability to abridge an individual's freedom of, and privacy in, association); the Third Amendment (the unconsented peacetime quartering of soldiers intrudes on privacy); and the Fifth Amendment's right against self-incrimination.

93. *Whalen v. Roe*, 97 S.Ct. 869 at 877 (1977).

94. Ibid.

95. Ibid.

96. *In re Search Warrant*, 810 F.2d 67 at 71 (3rd Cir., 1987), *cert.* denied, 107 S.Ct. 3233 (1987); *Schaill by Kross v. Tippecanoe School Corp.*, 864 F.2d 1309 at 1322 (7th Cir., 1988) rehearing denied (1989); *General Motors v. Director of the Institute for Occupational Safety and Health*, 636 F.2d 163 at 165 (6th Cir., 1980), *cert* denied, 102 S.Ct. 357 (1981).

97. *Doe v. City of New York*, 15 F.3d 264 at 267, (2d Cir., 1994).

98. *Plowman v. United States,* 698 F.Supp. 627 at 632 (E.D.Va., 1988).

99. 104th Cong., 1st Sess. S.1360 (October 24, 1995).

100. 5 U.S.C.A. §552a (West 1996).

101. 42 U.S.C.S. §12112(d)(3)(B) (Law. Co-Op. 1995).

102. See 42 U.S.C.S. §300ff-46 (Law. Co-Op. 1996).

103. 42 U.S.C.A. §14011 (West 1996).

104. 42 U.S.C.A. §14011(5) and (6) (West 1994).

105. 42 U.S.C.A. §10607 (West 1995).

106. 38 U.S.C.A. §7332(b)(2)(C)(i) (West 1995).

107. N.Y. P.H.L. §2781(2)(b)c) (McKinney 1994); OH-ST-ANN §3701.242(A)(2) (West 1995); CT-ST-ANN §19a-582(b)(3)(4) (Law. Co-Op. 1994); DE-ST-ANN 16 §1202(b)(2) (West 1995); N.R.S. §71-531 (Law. Co-Op. 1994); IA-ST-ANN §141.22 (West 1994); OH-ST-ANN §3701.242 (Baldwin 1995); MT-ST-ANN §50-16-1003 (West 1993); Fla. Stat. §381.004 (Law. Co-Op. 1994); N.J. Stat. § 26:5C-2 (Law. Co-Op. 1994); 410 I.L.C.S. §305/2 (1995 Supplement).

108. N.Y. P.H.L. §2781(a) (McKinney 1995).

109. KY-ST-ANN §214.625(2) (West 1994); NY-PHL Art. 27 §2781(1) (McKinney 1994); M.C.A. 50-16-1007(2) (West 1994); CT-ST-ANN §19a-582 (West 1994).

110. MA-ST-ANN Ch. 111 @ 70F(3) (West 1995); CA HLTH & S §120980 (West 1995-96); (KY-St §214.625 (Michie-Butterworth 1995); NM-ST-ANN §24-2B-7 (West 1995); NY PHL §2780(9) (McKinney 1995); ND-ST-ANN §23.07.5-02 (West 1994).

111. "AIDS Confidentiality Act" 40 I.L.C.S. 305/8 (Law. Co-Op. 1995).

112. GA-ST-ANN §31-22-9.2(c), (g) (West 1995); ND-ST-ANN §23-07.5-02(3) (West 1995); FL-ST-ANN §381.004(3)(i)10; SC-ST-ANN §44-29-230 (West 1995).

113. 42 U.S.C.S. §300ff-46 (Law. Co-Op. 1995).

114. SC-ST-ANN §44-29-135 (West 1995); Colorado (C.R.S. 25-4-1402 (Law. Co-Op. 1995); WI-ST-ANN §252.15(7) (West, 1995); MO-ST-ANN §191.656 (Vernon 1994); "AIDS Confidentiality Act," 410 I.L.C.S. 305/9(d) (Law. Co-Op. 1995); ARK-ST-ANN §20-15-906 (1995); N.J. State §26:5C-6 (Law. Co-Op. 1994); AZ-ST-ANN §36-664 (West 1995); and LA. R.S. 40.1300.14(E)(a) (West 1994).

115. TX-HLTH & SAF. §81.103(e) (West 1995); GA ST §31-22-9.2(a) (West 1995); MD HLTH GEN §18-201(a)(3)(ii) (Michie Butterworth 1995).

116. N.J. ST §26:5C-6 (Law. Co-Op. 1994); C.R.S. §25-4-1405.5(2)(a)(I) (West 1995); UT-ST-ANN, §§26-6-3, 26-6-6 (West 1995).

117. "Illinois: Proposal for HIV Registry Alarms State's AIDS Activists," *BNA Health Law Reporter* (February 1, 1996).

118. "California Medical Association Rescinds Policy to Push for Mandatory HIV Reporting," *BNA Health Law Reporter* (March 21, 1996).

119. ID-ST-ANN §39-609 (West 1994); NJ-ST-ANN §26:5C-8b(3) (West 1995); NV-ST-ANN, §441A.220(5) (West 1995); N.Y. PHL §2782(1)(d); WI-ST-ANN §252.15(5)(2) (West 1995); "AIDS Confid. Act" 305-9(c); CA HLTH & S §120985 (West 1995); Tex. Health and Safety Code §81.103(b)(5) (Law. Co-Op. 1995); ND-ST-ANN §23-07.5-05(1)(b) (Michie-Butterworth, 1995); KY-ST §214.625(5)(C)(3) (Michie-Butterworth 1995); LA. R.S. 1300.14(2)(a) (West 1994);SC-ST-ANN §44-29-135(d) (West 1995).

120. *J.B. v. Bohonovsky*, 835 F. Supp. 796 (D.N.J., 1993); *United States v. Joseph*, 33 M.J. 960 (NMCMR, 1991), review granted, 36 M.J. 17 (CMA, 1992) aff'd 37 M.J. 392 (CMA, 1993); *United States v. Dumford*, 28 M.J. 836 (AFCMR, 1989), review granted, 29 M.J. 436 (CMA, 1989), aff'd 30 M.J. 137 (CMA, 1990) *cert* denied 111 S.Ct. 150 (1990).

121. 42 U.S.C.S. §300ff-83 (Law. Co-Op. 1995).

122. *Urbaniak v. Newton,* 277 Cal. Rptr. 354 (Cal.App. 1 Dist., 1991).

123. *Hillman v. Columbia County,* 474 N.W.2d 913 (1991), review granted 482 N.W.2d 105 (Wis. App., 1992).

124. *Doe v. Roe,* 190 A.D.2d 463, (N.Y.A.D. 4 Dept., 1993).

125. *Doe v. Borough of Barrington,* 729 F. Supp. 376 at 379 (D.N.J., 1990).

126. *Doe v. Town of Plymouth,* 825 F. Supp. 1102 (D.Mass., 1993).

127. *Doe v. New York City Department of Social Services,* 1995 WL 619864 (S.D.N.Y., 1995).

128. *Dunn v. White,* 880 F.2d 1188 (10th. Cir., 1989) *cert* denied 110 S.Ct. 871 (1990); *Harris v. Thigpen,* 727 F. Supp. 1564 (M.D.Ala., 1990) aff'd in part, vacated in part 941 F.2d 1495 (11th Cir., 1991); *Adams v. Drew,* 906 F.Supp. 1050 (E.D.Va., 1995).

129. OH-ST-ANN §3701.242(E)(4) (West 1995); NV-ST-ANN §209.385(1) (West 1995).

130. NM-ST-ANN §24-2B-5.1 (West 1995).

131. NY PHL §2782(a)(o) (McKinney 1994).

132. WI-ST-ANN §252.15(5)(a)13 (West 1995).

133. NV-ST-ANN §209.385 3 (West 1994).

134. CA-ST-ANN §121070 (c) (West 1996).

135. *Anderson v. Romero,* 72 F.3d 518 (7th Cir., 1995); *Moore v. Mabus,* 976 F.2d 268 (5th Cir., 1992); *Harris v. Thigpen,* note 128; *Muhammud v. Carlson,* 845 F.2d 175 (8th Cir., 1988) *cert* denied 109 S.Ct. 1346 (1989).

136. *Roe v. Fauver,* 1988 WL 47359 (N.J., May 1988).

137. *Hunnewell v. Warden,* 19 F.3d 7 (1st Cir., 1994); *Goss v. Sullivan,* 839 F.Supp. 1532 (D.Wyo., 1993); *Johnson v. U.S. States,* 816 F. Supp. 1519 (N.D.Ala., 1993); *Robbins v. Clarke,* 946 F.2d 1331 (8th Cir., 1991).

38. *Nolley v. County of Erie,* 776 F.Supp. 715, (W.D.N.Y., 1991).

39. 42 U.S.C.S. §300ff-47 (Law. Co-Op. 1996).

40. See, for example, MO-ST-ANN §191.656(3)(g) (Vernon 1994); CA HLTH & S §121055 (West 1995); FL-ST-ANN §381.004(3)(h)(i)6 (West 1994); SC-ST-ANN §16-15-255 (West 1993); KY-ST §214.625 (Michie-Butterworth 1995).

41. *Doe v. Burgos,* 638 N.E.2d 701 (Ill.App., 4 Dist. 1994), appeal denied 645 N.E.2d 1357 (Ill., 1994).

42. *Johnetta J. v. Municipal Court,* 267 Cal.Rptr. 666 (Cal.App. 1 Dist., 1990).

143. *Matter of Anonymous,* 156 A.D.2d 1028, (N.Y.A.D. 4 Dept., 1989), appeal granted 552 N.E.2d 176 (N.Y., 1990) aff'd 559 N.E.2d 670 (N.Y., 1990); *Conte v. Merrell,* Lexis 16245, (N.Y.A.D. 4 Dept., 1989).

144. *People v. Anonymous,* 153 Misc.2d 436, (N.Y.Co.Ct., 1992).

145. *Application of Gribetz,* 159 Misc.2d 550, (N.Y.Co.Ct., 1994).

146. *People v. Durham*, 146 Misc.2d 913, (N.Y.Sup., 1990).

147. *People v. McVickers*, 840 P.2d 955 (Cal., 1992) rehearing denied (1993); *Government of the Virgin Islands v. Roberts,* 756 F. Supp. 898 (D. Virgin Islands, 1991); *Matter of Juveniles A, B, C, D, E,* 847 P2d 455 (Wash., 1993); *In the Interest of J.G.,* 674 A.2d 625 (N.J.Super.A.D., 1996).

148. *In re Hershey Medical Center,* 634 A.2d 159 (Pa., 1993).

149. *McBarnette v. Feldman,* 153 Misc.2d 627, (N.Y.Sup., 1992).

150. *Martinez v. Brazen,* 1992 WL 93245 (S.D.N.Y., 1992).

151. *Doe v. State of New York,* 152 Misc.2d 922, (N.Y.Ct.Cl., 1991).

152. *Roth v. New York Blood Center,* 596 N.Y.S.2d 639 (N.Y. Sup., 1993); *Chambarry v. Mount Sinai Hospital,* 161 Misc.2d 1000 (N.Y.Sup., 1994); *Borzillieri v. American National Red Cross* 139 F.R.D. 284, (W.D.N.Y., 1991).

153. *People v. Thomas,* 580 N.E.2d 1353 (Ill.App. 2 Dist, 1991), appeal denied 587 N.E.2d 1023 (Ill., 1992).

154. *People v. Adams,* 597 N.E.2d 574 (Ill., 1992).

155. *Doe by Lavery v. Attorney General of the United States,* 814 F.Supp. 844 (N.D.Cal., 1992) rev'd 62 F.3d 1424 (9th Cir., 1995) *cert* granted, vacated and remanded on other grounds, 116 S.Ct. 2543 (1996), aff'd 95 F.3d 29 (9th Cir., 1996) (remand was for reconsideration of damages in accordance with *Lane v. Pena,* 1996 U.S. Lexis 4049 (June 1996).

156. *Kerins v. Hartley,* 33 Cal.Rptr.2d 172 (Cal.App. 2 Dist., 1994).

157. *Faya v. Almaraz,* 620 A.2d 327 (Md., 1993).

158. *Mussivand v. David,* 544 N.E.2d 265 (Ohio, 1989); *C.A.U. v. R.L.,* 438 N.W.2d 441 (Minn.App., 1989); *Doe v. Johnson,* 817 F. Supp. 1382 (W.D.Mich., 1993).

159. 154 Misc.2d 269 (N.Y.Sup., 1992).

160. *Selby v. Rapping,* 1992 WL 400739 (S.D.N.Y., 1992).

161. *Weston v. Carolina Medicorp, Inc.,* 402 S.E.2d 653 (N.C.App., 1991), review denied, 409 S.E.2d 611 (N.C., 1991).

162. 93 S.Ct. 705 (1973)

163. *Planned Parenthood v. Casey,* 112 S.Ct. 279 (1992).

164. *United States v. Vuitch,* 901 S.Ct. 1294 (1971).

165. *Colautti v. Franklin,* 99 S.Ct. 675 at 688 (1979) (A "woman's life and health must always prevail over the fetus' life and health when they conflict"). See also Justice White's concurrence in *Vuitch,* note 164 ("Everyone [is] on adequate notice the health of the mother . . . is the governing standard").

166. The U. S. government may preclude the use of federal funds for abortion (*Rust v. Sullivan,* 111 S.Ct. 1759 (1991). The "Hyde Amendments" contain this prohibition, which applies unless abortion is necessary to save the mother's life or where the pregnancy was caused by rape or incest. The Hyde Amendments are constitutional. States are not obliged to pay for medical services when federal support is withdrawn (*Harris v. McRae,* 100 S.Ct. 2671, (1980). A

state's decision which favors childbirth by funding needed medical services but which precludes use of state funds for abortions unless "medically necessary" does not violate a woman's constitutional right to obtain an abortion (*Maher v. Roe*, 97 S.Ct. 2376 (1977).

167. Sangree, note 13.

168. Gittler, Josephine, and Rennert, Sharon, "Symposium: HIV Infection Among Women of Reproductive Age, Children, and Adolescents: HIV Infection Among Women and Children and Antidiscrimination Laws: An Overview," *Iowa Law Review* 77 (1992): 1362.

169. *Roe v. Wade,* note 162.

170. Johnse, Dawn E., "The Creation of Fetal Rights: Conflicts with Women's Constitutional Rights to Liberty, Privacy, and Equal Protection," *Yale Law Journal* 95 (1986): 599; Shafer, Richard P., "Fetus as Person on Whose Behalf Action May Be Brought Under 42 U.S.C.S. Section 1983," *A.L.R. Fed* 64 (1996): 886; Zitter, Jay M., "Liability of Hospital, Physician or Other Medical Personnel for Death or Injury to Mother or Child Caused by Improper Diagnosis and Treatment of Mother Relating to and During Pregnancy," *A.L.R., Fifth* 7 (1995):1.

171. *In re Ruiz*, 500 N.E.2d 935 (Ohio Com.Pl., 1986); *Matter of Baby X*, 293 N.W.2d 736 (Mich.App., 1980).

172. *Stefanel Tyesha C., In re*, 556 N.Y.S.2d 280 (N.Y.A.D., 1 Dept., 1990), appeal dismissed, 565 N.E.2d 1267 (N.Y., 1990);*Troy D., In re,* 215 Cal.App.3d 889 at 897, (Cal.App. 4 Dist., 1989), review denied (1990).

173. See Sangree, note 13; Williams, John C., "Propriety of Conditioning Probation on Defendant's Remaining Childless or Having No Additional Children During Probationary Period," 94 *A.L.R.3d* 1218 (1993).

174. *People v. Ferrell*, 659 N.E.2d 992 (Ill.App., 1995), appeal denied, 664 N.E.2d 644 (Ill., 1996).

175. *United States v. Vaughn*, cited in Smith, George Bundy, and Dabiri, Gloria M., "Prenatal Drug Exposure: The Constitutional Implications of Three Governmental Approaches," *Seton Hall Constitutional Law Journal* (1991): n. 127.

176. *Prince v. Massachusetts*, note 22.

177. *A.D.H. v. State Department of Human Resources*, 640 So.2d 969 (ALA.Civ.App., 1994).

178. Zitter, Jay M., "Power of the Court or Other Public Agency to Order Medical Treatment Over Parental Religious Objections for Child Whose Life Is Not Immediately Endangered," 21 *A.L.R.5th* 248 (1995); Williams, John C., "Power of Court or Other Public Agency to Order Medical Treatment for Child Over Parental Objections Not Based on Religious Grounds," 97 *A.L.R.3d* 421 (1995).

179. *Cruzan v. Director of the Missouri Department of Health*, 110 S.Ct. 2841 (1990).

180. *Raleigh Fitkin-Paul Morgan Memorial Hospital v. Anderson*, 201 A.2d 537 (N.J. 1964), *cert* denied, 84 S.Ct. 1894, (1964); *Crouse Irving Memorial Hospital, Inc. v. Paddock,* 127 Misc.2d 101 (N.Y.Sup., 1985).

181. *Jefferson v. Griffin Spalding County Hospital*, 274 S.E.2d 457 (Ga., 1981).

182. *In re Baby Boy Doe*, 632 N.E.2d 326 (Ill.App. 1 Dist., 1994).

183. *Taft v. Taft*, 446 N.E.2d 395 (Mass., 1983) cited in *In re Baby Boy Doe* Note 182 at 333.

184. *In re A.C.*, 573 A.2d 1235 (D.C.App., 1990).

185. *In re Jamaica Hospital*, 128 Misc.2d 1006 (N.Y.Sup., 1985).

186. *Skinner v. Oklahoma*, 62 S.Ct. 1110 (1942).

187. "The Basics of Counseling and Testing Pregnant Women," *AIDS Alert* 10 (1995): 1.

188. 608 N.Y.S.2d 518 (N.Y.A.D., 1994).

189. Sangree, note 13: 342–343.

190. Ibid. 343.

191. *The Blue Sheet* 38 (May 17, 1995): 8–10.

192. United States House of Representatives "Newborn Infant Notification Act," 104th Cong., 1st Sess. H.R. 1289 (1995). This legislation was dropped in favor of the counseling and testing provisions in the 1996 reauthorization of the CARE Act. See notes 34 and 35 and accompanying text. The Protocol Study is described in Connor, Edward M., et al., "Reduction of Maternal-Infant Transmission of Human Immunodeficiency Virus Type 1 with Zidovudine Treatment," *New England Journal of Medicine* 331 (1994): 1173–1180.

193. Lowe, David, "HIV Study Raises Ethical Concerns for the Treatment of Pregnant Women," *Berkeley Women's Law Journal* 10 (1995): 176 (The chief of pediatrics at the National Cancer Institute, Dr. Philip Pizzo, insists that mandatory testing is necessary to identify every pregnant woman with HIV); Hoffman, Christopher A., and Munson, Ronald, "Letters to the Editor" *New England Journal of Medicine* 332 (1995): 891–892 (Compulsory testing, although not treatment, may be justified by the Protocol 076 data).

194. Kolder, Veronika E. B., Gallagher, Janet, Parsons, Michael T., "Court-Ordered Obstetrical Interventions," *New England Journal of Medicine* 316 (1987): 1192–1196.

195. Bayer, Ronald, "Ethical Challenges Posed by Zidovudine Treatment to Reduce Vertical Transmission of HIV," *New England Journal of Medicine* 331 (1994): 1223–1225.

196. Minkoff, Howard, and Willoughby, Anne, "Pediatric HIV Disease, Zidovudine in Pregnancy, and Unblinding Heelstick Surveys: Reframing the Debate on Prenatal HIV Testing," *Journal of the American Medical Association* 274 (1995): 1165.

197. United States Department of Health and Human Services, Public Health Service, Centers for Disease Control, "Recommendations of the U.S. Public Health Services Task Force on the Use of Zidovudine to Reduce Perinatal Transmission of the Human Immunodeficiency Virus," *Morbidity and Mortality Weekly Report* 43 (1994): 4–5.

198. Bayer, note 195.

199. Connor et al., note 192.

200. United States Department of Health and Human Services, Public Health Service, Centers for Disease Control, *Morbidity and Mortality Weekly Report* 44 (1995): 1–14.

201. Kent, Christina, "States Pushed to Test Newborns for HIV; Reauthorization of 1990 Ryan White Act," *American Medical News* 39 (1996): 1.

202. [Editorial], "Perinatal HIV Transmission Declines," *AIDS Alert*, 11 (1996): 108.

203. 60 FR 10086 (February 23, 1995).

204. Navarro, Mireya, "Testing Newborns for AIDS Virus Raises Issue of Mothers' Privacy," *N.Y. Times*, (August 8, 1993) §1, Col. 5: 1.

205. Faden, Ruth R., Gielen, Nancy Kass, O'Campo, Patricia O., et al., "Prenatal HIV-Antibody Testing and the Meaning of Consent," *AIDS and Public Policy Journal* 9 (1994): 151–159.

206. Kent, note 201.

207. Landers, Daniel V., and Sweet, Richard L., "Reducing Mother-to-Infant Transmission of HIV—The Door Remains Open," *New England Journal of Medicine* 334 (1996): 1664–1665.

208. Wiznia, Andrew A., Crane, Marilyn, Lambert, Genevieve, "Zidovudine Use to Reduce Perinatal HIV Type 1 Transmission in an Urban Medical Center," *Journal of the American Medical Association* 275 (1996): 1504.

209. *Lancet* 345 (1995): 531.

210. Faden, Gielen, and O'Campo, note 205.

CHAPTER 6

1. Levine, Arnold J., et al. *Report of the NIH AIDS Research Program Evaluation Working Group of the Office of AIDS Research Advisory Council*, (Washington, D.C.: National Institutes of Health, 1996): 4.

2. Bayer, Ronald, and Healton, Cheryl, "Controlling AIDS in Cuba: The Logic of Quarantine," *New England Journal of Medicine* 320 (1989):1022–1024.

3. United States Department of Health and Human Services, Public Health Service, Centers for Disease Control and Prevention, "HIV/AIDS Surveillance Report, 1995," 7: 5–39.

4. St. Louis, Michael E., Conway, George A., Hayman, Charles R., et al., "Human Immunodeficiency Virus Infection in Disadvantaged Adolescents: Findings from the US Job Corps," *Journal of the American Medical Association* 266 (1991): 2387.

5. Burke, Donald S., Brundage, John F., Goldenbaum, Mary, et al., "Human Immunodeficiency Virus Infections in Teenagers: Seroprevalence Among Appli-

cants for US Military Service," *Journal of the American Medical Association* 263 (1990): 2074.

6. Gayle, Helene D., Keeling, Richard P., Garcia-Tunon, Miguel, et al., "Prevalence of the Human Immunodeficiency Virus Among University Students," *New England Journal of Medicine* 323 (1990): 1538–1541.

7. Until 1989, the Job Corps rejected HIV-positive youth. This policy changed after James Dorsey sued the government, alleging disability-based discrimination in violation of the VRA. In 1989, while his suit was pending, he was notified that he could reapply to the Job Corps and he was admitted (*Dorsey v. U.S. Department of Labor*, 41 F.3d 1551 (D.C. Cir., 1994).

8. Sweeny, Patricia, Lindegren, Mary Lou, Buehler, James W., et al., "Teenagers at Risk of Human Immunodeficiency Virus Type 1 Infection: Results from Seroprevalence Surveys in the United States," *Archives of Pediatrics & Adolescent Medicine* 149 (1995): 521.

9. "Revised HIV Estimates Lower Than 1 Million: Study Finds Sobering Trend Among Youth," *AIDS Alert* 11 (1996): 9.

10. Data compiled by the author from the AIDS Public Information Data Set, provided by the United States Department of Health and Human Services, Public Health Service, Centers for Disease Control (1994).

11. Office of National AIDS Policy, *Youth and HIV/AIDS: An American Agenda: A Report to the President,* (Washington, D.C.: The White House, 1996).

12. The National Commission on AIDS, *Preventing HIV/AIDS in Adolescents,* (Washington, D.C.: 1993): 4; [Editorial], "Societal Factors Lead to Spread of HIV. 11th International Conference on AIDS," *AIDS Weekly Plus*, (July 15, 1996): 7.

13. National Commission, note 12.

14. Gaiter, Juarlyn L., and Berman, Scott M., "Risky Sexual Behavior Imperils Teens," *Brown University Child & Adolescent Behavior Letter* 10 (1994): 1.

15. United States Public Health Service, Centers for Disease Control, "Trends in Sexual Risk Behavior Among High School Students—United States, 1990, 1991, and 1993," *Morbidity and Mortality Weekly Report* 44 (1995): 124.

16. [Editorial], "CDC Data Presented on Youth and HIV/AIDS Risk: Centers for Disease Control and Prevention," *AIDS Weekly Plus*, 1069 (1996): 17 (Discusses data presented by researchers from the CDC at the 11th International Conference on AIDS held in Vancouver, British Columbia, July 1996).

17. Sonenstein, Freya L., Pleck, Joseph H., and Ku, Leighton, "Why Young Men Don't Use Condoms: Factors Related to the Consistency of Utilization," (Washington, D.C.: The Urban Institute, 1995).

18. On perception of risk among women over the age of 20, see Kennedy, Bobbe-Lynne Urchin, "AIDS, Sexual Attitudes and Interpersonal Influence: Impact on HIV Risk-Reduction Among Middle-Class Women," Doctoral Dissertation, Columbia University School of Social Work, 1994: 87. On perception of risk among adolescents, see Gaiter and Berman, note 14; Berger, David K., Rivera, Miriam, et al., "Risk Assessment for Human Immunodeficiency Virus Among Pregnant Hispanic Adolescents," *Adolescence* 28 (1993): 597–607.

19. Gaiter and Berman, note 14; Berger and Rivera, note 18.

20. Berger, Rivera, et al., note 18.

21. [Letter], "Students' Belief That Condoms Prevent AIDS Influences Use," *Brown University Child & Adolescent Behavior* 8 (1992): 5 (The reported data were compiled from interviews with 403 sexually active students in grades 7 through 9. Twenty-five percent report that they never use condoms and 15 percent report that their use of condoms is rare).

22. Sonenstein, Pleck, and Ku, note 17.

23. Letter, note 21.

24. "Women's Risks of Contracting AIDS Rise with Partners," *AIDS Weekly*, October 3, 1994:11.

25. Sonenstein, Pleck, and Ku, note 17.

26. Committee on Adolescence: 1994 to 1995, American Academy of Pediatrics, "Sexually Transmitted Diseases," *Pediatrics* 94 (October 1994): 568–572.

27. Fanburg, Jonathan T., Kaplan, David W., Naylor, Kelly E., "Student Opinions of Condom Distribution at a Denver, Colorado, High School," *Journal of School Health* 65 (1995): 181.

28. Ibid.

29. "Trends in Sexual Risk Behavior," note 15.

30. Kipke, Michele D., O'Connor, Susan, et al., "Street Youth in Los Angeles: Profile of a Group at High Risk for Human Immunodeficiency Virus Infection," *Archives of Pediatrics & Adolescent Medicine* 149 (1995): 513.

31. Ibid.

32. 42 U.S.C.S. §300ee(a) *et seq.* (Law. Co-Op. 1996).

33. 42 U.S.C.S. §300ee-12(3) (Law. Co-Op. 1996).

34. As originally proposed by Senator Helms this statutory provision made no reference to heterosexual activity. [P. L. 100-202, 514(a) codified at 101 Stat. 1329-289 (1988).] Congress adopted an amendment proposed by Senators Kennedy and Cranston which added heterosexual to this proscriptive language. [P.L. 100-436, codified at 102 Stat. 1692 (1988).] See Tourk, Jessica M., "Controlling Expression: The Stagnant Policy of the Centers for Disease Control in the Second Decade of AIDS," *Cardozo Arts & Entertainment Law Journal* 13 (1993): 602–603.

35. 42 U.S.C.S. §300ee-5 (Law. Co-Op. 1996).

36. 42 U.S.C.S. §30033-12(7) (Law. Co-Op. 1996).

37. 42 U.S.C.S. §300ee-16(6)(B)(i)-(iii)(C) (Law. Co-Op. 1996).

38. Schonfeld, David J., O'Hare, Linda L., Perrin, Ellen C., et al., "A Randomized, Controlled Trial of a School-Based, Multi-Faceted AIDS Education Program in the Elementary Grades: The Impact on Comprehension, Knowledge and Fears," *Pediatrics* 95 (1995): 480–486.

39. United States Department of Health and Human Services, Public Health Service, Centers for Disease Control, "School-Based HIV-Prevention Education— United States," 45 *Morbidity and Mortality Weekly Report* 35 (1996): 760.

40. National Commission on AIDS, *Preventing HIV/AIDS in Adolescents* (Washington, D.C.: 1993): 17.

41. "School-Based HIV-Prevention Education—United States," note 39.

42. Backstrom, Charles, and Robins, Leonard, "State AIDS Policy Making: Perspectives of Legislative Health Committee Chairs," *AIDS and Public Policy Journal* 10 (1996): 238–248.

43. Kirby, Douglas, Shor, Lynn, Collins, Janet, et al., "School-Based Programs to Reduce Sexual Risk Behaviors: A Review of Effectiveness," *Public Health Reports* 109 (1994): 339–360.

44. *Brown v. Hot, Sexy and Safer Productions, Inc.*, 68 F.3d 525 (1st Cir., 1995), *cert* denied, 116 S.Ct. 1044 (1996).

45. *Ware v. Valley Stream High School,* 150 A.D.2d 14 (N.Y.A.D., 1989); aff'd 550 N.E.2d 420 (N.Y., 1989).

46. *Board of Education of the City of New York v. Sobol,* 613 N.Y.S.2d 792 (N.Y.Sup., 1993).

47. *Alfonso v. Fernandez*, 151 Misc.2d 899 (N.Y.Sup.,1992) rev'd 606 N.Y.S.2d 259 (N.Y.A.D., 1993).

48. United States Senate, The Parental Rights and Responsibilities Act of 1995, 104th Cong., 2d Sess. S. 984 (1995).

49. *AIDS Action Committee of Massachusetts, Inc. v. Massachusetts Bay Transportation Authority*, 849 F.Supp. 79, (D.Mass., 1993), aff'd 42 F.3d 1 (1st Cir., 1994).

50. *Gay Men's Health Crisis v. Sullivan,* 733 F. Supp. 619 (S.D.N.Y.) (GMHC I); *Gay Men's Health Crisis and others v. Sullivan,* 792 F. Supp. 278 (S.D.N.Y., 1992) (GMHC II). In 1973, in *Miller v. California,* 413 U.S. 15, the Supreme Court established a test for determining whether material is obscene. The test is vague and difficult to apply but nevertheless sets a standard to which courts must adhere. For an excellent discussion of the law regarding obscenity and the social issues it gives rise to, see Strossen, Nadine, *Defending Pornography: Free Speech, Sex, and the Fight for Women's Rights,* (New York: Scribner, 1995).

51. United States House of Representatives, *The Politics of AIDS Prevention: Science Takes a Time Out,* 102d Cong., 1st Sess. Rep. No. 102-1047 (1992).

52. Switzerland has mounted a multimedia educational campaign to encourage 17- to 30-year-olds to use condoms. Data show an increase in condom use with casual sex partners from 8 percent in 1987 to 50 percent in 1991. Among 17- to 20-year-olds, condom use has increased from 19 percent to 73 percent. See Stryker, Jeff, Coates, Thomas J., DeCarlo, Pamela, et al., "Prevention of HIV Infection: Looking Back, Looking Ahead," *Journal of the American Medical Association* 273 (1995).

53. "The Politics of AIDS Prevention," note 51.

54. The campaign is titled "Respect Yourself, Protect Yourself." See "Revised HIV Estimates," note 9.

55. See Kirby, Shor, and Collins, note 43.

56. "HIV Prevention Programs Can Be Effective," *AIDS Weekly* (October 24, 1994):9; Blair, Jill F., and Hein, Karen K., "Public Policy Implications of HIV/AIDS in Adolescents," *The Future of Children: Critical Health Issues for Children and Youth* 4 (1994): 73–93.

57. Hein, Karen, Dell, Ralph, Futterman, Donna, et al., "Comparison of HIV+ and HIV− Adolescents: Risk Factors and Psychosocial Determinants," *Pediatrics* 95 (1995): 96–104.

58. Stryker, Coates, and DeCarlo, note 52.

59. Ibid.

60. See C. Everett Koop, M. D., Surgeon General, "Introductory Statement, Report on AIDS," in "Politics of AIDS Prevention," note 51.

61. Blair and Hein, note 56.

62. Klein, Nicole Aydt, Goodson, Patricia, Serrins, Debra S., et al., "Evaluation of Sex Education Curricula: Measuring Up to the SIECUS Guidelines; Sex Information and Education Council of the US," *Journal of School Health* 64 (1994): 328.

63. United States Department of Health and Human Services, Public Health Service, Centers for Disease Control, "Contraceptive Method and Condom Use Among Women at Risk for HIV Infection and Other Sexually Transmitted Diseases—Selected U.S. Sites, 1993–1994," *Morbidity and Mortality Weekly Report* 49 (September 1996).

64. "Youth and HIV/AIDS," note 11: 7.

65. Stanton, B. F., Li, X., Galbraith, J., et al., "Sexually Transmitted Diseases, Human Immunodeficiency Virus, and Pregnancy Prevention: Combined Contraceptive Practices Among Urban African-American Early Adolescents," *Archives of Pediatrics & Adolescent Medicine* 150 (1996): 17.

66. Higgins, Donna L., Galavotti, Christine, O'Reilly, Kevin R., et al., "Evidence for the Effects of HIV Antibody Counseling and Testing on Risk Behaviors. Human Immunodeficiency Virus," *Journal of the American Medical Association* 266 (1991): 2419.

67. Holtgrave, David R., Qualls, Noreen L., Curran, James W., et al., "An Overview of the Effectiveness and Efficiency of HIV Prevention Programs," *Public Health Reports* 110 (1995): 134.

68. Schonfeld and O'Hare, note 38.

69. "HIV Prevention Programs Can Be Effective," *AIDS Weekly* (October 24, 1994): 9.

70. "Preventing HIV/AIDS in Adolescents," note 40; Hunter, Joyce, and Schaecher, Robert, "AIDS Prevention for Lesbian, Gay, and Bisexual Adolescents," *Journal of Contemporary Human Services* (1994): 346–354.

71. Cited in "Preventing HIV/AIDS in Adolescents," note 40: 13.

72. Holtgrave, Qualls, and Curran, note 67.

73. See also Sikkema, Kathleen J., Koob, Jeffrey J., Cargill, Victoria C., et al., "Levels and Predictors of HIV Risk Behavior Among Women in Low-Income Public Housing Developments," *Public Health Reports* 110 (1995): 707–713.

74. Walter, Heather J., and Vaughan, Roger D., "AIDS Risk Reduction Among a Multiethnic Sample of Urban High School Students," *Journal of the American Medical Association* 270 (1993): 725.

75. Stanton, Li, and Galbraith, note 65.

76. Goodson, Patricia, and Edmundson, Elizabeth, "The Problematic Promotion of Abstinence: An Overview of Sex Respect; Abstinence-Based Sex Education Curriculum," *Journal of School Health* 64 (1994): 205.

77. DiClemente, Ralph J., and Wingood, Gina M., "A Randomized Controlled Trial of an HIV Sexual Risk-Reduction Intervention for Young African-American Women," *Journal of the American Medical Association* 274 (1995): 1271.

78. Stryker, Coates, and DeCarlo, note 52.

79. Holtgrave, Qualls, and Curran, note 67.

80. Walter and Vaughn, note 74.

81. Holtgrave, Qualls, and Curran, note 67.

82. Higgins, Galavotti, and O'Reilly, note 66.

83. Johnson, Anne M., "Condoms and HIV Transmission," *New England Journal of Medicine* 331 (1994): 391–392.

84. Choi & Coates, cited in "HIV Prevention Programs Can Be Effective," *AIDS Weekly* (October 24, 1994): 9.

85. "The Politics of AIDS Prevention," note 51.

86. National Commission on AIDS, note 40: 4–5.

87. Schietinger, Helen, Coburn, Jay, and Levi, Jeffrey, "Community Planning for HIV Prevention: Findings from the First Year," *AIDS and Public Policy Journal* 10 (1995): 140–147.

88. Holtgrave, Qualls, and Curran, note 67.

89. DiClemente and Wingood, note 77.

90. Holtgrave, Qualls, and Curran, note 67.

91. Ibid.

92. "Peer Counselors Key for Hardest-to-Reach Groups? Data from Three Projects Look Good, Directors Say; Injecting-Drug Users, Female Sex Workers, Men Who Have Sex with Men but Don't Consider Themselves to Be Homosexual," *AIDS Alert* 11 (1996): 19.

93. Stevenson, Howard C., and Davis, Gwendolyn, "Impact of Culturally Sensitive AIDS Video Education on the AIDS Risk Knowledge of African-American Adolescents," *AIDS Education and Prevention* 6 (1994): 40–52.

94.   Ibid. 49.

95.   United States Department of Health and Human Services, Public Health Ser-
      vice, "Syringe Exchange Programs—United States, 1994–1995," *Morbidity
      and Mortality Weekly Report* 44 (1995): 684.

96.   Commission on Behavioral and Social Sciences and Education, National Re-
      search Council, *Preventing HIV Transmission: The Role of Sterile Needles and
      Bleach*, (Washington, D.C.: National Academy Press, 1995): 204–262. The
      academy review included (1) studies conducted by the United States General
      Accounting Office and the University of California, (2) papers presented at
      professional conferences, and (3) articles published in refereed journals. The
      review covers programs implemented in the United States, Canada, and West-
      ern Europe.

97.   Ibid. 200–201.

98.   Jarlais, Don C Des., Marmor, Michael, Paone, Denise, et al., "HIV Incidence
      Among Injecting Drug Users in New York City Syringe-Exchange Pro-
      grammes," *Lancet* 348 (1996): 987–991.

99.   Ibid. 251.

100. Ibid. 252.

101. United States Department of Health and Human Services, Public Health Ser-
      vice, Centers for Disease Control, "AIDS Community Demonstration Projects:
      Implementation of Volunteer Networks for HIV-Prevention Programs—
      Selected Sites, 1991–1992," *Morbidity and Mortality Weekly Report* 41 (1992):
      868. The history and evolution of these projects is described in O'Reilly, Kevin
      R., and Higgins, Donna L., "AIDS Community Demonstration Projects for HIV
      Prevention Among Hard-to-Reach Groups," *Public Health Reports* 106 (1991):
      714.

102. Commission on Behavioral and Social Sciences, note 96: 64–66; 95–99 and
      179–180.

103. Stryker, Coates, and DeCarlo, note 52: 1143.

104. Commission on Behavioral and Social Sciences, note 96: 180–186.

105. "CDC Releases HIV/AIDS Trends; Centers for Disease Control and Preven-
      tion," *AIDS Weekly Plus* (December 11, 1995): 10.

CHAPTER 7

1.   "Contract with America Advancement Act of 1996," P.L. 104-121, codified at
     110 Stat. 847 (March 29,1996).

2.   *Personal Responsibility and Work Opportunity Reconciliation Act of 1996-H.R.
     3734*, Part A—Block Grants for States for Temporary Assistance for Needy
     Families, Sec. 402(B)(3), 104th Cong., 2d Sess. 142, Slip Opinion, (August 8,
     1996) (hereafter PRA).

3.   Children born in the United States are automatically citizens regardless of the
     citizenship of their parents. Precisely what benefits, if any, such a child would

be entitled to receive is not clear under the new law. In 1996, the Republican Party adopted as part of its convention platform a proposal to amend the federal constitution to deny citizenship to a child born in the United States to anyone not a legal immigrant. Pear, Robert, "Platform Committee Attacks Constitution on Citizenship," *N.Y. Times* (August 7, 1996), Sect. A, col. 1: 13.

4. Excepted are political refugees, including individuals receiving asylum, honorably discharged veterans and active duty military personnel, and noncitizens with permanent resident status whose work history (in combination with the work history of their spouse and parents) equals ten years. PRA, note 2, Sec. 402(a)(2)(A)-(C) and Conference Report on H.R. 3734, "Limited Eligibility of Qualified Aliens for Certain Federal Programs," 142 *Cong. Rec.* H8829-02 (Tuesday, July 30, 1996).

5. 104th Cong., 2d Sess. "Omnibus Consolidated Appropriations Act, 1997," 142 *Cong. Rec.* 138, S11860 (September 30, 1996).

6. Pear, Robert, "Reward and Penalties Vary in States' Welfare Programs," *N.Y. Times* (February 23, 1997) National: 26. Further protection for noncitizen legal aliens may be provided by a 1971 Supreme Court decision that forbids states to deny assistance to legal immigrants solely because of their immigrant status. See *Graham v. Richardson,* 403 U.S. 365 (1971). To protect states against liability for denying benefits to legally admitted noncitizens, the PRA provides that a state that uses the federal classification system for determining the eligibility of non-citizens for public assistance shall be considered to have chosen the least restrictive means for achieving a compelling governmental interest. "PRA," note 2, Sec. 400(7). Whether courts will agree with Congress's effort to exonerate the states from liability remains to be seen.

7. PRA, note 2, Sec 403(a).

8. Sanger, Mary Bryna, "Essays: Welfare Reform within a Changing Context: Redefining the Terms of the Debate," *Fordham Urban Journal* 23 (1996): 273; Peterson, George E., "A Block Grant Approach to Welfare Reform," in Sawhill, Isabel V. (Ed.) *Welfare Reform: An Analysis of the Issues*, (Washington, D.C.: The Urban Institute, 1995): Ch. 1.

9. On March 24, 1995, the House of Representatives passed the Personal Responsibility Act, which in modified form passed the Senate as the Personal Responsibility and Work Opportunity Act of 1995. (United States House of Representatives, "Personal Responsibility and Work Opportunities Act of 1995," H.R. Conf. Rept. 430, 104th Cong., 1st Sess. (1995). The legislation was vetoed by President Clinton on January 9, 1996. On May 22, the Personal Responsibility and Work Opportunity Act (PRWO) of 1996 (House Bill 3734) was introduced in the House and the Senate. This legislation passed both Houses in midsummer and was signed by President Clinton on August 22, 1996.

10. Despite the claim for less regulation, TANF has approximately forty-three separate rules that the states must meet to receive federal funds, and the legislation is replete with references to regulations that must be issued by the Secretary of Health and Human Services. PRA, note 2.

11. Concerned that the states would not be able to meet an increased demand for aid following a recession, Congress included a "rainy-day" loan fund of $1.7 billion from which states could borrow in times of emergency. PRA, note 2.

12. 42 U.S.C.S. §601 (West 1995).

13. PRA, note 2.

14. Conference Report, note 4, Sec. 7 "Grants to the States, Family Assistance Grant."

15. PRA, note 2, Sec. 404(d).

16. Ibid. Sec. 402 (1)(A)(i).

17. Ibid. Sec. 402 (B)(iii).

18. Ibid. Sec. 402 (1)(A)(ii).

19. Ibid. Sec. 407(2)(B).

20. Ibid. Sec. 407(a)(1).

21. Ibid. Sec. 408(7).

22. Ibid. Sec. 408(5)(A)(i).

23. Ibid. Sec. 408(4)(A)(B).

24. Conference Report, note 4, Sec. 45 "Prohibitions; Requirements—Medical Assistance Required to Be Provided for Families Becoming Ineligible for Assistance Due to Increased Earnings or Collection of Child Support."

25. PRA, note 2, Sec. 408(7)(C).

26. Ibid. Sec. 407(3)(B)(5).

27. Ibid. Sec. 407(2).

28. Ibid. Sec. 407(b)(3).

29. Pear, Robert, "Budget Agency Says Welfare Bill Would Cut Rolls by Millions," *N.Y. Times* (July 16, 1996) A12.

30. United States General Accounting Office, *Health, Education, and Human Services Division Reports*, Rep. No. 96-15W (1995).

31. United States General Accounting Office, *Welfare to Work—State Programs Have Tested Some of the Proposed Reforms*, Rep. No. 95-26 (1995): 103. Services included education and training, help in preparing for the high school equivalency examination, assistance in acquiring proficiency in English, acquisition of job skills, and training for job readiness. For a discussion of how states handled child care, see Hagen, Jan L., and Lurie, Irene, "The Job Opportunities and Basic Skills Training Program and Child Care: Initial State Developments," *Social Service Review* 67 (1993): 198–216.

32. See "Welfare to Work," note 31.

33. Public Welfare Amendments of 1962, P.L. 87-543, codified as amended at 42 U.S.C.S §1315 (Law. Co-Op. 1996).

34. PRA, note 2, Sec. 415(a)(1).

35. Ibid. Sec. 415 (a)(2)(A).

36. For a review of the diverse provisions contained in state waiver programs, see Savner, Steve, and Greenberg, Mark, *The CLASP Guide to Welfare Waivers: 1992–1995*, (Washington, D.C.: Center for Law and Social Policy, 1995).

37. *C.K. v. Shalala*, 883 F. Supp. 991 (D.N.J., 1995), aff'd, 92 F.3d 171 (3d. Cir., 1996).

38. *Jones v. Milwaukee County*, 485 N.W.2d 21 (Wis., 1992); reconsideration denied, 491 N.W.2d 771 (Wis., 1992). Excepted from the waiting period are those who were (1) born in the state; (2) previous residents who had lived in the state for at least 365 days, (3) moving to Wisconsin to join a close relative who had resided in state for at least 180 days prior to the applicant's arrival; and (4) offered employment before moving to the state. Also, the statute provided an exception for medical emergencies and "cases of unusual misfortune or hardship" (485 N.W. 2d 21@22).

39. *Shapiro v. Thompson*, 89 S. Ct. 1322 (1969); *Memorial Hospital v. Maricopa County*, 94 S. Ct. 1076 (1974).

40. *Green v. Anderson*, 811 F. Supp. 516 (E.D.Cal., 1993), Aff'd, 26 F.3d 95 (9th Cir., 1994), *cert* granted, 115 S. Ct. 306 (1994), vacated and dismissed, 115 S.Ct. 1059 (1995). California was enjoined from implementing its residency requirement in a related case (*Beno v. Shalala*, 30 F.3d 1057 (9th Cir., 1994), which the state did not appeal, rendering moot its appeal in *Anderson*.

41. The exclusion for illness or incapacity is found at 42 U.S.C.A. §602(a)(19)(A) & (B) (i)-(ix) (West 1996) and the exclusion for recipients of SSI or SSDI is found at 42 C.F.R. §233.90.

42. *Beno v. Shalala,* note 40.

43. See AZ-ST-ANN §41-2027, Sect. 8 E(2) (1995); CT Public Act 95-194(1) (1995); WI-ST-ANN 49.27 (5)(1)(e) (1994); MN-ST-ANN §256.035 Sub. 2a(3) (1995); NJ-ST-ANN §10:86-3.2(b) (1995); IA-ST-ANN §249C.1(3)(c) (1994); FLO-ST-ANN §409.927(3)(a) (1996); GA-ST-ANN §49-4-116(n) (1995); CO-ST-ANN §26-2-410(2) (1995).

44. See FLO-ST-ANN §409.927(3)(a) (1996); GA-ST-ANN §49-4-116(n) (2) (1995); MN-ST-ANN §256.035 Sub. 2a(4) (1995); NJ-ST-ANN §10:86-3.2(b)(viii) (1995); IA-ST-ANN §249C.1(3)(e) (1994).

45. See AZ-ST-ANN §41-2027, Sect. 8 E(6) (1995); MN-ST-ANN §256.035 Sub. 2a(1) (1995); IA-ST-ANN §249C.1(3)(f) (1994); CO-ST-ANN §26-2-410(2)(a) (1995).

46. See Fla. Admin. Code Ann. r 10C-1.510; IA-ST-ANN §249c.1(g); WI-ST-ANN §49.27 (1994); N.J. Admin. Code tit. 10 § 86-3.4(a) 4).

47. 1995 Wisconsin Senate Bill No. 359, Wisconsin 92nd Legislative Session—1995–96 Regular Session (hereafter, Wisconsin Works).

48. Emergency medical care would be available under the Emergency Medical Treatment and Active Labor Act, 42 U.S.C.A. §1395dd (West 1995).

49. Wisconsin Works, §70 49.145(2)(n), note 47.

50. Ibid. §77 49.153(3)(a) 2.

51. Ibid. §78 49.155(a).

52. The statute does not expressly state this but it is not likely that the legislature would contemplate a longer benefit period for this one class of children.

53. Wisconsin Works, §72 49.147(5)(1), note 47.

54. "Contract with America Advancement Act," §105, note 1.

55. United States General Accounting Office, *Social Security—Major Changes Needed for Disability Benefits for Addicts*, Rep. No. 94-128 (1994).

56. Ibid.

57. United States Department of Health and Human Services, Public Health Service, Centers for Disease Control and Prevention, *HIV/AIDS Surveillance Report, 1995* 7 (1995): 6.

58. The General Accounting Office estimates that 50 percent of women and men receiving SSI on the basis of an addiction to drugs or alcohol have secondary medical conditions. (See note 55.)

59. Colvin, Carolyn, Deputy Commissioner for Programs and Policy of the Social Security Administration. Address to the California State Senate, Health and Human Services Committee, October 10, 1996.

60. 104th Cong., 1st Sess. Senate Report 104-96 (June 9, 1995).

61. Holahan, John, Coughlin, Teresa, and Liu, Korbin, et al., *Cutting Medicaid Spending in Response to Budget Caps*, (Washington, D.C.: The Urban Institute, 1995).

62. "Personal Responsibility and Work Opportunities Act of 1996," P.L. 104-193, codified at 110 Stat. 2105 (1996).

63. Holahan et al., note 61: 17–21. Studies dealing with this subject show mixed results: some report program savings, while others report that costs are similar to or greater than those associated with fee-for-service programs. See also Newacheck, Paul W., Hughes, Dana C., English, Abigail, et al., "The Effect on Children of Curtailing Medicaid Spending." Commentary, *Journal of the American Medical Association* 274 (1995): 1468.

64. United States General Accounting Office, *Arizona Medicaid—Competition Among Managed Care Plans Lowers Program Costs,* Rep. No. 96-2 (October 4, 1995). See also Holahan et al., note 61: 18.

65. Thorpe, Kenneth E., Shields, Alexandra E., Gold, Heather, et al., *Anticipating the Number of Uninsured Americans and the Demand for Uncompensated Care: The Combined Impact of Proposed Medicaid Reductions and the Erosion of Employer-Sponsored Insurance*, [draft] (Waltham, Mass.: Council on the Economic Impact of Health Care Reform, Heller Graduate School, Brandeis University, November 1995).

66. Thorpe, Kenneth E., Shactman, David, et al., *The Combined Impact on Hospitals of Reduced Spending for Medicare, Medicaid and Employer Sponsored Insurance*, [draft] (Waltham, Mass.: Council on the Economic Impact of Health Care Reform, Heller Graduate School, Brandeis University, November 1995); Rosenthal, Elizabeth, "Groups Predict New York Hospital Closings," *N.Y. Times* (April 7, 1996) A1.

67. "Medicaid AIDS Coverage Unfair; Not Likely to Change: Block-Grant Plan Could Be More Bad News," *AIDS Alert* 10 (1995): 103; "Statelines New York: Public Advocate's Report Blasts HMOs," *American Health Line* 4 (1996).

68. United States General Accounting Office, *Hospital Costs — Cost Control Efforts at 17 Texas Hospitals*, Rep. No. 95-21 (1994).

69. Ibid.

70. Rosenthal, Elizabeth, "Managed Care Has Trouble Treating AIDS, Patients Say," *N.Y. Times* (January 15, 1996) A1.

71. Fein, Esther B., "Report Says Plan Would Hurt AIDS Cases," *N.Y. Times* (October 4, 1995) B1.

72. The literature on AIDS is rife with suggestions that people can be classified as the "true victims" of AIDS and those who are blameworthy for their condition. An excellent discussion of the phenomena that give rise to this "blaming" is found in Susan Sontag's *AIDS and Its Metaphors*, (New York: Anchor Books/Doubleday, 1988).

73. PRA, Sec. 400, "Statement of National Policy Concerning Welfare and Immigration."

74. United States General Accounting Office, *Welfare Reform — Implications of Proposals on Legal Immigrants' Benefits,* Rep. No.95-58 (February 2, 1995).

75. United States General Accounting Office, *Social Security-New Functional Assessments for Children Raise Eligibility Questions,* Rep. No. 95–66 (1995).

76. Sawhill, Isabel V., "Overview," in Sawhill, Isabel V. (Ed.) *Welfare Reform: An Analysis of the Issues*, (Washington, D.C.: The Urban Institute, 1995): xi.

77. Zedlewski, Sheila, and Clark, Sandra, et al., *Potential Effects of Congressional Welfare Reform Legislation on Family Incomes* (Washington, D.C.: The Urban Institute, 1996): 6.

78. Ibid.

TABLE OF CASES

A.C., In re, 573 A.2d 1235 (D.C.App., 1990).

A.D.H. v. State Department of Human Resources, 640 So.2d 969 (ALA.Civ.App., 1994).

Abbott v. Bragdon, 912 F.Supp. 580 (D.Me., 1995).

Adams, People v., 597 N.E.2d 574 (Ill., 1992).

Adams v. Drew, 906 F.Supp. 1050 (E.D.Va., 1995).

AIDS Action Committee of Massachusetts, Inc. v. Massachusetts Bay Transportation Authority, 849 F.Supp. 79, (D.Mass., 1993), aff'd 42 F.3d 1 (1st Cir., 1994).

Alfonso v. Fernandez, 151 Misc.2d 899 (N.Y.Sup., 1992) rev'd 606 N.Y.S.2d 259 (N.Y.A.D., 1993).

Alfredo S., In the Matter of, 568 N.Y.S.2d 123 (N.Y.A.D., 1991).

Alle, In re Welfare of, 230 N.W.2d 574 (Minn., 1975).

Allen v. Allen, 330 P.2d 151 (Or., 1958).

Anderson v. Mayer, Lexis 4736 (E.D.Tx., 1996).

Anderson v. Romero, 72 F.3d 518 (7th Cir., 1995).

Anderson v. Shalala, 1993 WL 289203 (D.Kan., 1993) on remand from the 10th Circuit, 34 F.3d 1076, 1994.

Angel Lace M., In the Interest of, 516 N.W.2d 678 (Wis., 1994).

Anonymous Firemen v. City of Willoughby, 779 F. Supp. 402 (N.D.Ohio, 1991).

Anonymous, Matter of, 156 A.D.2d 1028, (N.Y.A.D. 4 Dept., 1989), appeal granted 552 N.E.2d 176 (N.Y., 1990) aff'd 559 N.E.2d 670 (N.Y., 1990).

Anonymous, People v., 153 Misc.2d 436, (N.Y.Co.Ct., 1992).

Application of Gribetz, 159 Misc.2d 550, (N.Y.Co.Ct., 1994).

Association of Relatives & Friends of AIDS Patients v. Regulations & Permits Administration, 740 F Supp 95 (D.Puerto Rico, 1990).

B.L.V.B., Adoption of, 628 A.2d 1271 (Vt., 1993).

Baby Boy Doe, In re, 632 N.E.2d 326 (Ill.App. 1 Dist., 1994).

Baby "K," In the Matter of, 832 F. Supp. 1022 (E.D.Va., 1993), aff'd 16 F.3d 590 (4th Cir., 1994), *cert* denied, 115 S.Ct. 91 (1994).

Baby Neal v. Casey, 821 F.Supp. 320 (E.D.Pa., 1993), denial of class certification rev'd and remanded 43 F.3d 48 (3rd Cir., 1994).

Baby X, In the Matter of, 293 N.W.2d 736 at 739 (Mich.App., 1980).

Barlow v. Ground, 943 F.2d 1132 (9th Cir., 1991) *cert* denied 112 S. Ct. 2995 (1992).

Baxter v. Belleville, 720 F Supp 720 (S.D.Ill., 1989).

Bell v. A.R.H., 654 N.E.2d 29 (Ind.App., 1995).

Beno v. Shalala, 30 F.3d 1057 (9th Cir., 1994).

Board of Education of the City of New York v. Sobol, 613 N.Y.S.2d 792 (N.Y.Sup., 1993).

Borzillieri v. American National Red Cross 139 F.R.D. 284, (W.D.N.Y., 1991).

Bradley v. University of Texas A & M Medical Center, 3 F.3d 922 (5th Cir., 1993), cert denied 114 S.Ct. 1071 (1994).

Breithaupt v. Abram, 77 S.Ct. 408 (1957).

Brown v. Hot, Sexy and Safer Productions, Inc., 68 F.3d 525 (1st Cir., 1995), *cert* denied, 116 S.Ct. 1044 (1996).

Burr v. Board of Commissioners, 491 N.E.2d 1101 (Ohio, 1986).

C.A.U. v. R.L., 438 N.W.2d 441 (Minn.App., 1989).

C.K. v. Shalala, 883 F. Supp. 991 (D.N.J., 1995) aff'd, 92 F.3rd 171 (3rd Cir., 1996).

Cain v. Hyatt, 734 F.Supp. 671 (E.D.Pa., 1990).

Carparts Distribution Center, Inc. v. Automotive Wholesaler's Association of New England, 826 F. Supp. 583 (D.N.H., 1993) vacated and remanded, 37 F.3d 12 (1st Cir., 1994).

Chalk v. United States, 840 F.2d 701, (9th Cir., 1988).

Chambarry v. Mount Sinai Hospital, 161 Misc.2d 1000, (N.Y.Sup., 1994).

City of Cleburne v. Cleburne Living Center, 105 S.Ct. 3249 (1985).

Clarkson v. Coughlin, 898 F.Supp. 1019 (S.D.N.Y., 1995).

Cohen v. Chater, 1995 WL 405028 (E.D.N.Y., 1995).

Colautti v. Franklin, 99 S.Ct. 675 at 688 (1979).

Commonwealth v. Pellegrini, 608 N.E.2d 717 (Mass., 1993).

Conte v. Merrell, Lexis 16245, (N.Y.A.D., 4 Dept. 1989).

County Department of Public Welfare v. Morningstar, 151 N.E.2d 150 (Ind.App., 1958).

Crouse Irving Memorial Hospital, Inc. v. Paddock, 127 Misc.2d 101 (N.Y.Sup., 1985).

Cruzan v. Director of the Missouri Department of Health, 110 S.Ct. 2841 (1990).

D'Amico v. New York State Board of Law Examiners, 813 F.Supp. 217 (W.D.N.Y., 1993).

D.B. v. Bloom, 896 F.Supp. 166 (D.N.J., 1995).

District 27 Community School Board v. Board of Education, 130 Misc.2d 398 (N.Y.Sup., 1986).

Doe v. Attorney General of the United States, 814 F.Supp. 844 (N.D.Cal., 1992). On remand from the 9th Circuit for findings on the merits (941 F.2d 780 9th Cir., 1991) rev'd, 62 F.3d 1424, unpublished disposition, 1995 WL 392178 (1995), *cert* granted for redetermination of damages award, 1996 WL 341602 (1996).

Doe v. Belleville Public Schools District, 672 F. Supp. 342 (S.D.Ill., 1987).

Doe v. Borough of Barrington, 729 F. Supp. 376 (D.N.J., 1990).

Doe v. Burgos, 638 N.E.2d 701 (Ill.App., 4 Dist., 1994), appeal denied 645 N.E.2d 1357 (Ill., 1994).

Doe v. City of Chicago, 883 F. Supp. 1126 (N.D.Ill., 1994).

Doe v. City of New York, 15 F.3d 264 at 267, (2d Cir., 1994).

Doe v. District of Columbia, 796 F.Supp. 559 at 563 (D.D.C., 1992).

Doe v. Dolton Elementary School District No. 148, 694 F. Supp. 440 (N.D.Ill., 1988).

Doe v. Jamaica Hospital 608 N.Y.S.2d 518 (N.Y.A.D., 1994).

Doe v. Johnson, 817 F. Supp. 1382 (W.D.Mich., 1993).

Doe v. Kohn Nast & Graf, P.C., 866 F.Supp. 190 (E.D.Pa., 1994).

Doe by Lavery v. Attorney General of the United States, 814 F.Supp. 844 (N.D.Cal., 1992) rev'd 62 F.3d 1424 (9th Cir., 1995) *cert* granted, vacated, and remanded on other grounds, 116 S.Ct. 2543 (1996), aff'd 95 F.3d 29 (9th Cir., 1996).

Doe v. New York City Department of Social Services, 1995 WL 619864 (S.D.N.Y., 1995).

Doe v. Roe 190 A.D.2d 463, (N.Y.A.D. 4 Dept., 1993).

Doe v. State of New York, 152 Misc.2d 922, (N.Y.Ct.Cl., 1991).

Doe v. Town of Plymouth, 825 F. Supp. 1102 (D.Mass., 1993).

Doe v. University of Maryland, 50 F.3d 1261 (4th Cir., 1995).

Doe v. Washington University, 780 F.Supp. 628 (E.D.Mo., 1991).

Dorsey v. U.S. Department of Labor, 41 F.3d 1551 (D.C.Cir., 1994).

Dunn v. White, 880 F.2d 1188 (10th. Cir., 1989) *cert* denied 110 S.Ct. 871 (1990).

Durham, People v., 146 Misc.2d 913, (N.Y.Sup., 1990).

Dustin T., In re, 93 Md.App. 726 at 732, (Md.App., 1992) *cert* denied 620 A.2d 350 (Md., 1993).

E.E.O.C. v. Mason Tenders, No. 93-3865 (S.D.N.Y., 1995).

Elaine W. v. Joint Diseases North General Hospital, 613 N.E.2d 523 at 525 (N.Y., 1993).

Encoe, People v., 885 P.2d 596 (Nev., 1994).

Eric L. v. Harry Bird, 848 F.Supp. 303 (D.N.H., 1994).

Faya v. Almaraz, 620 A.2d 327 (Md., 1993).

Ferrell, People v., 659 N.E.2d 992 (Ill.App., 1995), appeal denied, 664 N.E.2d 644 (Ill., 1996).

Finley v. Giacobbe, 827 F. Supp. 215 (S.D.N.Y., 1993).

Gay Men's Health Crisis v. Sullivan, 733 F. Supp. 619 (S.D.N.Y., 1989) (GMHC I).

Gay Men's Health Crisis and others v. Sullivan, 792 F. Supp. 278 (S.D.N.Y., 1992) (GMHC II).

General Motors v. Director of the Institute for Occupational Safety and Health, 636 F.2d 163 at 165 (6th Cir., 1980), *cert* denied, 102 S.Ct. 357 (1981).

Glanz v. Vernick, 750 F. Supp. 39 (D.Mass., 1990), 756 F. Supp. 632 (D.Mass., 1991).

Glover v. Eastern Nebraska Community Office of Retardation, 867 F.2d 461 (8th Cir., 1989) *cert* denied 110 S.Ct. 321 (1989).

Gorski v. Troy, 714 F. Supp. 367 (N.D.Ill., 1989) rev'd 929 F.2d 1183 (7th Cir., 1991).

Goss v. Sullivan, 839 F.Supp. 1532 (D.Wyo., 1993).

Government of the Virgin Islands v. Roberts, 756 F. Supp. 898 (D. Virgin Islands, 1991).

Graham v. Richardson, 403 U.S. 365 (1971).

Gray, State v., 584 N.E.2d 710 (Ohio, 1992).

Green v. Anderson, 811 F. Supp. 516 (E.D.Cal., 1993), aff'd, 26 F.3d 95 (9th Cir., 1994), *cert* granted, 115 S. Ct. 306 (1994), vacated and dismissed, 115 S.Ct. 1059 (1995).

Guardianship of Williams, Matter of 869 P.2d 661 (Kan., 1994).

H.N.R., In the Matter of the Adoption of Two Children, 666 A.2d 535 (N.J.Super.A.D., 1995).

Hardy, People v., 471 N.W.2d 619 (Mich., 1991).

Harris v. McRae, 100 S.Ct. 2671, (1980).

Harris v. Thigpen, 727 F. Supp. 1564 (M.D.Ala., 1990) aff'd in part, vacated in part 941 F.2d 1495 (11th Cir., 1991).

Herrod, In re Estates of, 254 Ill.App.3d 1061 (Ill.App. 1 Dist., 1993).

Hershey Medical Center, In re, 634 A.2d 159 (Pa., 1993).

Hillman v. Columbia County, 474 N.W.2d 913 (1991), review granted 482 N.W.2d 105 (Wis. App., 1992).

Hogar Agua y Vida en el Desierto v Suarez-Medina, 829 F.Supp. 19 (D.Puerto Rico, 1993) vacated by 36 F.3d 177 at 177 (1st Cir., 1994).

Hunnewell v. Warden, 19 F.3d 7 (1st Cir., 1994).

J.B. v. Bohonovsky, 835 F. Supp. 796 (D.N.J., 1993).

J.G., In the Interest of, 674 A.2d 625 (N.J.Super.A.D., 1996).

Jacob, In the Matter of, 660 N.E.2d 397 (N.Y., 1995).

Jacobson v. Com. of Massachusetts, 197 U.S. 11 (1905).

Jackson v. State, 833 S.W.2d 220 (Tex.App. 14 Dist., 1992).

Jamaica Hospital, In re, 128 Misc.2d 1006 (N.Y.Sup., 1985).

Jeanine B. by Blondis v. Thompson, 877 F.Supp. 1268 (E.D.Wi., 1995).

Jefferson v. Griffin Spalding County Hospital, 274 S.E.2d 457 (Ga., 1981).

Jew Ho v. Williamson, 103 F. 10 (N.D.Cal., 1900).

John T., In the Interest of, 538 N.W.2d 761 (Neb.App., 1995).

Johnetta J. v. Municipal Court, 267 Cal.Rptr. 666 (Cal.App. 1 Dist., 1990).

Johnson, Matter of Adoption of, 612 N.E.2d 569 (Ind.App. 1 Dist., 1993).

Johnson v. State, 578 So.2d 419 (Fla. App. 5 Dist., 1991) rev'd, 602 So.2d 1288 (Fla., 1992).

Johnson v. U.S. States, 816 F. Supp. 1519 (N.D.Ala. 1993).

Johnston v. Morrison, Inc., 849 F.Supp. 777 (N.D.Ala. 1994).

Jones v. Milwaukee County, 485 N.W.2d 21 (Wis., 1992); reconsideration denied, 491 N.W.2d 771 (Wis., 1992).

Juman v. Louise Wise Services, 620 N.Y.S.2d 371 (N.Y.A.D., 1995).

Juveniles A, B, C, D, E, Matter of 847 P2d 455 (Wash., 1993).

K.M., In re, Petition of 653 N.E.2d 888 (Ill.App. 1 Dist., 1995).

Kerins v. Hartley, 33 Cal.Rptr.2d 172 (Cal.App. 2 Dist., 1994).

King v. McMahon, 186 Cal.App.3d 648 (Cal.App. 1 Dist., 1986).

LaShawn A. v. Dixon, 762 F.Supp. 959 (D.D.C., 1991).

Leckelt v. Board of Commissioners of Hospital District No. 1, 714 F.Supp. 1377 (E.D.La., 1989) aff'd 909 F.2d 820 (5th Cir., 1990).

Lipscomb v. Simmons, 962 F.2d 1374 (9th Cir., 1992).

Local 1812, American Federation of Government Employees v. United States Dept. of State, 662 F. Supp. 50 (D.D.C., 1987).

Luster, State v., 419 S.E.2d 32 (Ga.App., 1992), *cert* denied (1992).

McBarnette v. Feldman, 153 Misc.2d 627, (N.Y.Sup., 1992).

McGann v. H & H Music Co., 742 F.Supp. 392 (S.D.Tx., 1990) aff'd 946 F.2d 401 (5th Cir., 1991), *cert* denied, 506 U.S. 981(1992).

McGuffin v. Overton, 542 N.W.2d 288 (Mich.App., 1995).

McNemar v. Disney Stores, 1995 WL 390051 (E.D.Pa., 1995), aff'd 91 F.3d 610 (3rd. Cir., 1996).

McVickers, People v., 840 P.2d 955 (Cal., 1992) rehearing denied (1993).

M.M.D., In re, 662 A.2d 837 (D.C.App., 1995).

Maher v. Roe, 97 S.Ct. 2376 (1977).

Mallette v. Children's Friend and Service, 661 A.2d 67 (R.I., 1995).

Maricopa County Juvenile Action, In the Matter of the Appeal in, 845 P.2d 1129 (Ariz.App. Div.1, 1993).

Marisol v. Giuliani, 95 Civ. 10533, Lexis 8420 (S.D.N.Y., 1996).

Mark Kadinger, Estate of, v. International Brotherhood of Electrical Workers, Local 110, Civil Action No. 3-93-159, 1993 U.S. Dist. Lexis 18982 (Mn. Dist. Ct., December 21, 1993).

Martinez v. Brazen, 1992 WL 93245 (S.D.N.Y., 1992).

Martinez v. School Board of Hillsborough County, 675 F.Supp. 1574, (M.D.Fla., 1987), 692 F.Supp. 1293, (M.D.Fla., 1988) Vacated, 861 F.2d 1502, (11th Cir., 1988), on remand, 711 F.Supp. 1066, (M.D.Fla., 1989).

Mauro v. Borgess Medical Center, 886 F.Supp. 1349 (W.D.Mich., 1995).

Memorial Hospital v. Maricopa County, 94 S. Ct. 1076 (1974).

Michael J. v. County of Los Angeles Department of Adoptions, 247 Cal.Rptr. 504 (Cal.App. 2 Dist., 1988).

Miller v. Spicer, 822 F. Supp. 158 (D.Del., 1993).

Miller v. Youakim, 440 U.S. 125 (1979).

Mills v. District of Columbia, 348 F. Supp. 866 (D.C.D.C., 1972).

Mohr v. Commonwealth, 653 N.E.2d 1104 (Mass., 1995).

Moore v. Mabus, 976 F.2d 268 (5th Cir., 1992).

Muhammud v. Carlson, 845 F.2d 175 (8th Cir., 1988) *cert* denied 109 S.Ct. 1346 (1989).

Mussivand v. David, 544 N.E.2d 265 (Ohio, 1989).

Nelson v. Thornburgh, 567 F.Supp. 369 (E.D.Pa., 1983), aff'd 732 F.2d 146 (3d Cir., 1984), *cert* denied 105 S.Ct. 955 (1985).

New York State Society of Surgeons v. Axelrod, 572 N.E.2d 605, (N.Y., 1991).

New York State Association for Retarded Children, Inc. v. Carey, 466 F. Supp. 479 (E.D.N.Y., 1978), aff'd 612 F.2d 644 (2d Cir., 1979).

Newton v. Riley, 899 S.W.2d 509 (Ky.App., 1995).

Nolley v. County of Erie, 776 F.Supp. 715, (W.D.N.Y., 1991).

Norcross v. Sneed, 573 F.Supp. 533 (W.D.Ark., 1983), aff'd 755 F.2d 113 (8th Cir., 1985).

Ordway v. County of Suffolk, 154 Misc.2d 269 (N.Y.Sup., 1992).

Pearlman, In re, No. 87-24926 DA (Fla. 17th Cir.Ct., 1989).

Pennsylvania Association for Retarded Children v. Commonwealth of Pennsylvania, 334 F. Supp. 1257 (E.D.Pa., 1971).

People v. Hardy, 469 N.W.2d 50 (Mich.App., 1990).

Phipps v. Saddleback Valley Unified School District, 204 Cal.App.3d 1110 (Cal.App. 4 Dist., 1988).

Planned Parenthood of Southeastern Pennsylvania v. Casey, 112 S.Ct. 2791 (1992).

Plowman v. United States, 698 F.Supp. 627 at 632 (E.D.Va., 1988).

Prince v. Massachusetts, 64 S.Ct. 438 (1944).

Raleigh Fitkin-Paul Morgan Memorial Hospital v. Anderson, 201 A.2d 537 (N.J., 1964), *cert* denied, 84 S.Ct. 1894, (1964).

Ray v. School District of DeSoto County, 666 F. Supp. 1524 (M.D.Fla., 1987).

Raytheon Co. v. Fair Employment & Housing Commission, 212 Cal. App.3d 1242 (Cal.App. 2 Dist., 1989).

Reinesto v. State, 894 P.2d 733 (Ariz.App. Div. 1, 1995).

Relf v. Weinberger, 372 F. Supp. 1196 (D.C.D.C., 1974).

Rene O.C., In the Matter of Guardianship of, 606 N.Y.S.2d 872 (N.Y.Sur., 1993).

Rescue Mission Alliance v. Mercado, 637 N.Y.S.2d 580 (N.Y.A.D. 4 Dept., 1996).

Reyes v. People, 141 Cal.Rptr. 912 (Cal.App. 4 Dist., 1977).

Reynolds v. Brock, 815 F.2d 571, (9th Cir., 1987), aff'd 985 F.2d 470 (9th Cir., 1993), rehearing denied, 994 F.2d 690 (9th Cir., 1993).

Rice v. The School District of Fairfield, 452 S.E.2d 352 (S.C.App., 1994), *cert* denied (1995).

Robbins v. Clarke, 946 F.2d 1331 (8th Cir., 1991).

Robertson v. Granite City Community Unit School District, 684 F. Supp. 1002 (S.D. Ill., 1988).

Rochin v. California, 72 S.Ct. 205 (1952).

Roe v. Catholic Charities of Springfield, 588 N.E.2d 354 (Ill.App., 1992).

Roe v. District of Columbia, 842 F.Supp. 563, (D.D.C., 1993), vacated and dismissed as moot (25 F.3d 1115 (D.C.Cir., 1994).

Roe v. Fauver, 1988 WL 47359 (N.J. May, 1988).

Roe v. Wade, 93 S.Ct. 705 (1973).

Rosetti v. Shalala, 12 F.3d 1216 at 1219 at 1220 (3rd Cir., 1993).

Ross v. Beaumont Hospital, 687 F.Supp. 1115 (E.D.Mich., 1988).

Roth v. New York Blood Center, 596 N.Y.S.2d 639 (N.Y. Sup., 1993).

Ruiz, In re, 500 N.E.2d 935 (Ohio Com. Pl., 1986).

Rust v. Sullivan, 111 S.Ct. 1759 (1991).

Santosky v. Kramer, 455 U.S. 745 at 745 (1982).

Schaill by Kross v. Tippecanoe School Corp., 864 F.2d 1309 at 1322 (7th Cir., 1988) rehearing denied (1989).

School Board of Nassau County v. Arline, 480 U.S. 273 (1987).

Scoles v. Mercy Health Corporation, 887 F.Supp. 765 (E.D.Pa., 1994).

Search Warrant, In re, 810 F.2d 67 (3rd Cir., 1987), *cert* denied, 107 S.Ct. 3233 (1987).

Selby v. Rapping, 1992 WL 400739 (S.D.N.Y., 1992).

Shapiro v. Thompson, 89 S. Ct. 1322 (1969).

Sharon Fletcher, In the Matter of, 533 N.Y.S.2d 241 (N.Y.Fam. Ct., 1988).

Skinner v. Railway Labor Executives' Association, 109 S.Ct. 1402 (1989).

Smith v. Dovenmuehle Mortgage, Inc., 859 F.Supp. 1138 (N.D. Ill., 1994).

Smith v. Robinson, 468 U.S. 992 at 1017 (1984).

Southeastern Community College v. Davis, 442 U.S. 397 (1979).

Stanley v. Illinois, 405 U.S. 645 (1972).

Stefanel Tyesha C., In re, 556 N.Y.S.2d 280 (N.Y.A.D., 1 Dept., 1990), appeal dismissed, 565 N.E.2d 1267 (N.Y., 1990).

Steven L. v. Dawn L., 148 Misc.2d 779 (N.Y. Fam. Ct., 1990).

Stewart B. McKinney Foundation, Inc. v. Town Plan & Zoning Commission, 790 F Supp 1197 (D.Conn., 1992).

Sullivan v. Zebly, 110 S.Ct. 885 (1990).

Support Ministries for Persons with AIDS, Inc. v. Village of Waterford, 808 F. Supp. 120 (N.D.N.Y., 1992).

Suter v. Artist, 112 S.Ct. 1360 at 1368 (1992).

T.E.P. and K.J.C. v. Leavit, 840 F. Supp. 110 (D. Utah, 1993).

Taft v. Taft, 446 N.E.2d 395 (Mass., 1983).

Tammy, Adoption of, 619 N.E.2d 315 (Mass., 1993).

Thomas v. Atascadero Unified School District, 662 F. Supp. 376 (C.D.Cal., 1986).

Thomas, People v., 580 N.E.2d 1353 (Ill.App. 2 Dist, 1991), appeal denied 587 N.E.2d 1023 (Ill., 1992).

Toney v. U.S. Healthcare, Inc., 838 F.Supp. 201 (E.D.Pa., 1993), 840 F.Supp. 357 (E.D.Pa., 1994) aff'd 37 F.3d 1489 (3rd. Cir., 1994).

Troy D., In re, 215 Cal.App.3d 889 at 897, (Cal.App. 4 Dist., 1989), review denied (1990).

Tsetseranoe v. Tech Prototype, 893 F.Supp. 109 (D.N.H., 1995).

United States v. Dumford, 28 M.J. 836 (AFCMR, 1989), review granted, 29 M.J. 436 (CMA, 1989), aff'd 30 M.J. 137 (CMA, 1990) *cert* denied 111 S.Ct. 150 (1990).

United States v. Joseph, 33 M.J. 960 (NMCMR, 1991), review granted, 36 M.J. 17 (CMA, 1992) aff'd 37 M.J. 392 (CMA, 1993).

United States v. Morvant, 898 F.Supp. 1157 (E.D.La., 1995).

United States v. University Hospital, 729 F.2d 144 (2d Cir., 1984).

Urbaniak v. Newton, 277 Cal. Rptr. 354 (Cal.App. 1 Dist., 1991).

Valerie D., In re, 595 A.2d 922 (Conn.App., 1991), *cert* granted, 600 A.2d 1029 (Conn., 1991), rev'd 613 A.2d 748 (Conn., 1992).

Vaughn v. North Carolina Department of Human Resources, 252 S.E.2d 792 (N.C., 1979).

Vuitch, United States v., 901 S.Ct. 1294 (1971).

Ware v. Valley Stream High School, 150 A.D.2d 14 (N.Y.A.D., 1989); aff'd 550 N.E.2d 420 (N.Y., 1989).

Weaver v. Reagen, 701 F.Supp. 717 (W.D.Mo., 1988) Aff'd, 886 F.2d 194 (1989).

Weston v. Carolina Medicorp, Inc., 402 S.E.2d 653 (N.C.App., 1991), review denied, 409 S.E.2d 611 (N.C., 1991).

Whalen v. Roe, 97 S.Ct. 869 (1977).

White v. Western School Corp., IP 85-1192-C, slip op., (S.D.Ind., 1985).

Whitner v. State, 1996 WL 393164 (S.C., 1996).

Wisconsin v. Yoder, 406 U.S. 205 at 233 (1972).

Woolfolk v. Duncan, 872 F.Supp. 1381 (E.D.Pa., 1995).

BIBLIOGRAPHY

Aase, Jon M., "Clinical Recognition of FAS: Difficulties of Detection and Diagnosis; Fetal Alcohol Syndrome; Includes Bibliography; Special Issue: Alcohol-Related Birth Defects," *Alcohol Health & Research World* 18 (1994).

Acuff, Katherine L., "Prenatal and Newborn Screening: State Legislative Approaches and Current Practice Standards," in Faden, Ruth, Geller, Gail, and Powers, Madison (Eds.) *AIDS, Women and the Next Generation: Towards a Morally Acceptable Public Policy for HIV Testing of Pregnant Women and Newborns,* (New York: Oxford University Press, 1991).

American Academy of Pediatrics, Task Force on Pediatric AIDS, "Pediatric Guidelines for Infection Control of Human Immunodeficiency Virus (Acquired Immunodeficiency Virus) in Hospitals, Medical Offices, Schools, and Other Settings," *Pediatrics* 82 (1988).

American Academy of Pediatrics, Task Force on Pediatric AIDS, "Infants and Children with Acquired Immunodeficiency Syndrome: Placement in Adoption and Foster Care," *Pediatrics* 83 (1989).

American Academy of Pediatrics, Task Force on Pediatric AIDS, "Guidelines for Human Immunodeficiency Virus (HIV)-Infected Children and Their Foster Families," *Pediatrics* 89 (1992).

American Association for Protecting Children, *Highlights of Official Child Neglect and Reporting Laws, 1986*, (Denver: American Humane Association, 1988).

American Medical Association Council on Scientific Affairs, "Health Care Needs of Gay Men and Lesbians in the United States," *Journal of the American Medical Association* 275 (1996).

Anastos, Kathryn, and Vermund, Sten, "Epidemiology and Natural History," in Kurth, Ann (Ed.) *Until the Cure: Caring for Women with HIV,* (New Haven: Yale University Press, 1993).

Anderson, Gary R. (Ed.) *Courage to Care: Responding to the Crisis of Children with AIDS,* (Washington, D.C.: Child Welfare League of America, 1990).

Annas, George J., "Detention of HIV-Positive Haitians at Guantanamo—Human Rights and Medical Care," *New England Journal of Medicine* 329 (1993).

Antoine, Florence S., "Scientists Changing Therapy Outlook for AIDS Patients," *Journal of the National Cancer Institute* 82 (1990).

Arno, Peter S., "The Non-Profit Sector's Response to the AIDS Epidemic: Community-Based Services in San Francisco," *American Journal of Public Health* 76 (1986).

Backstrom, Charles, and Robins, Leonard, "State AIDS Policy Making: Perspectives of Legislative Health Committee Chairs," *AIDS and Public Policy Journal* 10 (1996).

Banks, Taunya L., "Reproduction and Parenting," in Burris, S., Dalton, H. L., et al., *AIDS Law Today*, (New Haven: Yale University Press, 1993).

Barnhart, Huiman X., Caldwell, M. Blake, Thomas, Pauline, "Natural History of Human Immunodeficiency Virus Disease in Perinatally Infected Children: An Analysis from the Pediatric Spectrum of Disease Project," *Pediatrics* 97 (1996).

Bayer, Ronald, and Healton, Cheryl, "Controlling AIDS in Cuba: The Logic of Quarantine," *New England Journal of Medicine* 320 (1989).

Bayer, Ronald, "Public Health Policy and the AIDS Epidemic: An End to HIV Exceptionalism?" *New England Journal of Medicine* 324 (1991).

Bayer, Ronald, "AIDS, Public Health, and Civil Liberties: Consensus and Conflict in Policy," in Reamer, Frederic G. (Ed.) *AIDS and Ethics*, (New York: Columbia University Press, 1991).

Bayer, Ronald, "Ethical Challenges Posed by Zidovudine Treatment to Reduce Vertical Transmission of HIV," *New England Journal of Medicine* 331 (1994).

Bennett, Charles L., Horner, Ronnie D., Weinstein, Robert A., et al., "Racial Differences in Care Among Hospitalized Patients with Pneumocystis Carinii Pneumonia in Chicago, New York, Los Angeles, Miami, and Raleigh-Durham," *Archives of Internal Medicine* 155 (1995).

Bennett, Susan, and Sullivan, Kathleen A., "Disentitling the Poor: Waivers and Welfare 'Reform,'" *University of Michigan Journal of Law* 26 (1993).

Berger, David K., Rivera, Miriam, et al., "Risk Assessment for Human Immunodeficiency Virus Among Pregnant Hispanic Adolescents," *Adolescence* 28 (1993).

Blair, Jill F., and Hein, Karen K., "Public Policy Implications of HIV/AIDS in Adolescents," *The Future of Children: Critical Health Issues for Children and Youth* 4 (1994).

Blendon, Robert J., and Donelan, Karen, "Discrimination Against People with AIDS: The Public's Perspective," *New England Journal of Medicine* 319 (1988).

Blendon, Robert J., Donelan, Karen, and Knox, Richard A., "Public Opinion and AIDS: Lessons for the Second Decade; Public Opinion and Health Care," *Journal of the American Medical Association* 267 (1992).

Bobinski, Mary Anne, "Women and HIV: A Gender-Based Analysis of a Disease and Its Legal Regulation," *Texas Journal of Women and the Law* (1994).

Bopp, James, Jr., and Gardner, Deborah Hall, "AIDS Babies, Crack Babies: Challenges to the Law," *Issues in Law & Medicine* 7 (1991).

Boskey, Jill A., and Malvey, Thomas J., "HIV Disability Claims: A Reference for the Advocate," *Social Security Reporting Service* 46 (1994).

Bradford, William A., Jr., Zavos, Michele A., et al., "The AIDS Epidemic and Health Care Reform," *John Marshall Law Review* 27 (1994).

Brandt, Alan M., "AIDS in Historical Perspective," in Pierce, Christine, and Van-DeVeer, Donald (Eds.) *AIDS: Ethics and Public Policy*, (Belmont, CA: Wadsworth Publishing Company, 1988).

Broers, Barbara, Morabia, Alfredo, and Hirschel, Bernard, "A Cohort Study of Drug Users' Compliance with Zidovudine Treatment," *Archives of Internal Medicine* 154 (1994).

Brookmeyer, Ron, and Gail, Mitchell, H. *AIDS Epidemiology: A Quantitative Approach*, (New York: Oxford University Press, 1994).

Buchanan, Robert J., "Medicaid Policies for the Nursing Facility Care Provided to Medicaid Recipients with AIDS," *AIDS and Public Policy Journal* 10 (1995).

Buchanan, Robert J., and Kircher, Fred G., "Medicaid Policies for AIDS-Related Hospital Care; Health Care Needs of Vulnerable Populations," *Health Care Financing Review* 15 (1994).

Buchanan, Robert J., and Colby, David, "Medicaid Policies for the Physicians' Services Provided to Medicaid Recipients with AIDS," *AIDS and Public Policy Journal* 11 (1996).

Burke, Donald S., Brundage, John F., Goldenbaum, Mary, et al., "Human Immunodeficiency Virus Infections in Teenagers: Seroprevalence Among Applicants for US Military Service," *Journal of the American Medical Association* 263 (1990).

Burkett, Elinor, *The Gravest Show on Earth: America in the Age of AIDS,* (New York: Houghton Mifflin, 1995).

Caldwell, M. Blake, Mascola, Laurene, Smith, Walter, et al., "Biologic, Foster, and Adoptive Parents: Care Givers of Children Exposed Perinatally to Human Immunodeficiency Virus in the United States," *Pediatrics* 90 (1992).

Chaisson, Richard E., Keruly, Jeanne C., Moore, Richard D., "Race, Sex, Drug Use, and Progression of Human Immunodeficiency Virus Disease," *New England Journal of Medicine* 333 (1995).

Charney, P., and Morgan, C. "Do Treatment Recommendations Reported in the Research Literature Consider Differences Between Women and Men?" *Clinical Research* 40 (1992).

Chasnoff and colleagues, "Cocaine Use in Pregnancy," *New England Journal of Medicine* 313 (1988).

Chavkin, Wendy, "Pneumocystis Carinii Pneumonia in Children with Perinatally Acquired HIV Infection." Letter to the Editor, *Journal of the American Medical Association* 271 (1994).

Child Welfare League of America, Task Force on Children and HIV Infection, Subcommittee on Family Foster Care, *Meeting the Challenge of HIV Infection in Family Foster Care*, (Washington, D.C.: 1991).

Child Welfare League of America, *Children's Legislative Agenda: 1995 Budget Updates and Issue Briefs*, (Washington, D.C.: Child Welfare League of America, 1995).

Children's Defense Fund, *The State of America's Children Yearbook: 1996* (Washington, D.C.: The Children's Defense Fund, 1996).

Chiriboga, Claudia A., Vibbert, Martha, Malouf, Renee, et al., "Neurological Correlates of Fetal Cocaine Exposure: Transient Hypertonia of Infancy and Early Childhood," *Pediatrics* 96 (1995).

Clemo, Lorrie, "The Stigmatization of AIDS in Infants and Children in the United States," *AIDS Education & Prevention* 41 (1992).

Closen, Michael J., Bobinski, Mary Anne, Herman, Donald H. J., et al., "Criminalization of an Epidemic: HIV-AIDS and Criminal Exposure Laws," *Arkansas Law Review* 46 (1994).

Clotet, B., Ruiz, L., Ibanez, A., et al., "Long-Term Survivors of Human Immunodeficiency Virus Type 1 Infection," *New England Journal of Medicine* 332 (1995).

Cohen, Felissa L., and Faan, Wendy M., "Foster Care of HIV-Positive Children in the United States," *Public Health Reports* 109 (1994).

Colvin, Carolyn, Deputy Commissioner for Programs and Policy of the Social Security Administration. Address to the California State Senate, Health and Human Services Committee, October 10, 1996.

Commission on Behavioral and Social Sciences, National Research Council, *The Social Impact of AIDS in the United States*, (Washington, D.C.: National Academy Press, 1993).

Commission on Behavioral and Social Sciences and Education, National Research Council, *Preventing HIV Transmission: The Role of Sterile Needles and Bleach*, (Washington, D.C.: National Academy Press, 1995).

Committee on Adolescence: 1994 to 1995, American Academy of Pediatrics, "Sexually Transmitted Diseases," *Pediatrics* 94 (1994).

Committee on Pediatric AIDS, 1995 to 1996, "Human Milk, Breastfeeding, and Transmission of Human Immunodeficiency Virus in the United States," *Pediatrics* 96 (1995).

Connor, Edward M., et al., "Reduction of Maternal-Infant Transmission of Human Immunodeficiency Virus Type 1 with Zidovudine Treatment," *New England Journal of Medicine* 331 (1994).

Council on Ethical and Judicial Affairs Report, "Ethical Issues Involved in the Growing AIDS Crisis," *Journal of the American Medical Association* 259 (1988).

Crossley, Mary A., "Of Diagnoses and Discrimination: Discriminatory Nontreatment of Infants with HIV Infection," *Columbia Law Review* 93 (1993).

Davis, Susan F., Byers, Robert H., Lindegren, Mary Lou, et al., "Prevalence and Incidence of Vertically Acquired HIV Infection in the United States," *Journal of the American Medical Association* 274 (1995).

Day, Nancy L., and Richardson, Gale A., "Comparative Teratogenicity of Alcohol and Other Drugs: Prenatal Exposure to Alcohol or Other Drugs Can Impair Physical, Intellectual, and Behavioral Development," *Alcohol Health & Research World* 18 (1994).

DeNoon, Daniel J., "Best Combination So Far: Indinavir + AZT + ddI: Anti-HIV Drugs," *AIDS Weekly Plus* (January 1996).

DiClemente, Ralph J., and Wingood, Gina M., "A Randomized Controlled Trial of an HIV Sexual Risk-Reduction Intervention for Young African-American Women," *Journal of the American Medical Association* 274 (1995).

Doughty, Roger, "The Confidentiality of HIV-Related Information: Responding to the Resurgence of Aggressive Public Health Interventions in the AIDS Epidemic," *California Law Review* 82 (1994).

Draper, Jane M., "Annotation: Rescission or Cancellation of Insurance Policy for Insured's Misrepresentation or Concealment of Information Concerning Human Immunodeficiency Virus (HIV), Acquired Immunodeficiency Syndrome (AIDS), or Related Health Problems, 15 *A.L.R.5th* 92 (1995).

[Editor] "Heterosexual Transmission of Acquired Immunodeficiency Syndrome and Human Immunodeficiency Virus Infection—United States; Morbidity and Mortality Weekly Report; Column," *Journal of the American Medical Association* 262 (1989).

[Editor] "Relationship of Syphilis to Drug Use and Prostitution—Connecticut and Philadelphia, Pennsylvania; Morbidity and Mortality Weekly Report; Column," *Journal of the American Medical Association* 261 (1989).

El-Bassel, Nabila, Ivanoff, Andre, Schilling, Robert F., et al., "Preventing HIV/AIDS in Drug Abusing Incarcerated Women Through Skills Building and Social Support Enhancement: Preliminary Outcomes," *Social Work Research* 19 (1995).

English, Abigail, "The HIV-AIDS Epidemic and the Child Welfare System: Protecting the Rights of Infants, Young Children, and Adolescents," *Iowa Law Review* 77 (1992).

English, Abigail, "Pediatric HIV Infection and Perinatal Drug or Alcohol Exposure: Legal Issues and Legal Advocacy," in Barth, Richard P., Pietrzak, Jeanne, and Ramler, Malia (Eds.) *Families Living with Drugs and HIV: Intervention and Treatment Strategies,* (New York: Guilford Press, 1993).

European Study Group on Heterosexual Transmission of HIV, "Comparison of Female to Male and Male to Female Transmission of HIV in 563 Stable Couples," *British Medical Journal* 304 (1992).

Faden, Ruth R., Gielen, Nancy Kass, O'Campo, Patricia O., et al., "Prenatal HIV-Antibody Testing and the Meaning of Consent," AIDS and Public Policy Journal 9 (1994).

Fahs, Marianne C., Waite, Douglas, Sesholtz, Marilyn, et al., "Results of the ACSUS for Pediatric AIDS Patients: Utilization of Services, Functional Status, and Social Severity; AIDS Costs and Service Utilization Survey," Health Services Research 29 (1994).

Fanburg, Jonathan T., Kaplan, David W., Naylor, Kelly E., "Student Opinions of Condom Distribution at a Denver, Colorado, High School," Journal of School Health 65 (1995).

Fauvel, Micheline, Henrard, Denis, Delage, Gilles, et al., "Early Detection of HIV in Neonates," New England Journal of Medicine (1993).

Field, Martha A., "Testing for AIDS: Uses and Abuses," American Journal of Law & Medicine 16 (1990).

Filice, Gregory, and Pomeroy, Claire, "Preventing Secondary Infections Among HIV-Positive Persons," Public Health Reports 106 (1991).

Fleishman, John A., Hsia, David C., and Hellinger, Fred J., "Correlates of Medical Service Utilization Among People with HIV Infection," Health Services Research 29 (1994).

Forsyth, Brian W. C., "A Pandemic Out of Control: The Epidemiology of AIDS," in Geballe, Shelley, Gruendel, Janice, and Andiman, Warren, Forgotten Children of the AIDS Epidemic, (New Haven: Yale University Press, 1995).

Frascino, Robert J., "Changing Face of HIV/AIDS Care—Mother-Fetal and Maternal-Child HIV Transmission," Western Journal of Medicine 163 (1995).

Gaiter, Juarlyn L., and Berman, Scott M., "Risky Sexual Behavior Imperils Teens," Brown University Child & Adolescent Behavior Letter 10 (1994).

Gallant, Joel E., McAvinue, Sharon M., Moore, Richard D., et al., "The Impact of Prophylaxis on Outcome and Resource Utilization in Pneumocystis Carinii Pneumonia," Chest 107 (1995).

Gayle, Helene D., Keeling, Richard P., Garcia-Tunon, Miguel, et al., "Prevalence of the Human Immunodeficiency Virus Among University Students," New England Journal of Medicine 323 (1990).

Gellert, George A., Berkowitz, Carol D., et al., "Testing the Sexually Abused Child for the HIV Antibody: Issues for the Social Worker," Social Work 38 (1993).

Gellert, George A., Durfee, Michael J., Berkowitz, Carol D., et al., "Situational and Sociodemographic Characteristics of Children Infected with Human Immunodeficiency Virus from Pediatric Sexual Abuse," Pediatrics 91 (1993).

Gerbert, Barbara, Maguire, Bryan T., Bleecker, Thomas, et al., "Primary Care Physicians and AIDS: Attitudinal and Structural Barriers to Care," Journal of the American Medical Association 266 (1991).

Gittler, Josephine, and Rennert, Sharon, "Symposium: HIV Infection Among Women of Reproductive Age, Children, and Adolescents: HIV Infection Among Women and Children and Antidiscrimination Laws: An Overview," Iowa Law Review 77 (1992).

Golden, Megan R., "When Pregnancy Discrimination Is Gender Discrimination: The Constitutionality of Excluding Pregnant Women from Drug Treatment Programs," *New York University Law Review* 66 (1991).

Goodson, Patricia, and Edmundson, Elizabeth, "The Problematic Promotion of Abstinence: An Overview of Sex Respect; Abstinence-Based Sex Education Curriculum," *Journal of School Health* 64 (1994).

Gostin, Larry O., "Public Health Strategies for Confronting AIDS: Legislative and Regulatory Policy in the United States," *Journal of the American Medical Association* 261 (1989).

Gostin, Lawrence O., "The AIDS Litigation Project: A National Review of Court and Human Rights Commission Decisions, Part I: The Social Impact of AIDS," *Journal of the American Medical Association* 263 (1990).

Green, Jesse, and Arno, Peter S., "The 'Medicaidization' of AIDS: Trends in the Financing of HIV-Related Medical Care," *Journal of the American Medical Association* 264 (1990).

Groze, Victor, McMillen, J. Curtis, and Haines-Simeon, Mark, "Families Who Foster Children with HIV: A Pilot Study," *Child and Adolescent Social Work Journal* 10 (1993).

Groze, Victor, Haines-Simeon, Mark, and Barth, Richard P., "Barriers in Permanency Planning for Medically Fragile Children: Drug Affected Children and HIV Infected Children," *Child and Adolescent Social Work Journal* 11 (1994).

Guinan, Mary E., "Artificial Insemination by Donor: Safety and Secrecy." Editorial, *Journal of the American Medical Association* 273 (1995).

Gutman, Laura T., Herman-Giddens, Marcia E., and McKinney, Ross E., "Pediatric Acquired Immunodeficiency Syndrome Barriers to Recognizing the Role of Child Sexual Abuse," *American Journal of Diseases of Children* 147 (1993).

Hagen, Jan L., and Lurie, Irene, "The Job Opportunities and Basic Skills Training Program and Child Care: Initial State Developments," *Social Service Review* 67 (1993).

Hamilton, John D., Hartigan, Pamela M., Simberkoff, Michael S., et al., "A Controlled Trial of Early Versus Late Treatment with Zidovudine in Symptomatic Human Immunodeficiency Virus Infection—Results of the Veterans Affairs Cooperative Study," *New England Journal of Medicine* 326 (1992).

Hein, Karen, Dell, Ralph, Futterman, Donna, et al., "Comparison of HIV+ and HIV− Adolescents: Risk Factors and Psychosocial Determinants," *Pediatrics* 95 (1995).

Hellinger, Fred J., "The Use of Health Services by Women with HIV Infection," *Health Services Research* 28 (1993).

Hellinger, Fred J., "The Lifetime Cost of Treating a Person with HIV," *Journal of the American Medical Association* 270 (1993).

Heymann, David L., "AIDS: Mother to Child," *World Health* 48 (1995).

Higgins, Donna L., Galavotti, Christine, O'Reilly, Kevin R., et al., "Evidence for the Effects of HIV Antibody Counseling and Testing on Risk Behaviors Human Immunodeficiency Virus," *Journal of the American Medical Association* 266 (1991).

Hoffman, Christopher A., and Munson, Ronald, "Letters to the Editor." *New England Journal of Medicine* 332 (1995).

Hoffman, Christopher A., Munson, Ronald, Thea, Donald M., et al., "Ethical Issues in the Use of Zidovudine to Reduce Vertical Transmission of HIV," *New England Journal of Medicine* 332 (1995).

Hoffman, Richard E., Spencer, Nancy E., and Miller, Lisa A., "Comparison of Partner Notification at Anonymous and Confidential HIV Test Sites in Colorado," *Journal of Acquired Immune Deficiency Syndromes and Human Retrovirology* 8 (1995).

Hofkosh, Dena, Pringle, Janice L., Wald, Holly P., et al., "Early Interactions Between Drug-Involved Mothers and Infants: Within-Group Differences." *Archives of Pediatrics & Adolescent Medicine* 149 (1995).

Holahan, John, Coughlin, Teresa, Liu, Korbin, et al., *Cutting Medicaid Spending in Response to Budget Caps*, (Washington, D.C.: The Urban Institute, 1995).

Holtgrave, David R., Qualls, Noreen L., Curran, James W., et al., "An Overview of the Effectiveness and Efficiency of HIV Prevention Programs," *Public Health Reports* 110 (1995).

Hoover, Donald R., Saah, Alfred J., Bacellar, Helena, et al., "Clinical Manifestations of AIDS in the Era of Pneumocystis Prophylaxis," *New England Journal of Medicine* 329 (1993).

Hopkins, Karen M., "Emerging Patterns of Services and Case Finding for Children with HIV Infection," *Mental Retardation* 27 (1989). Cited in Weimer, Deborah, "Beyond Parens Patriae: Assuring Timely, Informed, Compassionate Decisionmaking for HIV-Positive Children in Foster Care," *University of Miami Law Review* 46 (1991).

Hsia, David C., Fleishman, John A., et al., "Pediatric Human Immunodeficiency Virus Infection: Recent Evidence on the Utilization and Costs of Health Services," *Archives of Pediatrics & Adolescent Medicine* 149 (1995).

Hunter, Joyce, and Schaecher, Robert, "AIDS Prevention for Lesbian, Gay, and Bisexual Adolescents," *Journal of Contemporary Human Services* 12 (1994).

Hurley, Peter, and Pinder, Glenn, "Ethics, Social Forces, and Politics in AIDS-Related Research: Experience in Planning and Implementing a Household HIV Seroprevalence Survey," *Milbank Quarterly* 70 (1992).

Husson, Robert N., Mueller, Brigitta U., Farley, Maureen, et al., "Zidovudine and Didanosine Combination Therapy in Children with Human Immunodeficiency Virus Infection," *Pediatrics* 93 (1994).

Imperato, P. J., Feldman, J. G., Nayeri, K., DeHovitz, L. "For Patients with AIDS in a High Incidence Area," *New York State Journal of Medicine* 88 (1988).

Indyk, Debbie, Belville, Renate, Lachapelle, Sister Susanne, et al., "A Community-Based Approach to HIV Case Management: Systematizing the Unmanageable," *Social Work* 38 (1993).

Isbell, Michael T., *HIV & Family Law: A Survey, Lambda Legal Defense and Education Fund* (New York: 1992).

Isbell, Michael, T., "AIDS and Access to Care: Lessons for Health Care Reformers," *Cornell Journal of Law & Public Policy* 3 (1993).

Jarlais, Don C Des., Marmor, Michael, Paone, Denise, et al., "HIV Incidence Among Injecting Drug Users in New York City Syringe-Exchange Programmes," Lancet 348 (1996).

Johnse, Dawn E., "The Creation of Fetal Rights: Conflicts with Women's Constitutional Rights to Liberty, Privacy, and Equal Protection," *Yale Law Journal* 95 (1986).

Johnson, Anne M., "Condoms and HIV Transmission," *New England Journal of Medicine* 331 (1994).

Johnston, Margaret I., and Hoth, Daniel F., "Present Status and Future Prospects for HIV Therapies," *Science* 260 (1993).

Jones, Jeffrey L., Wykoff, Randolph F., Hollis, Shirley L., et al., "Partner Acceptance of Health Department Notification of HIV Exposure, South Carolina," *Journal of the American Medical Association* 264 (1990).

Kaplan, Jonathan E., Masur, Henry, et al., "Reducing the Impact of Opportunistic Infections in Patients with HIV Infection: New Guidelines." Editorial, *Journal of the American Medical Association* 274 (1995).

Karon, J. M., Rosenberg, P. S., Mcquillan, G., et al., "Prevalence of HIV Infection in the United States, 1984 to 1992," *Journal of the American Medical Association* 276 (1996).

Katsiyannis, Antonis, "Policy Issues in School Attendance of Children with AIDS: A National Survey," *Journal of Special Education* 26 (1992).

Kennedy, Bobbe-Lynne Urchin, "AIDS, Sexual Attitudes and Interpersonal Influence: Impact on HIV Risk-Reduction Among Middle-Class Women," Doctoral Dissertation, Columbia University School of Social Work, 1994.

Kent, Christina, "States Pushed to Test Newborns for HIV; Reauthorization of 1990 Ryan White Act," *American Medical News* 39 (1996).

Killackey, Elizabeth, "Kinship Foster Care," *Family Law Quarterly* 26 (1992).

Kipke, Michele D., O'Connor, Susan, et al., "Street Youth in Los Angeles: Profile of a Group at High Risk for Human Immunodeficiency Virus Infection," *Archives of Pediatrics & Adolescent Medicine* 149 (1995).

Kirby, Douglas, Shor, Lynn, Collins, Janet, et al., "School-Based Programs to Reduce Sexual Risk Behaviors: A Review of Effectiveness," *Public Health Reports* 109 (1994).

Klein, Jeffrey S., "With More Businesses Having to Accommodate HIV-Positive Employees, Companies Need Guidelines to Address Federal Disability Law and Privacy Rights," *National Law Journal* B5, col. 1 (1994).

Klein, Nicole Aydt, Goodson, Patricia, Serrins, Debra S., et al., "Evaluation of Sex Education Curricula: Measuring Up to the SIECUS Guidelines; Sex Information and Education Council of the US," *Journal of School Health* 64 (1994).

Kolder, Veronika E. B., Gallagher, Janet, Parsons, Michael T., "Court-Ordered Obstetrical Interventions," *New England Journal of Medicine* 316 (1987).

Kurth, Ann, "An Overview of Women and HIV Disease," in Kurth, Ann (Ed.) *Until the Cure: Caring for Women with HIV,* (New Haven: Yale University Press, 1993).

Lado, Marianne L. Engelman, "Breaking the Barriers of Access to Health Care: A Discussion of the Role of Civil Rights Litigation and the Relationship Between Burdens of Proof and the Experience of Denial," *Brooklyn Law Review* 60 (1994).

Land, Helen, "AIDS and Women of Color," *Families in Society: The Journal of Contemporary Human Services* 18 (1994).

Landers, Daniel V., and Sweet, Richard L., "Reducing Mother-to-Infant Transmission of HIV—The Door Remains Open," *New England Journal of Medicine* 334 (1996).

Landis, Suzanne E., Schoenbach, Victor J., Weber, David J., et al., "Results of a Randomized Trial of Partner Notification in Cases of HIV Infection in North Carolina," *New England Journal of Medicine* 326 (1992).

Lawrence, Jill, "Mother of Arcadia AIDS Family Recounts Rejection, Persecution," *N.Y. Times,* Sect. A, Col. 3 (September 11, 1987).

Leahy, Patrick, Testimony of Senator Patrick Leahy before the Senate Agriculture Committee Hearings on the Better Nutrition and Health for Children Act of 1993, Federal Document Clearing House, 1994 WL 224552 (March 1, 1994).

Letter, "Students' Belief That Condoms Prevent AIDS Influences Use," *Brown University Child & Adolescent Behavior* 8 (1992).

Levin, Betty Wolder, Krantz, David H., et al., "The Treatment of Non-HIV-Related Conditions in Newborns at Risk for HIV: A Survey of Neonatologists," *American Journal of Public Health* 85 (1995).

Levine, Arnold J., et al. *Report of the NIH AIDS Research Program Evaluation Working Group of the Office of AIDS Research Advisory Council,* (Washington, D.C.: National Institutes of Health, 1996).

Levine, Carol, (Ed.) *Orphans of the HIV Epidemic,* (New York: United Hospital Fund, 1993).

Lindsey, Duncan, *The Welfare of Children,* (New York: Oxford University Press, 1994).

Link, R. N., Feingold, A. R., Charap, M. H., et al., "Concerns of Medical and Pediatric House Officers About Acquiring AIDS from Their Patients," *American Journal of Public Health* (1988).

Lipsky, James J., "Antiretroviral Drugs for AIDS," *Lancet* 348 (1996).

Long, Iris L., "A Community Advocate's View of Clinical Research," in Kurth, Ann (Ed.) *Until the Cure: Caring for Women with HIV,* (New Haven: Yale University Press, 1993).

Love, Jamie, and Shearer, William T., "Zidovudine and Didanosine Combination Therapy in Children with Human Immunodeficiency Virus Infection," *Pediatrics* 96 (1995).

Lowe, David, "HIV Study Raises Ethical Concerns for the Treatment of Pregnant Women," *Berkeley Women's Law Journal* 10 (1995).

McCarthy, Michael, "Can HIV-1 Transmission Be Prevented During Pregnancy and Labor?" *Lancet* 348 (1996).

McCormick, Harvey L., "Evidence," in McCormick, H. L., *Social Security Claims and Procedures: Part VI. Supplemental Security Income Act*, (St. Paul: West Publishing Co., 4th Ed. 1995 Pocket Part).

McGovern, Theresa M., "S. P. v. Sullivan: The Effort to Broaden the Social Security Administration's Definition of AIDS," *Fordham Urban Law Journal* 21 (1994).

McKinney, Martha M., Wieland, Melanie K., Bowen, G. Stephen, et al., "States' Responses to Title II of the Ryan White CARE Act; Ryan White Comprehensive AIDS Resources Emergency Act of 1992," *Public Health Reports* 108 (1993).

McNutt, Briar, "The Under-Enrollment of HIV-Infected Foster Children in Clinical Trials and Protocols and the Need for Corrective State Action," *American Journal of Law & Medicine* 20 (1994).

Marks, Gary, Richardson, Jean L., Ruiz, Monica, S. et al., "HIV-Infected Men's Practices in Notifying Past Sexual Partners of Infection Risk," *Public Health Reports* 107 (1992).

Michaels, David, and Levine, Carol, "Estimates of the Number of Motherless Youth Orphaned by AIDS in the United States," *Journal of the American Medical Association* 268 (1992).

Miles, Steven A., Balden, Erin, Magpantay, Larry, et al., "Rapid Serologic Testing with Immune-Complex-Dissociated HIV p24 Antigen for Early Detection of HIV Infection in Neonates," *New England Journal of Medicine* 328 (1993).

Minkoff, Howard, and Willoughby, Anne, "Pediatric HIV Disease, Zidovudine in Pregnancy, and Unblinding Heelstick Surveys: Reframing the Debate on Prenatal HIV Testing," *Journal of the American Medical Association* 274 (1995).

Mohr, Penny E., "Patterns of Health Care Use Among HIV-Infected Adults: Preliminary Results," *ACSUS Report* No. 3 (1994).

National Commission on AIDS, *The Challenge of HIV/AIDS in Communities of Color*, (Washington, D.C.: 1992).

National Commission on AIDS, *Preventing HIV/AIDS in Adolescents*, (Washington, D.C.: 1993).

Newacheck, Paul W., Hughes, Dana C., English, Abigail, et al., "The Effect on Children of Curtailing Medicaid Spending." Commentary, *Journal of the American Medical Association* 274 (1995).

Nicholas, Stephen W., and Abrams, Elaine J., "The 'Silent' Legacy of AIDS: Children Who Survive Their Parents and Siblings." Editorial, *Journal of the American Medical Association* 268 (1992).

Nichols, Ronald L., "Percutaneous Injuries During Operation: Who Is at Risk for What?" *Journal of the American Medical Association* 267 (June 1992).

North, Richard L., and Rotherberg, Karen H., "Partner Notification and the Threat of Domestic Violence Against Women with HIV Infection," *New England Journal of Medicine* 329 (1993).

Office of National AIDS Policy, *Youth and HIV/AIDS:An American Agenda: A Report to the President,* (Washington, D.C.: The White House, 1996).

Olivero, O. A., Beland, F. A., Fullerton, N. F., and Poirer, M. C., "Vaginal Epithelial DNA Damage and Expression of Prenoplastic Markers in Mice During Chronic Dosing with Tumorigenic Levels of 3'-azido-2',3'-Dideoxythymidine," *Cancer Biotechnology Weekly* (1995).

Onorato, Ida M., Grinn, Marta, and Dondero, Timothy J., "Applications of Data from the CDC Family of Surveys," *Public Health Reports* 109 (1994).

O'Reilly, Kevin R., and Higgins, Donna L., "AIDS Community Demonstration Projects for HIV Prevention Among Hard-to-Reach Groups," *Public Health Reports* 106 (1991).

Ozawa, Martha N., Auslander, Wendy F., and Slonim-Nevo, Vered, "Problems in Financing the Care of AIDS Patients," *Social Work* 38 (1993).

Panlilio, Adelisa L., Shapiro, Craig N., Schable, Charles A., et al., "Serosurvey of Human Immunodeficiency Virus; Hepatitis B Virus, and Hepatitis C Virus Infection Among Hospital-Based Surgeons," *Journal of the American College of Surgeons* 180 (1995).

Pantaleo, Giuseppe, Menzo, Stefano, Vaccarezza, Mauro, et al., "Studies in Subjects with Long-Term Nonprogressive Human Immunodeficiency Virus Infection," *New England Journal of Medicine* 332 (1995).

Pavia, Andrew T., Benyo, Mary, et al., "Partner Notification for Control of HIV: Results After 2 Years of a Statewide Program in Utah," *American Journal of Public Health* 83 (1993).

Peterson, George E., "A Block Grant Approach to Welfare Reform," in Sawhill, Isabel V. (Ed.) *Welfare Reform: An Analysis of the Issues*, (Washington, D.C.: The Urban Institute, 1995).

Pinching, Anthony J., "Managing HIV Disease After Delta: Questions Remain About How to Manage Patients Already on Nucleoside Monotherapy; Delta Clinical Trial Compared AZT Monotherapy and Combination Therapy." Editorial, *British Medical Journal* 312 (1996).

Pinkney, Deborah S., "Motherless Child; The AIDS Epidemic Is Creating the Largest Orphan Crisis Since the Influenza Outbreak of 1918; How Can Physicians Help?" *American Medical News* 37 (1994).

Plotkin, Stanley A., Cooper, Louis Z., Evans, Hugh E., et al., "American Academy of Pediatrics: Task Force on Pediatrics AIDS Infants and Children with Acquired Immunodeficiency Syndrome: Placement in Adoption and Foster Care," *Pediatrics* 83 (1989).

Plotkin, Stanley A., Cooper, Louis Z., Evans, Hugh E., et al., "Task Force on Pediatric AIDS: Guidelines for Human Immunodeficiency Virus (HIV)-Infected Children and Their Foster Families," *Pediatrics* 89 (1992).

Ploughman, Penelope, "Public Policy versus Private Rights: The Medical, Social, Ethical, and Legal Implications of the Testing of Newborns for HIV," *AIDS and Public Policy Journal* 10 (1994).

Polonsky, Sara, Kerr, Sandra, Harris, Benita, et al., "HIV Prevention in Prisons and Jails: Obstacles and Opportunities," *Public Health Reports* 109 (1994).

Popola, Pamela, Alvarez, Mayra, and Cohen, Herbert J., "Developmental and Service Needs of School-Age Children with Human Immunodeficiency Virus Infection: A Descriptive Study," *Pediatrics* 94 (1994).

Povinelli, Maryanne, Remafedi, Gary, and Tao, Guoyu, "Trends and Predictors of Human Immunodeficiency Virus Antibody Testing by Homosexual and Bisexual Adolescent Males, 1989–1994," *Archives of Pediatrics & Adolescent Medicine* 150 (1996).

Presidential Advisory Council on HIV/AIDS, *Progress Report: Implementation of Advisory Council Recommendations,* (Washington, D.C.: 1996).

Presidential Advisory Council on HIV/AIDS, *Report Three, April 26, 1996, Continued Steps for Presidential Action,* (Washington, D.C. 1996).

Presidential Commission on the Human Immunodeficiency Virus Epidemic, "Report of Presidential Commission on the Human Immunodeficiency Virus Epidemic: Submitted to the President of the United States," (Washington, D.C.: The Commission, June 24, 1988).

Prince, Regina J., "The Child Welfare Administration's Early Permanency Planning Project," in Levine, Carol (Ed.) *Orphans of the HIV Epidemic,* (New York: United Hospital Fund, 1993).

Provisional Committee on Pediatric AIDS, American Academy of Pediatrics, "Perinatal Human Immunodeficiency Virus Testing," *Pediatrics* 95 (1995).

Rampino, Kenneth J., "Annotation: Power of Court or Other Public Agency to Order Medical Treatment Over Parental Religious Objections for Child Whose Life Is Not Immediately Endangered," 52 *A.L.R.3d* 1118. (Law. Co-Op. Publishing Co., 1995).

Rendon, Mario, Gurdin, Phyllis, et al., "Foster Care for Children with AIDS: A Psychosocial Perspective," *Child Psychiatry and Human Development* 19 (1989).

Robinson, Robert P., Monk, Elizabeth, Coon, Linda, et al., "Social Catastrophe: Orphaned by AIDS; Children of Parents with AIDS," *Journal of the American Medical Association* 269 (1993).

Rutherford, George W.,"Contact Tracing and the Control of Human Immunodeficiency Virus," *Journal of the American Medical Association* 259 (1988).

Sadovsky, Richard, "HIV-Infected Patients: A Primary Care Challenge," *American Family Physician* 40 (1989).

Samuels, J. E., Hendrix, J., and Hilton, M., "Zidovudine Therapy in an Inner-City Population; Journal Review," *AIDS Alert* 5 (1990).

Sanger, Mary Bryna, "Essays: Welfare Reform within a Changing Context: Redefining the Terms of the Debate," *Fordham Urban Journal* 23 (1996).

Sangree, Suzanne, "Control of Childbearing by HIV-Positive Women: Some Responses to Emerging Legal Policies," *Buffalo Law Review* 41 (1993).

Savner, Steve, and Greenberg, Mark, *The CLASP Guide to Welfare Waivers: 1992–1995,* (Washington, D.C.: Center for Law and Social Policy, 1995).

Scarlatti, Gabriella, "Pediatric HIV Infection," *Lancet* 348 (1996).

Schable, Barbara, Diaz, Theresa, Chu, Susan Y., et al., "Who Are the Primary Care-takers of Children Born to HIV-Infected Mothers? Results from a Multistate Surveillance Project," *Pediatrics* 95 (1995).

Schietinger, Helen, Coburn, Jay, and Levi, Jeffrey, "Community Planning for HIV Prevention: Findings from the First Year," *AIDS and Public Policy Journal* 10(3) (1995).

Schneider, Elizabeth M., "Symposium on Reconceptualizing Violence Against Women by Intimate Partners: Critical Issues: Epilogue: Making Reconceptual-ization of Violence Against Women Real," *Albany Law Review* 58 (1995).

Schonfeld, David J., O'Hare, Linda L., Perrin, Ellen C., et al., "A Randomized, Con-trolled Trial of a School-Based, Multi-Faceted AIDS Education Program in the Elementary Grades: The Impact on Comprehension, Knowledge and Fears," *Pediatrics* 95 (1995).

Schor, E. L., et al., Committee on Early Childhood, Adoption, and Dependent Care, 1993 to 1994, "Health Care of Children in Foster Care," *Pediatrics* 93 (1994).

Scott, Deborah E., Hu, Dale J., Hanson, Celine I., et al., "Case Management of HIV-Infected Children in Missouri," *Public Health Reports* 110 (1995).

Shafer, Richard P., "Fetus as Person on Whose Behalf Action May Be Brought Un-der 42 U.S.C.S. Section 1983," *A.L.R. Fed* 64 (1996).

Shilts, Randy, *And the Band Played On,* (New York: St. Martin's Press, 1987).

Siegel, Galia, "Ventures into the Unprecedented: The Challenge of Integrating Women's Drug Treatment, Family Preservation and HIV Services," *Georgetown Journal on Fighting Poverty* 1 (1993).

Sikkema, Kathleen J., Koob, Jeffrey J., Cargill, Victoria C., et al., "Levels and Pre-dictors of HIV Risk Behavior Among Women in Low-Income Public Housing Developments," *Public Health Reports* 110 (1995).

Simonds, R. J., Oxtoby, M. J., Caldwell, M. B., et al., "Pneumocystis Carinii Pneu-monia Among U.S. Children with Perinatally Acquired HIV Infection," *Journal of the American Medical Association* 270 (1993).

Simonds, R. J., Lindegren, Mary Lou, Thomas, Polly, et al., "Prophylaxis Against Pneumocystis *carinii* Pneumonia Among Children with Perinatally Acquired Human Immunodeficiency Virus Infection in the United States," *New England Journal of Medicine* 332 (1995).

Smith, James Monroe, "Legal Issues Confronting Families Affected by HIV," *John Marshall Law Review* (1991).

Sokal-Gutierrez, Karen, Vaughn-Edmonds, Holly, and Villarreal, Sylvia, "Health Care Services for Children and Families," in Barth, Richard P., Pietrzak, Jeanne, and Ramler, Malia (Eds.) *Families Living with Drugs and HIV: Inter-vention and Treatment Strategies,* (New York: Guilford Press, 1993).

Sonenstein, Freya L., Pleck, Joseph H., and Ku, Leighton, "Why Young Men Don't Use Condoms: Factors Related to the Consistency of Utilization," (Washington, D.C.: The Urban Institute, 1995).

Sontag, Susan, *AIDS and Its Metaphors,* (New York: Anchor Books/Doubleday, 1988).

Special Issue, "Legal Responses to Domestic Violence: New State and Federal Responses to Domestic Violence," *Harvard Law Review* 106 (1994).

St. Louis, Michael E., Conway, George A., Hayman, Charles R., et al., "Human Immunodeficiency Virus Infection in Disadvantaged Adolescents: Findings from the US Job Corps," *Journal of the American Medical Association* 266 (1991).

Stanton, B. F., Li, X., Galbraith, J., et al., "Sexually Transmitted Diseases, Human Immunodeficiency Virus, and Pregnancy Prevention: Combined Contraceptive Practices Among Urban African-American Early Adolescents," *Archives of Pediatrics & Adolescent Medicine* 150 (1996).

Stein, Theodore J., "The Custodial and Visitation Rights of Parents Who Are HIV Positive or Diagnosed with AIDS," *AIDS and Public Policy Journal* 9 (1994).

Stein, Theodore J., "Child Custody and Visitation: The Rights of Lesbian and Gay Parents," *Social Service Review* 70 (1996).

Stephenson, Joan, "New Anti-HIV Drugs and Treatment Strategies Buoy AIDS Researchers. Medical News & Perspectives," *Journal of the American Medical Association* 275 (1996).

Stevenson, Howard C., and Davis, Gwendolyn, "Impact of Culturally Sensitive AIDS Video Education on the AIDS Risk Knowledge of African-American Adolescents," *AIDS Education and Prevention* 6 (1994).

Strossen, Nadine, *Defending Pornography: Free Speech, Sex, and the Fight for Women's Rights* (New York: Scribner, 1995).

Stryker, Jeff, Coates, Thomas J., DeCarlo, Pamela, et al., "Prevention of HIV Infection: Looking Back, Looking Ahead," *Journal of the American Medical Association* 273 (1995).

Summers, Patrick F., "Comment: Civil Rights: Persons Infected with HIV: Stewart B. McKinney Foundation v. Town Plan & Zoning Commission: Forcing the AIDS Community to Live a Prophylactic Existence," *Oklahoma Law Review* 46 (1993).

Swartz, Katherine, "Dynamics of People without Health Insurance: Don't Let the Numbers Fool You; Caring for the Uninsured and Underinsured," *Journal of the American Medical Association* 271 (1994).

Sweeny, Patricia, Lindegren, Mary Lou, Buehler, James W., et al., "Teenagers at Risk of Human Immunodeficiency Virus Type 1 Infection: Results from Seroprevalence Surveys in the United States," *Archives of Pediatrics & Adolescent Medicine* 149 (1995).

Swenson, Victoria J., and Crabbe, Cheryl, "Pregnant Substance Abusers: A Problem That Won't Go Away," *Saint Mary's Law Journal* 25 (1994).

Task Force on Children and HIV Infection, *Report of the CWLA Task Force on Children and HIV Infection: Initial Guidelines,* (Washington, D.C.: Child Welfare League of America, no date).

Thea, Donald M., Lambert, Genevieve, Weedon, Jeremy, et al., "Benefit of Primary Prophylaxis Before 18 Months of Age in Reducing the Incidence of Pneumocystis carinii Pneumonia and Early Death in a Cohort of 112 Human Immun-odeficiency Virus-Infected Infants," *Pediatrics* 97 (1996).

Thorpe, Kenneth E., Shields, Alexandra E., Gold, Heather, et al., *Anticipating the Number of Uninsured Americans and the Demand for Uncompensated Care: The Combined Impact of Proposed Medicaid Reductions and the Erosion of Employer-Sponsored Insurance*, [draft] (Waltham, Mass.: Council on the Economic Impact of Health Care Reform, Heller Graduate School, Brandeis University, November 1995).

Thorpe, Kenneth E., Shactman, David, et al., *The Combined Impact on Hospitals of Reduced Spending for Medicare, Medicaid and Employer Sponsored Insurance*, [draft] (Waltham, Mass.: Council on the Economic Impact of Health Care Reform, Heller Graduate School, Brandeis University, November 1995).

Tourk, Jessica M., "Controlling Expression: The Stagnant Policy of the Centers for Disease Control in the Second Decade of AIDS," *Cardozo Arts & Entertainment Law Journal* 13 (1993).

Turano, Margaret Valentine, *Supplementary Practice Commentaries (1994) to New York's Surrogate's Court Procedure Act*, Chapter 59-A, Article 17, Guardians and Custodians (McKinney 1995).

United States Congress, *Ryan White CARE Act Amendments of 1996*, 104th Cong., 2d Sess. P.L. 104-146, 110 Stat. 1346 (May 1996).

United States Department of Health and Human Services, Public Health Service, Centers for Disease Control, *Recommendations for Preventing Transmission of Infection with Human T-Lymphotropic Virus Type III/Lymphadenopathy-Associated Virus in the Workplace, Morbidity and Mortality Weekly Report* 34 (1985).

United State Department of Health and Human Services, Public Health Service, Centers for Disease Control, "Partner Notification for Preventing Human Immunodeficiency Virus (HIV) Infection—Colorado, Idaho, South Carolina, Virginia," *Journal of the American Medical Association* 260 (1988).

United States Department of Health and Human Services, Public Health Service, Centers for Disease Control, "Recommendations for Preventing Transmission of Human Immunodeficiency Virus and Hepatitis B Virus to Patients During Exposure-Prone Invasive Procedures," *Morbidity and Mortality Weekly Report* 40 (1991).

United States Department of Health and Human Services, Public Health Service, Centers for Disease Control, "AIDS Community Demonstration Projects: Implementation of Volunteer Networks for HIV-Prevention Programs—Selected Sites, 1991–1992," *Morbidity and Mortality Weekly Report* 41 (1992).

United States Department of Health and Human Services, Public Health Service, Centers for Disease Control, "Investigations of Persons Treated by HIV-Infected Health-Care Workers in the United States," *Morbidity and Mortality Weekly Report* 42 (1993).

United States Department of Health and Human Services, Public Health Service, Centers for Disease Control, "School-Based HIV-Prevention Education—United States," Morbidity and Mortality Weekly Report 45 (1996).

United States Department of Health and Human Services, Public Health Service, Centers for Disease Control and Prevention, "Birth Outcomes Following Zidovudine Therapy in Pregnant Women; AZT," *Journal of the American Medical Association* 272 (1994).

United States Department of Health and Human Services, Public Health Service, Centers for Disease Control, "Recommendations of the U.S. Public Health Services Task Force on the Use of Zidovudine to Reduce Perinatal Transmission of the Human Immunodeficiency Virus," *Morbidity and Mortality Weekly Report* 43 (1994).

United States Department of Health and Human Services, Public Health Service, Centers for Disease Control and Prevention, *AIDS Public Information Data Set*, (Washington, D.C.: 1994).

United States Department of Health and Human Services, Public Health Service, Centers for Disease Control and Prevention, "HIV/AIDS Surveillance Report," (Washington, D.C.: December, 1995).

United States Department of Health and Human Services, Public Health Service, Centers for Disease Control, "Syringe Exchange Programs—United States, 1994–1995," *Morbidity and Mortality Weekly Report* 44 (1995).

United States Department of Health and Human Services, Public Health Service, Centers for Disease Control and Prevention, *HIV/AIDS Surveillance Report: Year End Edition* 7 (1995).

United States Department of Health and Human Services, Public Health Service, Centers for Disease Control, "Trends in Sexual Risk Behavior Among High School Students—United States, 1990, 1991, and 1993" *Morbidity and Mortality Weekly Report* 44 (1995).

United States Department of Health and Human Services, Public Health Service, Centers for Disease Control, "1995 Revised Guidelines for Prophylaxis Against Pneumocystis *carinii* Pneumonia for Children Infected with or Perinatally Exposed to the Human Immunodeficiency Virus," *Morbidity and Mortality Weekly Report* 44 (1995).

United States Department of Health and Human Services, Public Health Service, Centers for Disease Control and Prevention, "First 500,000 AIDS Cases—United States, 1995," *Morbidity and Mortality Weekly Report* 44 (1995).

United States Department of Health and Human Services, Public Health Service, Centers for Disease Control and Prevention, "Update: AIDS Among Women—United States, 1994," *Morbidity and Mortality Weekly Report* 44 (1995).

United States Department of Health and Human Services, Public Health Service, Centers for Disease Control, "Update: Mortality Attributable to HIV Infection Among Persons Aged 25–44 Years—United States, 1994," *Morbidity and Mortality Weekly Report* 45 (1996)

United States Department of Health and Human Services, Public Health Service, Centers for Disease Control, "Contraceptive Method and Condom Use Among Women at Risk for HIV Infection and Other Sexually Transmitted Diseases—Selected U.S. Sites, 1993–1994," *Morbidity and Mortality Weekly Report 45 (1996).*

United States Department of Health and Human Services, Health Resources and Services Administration, *AIDS Funding History—FY 1986–FY 1997*, (Washington, D.C.: 1996).

United States Department of Health and Human Services, Public Health Service, Centers for Disease Control and Prevention, "AIDS Among Children-United States, 1996" *Morbidity and Mortality Weekly Report* 45 (1996).

United States Department of Housing and Urban Development, Office of HIV/AIDS Housing, *HOPWA Formula Programs: 1994 Summary* (August 1995).

United States General Accounting Office, *Hospital Costs—Cost Control Efforts at 17 Texas Hospitals*, Rep. No. 95-21 (1994).

United States General Accounting Office, *Social Security—Major Changes Needed for Disability Benefits for Addicts*, Rep. No. 94-128 (1994).

United States General Accounting Office, *Social Security—New Functional Assessments for Children Raise Eligibility Questions,* Rep. No. 95-66 (1995).

United States General Accounting Office, *Arizona Medicaid—Competition Among Managed Care Plans Lowers Program Costs,* Rep. No. 96-2 (1995).

United States General Accounting Office, *Welfare to Work—State Programs Have Tested Some of the Proposed Reforms*, Rep. No 95-26 (1995).

United States General Accounting Office, *Health, Education, and Human Services Division Reports*, Rep. No. 96-15W (1995).

United States General Accounting Office, Rep. GAO/HEHS 95-208, Child Welfare—Complex Needs Strain Capacity to Provide Services, (1995).

United States General Accounting Office, Rep. GAO/HEHS 95-114, Foster Care—Health Needs of Many Young Children Are Unknown and Unmet, (1995).

United States General Accounting Office, *Health Insurance for Children—Many Remain Uninsured Despite Medicaid Expansion,* Rep. No. 95-175 (1995).

United States General Accounting Office, *Welfare Reform—Implications of Proposals on Legal Immigrants' Benefits,* Rep. No. 95-58 (1995).

United States General Accounting Office, *Health Insurance for Children—State and Private Programs Create New Strategies to Insure Children*, Rep. No. 96-35 (1996).

United States General Accounting Office, *Scientific Research—Continued Vigilance Critical to Protecting Human Subjects*, Rep. No. 96-72 (1996).

United States House of Representatives, "Fair Housing Amendments Act of 1988," 100th Cong. 2d Sess. House Rep. No. 711, (1988).

United States House of Representatives, "The Americans with Disabilities Act of 1990," 101st Cong. 2d Sess. House Rep. No. 485, Part II, (1990).

United States House of Representatives, *The Politics of AIDS Prevention: Science Takes a Time Out,* 102d Cong., 1st Sess. Report No. 102-1047 (1992).

United States House of Representatives, "The Americans with Disabilities Act of 1990," 101st Cong. 2d Sess. House Rep. No. 485, Parts I through IV (1990).

United States House of Representatives, "Family Preservation Act of 1992," H.R. Rep. No. 684I, 102d Cong. 2d Sess. (1992).

United States House of Representatives, Subcommittee on Human Resources and Intergovernmental Relations, "Women and HIV Disease: Falling Through the Cracks," 102d Cong., 2d Sess. Rep. No. 1086 (1992).

United States House of Representatives, "Standby Guardianship Act," 103rd Cong., 1st Sess. H.R. 1354 (1993).

United States House of Representatives, Subcommittee on Human Resources and Intergovernmental Relations, "AIDS Treatment and Care: Who Cares?" 101st Cong., 2d Sess. Rep. No. 674 (1994).

United States House of Representatives, "Newborn Infant Notification Act," 104th Cong., 1st Sess. H.R. 1289 (1995).

United States House of Representatives, "Personal Responsibility and Work Opportunities Act of 1995," H.R. Conf. Rep. No. 430, 104th Cong., 1st Sess. (1995).

United States House of Representatives, "Ryan White CARE Act Amendments of 1995," 104th Cong., 1st. Sess. Rep. No. 245 (1995).

United States House of Representatives, "Making Appropriations for the Department of Defense for the Fiscal Year Ending September 30, 1997, and for Other Purposes," 104th Cong., 2nd Sess. Rep. No. 863 (1996).

United States Justice Department, "Application of Section 504 of the Rehabilitation Act to HIV-Infected Individuals," (September 27, 1988).

United States Senate, "Grandparents Raising Grandchildren Assistance Act of 1993," 103rd Cong., 1st Sess. S. Bill 1016 (1993).

United States Senate, "The Parental Rights and Responsibilities Act of 1995," 104th Cong., 2d Sess. S. 984 (1995).

Vernon, T. M., Jr., "Partner Notification for Preventing Human Immunodeficiency Virus (HIV) Infection—Colorado, Idaho, South Carolina, Virginia," *Journal of the American Medical Association* 260 (1988).

Voelker, Rebecca, "Several New Drugs Shift Direction of Treatment and Research for HIV/AIDS," *Journal of the American Medical Association* 275 (1996).

Volberding, Paul A., Lagakos, Stephen W., Grimes, Janet M., et al., "A Comparison of Immediate with Deferred Zidovudine Therapy for Asymptomatic HIV-Infected Adults with CD4 Cell Counts of 500 or More per Cubic Millimeter," *New England Journal of Medicine* 333 (1995).

Volberding, Paul A., "Improving the Outcomes of Care for Patients with Human-immunodeficiency Virus Infection," *New England Journal of Medicine* 334 (1996).

Walter, Heather J., and Vaughan, Roger D., "AIDS Risk Reduction Among a Multiethnic Sample of Urban High School Students," *Journal of the American Medical Association* 270 (1993).

Wartenberg, Alan A., " 'Into Whatever Houses I Enter': HIV and Injecting Drug Use." Editorial, *Journal of the American Medical Association* 271 (1994).

Watters, John K., "HIV Test Results, Partner Notification, and Personal Conduct." Commentary, *Lancet* 346 (1995).

Waysdorf, Susan L., "Families in the AIDS Crisis: Access, Equality, Empowerment, and the Role of Kinship Caregivers," *Texas Journal of Women and the Law* (1994).

White, Jocelyn C., and Levinson, Wendy, "Lesbian Health Care: What a Primary Care Physician Needs to Know," *Western Journal of Medicine* 162 (1995).

Williams, John C., "Propriety of Conditioning Probation on Defendant's Remaining Childless or Having No Additional Children During Probationary Period," 94 *A.L.R.3d* 1218 (1993).

Williams, John C., "Annotation: Power of Court or Other Public Agency to Order Medical Treatment for Child Over Parental Objections Not Based on Religious Grounds," 97 *A.L.R.3d* 421 (Law. Co-Op. Publishing Co., 1995).

Williams, Robert M., "The Costs of Visits to Emergency Departments," *New England Journal of Medicine* 334 (1996).

Wiznia, Andrew A., Crane, Marilyn, Lambert, Genevieve, "Zidovudine Use to Reduce Perinatal HIV Type 1 Transmission in an Urban Medical Center," *Journal of the American Medical Association* 275 (1996).

Wykoff, Randolph F., Heath, Clark W., Hollis, Shirley L., et al., "Contact Tracing to Identify Human Immunodeficiency Virus Infection in a Rural Community," *Journal of the American Medical Association* 259 (1988).

Yunzhen Cao, Limo Qin, Linqi Zhang, et al., "Virologic and Immunologic Characterization of Long-Term Survivors of Human Immunodeficiency Virus Type 1 Infection," *New England Journal of Medicine* 332 (1995).

Zedlewski, Sheila, and Clark, Sandra, et al., *Potential Effects of Congressional Welfare Reform Legislation on Family Incomes,* (Washington, D.C.: The Urban Institute, 1996).

Zitter, Jay M., "Liability of Hospital, Physician or Other Medical Personnel for Death or Injury to Mother or Child Caused by Improper Diagnosis and Treatment of Mother Relating to and During Pregnancy," *A.L.R., Fifth* 7 (1995).

Zitter, Jay M., "Power of the Court or Other Public Agency to Order Medical Treatment Over Parental Religious Objections for Child Whose Life is Not Immediately Endangered," 21 *A.L.R.5th* 248 (1995).

Zolopa, Andrew R., Hahn, Judith A., Gorter, Robert, et al., "HIV and Tuberculosis Infection in San Francisco's Homeless Adults: Prevalence and Risk Factors in a Representative Sample," *Journal of the American Medical Association* 272 (1994).

Zuckerman, Barry, "Developmental Considerations for Drug- and AIDS-Affected Infants," in Barth, Richard P., Pietrzak, Jeanne, and Ramler, Malia (Eds.) *Families Living with Drugs and HIV: Intervention and Treatment Strategies,* (New York: Guilford Press, 1993).

I N D E X

A.C., In re., 205n184
A.D.H. v. State Department of Human Resources, 191n112, 204n177
Aase, J.M., 186n52
Abandoned Infants Act, 72–73, 186n47
Abbott, Sidney, 46
Abbott v. Bragdon, 46, 175n56
Abortion. *See* Medicaid Services; Reproductive Choice
Abrams, E. J., 183n4,7
Acer, David, 167n132
Acuff, K. L., 195n21
Adams v. Drew, 202n128
Adolescent(s), 116–39; *see also* AIDS, related deaths; AIDS, sources for compiling data; Education and program content; Sexually transmitted diseases, Transmission of HIV by methods listed in index
  AIDS compared to pediatric AIDS, 117
  autonomy in making medical decisions, 80, 83, 191n109
  condom use, 116, 122–24, 126, 138, 208n21
  rates of HIV infection, 118, 122
  risk factors, 11
  risk-taking behavior, 122–24, 138
  street youth, 124
  transmission, methods of, 9
  young women and increased incidence of HIV, xi
Adolescents and young adult(s), number and percent of cases of AIDS, 11, 119–22, 137–38
  by age, gender, and race, 10, 13, 120, 137–38
  compared to all age groups, 120
  women compared to men, 120–21
  among women, 121, 137
Adoption, 69–70, 82, 85–87; *see also* Permanency planning
Adoption Assistance and Child Welfare Act, 74–77, 86, 186n47; *see also* Foster care, federal support of

Adoption Opportunities Act, 86
Adoption subsidies, 82, 86–87
Adoptive parents, 83–84
Agency for Health Care Policy and Research, 199n77
AIDS
  bias in data collected, 8–9
  as a chronic illness, 51, 80
  costs of drug treatment, 52, 56
  Drug Reimbursement Program, 52, 56, 80, 150
  factors affecting evolution of federal policy, 5–7
  first cases diagnosed in the U.S., 1
  geographic distribution of cases, 12–13, 139
  in historical perspective, 3–5, 12–13
  as leading cause of death, 10, 13
  limitations in data collected, 7, 13
  medical care, costs of, 51
  number of cases, 7, 9–10, 13
  number of cases and new diagnostic criteria, 9, 158n48
  as a political issue, 1–3, 5–6, 12–13, 55, 152, 154n1, 156n30, 193n4; *see also* Social services, grassroots movement
  related deaths, 10, 13, 120
  research funding, 116, 155n10
  sources for compiling data, 117–18
  in U.S. workforce, 163n66
AIDS Action Committee of Massachusetts, Inc. v. Massachusetts Bay Transportation Authority, 209n49
AIDS clinical trial groups, 47
AIDS Foundation, 54
AIDS Medical Foundation, 54
Aid to Families with Dependent Children, 39, 50, 66, 76, 77, 86, 140, 141, 142, 149; *see also* Welfare reform, Temporary Assistance to Needy Families
Alcohol, Drug Abuse, and Mental Health Administration Reorganization Act, 53, 59–61, 63

Alcohol, Drug Abuse, and Mental Health (cont.)
Associate Administrator for Women's Services required by law, 61
mandatory drug and health care coverage for women, 60–61, 63
purpose of, 60
Alfonso v. Fernandez, 209n47
Alfredo S., In the Matter of, 73
Alle, In re Welfare of, 193n141
Allen v. Allen, 193n141
Altman, L., 169n153, 198n67,68,74
Alvarez, M., 189n96, 190n104
American Academy of Pediatrics, 25, 30, 45, 83, 111, 124, 140–142, 168n135
American Academy of Pediatrics, Committee on Adolescents, 122, 126
American Association for Protecting Children, 187n61
American College of Obstetricians and Gynecologists, 111
American Family Physician, 45
American Foundation for AIDS Research, 54
American Humane Association, 74
American Medical Association, 111
American Medical Association, Council on Ethical and Judicial Affairs, 46
American Medical Association, Council on Scientific Affairs, 157n36
Americans with Disabilities Act, 14, 16–19, 22, 38, 44, 46, 62, 71, 100, 160n4, 161n15, 174n43; see also Disability, definition of in Civil Rights statutes
accessibility to buildings, 17, 19
applicability of court rulings reached under the VRA, 17
contrasted with the VRA, 16–17
and direct threat defense, 22, 29, 33–34
and education of children, 20, 35
and employment criteria, 17–18, 23–24, 165n84
employment provisions of, 17–18
and essential job functions, 18, 27, 161n27
and health insurance as an employment benefit, 44
and non-discrimination by medical providers, 43
and non-discrimination by places of public accommodation, 19, 36
and non-discrimination by public entities, 18–19
and the otherwise qualified individual, 17, 22–27, 29, 36, 164n75, 169n155; see also VRA and the otherwise qualified individual
and public transportation, 18–19
and reasonable accommodation, 18, 27–28, 35; see also VRA and reasonable accommodation
titles of, 16, 17–19, 161n15
types of discrimination prohibited, 14–15, 16, 17–19, 21, 34–35, 168n138
and undue hardship defense, 27, 29, 35, 44
Anastos, K., 159n67, 176n70
Anderson v. Mayer, 174n45
Anderson v. Romero, 202n135
Anderson v. Shalala, 172n24
Anderson, G. R., 180n135
Angel Lace M., In the Interest of, 185n37
Annas, G. J., 157n32
Anonymous Firemen v. City of Willougby, 195n27
Anonymous, Matter of, 202n143
Antoine, F. S., 198n72
Armstrong, F.D., 190n101
Arno, P. S., 49, 177n89,95–96, 180n132–133

Association of Relatives and Friends of AIDS Patients v. Regulations and Permits Administration, 155n19, 169n146
Attitudes toward people with HIV and AIDS, general public; 4–7, 128, 193n4; see also Physicians, attitudes toward treating people with AIDS
Auslander, W.F., 173n40
Azidothymidine or AZT. See Zidovudine

B.L.V.B., Adoption of, 185n37
Baby Boy Doe, In re., 205n182
Baby "K," In the Matter of, 166n103
Baby Neal v. Casey, 186n42
Baby X, In the Matter of, 186n53, 204n171
Bacellar, H., 198n72, 199n82
Backstrom, C., 3, 126, 155n11, 209n42
Balden, E., 200n88
Banks, T.L., 68, 185n30
Barlow v. Ground, 196n36
Barnhart, H. X., 80, 99, 190n106, 200n90
Barr, S., 167n132
Barth, R. P., 189n98
Bayer, R., 109, 110, 156n31, 193n2, 195n18, 205n195, 206n198, 206n2
Baxter v. Belleville, 169n146–147
Beland, F.A., 198n71
Belville, R., 180n135
Bennett, C. L., 50, 177n99
Beno v. Shalala, 215n40,42
Benyo, M., 196n42,50
Berkowitz, C.D., 192n132,134
Berger, D. K., 207n18, 208n19–20
Berman, S.M., 122, 207n14,18, 208n19
Best Interests of the Child, 67–71, 87, 184n19
Blair, J. F., 129, 210n56
Bleach distribution and clean needles. See Education to prevent transmission of HIV, and intravenous drug users
Bleecker, T., 174n51
Blendon, R. J., 4, 5, 156n23,24
Board of Education of the City of New York v. Sobol, 209n46
Bobinski, M.A., 155n20, 156n29, 175n61
Bopp, J., Jr., 189n99, 190n102
Borzillieri v. American National Red Cross, 203n152
Boskey, J. A., 172n26
Bowen, G. S., 181n154
Bradford, W.A., Jr., 173n39, 174n42, 177n91
Bradley v. University of Texas A and M Medical Center, 166n113
Brandt, A. M., 3, 155n12–14,18
Breithaupt v. Abram, 195n23
Broers, B., 175n62
Brookmeyer, R., 157n38
Brown v. Hot, Sexy, and Safer Productions, Inc., 209n44
Brundage, J. F., 206n5
Buchanan, R.J., 174n46, 177n88,97, 178n107, 179n122
Buehler, J.W., 207n8
Burke, D.S., 206n5
Burkett, E., 180n129,131
Burr v. Board of Commissioners, 193n141
Byers, R. H., 159n68

C.A.U. v. R.L., 203n158
C.K. v. Shalala, 215n37

Cain v. Hyatt, 161n23, 166n117
Caldwell, M. B., 180n135, 183n190, 183n3–5,7, 184n8, 188n82, 189n98, 190n106, 199n85, 200n90
Cao, Y., 169n153, 191n107
Cargill, V.C., 211n73
Carparts Distribution Center, Inc. v. Automotive Wholesaler's Association of New England, 174n44
Centers for Disease Control, xi, 1, 7, 8, 9, 10, 11, 13, 24, 25, 30–32, 39, 42, 65, 80, 93, 94, 101, 109–11, 117, 118, 119, 122, 125, 126, 128, 156n22, 157n35, 159n65, 167n132, 168n138, 170n161, 171n23, 196n37, 197n63; *see also* U.S. Department of Health and Human Services, U.S. Public Health Service
   AIDS Community Demonstration Projects, 136
   Family of Surveys, 8
   Pediatric Spectrum of Disease Project, 65
   Prevention of HIV in Women and Infants Demonstration Project, 130
   School Health Policies and Programs Study, 126
   Survey of Childbearing Women, 8, 10
   Youth Risk Behavior Survey, 122
Center for Substance Abuse Treatment, 60
Chaisson, R. E., 97, 198n70
Chalk v. United States, 23, 164n79–82, 165n93
Chambarry v. Mount Sinai Hospital, 203n152
Charap, M.H., 174n48
Charney , P., 176n74–75
Chasnoff, I.J., 189n99
Chavkin, W., 199n87
Child Abuse Prevention and Treatment Act, 71–72
   protective services, 60
   reporting of babies born with a positive toxicology for drugs or evidence of fetal alcohol syndrome, 73–74, 87, 106, 186n51,53, 187n58
Child Care, in families with HIV, 64, 65–66, 71, 87–88; *see also* Grandparents as care givers
Child Welfare System, 64, 71–87; *see also* Abandoned Infants Act; Adoption; Adoption Assistance and Child Welfare Act; Adoption Opportunities Act; Adoption subsidies; Child Abuse Prevention and Treatment Act; Foster care
Child Welfare League of America, 30, 78, 168n135, 188n83,90
Childhood disability. *See* Supplemental Security Income and childhood disability; Welfare reform and SSI program changes; Childhood disability
Children, *see also* ADA and education of children; IDEA; Adolescents; Foster care; Ethical issues; Supplemental Security Income and childhood disability; VRA and education of children)
   classroom segregation of those with the HIV, 27, 35
   and drug trials, 147–148
   health of, 189n99
   litigation against child welfare agencies on behalf of, 71, 186n42, 189n93
   as orphans of the AIDS epidemic, 64, 77, 88
   with special needs, 86–87
   survival time of those born HIV-infected, 80
Chiriboga, C. A., 189n99

Chu, S.Y., 170n1, 183n1,4–7
City of Cleburne v. Cleburne Living Center, 170n163–164
Clark, S., 217n77,78
Clarkson v. Coughlin, 194n7
Clemo, L., 5, 156n25
Closen, M.J., 155n20, 156n29
Clotet, B., 191n107
Coates, T.J., 133, 209n52, 210n58,59, 211n78, 212n103
Coburn, J., 211n87
Cohen v. Chater, 172n24
Cohen, D., 190n101
Cohen, F. L., 188n81,85–86,88, 189n97
Cohen, H.J., 189n96, 190n104
Colautti v. Franklin, 203n165
Colby, D., 174n46, 177n97
Collins, J., 209n43, 210n55
Colvin, C., 216n59
Commission on Behavioral and Social Sciences, 159n74, 172n37, 180n130, 181n162, 188n87, 192n120, 194n12, 212n96–97,102,104
Commmittee on Adolescence, 208n26
Committee on AIDS Research, 82
Committee on Pediatric AIDS, 159n64
Commonwealth v. Pellegrini, 187n58
Concorde Study, 97
Confidential testing to assuage fear of discrimination, 91–92, 193n4
Confidentiality, 8, 16, 72, 78, 81, 83–84, 89–115, 165n84; *see also* Foster care, disclosure of a child's HIV status; Testing for HIV
   and disclosure of HIV information in general, 56, 90–91, 100, 102–3, 113–14
   and disclosure in prisons, 103–4
   and disclosure under court order, 104–5
   and federal laws, 100, 113
   and rationale for laws, 90–92, 113
   of medical records, 99–100
   state laws, 101–3, 113–14
   violations of, 90–91
Congressional appropriations, 154n1
Congressional Budget Office, 144, 148
Congressional hearings on the epidemic, 1–3, 48, 127–28, 134
Congressional Office of Information Technology, 131
Congressional Research Service, 154n1
Connor, E. M., 205n192, 206n199
Consolidated Omnibus Reconciliation Act of 1985, 174n42
Contact tracing and partner notification, 93–96, 114, 197n65
   and control of sexually transmitted diseases, 93, 94, 105
   funding for, 94, 114
   pros and cons of, 94–96, 197n65
   provider referral compared to partner referral; 93, 95–96
   Ryan White CARE Act provisions, 94, 114
   and spousal notification requirement, 94
   state approaches, 94–95, 96
   success of in making contacts, 94–96
   targeted notification, 96
   treatment and prevention as justification for, 95–99
Conte v. Merrell, 202n143
Conway, G.A., 206n4

Coon, L., 185n27–29
Cooper, L.Z., 192n130–131
Coughlin, T., 178n115, 216n61,63
Council on Ethical and Judicial Affairs, 46, 175n54
County Department of Public Welfare v. Morningstar, 193n141
Crabbe, C., 183n189
Crane, M., 206n208
Cranston, Senator Allen 208n34
Crossley, M.A., 80, 190n103
Crouse Irving Memorial Hospital, Inc. v. Paddock, 204n180
Cruzan v. Director of the Missouri Department of Health, 204n179
Curran, J.W., 210n67, 211n72,79,81,88,90
Custodial Rights of HIV positive parents, 67

D'Amico v. New York State Board of Law Examiners, 163n61
D.B. v. Bloom, 175n57
Davis, G., 211n93
Davis, S.F., 159n68, 135
Day, N.L., 189n99
DeCarlo, P., 209n52, 210n58–59, 211n78, 212n103
DeHovitz, L., 174n49
DeNoon, D. J., 198n76
DesJarlais, D.C., 212n98, 99–100
Delage, G., 200n88
Dell, R., 210n57
DiClemente, R.J., 132, 134, 211n77,89
Diaz, T., 170n1, 183n1,4–7
Directive counseling. *See* Reproductive choice
Disability, HIV and AIDS as disabling conditions, 23, 145, 160n4
   definition of in Civil Right Statutes, 16, 22, 23, 160n4, 164n68, 171n6
   definition of in income maintenance, health, social service programs, 40, 42, 145, 147–49
   definition of in welfare reform, 145, 147–49
Disclosure of HIV Status. *See* Confidentiality and disclosure; Foster care, disclosure of information regarding a child's HIV status
Discrimination. *See* AIDS, factors affecting federal policy; AIDS, as a political issue; ADA, types of discrimination prohibited; FHA, types of discrimination prohibited; IDEA, types of discrimination prohibited; VRA, types of discrimination prohibited; Attitudes toward people with HIV and AIDS; Confidential HIV testing to assuage fears of; Congressional hearings on the epidemic; Directive counseling; Gay men, discrimination against, homophobia; HIV and AIDS as uninsurable conditions, caps on insurance coverage; Litigation against medical providers for failure to serve; Physicians, attitudes toward treating people with AIDS; Presidential Commission on AIDS; Quarantine; Risk of transmission; Welfare reform and immigrants, managed care; Women and diagnosis of AIDS, disability-based employment discrimination, drug trials, natural history of the HIV
District 27 Community School Board v. Board of Education, 163n53,55, 165n92,93
Division of AIDS Treatment Research Initiative, 175n59
Doe, Carol, 46

Doe v. Belleville Public Schools District, 163n53
Doe v. Borough of Barrington, 194n8, 202n125
Doe v. Burgos, 202n141
Doe v. City of Chicago, 24, 165n87
Doe v. City of New York, 200n97
Doe v. District of Columbia, 34, 165n93
Doe v. Dolton Elementary School District No. 148, 165n92,93, 166n95
Doe v. Jamaica Hospital, 175n55, 108
Doe v. Johnson, 203n158
Doe v. Kohn Nast and Graf, P.C., 165n86
Doe v. Laborer's District Council, 174n44
Doe by Lavery v. Attorney General of the United States, 168n138, 203n155
Doe v. New York City Department of Social Services, 202n127
Doe v. Roe, 202n124
Doe v. State of New York, 203n151
Doe v. Town of Plymouth, 202n126
Doe v. University of Maryland, 166n116, 168n139, 169n154
Doe v. Washington University, 166n115, 167n124–26
Dondero, T.J., 157n40
Donelan, K., 156n23,24
Dorsey v. U.S. Department of Labor, 207n7
Doughty, R., 194n8, 195n18
Draper, J. M., 173n41
Drug Trials. *See* Women and drug trials; Children and drug trials
Dunn v. White, 202n128
Durfee, M.J., 192n134
Dustin T., In re., 186n53

E.E.O.C. v. Mason Tenders, 174n44
Early periodic screening, diagnosis and treatment, 52, 79, 178n114
Early Permanency Planning Project, 68
Edmundson, E., 211n76
Education to prevent transmission of HIV, 116, 124–37, 138
   federal funding for, 125–26
   federal rules and community involvement in developing curricula, 125–26
   forms of educational campaigns, 124–25
   goals of educational campaigns, 125
   and intravenous drug users, 135–37
      needle-exchange programs, 116, 125, 135–36, 212n96
      needle-exchange programs, no evidence of increased drug use or increased number of users, 136
   legislators attitudes toward, 126
   litigation concerning educational programs, 126–27, 209n50
   outreach programs for at-risk youth, 125, 126, 135, 136
   parent's rights in re, 125–27
   peer educators, use of, 134–35, 138
   state requirements for HIV and AIDS, 126, 138
Education, program content
   advancement of public health goals, 116, 126–30
   condom use, 127, 128, 129, 130, 131–33, 134–35, 209n52
   congressional dissatisfaction with, 127–28
   curricula content, abstinence, knowledge, and skills, 128, 129, 130, 138
   curricula focus on abstinence, 127, 130, 138
   curricula focus on abstinence, criticism of, 128, 129, 130

federal rules and control of, 125
general concerns affecting, 119, 126–28, 138
influenced by political factors, 127–28
knowledge and skills-based, no evidence of increase in sexual activity, 128–29, 139
targeted to specific groups, 134–35, 135–37, 138
Education, program evaluation, 127–28, 129, 130–37, 138
and counseling associated with testing as an educational tool, 133
and effective program components, 131–33, 134, 138
and outcome measures, 130–31, 131, 136
and program duration linked to behavior change and maintenance of change, 133, 138
and programs for intravenous drug users 136–37
school-based clinics, 126
settings for providing, 125, 126
Education for All Handicapped Children's Act. *See* Individuals with Disabilities in Education Act
El-Bassel, N., 158n57
Elaine W. v. Joint Diseases North General Hospital, 182n168
Emergency Medical Treatment and Active Labor Act, 170n162, 177n102
English, A., 176n85, 188n84, 216n63
Entitlement program, 39–40, 49, 75, 76
Eric. L. v. Harry Bird, 186n42
Equal protection. *See* Fourteenth Amendment
Ethical Issues, 45–46, 81–83, 111–13, 114–15
European Study Group, 159n67
Evans, H.E., 192n130–131

Faan, W.M., 188n81,85–86,88, 189n97
Faden, R. R., 111, 206n205,210
Fahs, M. C., 158n55, 191n119
Fair Housing Act, 15–16, 22, 160n4; *see also* Disability, definition of in Civil Rights Statutes
community opposition to creating housing for people with HIV and AIDS, 32–33, 36–37
and confidentiality, 16
and direct threat defense, 16, 29
disabled persons rights under, 15–16, 36–37
entities exempted from coverage, 15
litigation on behalf of homeless people with HIV and AIDS, 32–33
and the otherwise qualified individual, 164n75
property owner's rights, 16
and reasonable accommodation, 28, 34–35
types of discrimination prohibited, 14, 22, 15, 32–33, 34–35
Family Medical Leave Act, 167n118
Family Preservation, 74, 75–76, 88
Family Reunification. *See* Foster care, permanency planning
Fanburg, J. T., 208n27–28
Farley, M., 198n72
Fauvel, M., 200n88
Faya v. Almaraz, 203n157
Federal Government, response of to the AIDS epidemic. *See* AIDS, as a political issue
Federal Privacy Act, 100
Federal requirement for inclusion of women and children in federally funded programs, 47–48, 60–61, 63
Federal Office of Technology Assessment, 2
Fein, E.B., 217n71

Feingold, A.R., 174n48
Feldman, J.G., 174n49
Field, M., 4
Fifth Amendment, 200n92
Filice, G., 199n77
Finley, Joann, 21
Finley v. Giacobbe, 163n63
First Amendment, 127, 200n92
Fleishman, J. A., 178n110
Flemming, P., 183n3
Forsyth, B. W. C., 158n58, 183n1
Foster care, 18, 65, 76–85; *see also* Adoption; Adoption Assistance and Child Welfare Act; Adoption Opportunities Act; Adoption subsidies; Family preservation; Transmission of HIV, risk of in foster care
disclosure of information regarding a child's HIV status, 82, 83–84
federal support of, 66, 74–77
health of children in, 79–80
liability for failure to disclose a child's HIV-status possible, 84
medical decision making for children, 80–81, 82–83
number of children with HIV or AIDS, 77, 87
participation of children in drug trials, 81, 82–83
permanency planning, 68, 74–76, 77, 78, 84–85, 88; *see also* Legal planning options
policies developed by agencies caring for children with HIV or AIDS, 78
state responsibility for children placed, 77–78
state support of, 66
testing of children for HIV, 79, 81–83; *see also* Ethical issues
Foster Parents for children with HIV or AIDS, 66, 67, 72, 78, 83–84, 160n6
Fourth Amendment, 92–93, 196n36
Fourteenth Amendment, 80, 92–93, 100, 103, 111–12
Francis, Donald, 154n5
Frascino, R.J., 158n59, 192n122
Fullerton, N.F., 198n71
Futterman, D., 210n57

Gail, M. H., 157n38
Gaiter, J.L., 122, 207n14,18, 208n19
Galavotti, C., 210n66, 211n82
Galbraith, J., 210n65, 211n75
Gallagher, J., 205n194
Gallant, J.E., 176n78
Garcia-Tunon, M., 207n6
Gardner, D.H., 189n99, 190n102
Gay men, definition of disability linked to illness experienced by, 42, 171n23
discrimination against, 3, 4, 156n30, 193n4; *see also* Attitudes toward people with HIV and AIDS
as exclusive focus of research, 48
homophobia, 44, 128, 130
perception of AIDS linked to, xi, 1, 4
Gay Men's Health Crisis, 54, 127; *see also* Social services, grassroots movement
Gay Men's Health Crisis v. Sullivan (GMHC I and II), 209n50
Gay, C.L., 80, 190n101
Gayle, H.D., 207n6
Geffen, David, 179n128
Gellert, G.A., 83, 192n132,134
General Motors v. Director of the Institute for Occupational Safety and Health, 200n96

Gerbert, B., 174n51
Gielen, N. Kass, 111, 206n205,210
Gittler, J., 106, 163n64, 204n168
Glanz v. Vernick, 166n102, 172n31,
Glover v. Eastern Nebraska Community Office of Retardation, 196n36
Gold, H., 216n65
Golden, M.R., 182n163–64,167
Goldenbaum, M., 206n5
Goodson, P., 210n62, 211n76
Gorter, R., 169n145
Gorski v Troy, 160n6
Goss v. Sullivan, 202n137
Gostin, L.O., 194n6, 195n18, 197n60
Government of the Virgin Islands v. Roberts, 203n147
Graham v. Richardson, 213n6
Grandparents as care givers, 66
Green v. Anderson, 215n40
Green, J., 49, 177n89,95–96
Greenberg, M., 215n36
Gribetz, Application of, 202n145
Grimes, J.M., 198n69
Grinn, M., 157n40
Groze, V., 188n89, 189n98
Guinan, M.E., 159n63
Gurdin, P., 189n95
Gutman, L.T., 192n133

H.N.R., In the Matter of the Adoption of Two Children by, 185n37
Hagen, J.L., 214n31
Hahn, J.A., 169n145
Haines-Simeon, M., 188n89, 189n98
Hamilton, J.D., 198n66
Hanson, C.I., 180n135
Harris v. McRay, 203n166
Harris v. Thigpen, 202n128,135
Harris, B., 158n57
Hartigan, P.M., 198n66
Hatfield, Senator Mark, 184n13
Hayman, C.R., 206n4
Health care, *see also* Health insurance; Medicaid; Medicare; Ryan White CARE Act, funds for health care services; ADAMHA, mandatory drug and health care coverage for women; Welfare reform and Medicaid; Welfare reform and managed care
   access to, 43–44, 47, 50–51, 61–62, 81, 149–50
   litigation against medical providers for failure to serve, 46, 62, 175n58
   migrant health care centers, funding for, 56
   primary health care centers, funding for, 56, 57–58
   referrals prohibited under the ADA or VRA, 46
Health insurance, 43–44, 81; *see also* Medicaid; Consolidated Omnibus Reconciliation Act of 1985
   and caps on coverage, 44, 174n43–44; *see also* ADA and health insurance as an employment benefit
   discrimination by health insurance industry against people with HIV and AIDS, 173n40
   and HIV or AIDS as pre-existing conditions, 173n41
   and HIV or AIDS as uninsurable conditions, 44, 173n40,41
   uninsured adults and children, 43, 172n37
   use of Ryan White CARE Act funds to pay health insurance premiums, 56
Healton, C., 206n2

Heath, C.W., 197n51
Hein, K. K., 129, 210n56,57
Hellinger, F.J., 176n76, 178n109,111
Helms, Senator Jesse, 2, 156n30, 193n4, 208n34
Hendrix, J., 175n62
Henrard, D., 200n88
Herman, D. H. J., 155n20, 156n29
Herman-Giddens, M.E., 192n133
Herrod, In re. Estates of, 185n39
Hershey Medical Center, In re., 203n148
Heymann, D.L., 159n64,68,80, 190n105
Higgens, D.L., 133, 210n66, 211n82, 212n101
Hillman v. Columbia County, 202n123
Hilton, M., 175n62
Hirschel, B., 175n62
Hoffman, C.A., 193n2, 205n193
Hoffman, R.E., 196n49
Hofkosh, D., 183n191, 189n99
Hogar Agua y Vida en el Desierto v Suarez-Medina, 160n10
Holahan, J., 178n115, 216n61,63
Hollis, S.L., 197n51–52
Holtgrave, D.R., 131, 133, 134, 210n67, 211n72,79,81,88,90
Homosexual men. *See* Gay men
Hoover, D.R., 98, 198n,72, 199n82
Hopkins, K.M., 183n7
Horner, R. D., 177n99
Hoth, D.F., 175n63
Housing Opportunities for People with AIDS, 53, 58–59, 63
   funding for, 58–59
   purpose of, 58, 63
   use of funds, 58–59
HIV
   and child sex abuse, 83
   early detection of, 99, 200n88
   estimated number of people infected in the U.S., 9, 13
   immunity from infection, 169n153
   long-term survivors of, 169n153
   methods of compiling data, 7–9; *see also* surveys listed under Centers for Disease Control
   not covered under IDEA, 163n53
   selective bias in data collected, 8, 13
   sources for compiling data, 8; *see also* surveys listed under Centers for Disease Control
Hsia, D. C., 178n110
Hu, D.J., 180n135
Hughes, D.C., 216n63
Hunnewell v. Warden, 202n137
Hunter, J., 210n70
Hurley, P., 9, 157n44
Husson, R.N., 198n72

Ibanez, A., 191n107
Immigrants. *See* Welfare reform
Imperato, P.J., 45, 174n49
Individuals with Disabilities in Education Act, 15, 35, 162n48, 163n53; *see also* ADA and education; VRA and education
   definition of disability limited, 20
   disabled child's right to free public education, 19–20, 25, 35
   and the otherwise qualified child, 24–25, 164n75, 165n92
   and reasonable accommodation, 27
   types of discrimination prohibited, 15, 19–20, 24–26
Indian Health Service, 43, 172n33
Indyk, D., 180n135

Informed consent, 8, 47, 81, 83, 91, 101, 103
Interstate Compact on the Placement of Children, 86
Intravenous Drug Use, 65, *see also* Education; HIV and modes of transmission; Women and intravenous drug use; Attitudes toward people with HIV and AIDS and affect on child care
Intravenous drug users, compliance with drug testing programs, 175n62
    as focus of research, 48
Isbell, M.T., 173n40, 174n42, 184n17
Ivanoff, A., 158n57

J.B. v. Bohonovsky, 201n120
J.G., In the Interest of, 203n147
Jacob, In the Matter of, 185n37
Jacobson v. Com. of Massachusetts, 156n30
Jackson v. State, 187n58
Jamaica Hospital, In re., 205n185
Jeanine B. by Blondis v. Thompson, 186n42
Jefferson v. Griffin Spalding County Hospital, 205n181
Jew Ho v. Williamson, 194n10
Job Corps, 93, 113, 117, 118, 207n7
Job Opportunities and Basic Skills Training Program, 144, 214n31
John T., In the Interest of, 184n25
Johnetta J. v. Municipal Court, 202n142
Johnse, D.E., 204n170
Johnson, Matter of Adoption of, 185n26
Johnson v. State, 187n58
Johnson v. U.S. States, 202n137
Johnson, A.M., 133, 211n83
Johnston v. Morrison, Inc., 163n58
Johnston, M.I., 175n63
Jones v. Milwaukee County, 215n38
Jones, J.L., 197n52
Juman v. Louise Wise Services, 193n141
Juveniles A, B, C, D, E, Matter of, 203n147

K.M., In re. Petition of, 185n37
Kadinger, Mark, Estate of v. International Brotherhood of Electrical Workers, Local 110, 174n44
Kaplan, J. E., 199n81
Kaplan, D. W., 208n27,28
Kaposi's Sarcoma Education and Research Foundation, 54
Karon, J.M., 9, 158n49
Katsiyannis, A., 168n136
Keeling, R.P., 207n6
Kennedy, B.U., 207n18
Kennedy, Senator Ted, 208n34
Kent, C., 206n201,206
Kerins v. Hartley, 203n156
Kerr, S., 158n57
Keruly, J.C., 198n70
Killackey, E., 184n16
King v. McMahon, 184n12
Kinship Care, 65–66
Kipke, M.D., 124, 208n30,31
Kirby, D., 128, 132, 133, 209n43, 210n55
Kircher, F. G., 178n107, 179n122
Klein, J.S., 163n66, 129
Klein, N.A., 129
Knox, R.A., 156n23
Kolder V.E.B., 109, 205n194
Koob, J.J., 211n73
Krantz, D.H., 175n53

Ku, L., 123, 207n17, 208n22,25
Kurth, A., 155n18, 159n67

LaShawn A., v. Dixon, 189n93
Lachapelle, Sr. S., 180n135
Lado, M.L.E., 177n101
Lagakos, S.W., 198n69
Lambert, B., 193n4, 197n61
Lambert, G., 200n89, 206n208
Land, H., 197n57
Landers, D.V., 206n207
Landis, S.E., 196n44,47, 197n53–55
Lane v. Pena, 203n155
Lautenberg, Senator Frank R., 155n6
Lawrence, J., 155n15
Leahy, Senator Patrick, 186n49
Leary, W. E., 197n64
Leckelt, v. Board of Commissioners of Hospital District No. 1, 165n88
Legal Planning Options, 66–71, 87; *see also* Adoption; Foster care, permanency planning
    adoption by married spouse, 69–70
    adoption by second parent, 70, 185n37
    guardian, appointment of in a will, 69, 70
    guardianship, 69
    power of attorney, 68–69, 70
    standby guardianship, 70–71, 185n39
    and termination of parental rights, 69–70, 85
Lesbians, 7, 67, 157n36
    discrimination against, 3
Levi, J., 211n87
Levin, B.W., 175n53
Levine, A.J., 154n2, 206n1
Levine, C., 180n135, 183n1
Levinson, W., 157n37
Lewin, T., 156n30, 193n4, 194n9
Lindegren, M.L., 159n68, 200n91, 207n8
Lindsey, D., 188n75,77
Link, R.N., 45, 174n48
Lipscomb v. Simmons, 184n12
Lipsky, J.J., 199n77
Li, X., 210n65, 211n75
Liu, K., 178n115, 216n61,63
Local 1812, American Federation of Government Employees v. United States Dept. of State, 195n26
Long, I.L., 175n64
Love, J., 198n72
Lowe, D., 205n193
Lurie, I., 214n31

McAvinue, S.M., 176n78
McBarnette v. Feldman, 203n149
McCarthy, M., 159n65
McCormick, H.L., 171n16, 172n25
McGann v. H and H Music Co., 174n43
McGovern, T.M., 171n21,22
McGuffin v. Overton, 68, 185n32
McKinney, M.M., 181n154
McKinney, R.E., 192n133
McMillen, J.C., 188n89
McNemar v. Disney Stores, 165n90
McNutt, B., 192n121,125
McQuillan, G., 158n49
M.M.D., In re., 185n37
Magpantay, L., 200n88
Maguire, B.T., 174n51
Maher v. Roe, 203n161
Mallette v. Children's Friend and Service, 193n141
Malouf, R., 189n99
Malvey, T.J., 172n26

Maricopa County Juvenile Action, In the Matter of the Appeal in, 185n31
Marisol v. Giuliani, 186n42
Marks, G., 95, 197n58
Marmor, M., 212n98,99,100
Martinez v. Brazen, 203n150
Martinez v. School Board of Hillsborough County, 162n50, 163n54, 165n91–93, 166n96–97,111
Mascola, L., 180n135, 183n4
Masur, H., 199n81
Maternal and Child Health Services Act, 43
Mauro v. Burgess Medical Center, 166n113
Medicaid, 38, 43, 49–53, 58, 59, 61, 63, 79, 141, 172n33; *see also* ADAMHA, mandatory drug and health care coverage for women; Health care; Health insurance; Medicare; Ryan White CARE Act, funds for health care services; Welfare reform and Medicaid; Welfare reform and managed care
  abortion, coverage for, 106, 203n166
  eligibility for, 49–50
  as health insurance for people with AIDS, 49, 62
  low reimbursement rates and effect on health care received, 50–51, 62
  mandatory coverage for pregnant women and children; 50
  Mills, 50, 62, 177n100
  prescription drug coverage, 52; *see also* AIDS Drug Reimbursement Program; AIDS, cost of drug treatment
  services provided, 52
  waivers, 52–53, 63
Medicaid Transformation Act of 1995, 149
Medical care and the otherwise qualified individual, 25–27, 36
Medical Records Confidentiality Act, 100
Medicare, 43, 52, 172n33; *see also* Health insurance; Medicaid; Ryan White CARE Act, funds for health care services; ADAMHA, mandatory drug and health care coverage for women; Welfare reform and Medicaid; Welfare reform and managed care
Memorial Hospital v. Maricopa County, 215n39
Menzo, S., 169n153, 191n107
Michael J. v. County of Los Angeles Department of Adoptions, 193n141
Michaels, D., 183n1
Miles, S.A., 200n88
Miller v. California, 209n50
Miller v. Spicer, 175n58
Miller v. Youakim, 184n10
Miller, L.A., 196n49
Mills v. District of Columbia, 162n47
Minkoff, H., 110, 205n196
Mohr v. Commonwealth, 193n141
Mohr, P.E., 175n65
Monk, E., 185n27–29
Moore v. Mabus, 202n135
Moore, R.D., 176n78, 198n70
Morabia, A., 175n62
Morgan, C., 48
Mueller, B.U., 198n72
Muhammud v. Carlson, 202n135
Munson, R., 193n2, 205n193
Mussivand v. David, 203n158
Myers, Dr. Woodrow, 156n30, 193n4

National Academy of Sciences, 54
National AIDS Clearinghouse, 54

National AIDS Demonstration Research Projects, 137
National Adoption Information Exchange, 86
National Commission on AIDS, 129, 134, 178n113, 207n12,13, 209n40, 210n70, 211n71, 211n86
National Institute of Allergy and Infectious Diseases, 46–47, 48, 175n59
National Institute on Drug Abuse, 137
National Institute of Health, 46, 47, 49, 97, 150
National Survey of Adolescent Males, 123
Navarro, M., 206n204
Nayeri, K., 174n49
Naylor, K.E., 208n27,28
Needle exchange programs. *See* Education to prevent transmission of HIV and intravenous drug users
Neergard, L., 198n71
Nelson v. Thornburgh, 29, 167n130
New York State Society of Surgeons v. Axelrod, 196n40
New York State Association for Retarded Children, Inc. v. Carey, 195n16
Newacheck, P.W., 216n63
Newborns, blinded screening of, 109, 113, 115
Newton v. Riley, 67
Nichols, S.W., 183n4–5,7
Nichols, R.L., 168n133
Ninth Amendment, 99
Nolley, Louise, 103–4
Nolley v. County of Erie, 202n138
Norcross v. Sneed, 163n59
North, R.L., 197n57
North America Syringe Exchange Network 135

O'Campo, P. O., 111, 206n205,210
O'Connor, S., 208n30,31
O'Hare, L.L., 208n38, 210n68
O'Reilly, K.R., 210n66, 211n82, 212n101
Office of AIDS Research, 49, 176n82
Office of National AIDS Policy, 207n11, 210n64
Office of Research on Women's Health, 49
Olivero, O.A., 198n71
Omnibus Budget Reconciliation Act of 1989, 177n93
Omnibus Budget Reconciliation Act of 1990, 177n94
Onorato, I.M., 157n40
Ordway v. County of Suffolk, 105
Orphan Drug Act, 52
Otherwise Qualified. *See* specific statutory references
Oxtoby, M.J., 183n3, 188n82, 189n98, 199n85
Ozawa, M.N., 173n40

Panlilio, A.L., 168n134
Pantaleo, G., 169n153, 191n107
Paone, D., 212n98,99,100
Parental Rights and Responsibilities Act, 127
Parsons, M.T., 205n194
Partner notification. *See* Contact tracing
Pavia, A.T., 196n42, 50
Pear, R., 178n118, 212n3, 213n6, 214n29
Pearlman, In re., 185n34
Pediatric HIV and AIDS; *see also* Transmission, in-utero; Adolescent compared to pediatric AIDS
  defined, 9, 10
  as leading cause of death, 10
  new cases each year, xi, 10
  number of cases, 10, 13
  number of cases by race and ethnicity, 10
  and seroconversion, 10, 11, 81–82

sources for compiling data, 8; *see also* surveys
  listed under Centers for Disease Control
*Pennsylvania Association for Retarded Children v.
  Commonwealth of Pennsylvania*, 162n47
People v. Adams, 203n154
People v. Anonymous, 202n144
People v. Durham, 203n146
People v. Encoe, 187n58
People v. Ferrell, 204n174
People v. Hardy, 187n58
People v. McVickers, 203n147
People v. Reyes, 187n58
People v. Thomas, 203n153
Perrin, E.C., 208n38
Personal Responsibility and Work Opportunities
  Act, 140, 141
Peterson, G.E., 213n8
*Phipps v. Saddleback Valley Unified School Dis-
  trict*, 165n92, 166n107
Physicians, attitudes toward treating people with
  AIDS, 44–46, 62
Pinching, A.J., 198n76
Pinder, G., 9, 157n44
*Planned Parenthood of Southeastern Pennsylvania
  v. Casey*, 191n110, 203n163
Pleck, J.H., 123, 207n17, 208n22,25
Plotkin, S.A., 192n130–31
Ploughman, P., 199n79
Plowman v. United States, 200n98
Poirer, M.C., 198n71
Polonsky, S., 158n57
Pomeroy, C., 199n77
Popola, P., 79, 80, 189n96, 190n104
Poverty and AIDS, 39
Povinelli, M., 199n80
Presidential Advisory Council on HIV and AIDS,
  58, 176n82, 181n156
Presidential Commission of AIDS, 2, 5–6
Presidential Commission on the Human Immunod-
  eficiency Virus, 48
Prevention of foster care. *See* Family preservation;
  Legal planning options
Prevention of HIV infection. *See* Education
Prince v. Massachusetts, 195n22, 204n176
Prince, R., 185n27
Pringle, J.L., 183n191, 189n99
Privacy, right of, 92, 99–100, 101, 103–5, 114, 115,
  200n92
Prostitutes, 10
Protease inhibitors. *See* Treatment, "new" thera-
  pies
Protocol 076 Study. *See* Reproductive choice
Provisional Committee on Pediatric AIDS, 183n2,
  199n86
Purdham, T. S., 156n30, 193n4

Quarantine, 156n30, 193n4
Qin, L. 169n153, 191n107
Qualls, N.L., 210n67, 211n72,79,81,88,90

*Raleigh Fitkin-Paul Morgan Memorial Hospital v.
  Anderson*, 204n180
Rampino, K.J., 191n111
Ray v. School District of DeSoto County,
  162n92–93, 166n94,110
*Raytheon Co. v. Fair Employment and Housing
  Commission*, 34, 165n93, 170n156–60
Reasonable accommodation in higher education,
  28–29; *see also* ADA, FHA, IDEA and VRA
Reinesto v. State, 187n58

Relf v. Weinberger, 195n14
Remafedi, G., 199n80
Rendon, M., 189n95
Rene O.C., In the Matter of Guardianship of,
  186n41
Rennert, S., 106, 163n64, 204n168
Reproductive choice, 105–12, 114–15; *see also*
  Medicaid, abortion coverage for
  and court ordered medical treatment, 107–8, 115
  and constitutional issues, 111–12, 114–15,
    203n165
  and directive counseling, 108–9
  justification for state intervention on behalf of a
    fetus, 106–7
  and permissible state barriers to electing abor-
    tion, 105–6, 203n166
  and the Protocol 076 Study, 109–11
Rescue Mission Alliance v. Mercado, 194n5
Reynolds v. Brock, 163n57
Rice v. The School District of Fairfield, 21fn
Rich, F., 167n132
Richardson, G. A., 189n99
Richardson, J.L., 197n58
Risk of transmission. *See* Transmission, risk of;
  Universal precautions
Rivera, M., 207n18, 208n19,20
Robbins v. Clarke, 202n137
Robert Woods Johnson Foundation, 179n128
Robertson, Pat, 156n30, 193n4
*Robertson v. Granite City Community Unit School
  District*, 163n53, 165n92, 166n109
Robins, L., 3, 126, 155n11, 209n42
Robinson, R.P., 185n27–29
Rochin v. California, 195n24
Roe v. Catholic Charities of Springfield, 84
Roe v. District of Columbia, 170n160
Roe v. Fauver, 202n136
Roe v. Wade, 105, 107, 204n169
Rosenberg, P.S., 158n49
Rosenthal, E., 217n70
Rosetti v. Shalala, 171n23
Ross v. Beaumont Hospital, 163n60
Roth v. New York Blood Center, 203n152
Rotherberg, K.H., 197n57
Ruiz, L., 191n107
Ruiz, In re, 186n53, 204n171
Ruiz, M.S., 197n58
Rust v. Sullivan, 203n166
Rutherford, G.W., 197n60,62
Ryan White CARE Act, 7, 38, 43, 52, 53, 55–58,
    61, 63, 83, 93, 100, 141, 150, 155n20; *see
    also* Testing for HIV; Contact tracing and
    partner notification; Health care
  and confidential reporting of HIV test results,
    101–2
  and early intervention services, Title III, 56
  and the Emergency Relief Grant Program, Title
    I, 55
  federal funds allocated, 55, 180n36
  funds for health care services, 56–58, 63
  and grant program, Title II, 56
  and health services planning councils, 55
  and HIV care consortia, 56
  and priorities for women, 56–57
  and provisions for criminal prosecution for in-
    tentional transmission of HIV required,
    104
  purpose of, 55, 57, 63; *see also* separate titles of
    CARE Act
  services funded, 57–58
  Special Projects of National Significance, 57, 59

S.P. v. Sullivan, 42
Saah, A.J., 198n72, 199n82
Sadovsky, R., 174n47
Samuels, J.E., 175n62
Sanger, M.B., 213n8
Sangree, S., 106, 108, 195n13, 204n167,173
Santosky v. Kramer, 191n108
Savner, S., 215n36
Sawhill, I., 217n76
Scarlet, G., 158n52
Schable, B., 170n1, 183n1,4–7, 184n14
Schable, C.A., 168n134
Schaecher, R., 210n70
Schaill by Kross v. Tippecanoe School Corp.,
   200n96
Schietinger, H., 211n87
Schilling, R.F., 158n57
Schneider, E.M., 179n127
Schoenbach, V.J., 196n44,47, 197n53–55
Schonfeld, D.J., 208n38, 210n68
School Board of Nassau County v. Arline, 23, 25,
   163n56, 164n75,77–78, 169n155
Schor, E.L., 188n91
Scoles v. Mercy Health Corporation, 166n114,
   169n155
Scott, D.E., 180n135
Search Warrant, In re., 200n96
Second Family Program, 68
Selby v. Rapping, 105
Serrins, D.S., 210n62
Sesholtz, M., 158n55, 191n119
Sexually transmitted diseases, 3–4, 83
   adolescents at greater risk for, 124
   adolescents, rates of, 124
   rate of as an outcome measure for education
      programs, 130, 133
   and risk of in-utero transmission of HIV, 11
Shactman, D., 216n66
Shafer, R.P., 204n170
Shapiro v. Thompson, 215n39
Shapiro, C.N., 168n134
Sharon Fletcher, In the Matter of, 187n57
Shearer, W.T., 198n72
Shields, A.E., 216n65
Shilts, R., 154n1, 179n128, 180n129
Shipp, E.R., 156n27
Shor, L., 209n43, 210n55
Siegel, G., 180n135
Sikkema, K.J., 211n73
Simberkoff, M.S., 198n66
Simonds, R.J., 79, 99, 199n85, 200n91
Skinner v. Oklahoma, 205n186
Skinner v. Railway Labor Executives' Association,
   195n25
Slonim-Nevo, V., 173n40
Smith v. Dovenmuehle Mortgage, Inc., 165n89
Smith v. Robinson, 162n51
Smith, J.M., 184n17
Smith, W., 180n135, 183n4
Smothers, R., 193n4
Social Security Administration, 39, 41, 42, 63,
   171n23
Social Security Disability Income, 39–43, 61, 140,
   141
   eligibility for, 40–41, 61, 171n19–20
   eligibility process, 41–43, 171n5–6,19–20
Social services 38–39; *see also* Ryan White CARE
      Act
   grassroots movement, 53–54, 63, 179n127
   services provided by voluntary agencies, 54

Social welfare programs. *See* Abandoned Infants
      Act; Adoption Assistance and Child Wel-
      fare Act; Adoption Opportunities Act;
      Adoption subsidies; Child Abuse Preven-
      tion and Treatment Act; Family preserva-
      tion; Foster care; Housing opportunities for
      people with AIDS; Medicaid; Ryan White
      CARE Act; Social services, grassroots
      movement; Social Services Block Grant;
      Supplemental Security Income; Supplemen-
      tal Security Disability Income; Temporary
      Assistance for Needy Families; United
      States Deptartment of Health and Human
      Services; Welfare reform; Women and ser-
      vice priorities under federal law
Sokal-Gutierrez, K., 180n135
Sonenstein, F.L., 123, 207n17, 208n22,25
Sontag, S., 217n72
Southeastern Community College v. Davis, 28,
   161n26, 167n120–23
Spencer, N.E., 196n49
St. Louis, M.E., 206n4
Stanley v. Illinois, 184n18
Stanton, B.F., 130, 132, 210n65, 211n75
State sanctioned medical abuse, 91, 113
State v Gray, 187n58
State v. Luster, 187n58
States, governor's response to AIDS, 3
Stefanel Tyesha C., In re., 186n53, 187n55–56,
   204n172
Stein, T.J., 184n 20–22
Stephenson, J., 198n76
Steven L. v. Dawn L., 67
Stevenson, H.C., 135, 211n93
*Stewart B. McKinney Foundation, Inc. v. Town
      Plan and Zoning Commission*, 169n146
Strossen, N., 209n50
Stryker, J., 209n52, 210n58,59, 211n78, 212n103
Substance abuse, treatment for, 56–57; *see also*
      ADAMHA
Sullivan v. Zebly, 172n28–29
Summers, P.F., 169n144
Supplemental Security Income, 38, 39–43, 61, 140,
   141, 149
   and childhood disability, 20, 43, 171n6, 172n28
   eligibility for, 40–41, 61, 171n19
   eligibility process, 41–43, 171n5–6,23
   effects of welfare reform. *See* Welfare reform
*Support Ministries for Persons with AIDS, Inc. v.
      Village of Waterford*, 169n146, 148–51
Suter v. Artist, 187n68
Swartz, K., 172n37
Sweeny, P., 118, 207n8
Sweet, R.L., 206n207
Swenson, V.J., 183n189

T.E.P. and K.J.C. v. Leavit, 157n33
Taft v. Taft, 205n183
Tammy, Adoption of, 185n35,37
Tao, G., 199n80
Taylor, Elizabeth Foundation, 179n128
Temporary Assistance for Needy Families Block
      Grant. *See* Welfare reform
Termination of parental rights. *See* Legal planning
      options
Terry Beirn Clinical Research Program, 47, 175n59
Testing for HIV, 56, 60, 78, 89–115; *see also* Adoles-
      cents, autonomy in making medical deci-
      sions; Contact tracing; Ethical issues; Foster
      care, testing of children; HIV, early detection

anonymous and confidential testing, 56, 90, 100, 101, 113, 197n56
and confidentiality, 92–93, 101–2
justification for, 93, 94–99, 113, 197n65
mandatory testing, 81–82, 83, 90, 92–93, 103, 113–14, 115, 196n36
and Ryan White CARE Act provisions, 93, 104
targeted, 83
under court order, 104
voluntary testing, 90, 111, 113, 115
Thea, D.M., 99, 193n2, 200n89
Third Amendment, 200n92
Thomas v. Atascadero Unified School District, 165n92
Thomas, P., 190n106, 200n90,91
Thorpe, K.E., 216n65,66
Toney v. U.S. Healthcare, Inc., 166n101
Trafford, A., 156n30, 193n4
Transmission of the HIV, 10–11, 117; *see also* Universal precautions; Education; Adolescent compared to pediatric HIV
and artificial insemination, 10–11
and blood products, 9, 10–11, 122
and breast feeding, 10–11, 159n64
classifying cases by method of exposure, 157n35
classification method weighted against heterosexual exposure, 7, 13
and heterosexual intercourse, xi, 7, 10, 118, 119, 121–22
and homosexual intercourse, 7, 10–11, 118–19, 122
in-utero, 9, 10–11
and increased risk for women compared to men, 11–13
intentional transmission and criminal prosecution, 100, 104, 155n20
and intravenous drug use, 10–11, 59, 119, 121–22, 135
method of exposure, young women compared to young men, 118–19
no known risk factor, 4, 7, 11–12, 118, 119, 122
risk of during pregnancy, 11
risk of and employment discrimination, 23, 33–34, 36, 170n160–61
risk of and expert opinion, 23, 25, 33–34, 36, 165n93
risk of and food handling, 30
risk of and housing discrimination, 32–33
risk of, professional guidelines to reduce, 24, 30–32
risk of in contact sports, 31
risk of in day care, 31–32
risk of in foster care, 31–32
risk of in public school settings, 24–25, 31–32, 35
risk of in receipt of medical care, 28–29, 30–31, 33–34, 167n132, 168n138, 169n155
Treatment, "new" therapies, 52, 97–98
Troy D., In re, 186n53, 204n172
Tsetseranoe v. Tech Prototype, 163n62
Turano, M.V., 185n38
Tourk, J.M., 208n34

Uniform Marriage and Divorce Act, 184n19
U.S. Conference of Mayors, 135
U.S. Department of Health and Human Services, 30, 42, 47, 62, 121, 127–28, 150, 156n22, 157n47, 158n48,51,62, 159n73, 160n76, 163n65, 167n132, 168n135,

169n153, 170n161, 178n108, 180n136, 183n7, 198n73,75, 199n84, 205n197, 206n200, 206n3, 209n39,41, 210n63, 212n95,101
U.S. Department of Housing and Urban Development, 181n159
U.S. General Accounting Office, 79, 144, 147, 150, 172n36–37, 173n38, 177n87, 178n103, 181n151, 186n46, 189n92,94, 194n11, 195n15,17, 214n30–32, 216n55–56,58,64, 217n68–69,74–75
U.S. House of Representatives, 48, 57, 154n3, 155n7, 156n26, 159n75, 160n4, 161n19–20, 162n45, 164n68,72–73,75–76, 167n119, 169n143, 175n59, 176n72–73,77,83, 177n88,98,100, 178n104,112, 181n151,153, 182n165–166, 184n9, 188n76, 209n51, 210n53,60, 211n85, 213n9
U.S. Justice Department, 160n4
U.S. Public Health Service, 47, 48, 108, 207n15; *see also* U.S. Department of Health and Human Services
United States v. Dumford, 201n120
United States v. Joseph, 201n120
United States v. Morvant, 172n32, 175n57
United States v. University Hospital, 26, 166n99–100
United States v. Vuitch, 203n164
Universal precautions, 30, 36, 78, 168n138
Urban Institute, 152
Urbaniak, Richard, 102–103
Urbaniak v. Newton, 202n122

Vaccarezza, M., 169n153, 191n107
Valerie D. In re., 182n169
Vaughn v. North Carolina Department of Human Resources, 193n14
Vaughn, R.D., 131, 132, 211n74,80
Vaughn-Edmonds, H., 180n135
Venereal Disease. *See* Sexually transmitted diseases
Vermund, S., 159n67, 176n70
Vernon, T.M., 196n47,48,50, 197n59
Veteran's Administration, 43, 48, 100, 172n33
Veteran's Health Program Extension Act, 48
Vibbert, M., 189n99
Victim's Compensation Assistance Act, 100
Villarreal, S., 180n135
Violence Against Women Act, 100
Vocational Rehabilitation Act, 14, 22, 38, 46, 62, 71, 108, 160n4, 161n15; *see also* ADA; Disability, definition in Civil Rights statutes
accessibility to buildings, 17
contrasted with the ADA, 16–17
and direct threat defense, 29
and education of children, 20, 35
and essential job functions, 27
and non-discrimination by medical providers, 43
and non-discrimination by places of public accommodation, 19, 36
and the otherwise qualified individual, 22–27, 29, 36, 164n75, 169n155
and reasonable accommodation, 23, 27–28, 34–35
types of discrimination prohibited, 14–15, 21, 22–27, 34–35, 170n160
and undue hardship defense, 27, 29, 35, 44
Voelker, R., 198n76
Volberding, P.A., 97, 178n106, 198n69

Waite D., 158n55, 191n119
Wald, H.P., 183n191, 189n99
Walter, H.J., 131, 132, 211n74,80
Ware v. Valley Stream High School, 209n45
Wartenberg, A.A., 175n62
Watters, J.K., 196n46
Waysdorf, S.L., 191n118
Weaver v. Reagen, 178n117
Weber, D.J., 196n44,47, 197n53–55
Weedon, J., 200n89
Weimer, D., 183n7, 192n124
Weinstein, R. A., 177n99
Welfare Reform, 39, 76–77, 140–53, 213n9,11
    and AFDC-Waivers, 141, 144–45
    and effects on women with HIV and AIDS,
        145–48
    and children of non-citizen immigrants, 212n3
    and Managed care, 149–50
    and Medicaid, 141, 143, 146, 149–50
    and non-citizen immigrants, 141, 151, 213n4,6
    and political considerations, 151
    and SSI program changes, adults 141, 147–49
    and SSI Program changes, childhood disability,
        43, 148–49, 151
    The Temporary Assistance to Needy Families
        Block Grant (TANF), 66, 140–41, 141–47,
        152; *see also* Welfare reform and AFDC-
        Waivers
    and family caps, 144–45
    and regulations, 213n10
    and residency requirements, 145, 146
    and teenage parents, 143, 146, 151
    and work requirements, 143
    work requirements, hardship exemption, 143–44
Weston v. Carolina Medicorp, Inc., 203n161
Whalen v. Roe, 100
White v. Western School Corp., 166n108
White House Office of National AIDS Policy, 130
White, J.C., 157n37
Whitner v. State, 74, 187n58
Wieland, M.K., 181n154
Williams, Guardianship of, 185n33
Williams, J.C., 191n111, 204n178
Williams, R.M., 177n100
Willoughby, A., 110, 205n196
Wingood, G.M., 132, 134, 211n77,89
Wisconsin v. Yoder, 191n114
Witkin, G., 156n30, 193n4
Wiznia, A.A., 206n208
Women
    criminal charges sustained for in-utero trans-
        mission of drugs, 74
    diagnosis of HIV/AIDS, 42, 48–49, 62–63
    and disability-based employment discrimination,
        21, 35–36
    and drug treatment programs, access denied as
        sex discrimination, 59–60
    and drug treatment programs, lack of, 59–61,
        63, 73, 151; *see also* ADAMHA, mandatory
        drug and health care coverage for women;

ADAMHA, Associate Administrator for
    Women's Services required by law; CAPTA,
    reporting of babies born with a positive
    toxicology for drugs or evidence of fetal al-
    cohol syndrome
drug treatment programs, state response to lack
    of, 61
and drug use during pregnancy and child
    health, 79–80
and experimental drug trials, 46–48, 56–57, 62,
    175n59, 150, 151
and gender specific effects of medications,
    47–48, 97
and gynecological problems as symptoms of
    HIV, 48–49
and increased incidence of HIV and AIDS
    among, xi, 9–10, 13
as leading cause of death by age, 10, 13
as leading cause of death by race and ethnicity,
    10
and the natural history of HIV, 47–48, 48–49,
    61–62, 62–63, 151
and number of cases in U.S., 9
and number of cases in U.S. by race, 10
and number of cases of AIDS worldwide, 10
and planning for long-term care of their chil-
    dren, 66–67, 85; *see also* Permanency Plan-
    ning; Legal Planning Options
and programs to help mothers plan, 68
pregnancy and risk of transmission of HIV, 11,
    57
and primary health care, lack of for poor
    women, 50–51, 62, 149–50, 151
and the Protocol 076 study, 181n148, 198n71
and reliance on public assistance, 39; *see also*
    Welfare Reform topics
risk factors, 11–12, 13; *see also* Transmission,
    risk of
role of heterosexual intercourse in transmission
    of HIV, 11, 13
and service priorities under federal law, 56–58,
    60–61, 63, 150
as single parents, xii, 64, 65
and state intervention in medical decision mak-
    ing, 92, 109–11, 106–8
and testing for HIV. *See* Testing
and work. *See* Welfare reform
Woolfolk v. Duncan, 26, 166n101,104–5
World Health Organization, 10, 157n35
Wykoff, R.F., 197n51,52

Zavos, M.A., 173n39, 174n42, 177n91
Zedlewski, S., 217n77,78
Zhang, L., 169n153, 191n107
Zitter, J.M., 204n170,178
Zolopa, A.R., 169n145
Zuckerman, B., 182n163, 183n191, 189n99
Zidovudine (ZDV), 82, 96–97, 98, 112, 197n65,
    198n71; *see also* Reproductive Choice and
    the Protocol 076 Study